D'ARTAGNAN'S
glorious game
COOKBOOK

D'ARTAGNAN'S
glorious game
COOKBOOK

ARIANE DAGUIN, GEORGE FAISON, *and* JOANNA PRUESS

Photographs by Tom Eckerle

LITTLE, BROWN AND COMPANY

Boston New York London

To Alix, who loves all kinds of animals:
wild, furry, . . . or cooked medium rare.
A.D.

To my wife, Carol, and my children,
Lisa and Spud.
G.F.

To my own three musketeers:
Nicole, Ben, and Justin.
J.P.

FIRST EDITION

Photograph on page xvii (left) by Cathy Vincent. Photographs on pages xvii (right), 25, 58, 121, 125, by Jean-Bernard Laffitte. Photograph on page 26 © The British Museum. Photograph on page 138 by Simon Lofthouse Photography. All other photographs by Tom Eckerle.
Book design by Julia Sedykh Design.

Library of Congress Cataloging-in-Publication Data
    Daguin, Ariane.
        D'Artagnan's glorious game cookbook / Ariane Daguin, George Faison, and
    Joanna Pruess; photographs by Tom Eckerle. — 1st ed.
            p.   cm.
        ISBN 0-316-17075-5
        1. Cookery (Game) 2. Game and game-birds. I. Faison, George. II. Pruess, Joanna.
    III. D'Artagnan's. IV. Title.
    TX751.D33   1999
    641.6'91 — dc21   99-19625

10 9 8 7 6 5 4 3 2

IM-S

Printed in Singapore

contents

acknowledgments

We feel honored that so many talented individuals and generous organizations helped us bring this book to fruition. Along with our favorite dishes, it includes those of many gifted chefs, cooks, and friends who willingly shared their recipes and support with us.

From the very beginning, our agent, Angela Miller, championed this project with unfailing effort and enthusiasm. She found answers to challenges large and small, while maintaining her sense of humor.

Jennifer Josephy, senior editor at Little, Brown and Company, contributed not only long hours but a genuine passion for producing the kind of book we dreamed of creating. Additionally, from Little, Brown, our copyeditor, Peggy Leith Anderson, persisted inexhaustibly and always with the right refinement. Dara Mandle, Jennifer's assistant, was tireless, cheerful, and willing to follow up on all the details that really do matter.

To all of the employees of D'Artagnan, we are grateful for your help in the office as well as your willingness to test our recipes in the evening. Sally and Gene Kofke, Wendy Raymont, and Jeanne Brooksbank were all dedicated testers and tasters. Kathy Sreedhar and her family were graciously hospitable and eager tasters for every new dish. Thanks go to Nicole Pruess for helping to input and rewrite recipes, especially when the pressure was intense. Along the way, some assistance came from Kim Graziano and Julie Lochow as well. All of the g me suppliers mentioned in this book also gave generously of their products.

Roger "Zizou" Duffour and master butcher Loic Jaffres shared years of expertise and enthusiasm for game cooking with us; Sutton Place Gourmet was ever willing to help with our food needs; Scaglio's Market in Katonah, New York, kindly became our Westchester delivery drop-off point for more game products than they ever imagined in a week's delivery; and Steve Nyburg, wine director of Green Lane Wines & Liquors in Bedford Hills, New York, offered many thoughtful wine suggestions.

Photographer Tom Eckerle, along with his wife, the elegant stylist Ceci Gallini, and the supremely gifted food stylists Mariann Sauvion and Grady Best, brought our game dishes temptingly to life in the studio and on location. Dominique Millée, of Bernardaud Porcelaines, graciously shared props for some of those pictures. We thank Fred and Abbie Wyman for lending us their beautiful home for the outdoor picnic and barbecue shots and Peter Josten for sharing his handsome Victorian home for the kitchen and dining room pictures. Additional thanks go to photographer Jean-Bernard Laffitte for his images of Gascony, and Cathy Vincent for her photo of Ariane with the D'Artagnan statue. Our book designer, Julia Sedykh, and jacket designer, Leslie Goldman, transformed the text and images into a handsome, tempting volume.

Finally, we thank you, our customers — amateurs, chefs, and retailers — for sharing our love of these wonderful game meats.

introduction

In 1984 a revolution in American dining began. It centered on one of life's ultimate luxury foods: fresh foie gras. For the first time, chefs in New York and San Francisco could prepare Sauternes-infused terrines or slices of quickly seared, silky, fresh foie gras like those that connoisseurs swooned over in Europe. Previously, when a chef wanted foie gras in a dish, he had to open a can of processed duck or goose liver from France to comply with U.S. restrictions on importing raw meat. The dream that one might prepare fresh foie gras was just that — a fiction.

While the laws didn't change, in that year an American foie gras industry was born, and ever since, consumption of the rich livers has continued to escalate sharply each year. So popular are they today that a veritable *crise de foie gras* occurred during the 1997 holiday season, when suppliers simply could not meet the astonishing demands of restaurants, caterers, specialty stores, catalog sales, and home cooks. Lifting the ban on imported raw poultry from France, in December 1998, raised the availability and choices of foie gras while lowering the price.

Way before domestic foie gras made its debut, Long Island ducklings — albeit frozen — appeared with some frequency in markets. But who had heard of buying fresh duck breasts, particularly the meaty *magrets* of Moulards, to serve rare? Squab and quail were hard to come by for chefs, and almost impossible for home cooks to buy with any regularity. And venison was generally a hit-or-miss commodity, with unregulated standards of quality and size. Its usual destination was the hunter's stewpot.

Game was considered exotic and best savored on trips abroad and in "fancy" restaurants. Remember duck à l'orange, or venison marinated for days and then buried under a heavy cream sauce? Chances are, the duck's skin was flabby (or the meat dry) and the orange sauce was cloying; the deer meat tasted overwhelmingly of herbs and wine. Yet these dishes were considered the height of gastronomy.

This is the point at which a new company named D'Artagnan entered the food scene and created a business as colorful and adventurous as any Alexandre Dumas musketeer. It was to be a seminal event for lovers of great food, especially game.

D'Artagnan's tale begins with a fortuitous partnership between a proud Gascon, Ariane Daguin, and a passionate Texan, George Faison, who together left the Greenwich Village pâté business where both were working to support a newly launched domestic New York duck farm. The pair saw gold where others saw folly in a project to sell fresh American foie gras of a quality to match the finest from France. Were they headstrong? Absolutely! Were they mad? Judge for yourself.

Today the New Jersey–based company is the premier purveyor of game and foie gras in the United States; any discussion of game cooking in America must acknowledge their fundamental role. Getting to this point wasn't easy, but hefty doses of humor, total commitment, and old-fashioned chutzpah were useful tools. You can read about some of their trials and adventures in "The D'Artagnan Story," page xiv, and throughout this book. You'll also meet suppliers and friends who supported this enterprise and have worked alongside George and Ariane to improve industry standards and availability.

At the company's tenth anniversary party, held at Grand Central Station, more than two thousand chefs and friends came to celebrate. Florence Fabricant, of the *New York Times,* wrote that the "dynamic pair . . . changed American restaurant menus forever."

Today the revolution that D'Artagnan started with foie gras includes not only game meats, but charcuterie and prepared foods as well. Their confit of duck and foie gras terrine appear on prestigious restaurant menus nationwide. Caterers suggest squab to clients without fear of squeamish reactions. California Burrito Company regularly orders duck rillettes for its burritos. Even Sky Chef, a huge supplier of airline food, includes smoked magrets on in-flight meals.

Like mesclun, portobello mushrooms, and infused oils, game meats are making the transition from restaurants to home kitchens. In the years since their anniversary party, D'Artagnan's retail division has made available a variety and quality of game foods heretofore unimaginable in supermarkets, butcher shops, specialty stores, and by mail order.

Game is now considered chic and topical. Publications like *Bon Appétit, Food Arts,* and *Weight Watchers Magazine* describe venison as flavorful and healthful, "a perfect meat for modern times"; rabbits and game birds, they suggest, make savory feasts. When Kathie Lee Gifford told 8 million *Live! With Regis and Kathie Lee* viewers about the wonderful squab dinner her husband prepared, game cooking had truly arrived in the culinary mainstream.

FROM VENISON CHILI TO SILKY FOIE GRAS: NEW OPTIONS

What caused the shift from the perception that buffalo burgers and venison chili were the only kinds of game meats suitable for home kitchens? For starters, Americans are eating out more often and have tasted game dishes that have exciting seasonings and multiple textures but are simple and light. The birds, meats, and foie gras are being paired with stylish ingredients like fresh salsas and dried fruits or grains and bitter greens. Classics have been updated and lightened as well. Diners leave the table feeling sated, not weighted down.

When home cooks entertain, they want an exciting focal point for the meal. Above all, that means foods with flavor and style but not necessarily with a lot of fat. Boneless, skinless chicken breasts — no matter how healthful they are or how dramatic the presentation — aren't the answer. In addition, home cooks want dishes that can be prepared without investing days of free time. Convenience is important, but quality is essential. Today's game easily meets all these criteria. It's exotic and rich in flavor yet very nutritious. Venison has fewer calories and less fat than an equal portion of skinless chicken. It's raised without additives and growth hormones, and is recommended by the American Heart Association and American Dietetic Association as an excellent choice in protein.

A mouthful of wild boar is like the sweetest pork you ever tasted — actually, like pork before producers bred it to be "the other white meat." Buffalo is juicy and robust. Anyone who remembers what chickens used to taste like will be pleased to rediscover the original among today's free-range, organically fed chickens.

Many game birds are also free-range and organic. Farm-raised birds have a mild flavor because of their controlled diets. They are always processed at their most tender, unlike birds shot in the woods. (There's no buckshot in the meat, either.) And since in America we do not hang wild birds — a process favored in Europe to develop flavor and tenderize the meat — they never develop a high, somewhat ripe taste.

A wider variety of game is available today than ever before, including the days when our forefathers hunted it for their sustenance. Specialty cuts of boar, duck breasts, and semiboneless squab are all as close as your supermarket. You can capture your birds and beasts with a shopping cart.

Quality is strictly controlled and reliable. Because of modern technology, vacuum-packed meats keep fresh under refrigeration for many days. Once the package is opened, the meat should be used within 2 or 3 days. Be sure to read the introduction to each of the main sections of this book for food safety information.

FROM SHOPPING TO SERVING

What to do with a leg of venison once it's home is the question we address in this cookbook. *D'Artagnan's Glorious Game Cookbook* is meant for novice game cooks as well as the seasoned pro. Since these products might be new to you, we start each chapter with the basics: an introduction and a little history about the animal or group of related animals, general cooking instructions, a description of flavor, nutritional facts, uses, and storage ideas. As you prepare some of the dishes and become familiar with the category, we urge you to modify our recipes and create your own.

We use stocks again and again in our recipes. Today's greatly improved commercial products with relatively low sodium are good options if you can't make your own. Stores like Whole Foods offer shelf-stable boxes of stock with no chemical additives. Sutton

Place stores sell their own veal, chicken, and beef stock. We know that it's easier to open a can, but homemade is definitely superior and not hard to make. Many of our recipes show you how to do it as you go.

D'Artagnan sells a product that is convenient and magical at the same time: rich duck and veal demi-glace. Add a little to aromatic ingredients, along with some water or wine, and, *voilà,* you'll have a sublime sauce. Throughout this book we've liberally taken advantage of this shortcut, but we also tell you how to make your own demi-glace.

D'Artagnan's Glorious Game Cookbook includes commonsense information that we hope instills confidence. If you want to compare the intensity of flavor of different game, we provide a chart in the back of the book. Tips on how to present each dish with appropriate garnishes, as well as what to do ahead, are detailed in the recipes.

This cookbook is also personal, and it includes intimate reflections associated with hunting and the creation of D'Artagnan. George Faison is an expert shot with bow and arrow and guns. He is also a jovial raconteur who has developed a close relationship with the company's purveyors. He'll introduce you to personalities like Bill and Janet Odom, who raise quail at Manchester Farms, or George Rude, who supplies D'Artagnan with pheasants from Griggstown Farm. You'll learn firsthand what it takes to produce top-quality game meats.

Ariane Daguin grew up in Gascony, in a family immersed in food. Her father, André, is an eleventh-generation chef. She recalls the cooing of the birds in the *pigeonnier* (dovecote), the smell of the crisp, early morning air, and the sound of leaves crunching underfoot as she followed her father and the grown-ups into the fields as they hunted or collected cèpes. At age ten she helped in her father's Michelin two-star restaurant by stuffing goose necks. It was only natural for her to develop most of the prepared products now sold by D'Artagnan.

George and Ariane are both strongly opinionated! Ariane, for example, emphatically believes that duck fat is the *only* choice for sautéing. There are some convincing arguments to back up her point, and potatoes in duck fat are heavenly. But if you prefer, you can use unsalted butter, of course.

CONTEMPORARY AND CLASSIC DISHES FOR A YEAR OF FEASTS

Many of our own favorite game recipes, or personal interpretations of classics, are in these pages. So are recipes from many of this country's greatest chefs, as well as from talented friends who have used our products. All the recipes have been adapted for your kitchen. Most serve from 4 to 6, except for the terrines and pâtés, which generally serve at least 8.

D'Artagnan's Glorious Game Cookbook includes two large categories: game birds, including farm-raised, and game meats. A third section addresses charcuterie, sausages, and foie gras. Many dishes are relatively easy to prepare, requiring modest cooking times and basic equipment. Some, such as Duck Quesadillas, are very simple. With more complicated dishes, where possible, we've indicated steps that can be done ahead of time, along with suitable substitutions and shortcuts.

The flavors you'll encounter reflect today's international pantry: a Persian-inspired duck with pomegranate sauce, boneless squabs with mole sauce on thyme-flecked polenta, and red snapper and foie gras with black truffle sauce. Some are subtle, others bold.

Until recently game was thought of as heavy, cold-weather food. We disagree. Game meats are in fact extremely lean. There are dishes for every season of the year and all kinds of dining experiences. Custardy-smooth seared foie gras with grapes and balsamic vinegar would make a stellar prelude to a grand dinner. Serve warm salad of duck breast, asparagus, and blackberries as a refreshing and elegant summer lunch or first course. For a sultry evening, try grilled venison chops with cool watercress salad.

Appropriate side dish recipes for many of the main courses are included as helpful suggestions to get you started. Many are inspired and worth trying in combination with other game dishes. Medallions of venison with fresh and dried fruit are served with twin jewel-toned purées, one of beets, the other of sweet potatoes. Either or both vegetables would be great with roast goose or sautéed duck breasts.

Game, you'll discover, is hardly an acquired taste. It's meat and birds with real flavor. Follow our directions and you'll see how remarkably easy it is to prepare. We hope we inspire you to create your own luscious and exciting feasts.

the d'artagnan story: a conversation

GEORGE FAISON: Ariane and I were inspired to create our own company when domestically raised Moulard duck and its liver, the foie gras, first became available in the United States. In the autumn of 1983 we were employees of a New York City pâté company; it was here that we first heard about a newly launched duck farm providing these previously unavailable products. Both of us saw it as a golden opportunity to advance the art of charcuterie in America. Not so our employers.

With substantial encouragement from Ariane's father, Michelin two-star chef André Daguin, and Jean Banchet of Le Français in Wheeling, Illinois, along with every penny we had ($15,000), we made a fateful move.

ARIANE DAGUIN: First, we needed a name. Our intention was to sell the breast, or *magret*, the legs, and the livers of Moulard ducks in their raw state, and processed as terrines, confits, sausages, and smoked and dry-cured duck breasts. We wanted our moniker to reflect my Gascon heritage — of which foie gras is a large part — and our association with American foie gras ducks.

Nonetheless, the first name we came up with was Fada — the first syllables of our last names. It means loco or crazy in French slang, and it aptly described the two of us. When we did the name search that is required before incorporation, however, we found that restaurateurs of Provençal descent in New York City had already claimed it.

GEORGE: Several weeks later, over a few pastises at a favorite hangout, we decided on D'Artagnan.

ARIANE: Most people know D'Artagnan as the protagonist of Alexandre Dumas's novel *The Three Musketeers*. In fact he was also a real-life seventeenth-century personality

known for his flamboyant, daring panache, a sincere commitment to responsibility, and undying loyalty to family, friends, and associates; providentially, he hailed from a village just outside Auch, my hometown. As the heroic patron of Gascony, D'Artagnan was the perfect role model for two young entrepreneurs seeking to make their mark in life!

GEORGE: On that same fateful night, the friendly bartender (who happened to be an artist) heard the discussion and, on the back of a napkin, drew the duck that would become the company's logo. It was his inspiration to cover the duck's head with a musketeer's flamboyantly plumed hat and drape a banner across its chest proclaiming "D'Artagnan."

ARIANE: Unbeknownst to André, the artistic bartender, the colors he selected, red and white, were the colors of Auch, my hometown.

GEORGE: Finding the name, as it turned out, was the easy part. The original notion of promoting everything based on Moulard ducks proved to be more challenging. When we discussed our plans with a good friend, Steve Robbins of Preferred Meats in Dallas, he suggested we include complementary lines of fresh game meats and poultry in our distribution program. He had recently started offering these items to his North Texas clientele, and out of concern that Ariane and I might starve before foie gras caught on, he directed us to some of his suppliers.

Up until that time, distribution of game in the Northeast was minimal, with the majority of these items being available only frozen. As freezing has a particularly detrimental effect on lean game meats, most quality chefs refused to place them on their menus unless specifically requested by a client.

⌃ Ariane with statue of D'Artagnan, patron of Gascony

Auch, in southwest France, the heart of foie gras country ⌃

The farmers were delighted to join with a young company that would promote their fresh meats as a primary business rather than as an afterthought. For D'Artagnan, the suggestion offered a totally different perspective on where we were going. We plunged into the market and started showing these meats right away; the response was overwhelming.

ARIANE: We were completely buried under. Having incorporated in July of 1984, by the first of September, we started to make deliveries. The "we" at that point was just the two of us, and we did everything from start to finish. When a customer's bookkeeper insisted on speaking to accounting, we just switched the phone from one ear to the other. When foie gras needed to be picked up, off we'd drive to the farm. We went to the airport to receive venison from New Zealand, or squab from California, and then we came back and made our deliveries.

GEORGE: Within a year, our initial sales plan of a fifty-fifty split between fresh foie gras and ducks and prepared duck products had evolved to 30 percent fresh and prepared foie gras and duck and 70 percent fresh game. No one could have foreseen the willingness of New York chefs to place game meats on their menus so quickly. Nothing like this repertoire of fresh meats had been offered from one consolidated location before. A single call could convey wild boar from Texas, quail from South Carolina, New Jersey free-range pheasants, and (from mid-September to February) fresh wild Scottish game to a restaurant's kitchen.

By providing chefs with reliable fresh deliveries of consistent quality products, D'Artagnan effectively changed a menu mix that had remained relatively stagnant since the 1920s and 1930s, when federal game laws prohibited the commercial resale of hunted game. David Waltuck, chef-owner of Chanterelle, a New York City four-star restaurant, summed it up quite simply when he said: "I would never have put squab on my menu if you had not been in business."

ARIANE: We were very lucky with our timing!

GEORGE: Many game farms, which had provided birds for hunt clubs for decades, found that by the 1980s, preserve hunting had declined in popularity and the owners were looking for ways to change the direction of sales. Bill Odom of Manchester Farms (see page 113) was just starting and was convinced that quail, if farmed and processed like chicken, could find a successful niche in restaurants and retail stores nationwide. The "table trade" was ripe for growth.

We also worked with farmers and suppliers to create products when we saw a need to be filled. We knew, for example, that it was legal to bring wild Scottish game into the United States, but no one had ever tried to bring it in fresh. I made a quick trip to Scotland, and within three weeks fresh grouse, wood pigeon, hare, partridge, pheasant, red deer, and roe deer were on America's menus.

Fostering products grown to our own stringent standards was another aspect of the job. Organic, free-range chicken is a case in point. In 1985 the desire for "real" chicken had created a niche market for small farmers willing to invest the extra effort and cost of raising birds without antibiotics, hormones, or animal by-products, and in outdoor, open-pen environments. As demand for these full-flavored, firmer-textured chickens escalated, the ability of small farms to successfully expand their business while maintaining quality suffered.

At this point, we contacted Bob Eberly of Eberly Poultry (see page 8) in central Pennsylvania. Luckily, he was already of a similar mind. We convinced him to go all the way: raise the birds organically, utilizing feed that had been grown without pesticides, hormones, or chemical fertilizer, and to let them range freely outdoors. Of course, this increased the cost enormously. But it gave us, and our market, a chicken that was truly like the chicken our grandparents had. This willingness to put quality ahead of cost, whether it be increased feed or transportation costs, has been at the core of our business philosophy since we began.

Working with the farmers has probably been the most fun, because we've learned, they've learned, and we've all grown our businesses together with mutual trust.

ARIANE: George, you're giving people the impression that all we do is work all the time.

GEORGE: Well, we have invested a hell of a lot of energy, time, and passion in D'Artagnan. But what good is hard work without hard play? And besides, as you know, the lines blur pretty often.

ARIANE: That's for sure. Parading in and out of hundreds of kitchens to explain to chefs the finer points of our products, or prancing around at the Fancy Food Show in musketeer costumes, offering samples of our terrines is necessary, and so we try to make it fun. Remember how we met Julio Iglesias feeding him French Kisses at a charity dinner? After a few bites he said, "I'm a Latin lover, but I prefer D'Artagnan French Kisses."

GEORGE: Yes. Teaching people about products is essential. It's really grown D'Artagnan and established great loyalty. No one ever accused either of us of being quiet and reserved! And parties are a way of sharing and communicating.

ARIANE: Agreed. That brings me back to Lady Luck and timing. It seems to us that now is the time to share some of what we've learned with a wider audience.

GEORGE: Right, because a lot of retail customers order from us, and they're always asking for recipes for venison, quail, and foie gras. They want directions and serving ideas, too. We have so many recipes of our own, or those shared with us by customers and friends, that this book is one way to help everyone.

Early on in our business, in 1984, Balducci's in New York bought game for their retail customers. In 1987 the Food Emporium stores did the same. They were truly pioneers. Today game is available in many gourmet stores and supermarkets across the entire country. People are getting into quality game products because they tie in with Americans' changing eating and health philosophies. Plus, there's a new desire for full flavor and variety in foods. One fantastic venison chop that's low in cholesterol and fat but loaded with flavor is a lot more pleasing than a bland veal chop.

ARIANE: Realistically, though, a lot of people who eat game in restaurants get a little nervous when they try cooking it at home for the first time.

GEORGE: They should throw a few quail on the grill to see how simple it is! Or sauté a duck breast and then fan it with some fresh salsa.

ARIANE: That's the point. We want to help make their meals great events. And that's not *fada!*

All game birds, game meats, and sausages used in this book, as well as rendered duck fat and duck and veal demi-glace, can be purchased from your local butcher or ordered from D'Artagnan at:

www.dartagnan.com

or 1-800-DARTAGN

---

game birds

and farm-raised poultry **1**

working
with game birds
and farm-raised
poultry

In this section, we give each bird its own chapter to highlight some of the flavors and preparations that work best for each one. There is a remarkable variety of tastes, colors, and textures. Cut-up and small birds all take well to sautéing, grilling, and baking. Larger birds can be roasted, poached, and, with special preparation, barbecued. In the following recipes we have tried to demonstrate how versatile game birds are.

There are some general guidelines to handling birds that are useful to review. We are great advocates of fresh birds, not only from the standpoint of food safety and avoiding food-borne bacteria but, most important, for optimal flavor and enjoyment. Ideally, poultry should not be frozen. However, if there is a chance that you won't use it within the appropriate time frame (1 to 2 days after purchase if fresh, 3 to 4 days if vacuum-packed), it is preferable to freeze it rather than let the bird deteriorate.

PREPARATION AND SAFETY TIPS BEFORE COOKING

Fresh poultry should be stored in the coldest part of your refrigerator and used as quickly as possible (see above). Place it on paper towels to absorb any juices that might leak.

When ready to begin preparation, remove giblets and neck, and reserve if recipe calls for them. If you will be using them in another recipe to be prepared later or saving for stock, remove before storing bird and freeze immediately in an airtight container.

Rinse birds under cool water, pat dry, and remove excess fat and skin when necessary. Turn wing tips under or remove first 2 wing joints.

If poultry is to be used boneless, use a sharp knife to bone. Reserve bones and trimmings for stock, if desired, in a heavy resealable plastic bag. Some recipes ask that you

◀ Raspberry-Glazed Poussin with Wild Mushroom Ragout
on Wild Rice Pancakes (page 12)

leave the drummette on the breast; this is the section of the wing that is attached to the body.

Always use a sharp knife when boning or cutting poultry. A sturdy pair of kitchen scissors or poultry shears is very valuable for cutting up a bird.

Never leave cooked or raw poultry outside the refrigerator for more than 1 hour. Do not reuse the same dish to serve from that you used for marinating without first washing it thoroughly.

Always wipe off the counters with soapy water or a disinfectant where you have cut up poultry.

COOKING NOTES

In this section you'll find some whole roasted poultry dishes, especially with smaller birds like quail and squab. Since the breasts cook to perfection before the legs are done, many recipes have you remove that part first or even cook the parts separately. Here an instant-read thermometer is extremely useful as a gauge to indicate when each portion is done to its best; the recipes will tell you when a specific temperature is recommended.

When you have leftover legs and/or trimmings, save them raw or cooked and use them in pâtés or ragùs.

STOCKING UP FOR STOCKS

To make a brown stock, game bird (or other) bones are first browned in a hot oven or over high heat, then combined with aromatic vegetables (celery, onion, carrot), herbs, water, and/or wine. For a light-colored stock, the bones are first simmered in water and not browned before adding the vegetables. In both cases, the water is skimmed to remove impurities that rise to the surface as the liquid slowly reduces. It is then poured through a fine strainer to remove bones and other solids. The recipes throughout the book will tell you which approach to use in making the stocks you need.

Since making stock requires some time, we suggest you rely on the "rollover" method. Keep game stock in your freezer to use as needed, and save bones and trimmings from the current recipe for the next batch of stock. Bones from one or several kinds of birds can be interchanged. Store bones in resealable plastic bags, separated into birds and meat, if you prefer a bird or meat stock; otherwise, they may be combined. Once you have enough bones on hand, you can make stock to replenish your freezer supply.

I want there to be no peasant in my kingdom so poor
that he is unable to have a chicken in his pot on Sundays.

— Henri IV of France, 1553–1610

chicken, poussin, and capon

GEORGE: One of the first items to really catch on at D'Artagnan wasn't a game bird, but a chicken. In this case a baby chicken, or *poussin.* As veal is to beef, the little bird is younger and more tender than an older chicken. What a poussin is *not* is a Rock Cornish hen, which is actually a mature but small breed of chicken that is tougher and less flavorful. In 1984, when we started, nobody was serving poussin in New York, or anywhere else in the country.

In France and most of Europe, poussin are very popular and have been regularly available since the domesticated wild red jungle fowl from India first arrived in Central Europe, around 1500 B.C. Poussin is simply one stage of the chicken's life. *Poussin* is the first stage. Next is the *poulet* (or, as we call it, a *pullet*). Mature females, or hens, are *poules,* and mature males are *coqs.* Typically, a European goes to market with a specific type of chicken in mind for a particular recipe.

If a recipe involves stewing a bird with wine for a long time, as in coq au vin, an old male is purchased. Its fuller flavor stands up to the wine, and its firm texture holds up to the long cooking process without falling apart in the broth. Poule au pot, or hen in the pot, requires a mature female to slowly stew in broth with aromatic vegetables. Here the coq's pronounced flavor is considered undesirable. In America, when poules aren't readily available, we suggest a capon.

A capon is a male pullet that is gelded and then fed a rich diet of milk or porridge until it reaches 6 to 10 pounds, at between 5 and 6 months. The flesh is very white and, unlike that of other chickens, marbled with fat. In early Rome and through the Middle Ages, capons were popular, especially with the clergy and kings. In present-day France and Italy, capons are traditionally served at Christmas.

For everyday roasting or other dry-cooking methods, choose a poulet, or pullet, for a bird that will be juicy and tender. For extraordinary tenderness, choose a poussin.

Poussin are 3½-to-4-week-old chickens. (By comparison, organic chickens mature in 9 weeks; mass-produced birds do so in 6 weeks.) They weigh between 14 and 18 ounces, and are fed a diet of only pure grain. The little birds have a delicate flavor and are extremely tender. They are lower in fat than a fully grown chicken. Because of these properties, poussin lend themselves beautifully to all types of cuisines and methods of dry-heat cooking, from the oven to the grill to the rotisserie. Brushed with olive oil and dusted with herbs and salt and pepper, then grilled; or stuffed with fresh black truffle slices under the skin and roasted — poussin's versatility is limited only by your imagination.

In the United States, according to government standards terminology, *fryers* are birds of either sex that weigh up to 3½ pounds. Birds up to 5 pounds, of either sex, are *roasters. Capons,* as noted, weigh between 6 and 10 pounds.

Poussin were pivotal to D'Artagnan's early success, and they still hold a place of honor. My first order, for three dozen of these birds, was from the late chef Patrick Clark. At the time, he was at the Odeon Cafeteria in lower Manhattan. (Later he went to the Hay-Adams in Washington, D.C., and then returned to New York City, as executive chef of Tavern on the Green, on Central Park West.) Odeon was one of the first restaurants in New York to crack the stuffy "continental" service mold that had predominated in the city during the fifties.

Whether Patrick was initially impressed by our poussin or simply felt some sympathy for me just getting started, I'm not sure. He was our very first customer, and poussin became a mainstay of his menu for more than two years.

While poussin is a luxurious indulgence, chicken is generally considered a dish for common folk. Long before the Republicans used a variation of the phrase in 1928, Henri IV, of Gascony, proclaimed at his coronation that he wished every peasant in his realm might have "a chicken in his pot on Sundays," as a sign of prosperous times to come.

Although chickens are not mentioned among the birds in the Bible, Egyptian tomb paintings illustrate that they were common more than thirteen hundred years before the Christian era. Records from the Emperor Trajan, who ruled Rome from A.D. 98 to 117, show chicken was a staple in an era when food appreciation had reached its height.

Today, good times in chicken farming mean that no one has to eat bland, chemically pumped up chicken bred in a claustrophobic coop. We've seen flavorful chicken make a big comeback.

crispy oven-roasted chicken
with sautéed parsleyed potatoes

SERVES 4

Perfectly crisp and juicy roasted chicken with no fuss — guaranteed — and a delicious sauce made from the vegetables that serve as the rack for the chicken and caramelize along the way. Allowing the chicken's skin to tighten in the refrigerator overnight seals in flavor and moisture. Once you taste chicken cooked this way, you'll be won over, and tempted to try turkey and other birds using the same technique. Enjoy a Côtes du Rhône or Beaujolais with this chicken.

1 chicken, 3 pounds

Salt and freshly ground pepper

5 cloves garlic, coarsely chopped

2 sprigs rosemary

½ lemon

2 tablespoons unsalted butter or rendered
    duck fat, melted

2 carrots, coarsely chopped

2 ribs celery, coarsely chopped

1 large onion, coarsely chopped

¾ cup white wine

¾ cup chicken stock

Sautéed Parsleyed Potatoes (recipe follows)

2 tablespoons chopped flat-leaf parsley

1. Season chicken cavity with salt and pepper, add half of the garlic and all the rosemary, and squeeze in lemon juice. Leave squeezed lemon half inside cavity.

Place chicken on a cake rack over a plate, and leave uncovered in refrigerator overnight, or for at least 8 hours.

2. Preheat oven to 450°F.

3. Put 1 tablespoon of the butter in the bottom of a heavy gratin or shallow roasting pan just large enough to hold the chicken. Add carrots, celery, onion, and remaining garlic. Brush remaining butter over chicken and place bird, breast up, on the vegetables. Put pan in oven with legs facing toward back of oven.

4. Turn heat down to 400°F and roast until skin is rich brown and leg moves easily in the socket, about 1 hour and 20 minutes, basting with pan drippings every 20 minutes. After 1 hour, pour wine and stock over vegetables, and continue roasting until chicken is done.

5. Meanwhile, while chicken is roasting, prepare Sautéed Parsleyed Potatoes.

6. Turn oven off, transfer chicken to a platter, and keep warm in oven while finishing sauce. Scrape vegetables and pan drippings into a food processor or electric blender and purée until almost smooth. Season with salt and pepper, then stir in parsley.

7. Cut chicken into serving pieces and put on plates or serving platter. Spoon on a small amount of sauce and pass remainder at table.

sautéed parsleyed potatoes

1½ pounds Yukon Gold or Red Bliss potatoes

2 to 3 tablespoons rendered duck fat

3 large cloves garlic

¼ cup flat-leaf parsley leaves

Salt and freshly ground black pepper to taste

EBERLY POULTRY

Levi W. Eberly grew up in the same hilly Lancaster County, Pennsylvania, countryside that is still home to the poultry business run by his sons Bob and George. In many ways little has changed since earlier generations of Eberlys settled in this area. Horse-drawn buggies filled with Amish farmers still crisscross the community. And Eberly's is still a small family-owned business that takes pride in its poultry.

What has changed since 1935 is how business is conducted. Grandfather Harvey Eberly sold live chickens to people going to local farmers markets. They in turn resold the birds. Today's generation of Eberlys now stays at the plant, committed to processing chickens and specialty poultry that taste as good as their grandfather's did, with a mix of old and new techniques.

BOB EBERLY: When I met George Faison in 1986, we were just getting into producing organic turkeys. If you know George, you know he's a pretty passionate kind of guy. He got wildly enthusiastic about the whole idea, and convinced us that we needed to do organic chickens as well. Soon Ariane had us free-ranging our birds too, because she believes they have a dramatically improved flavor. She was right. Then in 1989, NOFA (Northeast Organic Farming Association) certified us. Today we are the country's largest certified organic poultry farm.

In the past, other people have gotten wild about an idea like free-range and organic, and then they don't carry through. The difference about George and Ariane is they turn ideas into realities. D'Artagnan supports and protects their suppliers. They are very demanding about quality, but if they are committed to 8,000 chickens, for example, they don't call up and say send 4,000.

For a bird to be "certified organically raised — free range," it must meet the strict growing conditions supervised by NOFA and the USDA (U.S. Department of Agriculture). It has to be fed exclusively on certified organic grains (which come from fields free from pesticides and herbicides for at least three years), without animal by-products, protein supplements, growth hormones, tranquilizers, or antibiotics. The bird drinks pure spring-fed well water, without chlorine or fluorine added. That's the "organic" part.

To be "free-range," the birds must be able to forage outdoors, have access to natural light, and have at least 1½ square feet while indoors, overnight, or during inclement weather, compared to less than ½ square foot of space and artificial lighting for the entirety of a mass-produced bird's life!

It costs more to raise birds this way. It also takes 8 weeks to grow them, as opposed to 5 to 6 weeks. But the result is a healthier, leaner bird with a distinctly rich flavor. In fact, it's chicken as nature intended! For consumers who genuinely care about what their poultry tastes like, as well as how it's been raised, our standards matter.

ARIANE: Once in a while a new marketing ploy appears, with chickens identified as "Amish," "free-roaming," or, most common, "natural." Don't allow yourself to be confused by these terms, which provide no real substantiation of the quality of the bird you buy. "Amish" refers to the farmer who raised the bird, not to the bird itself; not all Amish and Mennonites raise birds according to free-range, organic standards. The term "free-roaming" has been disallowed by the USDA; it means absolutely nothing. And "natural" on a poultry bag means only that nothing was added at the slaughter plant; it does not imply anything about how the bird was raised or fed.

1. Peel potatoes, cut into ⅜-inch cubes, and place in a large bowl of cold water to cover. Once all potatoes are cut, drain water from bowl, and fill again. *Potatoes may be left in water for several hours.*

2. Heat duck fat in a large nonstick skillet over medium-high heat. Drain potatoes, and blot dry on paper towels. Add to hot fat and cook until crisp and browned on all sides, turning occasionally, about 15 minutes. While potatoes are cooking, finely mince garlic and parsley together. Season potatoes with salt, pepper, and garlic-parsley mixture, turning to coat evenly.

chicken with yams, fennel, and ginger

SERVES 4 TO 6

A chicken casserole probably unlike any you've tasted before. The ethereal blend of flavors, combined with chicken so tender it falls from the bones, is the perfect Sunday night supper or ready-when-you-are one-dish meal. Drink a chilly California Chardonnay.

2 tablespoons clarified butter

1 tablespoon fruity olive oil

4 to 6 pieces of chicken, white or dark meat, skinned and patted dry

½ cup good Armagnac or Cognac

1 cup chicken stock

½ cup dry white wine

2 cups very thinly sliced fennel

3 tablespoons sliced shallots

2 tablespoons sliced garlic

3 cups peeled yams, cut into ½-inch-thick slices (about 1¼ pounds)

1 cup loosely packed dried apricots, cut into ¼-inch dice (whole pitted rather than halves, if possible)

1 tablespoon finely julienned fresh gingerroot

5 (4-inch) sprigs rosemary; *do not* use loose leaves

2 (4-inch) sprigs thyme

Salt and freshly ground black pepper to taste

⅓ cup toasted sunflower seeds, to garnish (optional)

1. Preheat oven to 325°F.

2. Heat clarified butter and oil in a large skillet over medium-high heat until hot but not smoking. Add chicken pieces and brown on both sides, 5 to 7 minutes on each side. Transfer to a deep enamel or cast iron casserole with a tight-fitting lid.

3. Pour off butter-oil mixture and set aside. Deglaze pan with Armagnac, stirring up any browned cooking bits. Add stock and wine, turn heat to high, and boil until liquid is reduced by one-quarter. Pour liquid over the chicken in casserole.

4. Wipe out skillet. Heat 2 tablespoons of the reserved butter-oil mixture until hot. Add fennel, shallots, and garlic, cover, and sweat over medium heat until softened, 5 to 6 minutes, then scrape into the casserole.

5. Add yams, apricots, ginger, herbs, salt, and pepper to chicken, and mix to distribute the flavors. Cover tightly and bake for 1¾ to 2 hours, or until the meat falls off the bones. Sprinkle with toasted sunflower seeds and serve.

Adapted from Len Allison and the late Karen Hubert Allison, Hawaii

chicken provençal
with grilled vegetables

SERVES 4

This lavender, rosemary, and thyme–rubbed chicken grilled with colorful vegetables will carry your thoughts and spirits to sunny southern France. Add salad and a loaf of crusty bread. Serve a chilled Provençal wine, like a Bandol, and follow the meal with a platter of cheese and fruit.

1 tablespoon plus ⅓ cup olive oil

2 teaspoons plus 1 tablespoon minced garlic

1 tablespoon *each* dried thyme, rosemary, and lavender

1 chicken, 3½ to 4 pounds, cut into 8 parts

Coarse salt and freshly ground black pepper to taste

1 medium eggplant, cut crosswise into ½-inch slices

2 medium zucchini, cut crosswise into 1-inch slices

2 bunches scallions, roots and half of green parts removed

1 *each* red and yellow bell peppers, cored and seeded, cut into 1-inch-wide rings

¼ cup balsamic vinegar

1. Combine 1 tablespoon of the olive oil and 2 teaspoons of the garlic in a small bowl. Add the thyme, rosemary, and lavender, rubbing leaves between your hands to crush slightly, and stir to blend. Rub about 2 tablespoons of the mixture over the chicken. Season with salt and pepper, and set aside. *This may be done the day before except for the salt. Cover and refrigerate overnight.*

An hour before grilling, remove from refrigerator, add salt, and allow to sit at room temperature.
2. Lay eggplant slices on paper towels and sprinkle with salt to extract moisture. After 10 minutes, blot dry and turn over. Lightly salt again and let stand 10 minutes longer, then blot dry. Combine with zucchini, scallions, and peppers in a large flat pan.
3. Combine the remaining ⅓ cup of olive oil with balsamic vinegar, and pour over vegetables, tossing to coat evenly. Sprinkle on the remaining tablespoon of garlic, the remaining herb mixture, salt, and pepper, and toss again to make sure each vegetable is well coated. Add more oil if needed. Let vegetables marinate at room temperature.
4. Light a gas or charcoal grill and, when hot, place chicken parts skin side down to start cooking. Be careful not to burn skin. Adjust heat down to medium, and grill until chicken is crisp and is just cooked through, turning once or twice, 30 to 35 minutes. Times can vary a lot, depending on the kind of grill and temperature of the fire, as well as the size of the chicken. Remove and let stand at least 5 to 10 minutes before serving.
5. Place vegetable pieces on grill over medium heat and cook until soft, turning once or twice. Serve with chicken.

bangkok chicken thighs

SERVES 4

Rub skinless chicken thighs (or breasts) with a paste of garlic, tamarind, basil, and coriander, and you might discover one of the tastiest and easiest dishes to prepare for 4 or 40 friends. The marinade infuses a faraway taste that will satisfy even the most blasé diner. Heavy resealable plastic bags keep cleanup to a minimum. Serve with jasmine rice and sugar snap peas. Thai beer or a Zinfandel is our choice to quench your thirst.

4 to 5 large cloves garlic

6 tablespoons firmly packed dark brown sugar

¼ cup Thai fish sauce (nam pla, available at Asian markets)

2 tablespoons tamarind paste (available at Indian markets)

4 teaspoons dried basil

4 teaspoons ground coriander

½ to 1 teaspoon cayenne

4 to 6 large chicken thighs, skin and fat removed

Chopped cilantro, to garnish

1. Combine garlic, brown sugar, fish sauce, tamarind, basil, coriander, and cayenne in a blender, and purée until smooth. Scrape mixture into a resealable plastic bag or bowl, add thighs, seal or cover, turn contents over a couple of times to coat completely, then marinate 8 hours or overnight. *You may do this up to 2 days ahead.*
2. Preheat oven to 350°F.
3. Heat a large, ovenproof nonstick skillet over high heat. Add thighs flesh side down and brown quickly, about 2 to 3 minutes. Do not crowd or chicken will steam. Turn thighs over and transfer to oven. Bake for 30 minutes.
4. Meanwhile, drain remaining marinade into a small saucepan and boil to reduce by half. After chicken has baked for 15 minutes, brush with reduced marinade. When thighs are done, remove from oven, garnish with cilantro, and serve.

raspberry-glazed poussin
with wild mushroom ragout on wild rice pancakes

SERVES 4

Plump poussin, lacquered with sweet raspberry glaze, play against earthy wild mushrooms and toothsome, hearty wild rice pancakes. It's a luxurious combination of tastes and textures to tempt the most refined diner. Serve with steamed asparagus or green beans.

Wild Mushroom Ragout and Wild Rice Pancakes (recipes follow)

⅔ cup red wine

½ cup raspberry vinegar

¼ cup soy sauce

1 cup raspberry preserves, strained

4 poussin, about 1 pound each

2 teaspoons canola oil

Freshly ground black pepper to taste

Small sprigs parsley, to garnish

1. Prepare Wild Mushroom Ragout and Step 1 of Wild Rice Pancakes.

2. Combine wine, vinegar, soy sauce, and preserves in a small nonreactive saucepan, and bring to a boil over high heat. Continue cooking until glaze is reduced to 1 cup. Set aside.

3. Preheat oven to 400°F.

4. With a sharp knife or poultry shears, remove backbones, wings, and necks from poussin (discard or save for stock), and trim excess skin. Cut each bird into 1 whole breast and 2 drumstick-thigh combinations. Rinse and pat dry.

5. Heat oil in a large skillet or shallow roasting pan over medium-high heat until hot and almost smoking. Add poussin pieces, skin side down, and cook until browned, about 2½ minutes. Turn, brush each bird with about 2 tablespoons of glaze, and season with pepper. Transfer pan to oven. Bake until poussin are just about done, 10 minutes. Turn off oven. Brush birds with some of the remaining glaze, and leave in oven while finishing Step 2 of pancakes.

6. To serve, place a pancake at the top center of each of 4 warmed dinner plates. Divide mushroom ragout among plates, spooning it into the center of plates, slightly overlapping lower edge of pancake. Place breasts on top of mushrooms and a leg on either side of each breast. Spoon on remaining glaze, add a small parsley sprig between each drumstick and thigh joint, and serve. Pass extra pancakes at table, if desired.

wild mushroom ragout

2 cups boiling water

2 ounces dried wild mushrooms, any variety

1½ teaspoons unsalted butter

½ cup finely chopped shallots

½ cup tawny port

Salt and freshly ground black pepper to taste

2 tablespoons minced flat-leaf parsley

1. Pour boiling water over mushrooms and soak until soft, about 20 to 30 minutes. Lift mushrooms from liquid; discard any coarse stems and remove any grit. Strain mushroom soaking liquid through a fine sieve lined with a dampened paper towel, and transfer it to a small saucepan. Boil it to reduce to about ½ cup.

2. Melt butter in a saucepan over medium heat. Add shallots and sauté until limp and beginning to brown, 1½ minutes. Stir in port and reduced soaking liquid along with mushrooms, and bring liquid to a boil over high heat. Continue cooking until liquid has almost completely evaporated. Season with salt and a liberal amount of pepper. Stir in parsley and leave on low heat, partially covered, while preparing poussin.

wild rice pancakes

MAKES 8 TO 10 PANCAKES

½ cup all-purpose flour

¼ cup buckwheat flour

1 teaspoon baking powder

¼ teaspoon salt

Freshly ground black pepper to taste

¼ cup finely chopped pecans

1 egg

1 cup low-fat milk

1 cup cooked wild rice

1 to 2 tablespoons canola oil

1. Combine flours, baking powder, salt, pepper, and pecans in a large bowl. Beat egg and milk together, then stir into dry ingredients until blended. Stir in wild rice.
2. Heat a large nonstick skillet over medium-high heat. Add 1 tablespoon of the oil and, when hot, pour in about ¼ cup of batter for each 3½-inch pancake. Cook until bubbles form on the surface and underside is golden brown (lift with a spatula to check), 1½ to 2 minutes. Turn and cook second side until golden brown, 1½ minutes. Transfer to warm oven and continue until all pancakes are cooked.

roast poussin with white truffle jus
with lavender-honey roasted butternut squash

SERVES 4

Because each guest is served a whole poussin, the small thyme-scented birds make an exquisite special-occasion dish. The sauce, made from the pan drippings, is enriched with white truffle oil and butter. Combine with the lavender-honey roasted squash, and you'll think it's heaven-sent. Serve on a bed of Sautéed Swiss Chard (see page 213).

4 poussin, about 1 pound each, patted dry

Salt and freshly ground black pepper to taste

Lavender-Honey Roasted Butternut Squash
    (recipe follows)

1 large carrot, diced

1 rib celery, diced

1 medium leek, trimmed, split, washed well, white and pale green parts cut into 1-inch pieces

3 tablespoons unsalted butter, melted, plus 4 tablespoons cold butter, cut into cubes

1 teaspoon dried thyme

1 cup dry white wine

1 tablespoon white truffle oil

1. Preheat oven to 450°F.
2. Remove neck and giblets from poussin and reserve. Season birds inside and out with salt and pepper. Tuck wings behind neck, and truss with kitchen string.
3. Prepare Lavender-Honey Roasted Butternut Squash.
4. Make a nest of the carrot, celery, and leek, along with the necks and giblets, in a roasting pan. Arrange poussin on top. Combine melted butter and thyme in a small bowl, and brush it over the birds. Roast poussin in oven for 15 minutes, then reduce temperature to 350°F.
5. Pour wine over poussin and roast until juices run clear when thickest part of thigh is pierced with a fork, 15 to 20 minutes more. If birds are not a beautiful golden brown color, place under broiler for a minute to crisp and brown skin, turning to brown backs as well.
6. Remove birds from pan. Strain pan juices into a small saucepan, discarding

vegetables and giblets. Spoon off any fat and discard. Reduce liquid over high heat to ⅓ cup. Remove pan from heat and slowly whisk in cold butter and white truffle oil, waiting to add each butter cube until previous one is incorporated. Season with salt and pepper. Top poussin with a little truffle jus and serve along with squash.

lavender-honey roasted butternut squash

1 small butternut squash

3 tablespoons unsalted butter, cut into ½-inch cubes

2 tablespoons honey

1 teaspoon dried lavender

1 teaspoon dried thyme

½ teaspoon salt or to taste

Freshly ground black pepper to taste

1. Preheat oven to 400°F.
2. Peel squash and split lengthwise. Scoop out seeds and cut squash into ½-inch dice. Spread in a single layer in a roasting pan. Dot squash with butter and drizzle with honey. Sprinkle on lavender, thyme, salt, and pepper. Cover with aluminum foil and roast until tender, about 30 minutes, stirring occasionally. (If roasting along with poussin, this will take about 40 to 45 minutes.) Serve immediately, *or cool to room temperature, cover, and refrigerate for up to 2 days. Reheat before serving.*

Adapted from Kevin von Klause, chef-partner, White Dog Café, Philadelphia

roasted capon with chestnut honey
with dirty rice

SERVES 6 TO 8

Capon is a luxurious bird perfect to serve for any year-end holiday meal. Spread an ambrosial mixture of goat cheese and chestnut honey under the skin, and the juicy bird becomes celestial. As the bird roasts, the mixture melts, perfuming and basting the meat. Save the giblets for Dirty Rice, a Cajun favorite made with minced giblets, which give this dish its name.

1 capon, 8 pounds, giblets, neck, and excess fat removed, patted dry

Salt and freshly ground black pepper to taste

½ cup *each* unsalted butter and goat cheese, softened

3 tablespoons chestnut honey (available at specialty food stores), or any honey

3 tablespoons finely chopped shallots

2 tablespoons Dijon mustard

2 tablespoons cooked bacon, ventrèche, or pancetta, chopped or crumbled

2 teaspoons chopped fresh thyme leaves

2 cups chicken stock

Dirty Rice (recipe follows)

1. Preheat oven to 400°F.
2. Season capon inside and out with salt and pepper. Turn wing tips under.
3. Mix butter, goat cheese, honey, shallots, Dijon mustard, bacon, and thyme into a smooth paste. Using your fingers, gently

separate breast and thigh skin from meat. Distribute cheese mixture under skin, massaging flesh to smooth it as evenly as possible over breast and thighs. Place bird on rack in a roasting pan, breast side up, and roast for 20 minutes. Turn oven to 325°F and continue roasting, basting occasionally with pan juices, until an instant-read thermometer registers 160°F when inserted deep into thigh and juices run clear, about 2½ hours. While capon roasts, prepare Dirty Rice.

4. Remove capon from oven to a warm platter, tent lightly with foil, and let rest at least 10 to 15 minutes. Meanwhile, discard as much fat as possible from roasting pan. Set pan on top of stove. Pour in chicken stock and deglaze pan over high heat, stirring up all browned cooking bits. Boil until reduced to a thin sauce consistency. Carve capon at table and spoon sauce over slices. Serve with Dirty Rice.

dirty rice

2 tablespoons rendered duck fat or unsalted butter

2 ribs celery, finely chopped

1 medium onion, finely chopped

1 red or green bell pepper, cored and seeded, finely chopped

1 tablespoon minced garlic

1 cup capon, duck, or chicken giblets, cleaned and finely chopped

2 cups long-grain rice

3 cups chicken stock

2 bay leaves

1 teaspoon dried thyme

Salt, freshly ground black pepper, and Tabasco to taste

½ cup chopped scallions, including green parts

Heat duck fat in a large skillet over medium-high heat. Stir in celery, onion, bell pepper, and garlic, and sauté until translucent, about 5 minutes, stirring occasionally. Add giblets and cook for 2 to 3 minutes. Stir in rice and pour in chicken stock. Add bay leaves, thyme, salt, pepper, and Tabasco, and bring to a boil. Cover and reduce heat to a simmer. Cook until rice is tender and liquid is absorbed, 15 to 20 minutes. Taste to adjust seasonings, stir in scallions, and serve.

Adapted from Susan Spicer, chef-owner, Bayona and Spice, Inc., New Orleans

stewed capon in sugarcane brandy

SERVES 6 TO 8

Typical Grenadian ingredients, including sugarcane brandy and tannias (similar to taro or cassava), plus an old French technique of sautéing a bird in caramelized cane sugar still used in the Caribbean, create this lush, exotically flavored capon. We list readily available substitutes so you can easily enjoy it. A simple rice pilaf made with chicken stock and minced red bell peppers will help you to soak up every drop of the sauce. Have plenty of chilled beer — like a Yuengling Black & Tan — on hand.

4 tablespoons coconut oil (available at Caribbean groceries) or vegetable oil

2 tablespoons raw cane sugar (available at some supermarkets and health food stores) or brown sugar

1 capon, 8 pounds, giblets, neck, and excess fat removed, cut into 18 pieces, patted dry

1 teaspoon sea salt or to taste

2 *each* small onions and tomatoes, diced

4 small tannias (or substitute taro root), peeled and diced (about 4 cups)

5 bay leaves

4 Grenadian seasoning chilies or 3 habanero (Scotch bonnet) chilies, seeded and minced

½ teaspoon ground mace

1 stick cinnamon

½ teaspoon freshly grated nutmeg

2 cups coconut milk

1 cup sugarcane brandy or dark rum

½ cup lime juice

1 teaspoon aromatic bitters

Sea salt and freshly ground black pepper to taste

1. Heat a large casserole over medium heat. Add oil and sugar and, stirring constantly, let sugar brown to a rich, dark mahogany color. Season capon with salt and carefully sauté pieces, in batches if necessary, to brown on all sides, taking care not to burn the sugar.

2. Add the onions and tomatoes to the browned capon pieces, stir a few times, then add the tannias, bay leaves, chilies, mace, cinnamon, nutmeg, coconut milk, brandy, and lime juice. Bring to a boil, cover, reduce heat, and simmer until capon is tender, 40 to 45 minutes. Remove capon to a platter, lightly tent with foil, and keep warm.

3. Remove bay leaves and cinnamon from sauce and discard. Bring sauce to a boil over high heat and reduce by half to thicken, about 10 minutes. Season with aromatic bitters and salt and pepper to taste. Spoon sauce over capon and serve.

Adapted from Wayne Nish, chef-owner, March Restaurant, New York City

A TASTE OF GRENADA

WAYNE NISH: Recently I went to Grenada. Although I had heard many favorable things about their cooking, my expectations were surpassed. Unlike the situation in many other Caribbean nations, where international hotel food is the norm, a real restaurant culture has developed in Grenada, by and for the local people. Stewed Capon in Sugarcane Brandy is a good example of Creole cooking with local ingredients. Many of the ingredients can be found in the United States in local Chinatowns, as there is a historic connection with Chinese immigration to the West Indies in the late nineteenth and early twentieth centuries. Sautéing birds in caramelized sugar is an old French technique still used locally, if nowhere else anymore.

roast capon with cognac-mushroom sauce

SERVES 10

Bresse, a region of eastern France, is celebrated for raising some of that country's finest poultry. The capon is considered the "king of the table" by many local aficionados of chicken. This superb recipe does justice to that title, making you feel a bit noble as you serve it. The bird and its luscious sauce are worth an indulgence. Don't worry about adding any fat to the pan; the bird begins roasting on its back and quickly starts to render its fat. Serve with Sautéed Parsleyed Potatoes.

1 pound mushrooms (domestic white, wild, or a mixture), wiped clean and thinly sliced (about 7 cups)

1½ cups dry white wine

1 capon, 8 pounds, giblets, neck, and excess fat removed, patted dry

1¼ teaspoons *each* salt and freshly ground black pepper, or to taste

1 teaspoon herbes de Provence

Sautéed Parsleyed Potatoes (page 7)

1 tablespoon Cognac

1 cup heavy cream

1 teaspoon potato starch dissolved in 1 tablespoon water

1 tablespoon chopped fresh tarragon

1. Preheat oven to 400°F.

2. Combine mushrooms and wine in a saucepan, and bring to a boil over high heat. Cover, reduce heat to low, and boil gently for 10 minutes. Set pan aside off heat.

3. Season capon with 1 teaspoon each of the salt and pepper, and the herbes de Provence, and place bird on its back on a rack in a roasting pan. Turn wing tips under. Roast in oven for 30 minutes, then turn over and roast it, breast side down, for 60 minutes. Finally, turn capon on back again, and roast for 10 additional minutes, for a total roasting time of 1 hour 40 minutes. (A thermometer inserted into the deepest part of the thigh should register at least 160° to 170°F.) Transfer capon to an ovenproof platter, and keep warm in a 180°F oven.

4. Meanwhile, while capon is roasting, prepare Sautéed Parsleyed Potatoes.

5. After capon is done and is resting in a warm oven, prepare the sauce: Remove as much fat as possible from drippings in roasting pan and drain juice from mushrooms into pan. Heat mixture over high heat for a few seconds, stirring constantly to dissolve any browned cooking bits in pan, then pour resulting glaze through a strainer set over mushrooms. Add Cognac and cream to mushroom mixture, bring to a boil, and stir in dissolved potato starch. Mix in the remaining ¼ teaspoon of salt and pepper, and the tarragon.

6. Carve capon and serve it, with or without bones, with some of the sauce.

Adapted from Jacques Pépin, cookbook author, public television personality, dean of studies, French Culinary Institute, New York City

poule au pot
with gros sel sauce

SERVES 8

Poule au pot, a favorite dish of Henri IV, is the pride and joy of many mothers in southwestern France. Their recipes are often fiercely guarded secrets passed down only to daughters. In restaurants the dish is served in three courses: the rich, elixir-like poaching broth first, with a spoonful of red wine in the last sip (called *le chabrot;* see page 263); next the vegetables and stuffing; and finally the sliced bird with a sauce made with coarse sea salt *(gros sel).* At home, all of the dishes are placed on the table, but the broth is always eaten first. We suggest a capon rather than the old hen, or *poule,* that is traditionally braised. It is served with an emulsified sauce made with mustard, hard-cooked eggs, some of the broth, plus oil and vinegar.

FOR THE STUFFING:

1 capon liver or 2 chicken livers, chopped

6 ounces chopped pork sausage meat

3 ounces unsmoked cured dry ham, such as Jambon de Bayonne or prosciutto, diced

3 ounces Grade B foie gras, diced (optional; see page 255)

1 shallot, chopped

½ cup chopped flat-leaf parsley

2 eggs, beaten

2 tablespoons Armagnac

1 tablespoon chopped garlic

Salt and freshly ground black pepper to taste

2 to 3 slices day-old country bread, about 2 ounces, torn into small pieces

1 cup milk

FOR THE CAPON:

1 capon, 8 pounds, giblets, neck, 2 wing joints, and extra fat removed

Salt and freshly ground black pepper to taste

8 medium turnips, quartered

3 onions, each studded with 3 whole cloves

3 carrots, cut into 2-inch pieces

2 ribs celery, cut into 2-inch pieces

2 leeks, trimmed and washed, cut into 2-inch pieces

3 bay leaves

2 bunches fresh thyme

1 head garlic, separated into cloves, with skin left on

4 quarts chicken stock

1 head Savoy cabbage, large ribs removed, cored, quartered, and blanched

TO FINISH:

Gros Sel Sauce (recipe follows)

8 ounces dried vermicelli pasta

Capers, pickled onions, cornichons, and mustard, to garnish (optional)

1. Prepare stuffing. Blend liver, sausage, ham, and foie gras, if using, in a bowl. Add shallot, parsley, eggs, Armagnac, garlic, salt, and pepper. Soak bread in milk, then gently squeeze to remove excess milk. Add to meat mixture, and mix well. Cover and refrigerate until needed.
2. Season inside of capon well with salt and pepper. Fill cavity with the stuffing

and sew closed with butcher's twine, making sure twine is very tight. (Or roll stuffing into a log in a double layer of cheesecloth and tie ends closed. Add to bouillon about ½ hour before bird is done cooking, and poach until firm.)

3. Add turnips, onions, carrots, celery, and leeks to a large, deep pot. Place stuffed capon on vegetables, add bay leaves, thyme, and garlic. Add a generous sprinkling of salt and pepper, and pour in stock. It should completely cover bird and vegetables. Add a little water if needed. Bring liquid to a boil, reduce heat, and simmer gently until meat is very tender and almost falling off the bones, at least 2½ hours. Cook the cabbage in the bouillon for the last ½ hour of cooking time.

4. While capon cooks, prepare Gros Sel Sauce.

5. Carefully remove capon and vegetables from pot with large slotted spoons. Lightly tent with foil. Strain broth, then bring to a boil for 5 minutes. Taste to adjust seasonings, add pasta, and cook until tender, about 8 to 10 minutes. While pasta cooks, cut capon into serving portions. Remove the stuffing from the cavity and cut into slices (or unwrap and slice). Arrange vegetables around capon and cover with foil. Keep in a warm (180°F) oven.

6. Ladle broth with vermicelli into bowls, and serve. Don't forget to pass a bottle of red wine for the *chabrot*. Following the broth, serve the stuffing, vegetables, and capon, pouring some of the hot broth over them before serving. Garnish with capers, pickled onions, cornichons, and mustard. Serve with Gros Sel Sauce.

WHY AN APRON IS THE MOST IMPORTANT TOOL IN A GASCON WOMAN'S LIFE, AND DEBATING POULE AU POT

While Laurent Manrique was chef at the New York Waldorf Astoria's Peacock Alley restaurant, he decided to serve poule au pot, a traditional Gascon supper. The stewed hen, with sausage stuffing and vegetables, is considered the pride of Gascon matriarchs, so Manrique invited his own mother, Nicole, and two other accomplished home cooks, Lucette and Mimi, to fly over and join him in the kitchen.

On the fateful day, in the middle of the elegant restaurant stood Lucette, proudly ladling out the soup. Nicole, meanwhile, circulated among the guests, explaining how important an apron is in a Gascon woman's life:

She gathers her apron in one hand, fills it with cereal, then uses the other hand to feed the barnyard animals. A woman carries fresh vegetables and eggs in her apron. At the river, an apron protects the upper body while washing the linens. An apron makes a perfect sling to carry a baby. Finally, your apron is right there when you need to dust the table.

At this, a patron asked Nicole: *If you never take it off, when do you wash it?*

Meanwhile, reports Manrique, the three friends had debated the fine points of their own recipes for the dish. Mimi was against putting pork in the sausage. Lucette said the stuffing should be put inside the bird, not wrapped in a cheesecloth and poached separately. Whose recipe did chef Manrique finally settle on? That of *la mère* Nicole, of course, because sons want to please their moms.

gros sel sauce

MAKES ABOUT 4 CUPS

4 hard-cooked eggs, chopped

2 tablespoons Pommery mustard

½ cup sherry vinegar

¼ cup mixed chopped tarragon, flat-leaf
parsley, chives, and chervil

2 cups grapeseed or canola oil

1 cup warm broth (reserved from above)

2 to 3 tablespoons coarse sea salt

Combine eggs, mustard, vinegar, and
herbs in a bowl. Slowly stir in oil, then add
the broth. Season to taste with sea salt.

Adapted from Laurent Manrique, chef, Campton Place Hotel,
San Francisco

 duck

Duck is one of the most delicious birds to eat. It is also one of the most versatile and easiest to prepare. It takes amiably to flavors from around the world, and in spite of what some frustrated cooks might say, duck isn't greasy and fatty when well prepared. To make things simpler, today's shoppers can buy different breeds of ducks, ducks that are whole or cut up, duck breasts or duck legs, smoked duck, or duck confit. As the recipes in this chapter illustrate, duck isn't only for "fancy meals."

The introduction to this book relates how George Faison and Ariane Daguin started D'Artagnan by selling fresh (i.e., raw) foie gras, the fatted liver of the Moulard duck. To this day, Moulard ducks and their liver are a cornerstone of the company. Ducks have also been part of Ariane's patrimony and everyday life since her birth. André Daguin, Ariane's father and the two-star chef-owner of the Hôtel de France in Auch, almost single-handedly created a worldwide passion for rare-cooked *magrets,* the breasts of fatted Moulard ducks.

These sizable birds are the sterile offspring of a female Pekin and a male Muscovy duck. The crossbred ducks have large breasts (each half breast weighs about a pound and easily serves two). The meat is slightly more gamy tasting than that of other ducks, with a hint of foie gras aroma. It looks a lot like red meat with a fine grain and a somewhat firm texture.

ARIANE: In Gascony, Moulard ducks are the backbone of all gastronomic traditions. For local inhabitants, there is almost a religious reverence about the birds, with centuries of tradition ingrained in their souls. In fact, one day we will probably discover that

Gascons have a region in their brains that preserves all duck lore and recipes. This would include memories of the Gauls who lived just above the Pyrenees — my ancestors — who taught themselves how to domesticate these migratory waterfowl.

The Gascon love of duck is centuries old. Before the early Romans set their sights on Gaul, they invaded Egypt. When they returned, they brought back from the rich land of the Nile a very interesting way to care for their web-footed animals: they were separated into pens and force-fed twice or three times a day with little balls of cereal or a mixture of dried figs.

The effect of this regime on the birds was the same as what occurs naturally when the air cools and the leaves change colors: ducks and geese begin to gorge themselves on any piece of grass, grain, insects, and even fish they can find. Within just 15 days, they double in weight and create a thick layer of fat all over their body; this enables them to withstand the brutally cold temperatures of high altitude during migration. Most important, they also create a magnificent huge, pale, fat liver that serves as an energy storehouse. It is located exactly in the middle of the body for perfect aerodynamic equilibrium.

Twice a year this happens, with time-clock precision: in the wild, migratory ducks and geese eat and drink like crazy before the long, nonstop flight north or south, depending on the season. Once they arrive, they resume their normal regimen and the enlarged liver, which may weigh up to 2 pounds, shrinks to its normal size, about 2 ounces.

The Egyptians recognized the superiority of fat birds and did everything to promote their growth. Tomb paintings from as early as the Fourth Dynasty (about 2600 B.C.) depict the daily ritual of feeding the domesticated birds. Ducks and geese were considered so

Moulard ducks ⌃

important by the Pharaohs and other royalty that they carried the birds with them, as sacred symbols, into the afterlife.

Like the Egyptians, Romans thought the soul of a goose was in its liver. Yet this did not prevent them from eating this foie gras that Apicius and Lucullus prepared and enjoyed in so many different ways.

Eventually, the custom of force-feeding followed the Jewish exodus and resettlements to pockets of Eastern Europe, Alsace, and Gascony. Following the normal life cycle of the birds, Gascons force-fed ducks and geese in the fall as they reached adult size. The timing was perfect, as provisions were needed to survive the coming winter. And never has the art of preserving foods been more effective or tastier than with the meat of these birds, preserved, or "confited," in their own fat. (*Confit* is the past participle of the French verb *confire,* "to preserve.") All parts of the bird, including the giblets and famous foie gras, were salted, simmered in fat, and then stored in big earthenware pots, buried in goose or duck fat, to be eaten much later. Peasants regularly ate slabs of foie gras on bread. Our Gascon king, Henri IV, sent for whole barrels of the stuff, since nobody in Paris made confit.

Foie gras became the noble, expensive, aristocratic delight that it is today only after the infamous Alsatian chef of Maréchal de Condale, Jean-Pierre Clause, incorporated it into a pâté, in 1778. (*Pâté* at that time still meant a hot or cold meat mixture surrounded by pastry, what we call pâté en croûte today.) That nobody in Gascony thought of committing such a crime — mixing and grinding foie gras with less noble ingredients like pork — is not astonishing. We simply love the taste of duck liver and we respect it.

▲ Mural from the tomb of Nebamun, at Thebes,
showing domesticated geese

But enough about foie gras and confit, which are dealt with in detail in Part 3. In this chapter you will find several recipes for magrets, the breasts of these Moulard ducks, as well as for breasts of Muscovy ducks. To prepare them for cooking, trim away excess fat that extends beyond the edge of the meat. Using a very sharp knife, score skin and fat on the diagonal into ¼-inch squares, being careful not to cut the flesh. Cook skin side first in a medium-hot pan to completely render the fat, then turn and cook flesh side until rare or medium rare for maximum juiciness and flavor. These breasts taste like red meat and that is how they are best enjoyed.

Also, there are a few recipes for whole ducks. Aside from a mallard recipe, they are mostly for Pekins, the ones you find most readily in markets. No matter which variety of duck you choose, you will have to make a compromise of sorts. Breasts are usually best when the flesh is rare or medium rare. Drumsticks and thighs can be tough and stringy at this point. They need longer, slower cooking. Often the solution is to treat the sections separately, even removing the breast from the bird when it is done, while leaving the legs to cook, or disjointing the bird before cooking.

While we've given top billing to Moulards and their magrets, there are other breeds of duck commercially available in the United States. For many Americans, the duck they still encounter most often is a Pekin. These are perfectly good birds, as long as you buy them fresh.

The Pekin (not to be confused with Peking, which is a style of cooking duck) originally came from China, where it is known to have been domesticated for more than a thousand years. How they got from there to Long Island, New York, and mass acceptance, is a subject for conjecture.

One version of the story says that some Pekins first arrived in San Francisco in the 1870s from China, and that by 1901 Reichart Farms, located just north of the Bay in Sonoma, California, had begun selling ducks raised from the original stock. The market for ducks was underwhelming, to say the least, since the birds were irregularly sized and the ratio of meat to bones was poor. The only people who regularly cooked them were immigrants who knew them from their homeland cuisines.

Somehow, through an entrepreneurial scheme, ducks made it across the country and reached Long Island, a naturally perfect habitat for them. Thanks to a persistent marketing campaign, and improved husbandry, the white-feathered Pekin became a success. The supply became consistent, and the birds of a standard size and weight, about 4 to 5 pounds. Although this seems a generous size, by the time the fat is rendered, one duck will only feed two people, unless it is cut up into a stew. Probably what recommends them most to Americans is their mild-tasting flesh and attractive price. For farmers, the appeal is the ease and speed of breeding.

Muscovy ducks, originally from Central America, are another commercially available breed. Also known as Barbary (or Barbarie), they are leaner than Pekins, with redder meat and a more pronounced flavor. Males average about 7 to 8 pounds; a whole boneless breast weighs about 2 pounds. Females are about half the size of males. This difference can be helpful when choosing the size of a serving portion.

When the breast is skinned, the meat is 98 percent fat free. Thighs and drumsticks are large, and delicious in stews and any dish where long, slow cooking is required. Like the Moulard's, the Muscovy's liver can become enlarged into a foie gras. Only the male's liver is useful, as female livers remain small and veiny, and become spongy when sliced, sautéed, or used in a terrine. The Muscovy's large size and special upbringing make it much more expensive to breed than the Pekin (10 weeks to full growth instead of 6). Aside from some distinctive physical attributes, the Muscovy duck's most unique characteristic is that it doesn't quack, it hisses.

Additionally, hunters regularly shoot several varieties of wild duck, including the teal, canvasback, and mallard. Typically, these birds are smaller than their domesticated cousins, making a single bird a generous serving for one but inadequate for two diners to share. Of the wild ducks, mallards are the most readily available when commercially farm-raised. Like other animals from the wild, these ducks have far less fat and a stronger flavor than the farm-raised ones. Wild birds that feed inland on grains and wild berries taste milder than ducks forced to rely on fish and water animals in brackish marshes. Under the latter conditions, ducks can develop an oily, unpleasantly aggressive taste that many seasoned hunters have encountered.

The gaminess of wild duck is sought after by many aficionados, who like their birds barely cooked to a rare stage.

EVERYTHING BUT THE QUACK

ARIANE: If there is one thing my father taught me, it was respect for the prime ingredients. To abide by this rule, at D'Artagnan we use everything in the duck but the quack! (Recipes to help you make your own versions of some of these dishes are found throughout this book.)

DRUMSTICKS AND THIGHS

- *Duck rillettes.* Duck simmered in an aromatic stock until the meat naturally shreds and falls off the bones. (See page 292.)
- *Duck Terrine Mousquetaire.* A classic country-style terrine enhanced with prunes and Armagnac. First we debone the bird and grind the meat with the spices, then cook it as a terrine. (Terrine recipes are in Part 3.)
- *Duck leg confit.* Whole legs are cured in salt and spices, then slowly cooked in duck fat. (See page 291.)
- *Duck sausage with Armagnac.* A must in garbure and cassoulet (see pages 32 and 293); it is also great just grilled.
- *Duck and cornbread stuffing.* Chefs use it in lasagnas and meat loaves.

BREASTS AND WINGS

- *Duck prosciutto.* Individual breasts cured in salt and herbs, then hung to slowly dry, while constantly being brushed with olive oil. (See page 289.)
- *Smoked duck breast.* Seasoned only with salt and cracked pepper, the breasts are hot-smoked very slowly over hickory chips.
- *Duck pastrami.* Same idea as smoked duck breasts, but they are first marinated in molasses and traditional pastrami spices.
- *Smoked duck wings.* Confited and smoked, they are a terrific snack dipped in Roquefort dressing.

BONES

- *Demi-glace.* Bones give it the collagen necessary for the gelatinous texture, and the 3 days' cooking time naturally concentrates flavor. (See page 33.)

WHOLE DUCK DEBONED

- *Duck galantine.* A deboned whole duck is stuffed with a mixture of the ground meat, a roll of foie gras, and some apricots marinated in Pousse Rapière (a liqueur of Armagnac with orange essence). The whole thing is then carefully wrapped and slowly poached in duck stock.

SKIN

- *Rendered duck fat.* The "butter" (but better) of Gascony can be used to cook everything: eggs, vegetables, wild mushrooms, potatoes, meat, and even a dessert, the pastis Gascon. (See Step 1, page 291.)
- *Cracklings.* This is what's left when you render fat. These crispy bits of fried skin are delicious when salted and eaten straight out of the pan; they are only good when freshly made. (See Step 3, page 37.)

GIBLETS

- *Foie gras.* These enlarged duck livers are available fresh (raw) and in a variety of preparations. (See Part 3.)
- *Gizzards confit.* Delicious when sliced warm in salads. (See page 291.)
- *Hearts.* Skewered with cèpes and grilled, they are the fast food of Gascony.
- *"White olives."* Found only in male ducks, they are seared in duck fat for maximum flavor. (See page 291.)

duck quesadillas

MAKES 6 WEDGES

A speedy hors d'oeuvre that can be tailored to your own tastes and invention. Between a pair of flour tortillas, you can let your creativity go wild. Spread a little ancho chili paste, honey mustard, or mole sauce. Sprinkle on cheeses like shredded Monterey Jack, Cheddar, Manchego, or blue. Then top with marinated artichoke hearts or roasted peppers. Surely you can think of many other variations. Serve with icy beer or margaritas.

⅓ cup grated Gouda cheese

1 scallion, thinly sliced

¼ avocado, peeled and thinly sliced

1 to 2 ounces smoked duck breast, fat removed and thinly sliced, or Duck Rillettes (see page 292), or shredded duck confit (see page 291)

3 to 4 pickled jalapeño slices, chopped

2 (8-inch) flour tortillas

1. Arrange Gouda, scallion, avocado, duck, and jalapeño on 1 tortilla. Cover with the second tortilla.
2. Heat a 10-inch nonstick skillet over medium-high heat. Put quesadilla in skillet and cook until bottom side is lightly colored, about 4 to 5 minutes. Turn and cook until second side is lightly colored and cheese is melted, 3 to 4 minutes.
3. Remove from skillet, cut into 6 wedges using a pizza cutter or sharp knife, and serve immediately.

Adapted from Ann Brody, specialty food consultant, Bethesda, Maryland

curried duck soup with cucumber-rice salad

SERVES 4

What to do with a duck carcass and leftover bits of duck? This creamy, mildly spicy hot soup, served with a mound of cool rice salad in the center, will put them to festive use. By heating the curry spices, you lightly toast them and enrich the flavor. A chilled Gewürztraminer will balance the flavors.

1 tablespoon Madras curry powder

2 tablespoons rendered duck fat

1 small onion, diced

½ small rib celery, diced

1 small carrot, diced

½ cup dry white wine

2 cups duck stock made with duck carcasses (see page 33)

½ cup cooked jasmine rice

½ small cucumber, peeled, seeded, and cut into ⅛-inch dice

1 tablespoon chopped cilantro, plus cilantro sprigs, to garnish

2 tablespoons sour cream

1 tablespoon minced red onion

½ tablespoon lime juice

Salt and freshly ground black pepper to taste

1 cup coconut milk

1 cup half-and-half

1 Thai (or other small hot) chili, thinly sliced

Grated zest 1 lime

4 to 6 tablespoons minced cooked duck meat

Curried Duck Soup with Cucumber-Rice Salad ❯

1. Heat curry powder in a small skillet over medium-high heat until lightly toasted, shaking pan often. Melt duck fat in a heavy casserole over medium heat. Add onion, celery, carrot, and curry powder. Cover and sweat until vegetables are tender, about 5 minutes, stirring occasionally. Add wine, raise heat, and boil until reduced by half. Pour in stock, partially cover pan, and simmer soup for 40 minutes.

2. Meanwhile, prepare cucumber-rice salad: Mix rice, cucumber, chopped cilantro, sour cream, red onion, and lime juice together in a small bowl. Season with salt and pepper, then chill until needed.

3. After soup has simmered, add coconut milk, half-and-half, Thai chili, and lime zest, and simmer 5 minutes longer, then strain. Return soup to casserole, stir in duck meat, and keep hot until serving. Fill 4 bowls with soup. Spoon a small mound of cool rice salad in center and add a sprig of cilantro. Serve at once.

Adapted from Thomas Salamunovich, chef, Vail, Colorado

hearty duck and cabbage soup (garbure)

SERVES 4 TO 6 GENEROUSLY

A rustic, peasant-style duck and cabbage soup meal from Gascony. Enjoy it on a chilly evening, with thick slices of country bread. There are as many varieties of this much-loved classic as there are cooks in the region. Some use goose instead of duck, others add large white dried beans called *cocos* as soon as the stock boils.

A piece of rind from an old hanging Jambon de Bayonne is considered essential to the flavor in southwestern France. If you have a nice piece available, it is the secret to a perfect garbure; otherwise, don't skimp on the ventrèche.

2 quarts Duck Stock (recipe follows), or 1½ cups duck and veal demi-glace (see page 33) plus 6½ cups water

12 cloves garlic

½ cup rendered duck fat

2 onions, chopped

2 ribs celery, chopped

½ pound ventrèche or pancetta, diced

1 rind from an old prosciutto (optional)

6 eggs

1 pound raw duck or pork sausage meat, casing removed, broken into small pieces

¼ cup chopped flat-leaf parsley

2 duck legs confit, cut in half at the joint (see page 291)

1 head Savoy cabbage

4 carrots, cut into 1-inch pieces

Salt and freshly ground black pepper to taste

4 duck gizzards confit, thinly sliced

12 cloves garlic confit (see Step 4, page 76)

1. Prepare Duck Stock.

2. Chop 6 cloves of the garlic. Heat 2 tablespoons of the duck fat in a large pot or Dutch oven over medium-high heat. Stir garlic, onions, celery, and ventrèche into pot and sauté until tender, 5 minutes. Pour in Duck Stock and bring liquid to a boil. Reduce to a simmer.

3. Meanwhile, beat eggs with sausage meat and parsley. Heat 2 more tablespoons of the duck fat in a large nonstick skillet, over medium heat. Pour in egg mixture and cook until first side is golden brown. Slide omelet onto a large plate, cover it with a second plate and invert it, then slide it back into pan. Cook second side until brown. Slide omelet and duck legs confit into stock. Simmer for 30 minutes.

4. Remove blemished leaves from cabbage and discard. Core cabbage and cut into 4 or 6 wedges. Bring a large pot of salted water to a boil, add cabbage, and blanch for 5 minutes, then drain well. Heat 2 tablespoons of the duck fat in a saucepan. Add cabbage, turning to coat evenly, and adding more fat if needed. Transfer cabbage and carrots to soup pot and cook for 30 minutes longer. Season to taste with salt and pepper. *Recipe may be made ahead to this point and refrigerated for several days — it gets better as it sits.*

5. Ten minutes before serving, add sliced gizzards and garlic confit. Ladle garbure into warmed large flat bowls, dividing duck, omelet, and vegetables evenly, and serve.

duck stock

MAKES 2 QUARTS

3 pounds duck bones, chopped into pieces

2 tablespoons rendered duck fat

1 cup *each* thinly sliced onion, carrot, and celery

2 teaspoons salt

2 quarts water

4 sprigs flat-leaf parsley

2 sprigs thyme

2 bay leaves

1 large clove garlic, unpeeled

10 black peppercorns

1. Preheat oven to 375°F.

2. Spread bones on a heavy baking sheet. Drizzle on fat, tossing to coat. Roast for 30 minutes, turning occasionally. Add

---

DEMI-GLACE: SHORTCUT TO MAXIMUM FLAVOR

D'Artagnan's duck and veal demi-glace is made according to traditional methods whereby duck bones are combined with veal bones to make stock. The stock is slowly simmered until reduced by about half its volume. This takes 3 days and imparts great depth of flavor. The liquid is strained, then red wine is added, and again it's reduced by half. Finally, a little tomato paste is stirred in. No additional gelatin is needed because the bones are rich in natural collagen. Nor is any salt or flour added. The result is a very concentrated stock.

At home, we store demi-glace in its original container in the freezer, next to the duck fat. We simply use a hot spoon to remove the amount needed. Our duck and veal demi-glace is available at many fine specialty stores as well as directly from D'Artagnan. It's simply the easiest and best shortcut for making great soups and sauces.

If you want to make demi-glace at home but don't want to spend 3 days doing it, a quick option is found on page 88.

onion, carrot, and celery, turn to coat with oil, and continue roasting until vegetables are richly browned but not scorched, about 25 minutes.

3. Transfer bones and vegetables to a stockpot. Deglaze the roasting pan with enough hot water to dissolve all browned spots and add to pot. Add salt and 2 quarts water, or more if needed to cover bones. Bring liquid to a boil, then turn heat down so liquid is simmering fairly quickly. Simmer uncovered for 45 minutes, skimming any fat and impurities that rise to the surface.

4. Add parsley, thyme, bay leaves, garlic, and peppercorns. Simmer uncovered for 3 hours, adding hot water as necessary to keep bones and vegetables covered. Pour through fine sieve, pressing with a wooden

spoon to extract as much liquid as possible. Discard solids and pour liquid through a strainer lined with several layers of dampened cheesecloth. If there are more than 2 quarts of stock, boil to reduce. *Stock may be refrigerated 3 to 4 days, or chilled and then frozen for several weeks. Remove the solidified fat on the top before reheating.*

A FLAVORFUL TAPENADE FOR BREAD

Garbure will sate even the most serious of appetites. However, if you want a little something extra to spread on your slices of country bread, purée some of the white beans that have been cooked in the garbure together with garlic, parsley, and a little duck fat in an electric blender or food processor until smooth. Season with coarse salt to taste. It's scrumptious! Use the same spread with duck prosciutto or other fillings in a pita bread sandwich. It's also a good hors d'oeuvre.

warm curried moulard duck and apple salad

SERVES 4 AS A LIGHT MAIN COURSE

This warmly spiced salad will rouse your palate if you are a curry lover. Thin slices of lean, rosy duck breast rest on a tangy green apple salad laced with cumin-anise oil and balsamic vinegar. Do not score the breast fat before searing, so the skin can be removed in a single piece. The flavors in this simple dish are exciting, so long as you don't stint with the salt and pepper. Star anise and aniseed are available in many supermarkets, as well as at Asian or Middle Eastern groceries. Grapeseed oil and soybean oil are often found in specialty or health food stores. If they are unavailable, use canola oil.

¼ cup *each* grapeseed oil and soybean oil, or
  ½ cup canola oil

6 star anise

¼ tablespoon aniseeds

1½ tablespoons ground cumin

1 whole Moulard duck breast, cut into
  2 magrets, patted dry

2 tablespoons unsalted butter

4 chopped shallots

1 teaspoon chopped garlic

4 tablespoons hot or mild curry powder, according to taste

4 tablespoons grated fresh gingerroot

4 tablespoons honey

4 tablespoons thinly sliced chives or chopped scallion greens

Salt and freshly ground black pepper to taste

4 Granny Smith or other tart green apples, cored and cut into small dice

1 tablespoon balsamic vinegar

1. Heat the oils in a saucepan to 165°F. Add star anise, aniseed, and ground cumin. Cover, remove from heat, and steep for about 30 minutes, then strain through a double layer of cheesecloth or a clean kitchen towel. Cool and reserve.

2. Heat a heavy skillet over medium-high heat until hot. Place duck magrets skin side down in skillet and sear until skin is crisp. Turn and sear second side for 3 to 4 minutes. Remove to a warm plate, let rest for 15 minutes, then remove skin and fat from breasts and discard. Cut meat across the grain into thin slices and put aside. Breast will be quite rare.

3. Melt butter in a skillet over medium-high heat. Stir in shallots, garlic, 2 tablespoons of the curry powder, 2 tablespoons of the ginger, and all of the duck slices. Stir in 2 tablespoons of the honey, and cook until breast is rare to medium rare, 1 to 2 minutes. Sprinkle with 2 tablespoons of the chives, season with salt and pepper, and set aside.

4. Heat 2 tablespoons of the reserved cumin-anise oil in a skillet over medium-high heat until hot. Add apples and sauté until warmed through, 2 to 3 minutes, then stir in the remaining 2 tablespoons each of the curry powder, ginger, honey, and chives. Season with salt and pepper, and divide among 4 plates. Lay duck slices over apples. Blend 4 tablespoons of the cumin-anise oil with balsamic vinegar, drizzle over duck, and serve.

Adapted from Thierry Rautureau, chef-owner, Rover's Restaurant, Seattle

pekin duck breast salad with blackberries, asparagus, and cracklings

SERVES 2 AS A MAIN COURSE SALAD
OR 4 AS AN APPETIZER

Combine thin slices of duck breast with brilliant green asparagus tips and jewel-like blackberries in this handsome salad. Poaching the skinless breasts in stock keeps the meat moist and flavorful without any fat. The bottom halves of the asparagus stalks are puréed with walnut oil and raspberry vinegar for a creamy-zingy dressing that tingles on the tongue. For croutons, make cracklings. But beware. They are addictive. Like the chip commercial says, you can't eat just one.

16 spears young asparagus (about 1 pound)

1 whole Pekin duck breast, cut into 2 cutlets

Coarse salt and freshly ground black pepper to taste

1½ cups duck or chicken stock

½ head red leaf lettuce, torn into bite-size pieces

½ small bunch watercress, coarse stems removed, broken into small pieces

7 tablespoons walnut oil

2½ tablespoons raspberry vinegar

1 tablespoon Dijon mustard

1 tablespoon minced fresh tarragon leaves, or 1 teaspoon dried tarragon

1 teaspoon green peppercorns packed in brine, rinsed

4 ounces blackberries or raspberries

1. Break the woody base from each asparagus stalk and peel stalks from just below tip. Bring a large pot of salted water to a boil, add asparagus, and cook until tender, just a few minutes. Drain, shock in cold water, and set aside, covered with a damp paper towel.

2. Remove skin and fat from each breast half by first sliding your fingers between the meat and skin on one side. Grab skin and gently pull. It should easily separate from most of the breast. At points where it is attached, use a sharp paring knife to free it. Season meat with salt and pepper and set aside.

3. Make cracklings: Cut skin into small squares, ½ to ¾ inch, and combine with 2 tablespoons water in a small saucepan. Set pan over high heat until a little fat is rendered, then reduce to medium heat and cook until all fat is rendered and the skin is light brown and crisp, stirring occasionally to prevent sticking. Remove cracklings to paper towels with a slotted spoon

and blot well. Toss with salt. Keep warm in a slow oven, or reheat before serving.

4. Meanwhile, heat a skillet over high heat. Remove 1 tablespoon of the duck fat from saucepan with cracklings and add to skillet. When hot, add breasts, and cook until lightly seared, about 1½ minutes, then turn and cook second side for 1½ minutes. Pour stock over duck, bring liquid to a boil, then adjust heat down so liquid simmers. Cook until breasts are medium rare, 6 minutes, turning once. Remove breasts from liquid and let cool.

5. Combine lettuce and watercress in a bowl. Pour on 1 tablespoon of the walnut oil and 1 teaspoon of the raspberry vinegar, and toss. Season with salt and pepper, toss again, then divide between 2 dinner plates.

6. Cut asparagus spears in half, leaving about 2 inches of stalk attached to each tip. Lay tips over lettuce, radiating in pairs from center of plate, like spokes. To make dressing, combine remaining stalk ends with the remaining 6½ teaspoons vinegar, the mustard, tarragon, and green peppercorns in a food processor or electric blender, and purée until smooth. Scrape down sides and, with motor running, slowly pour in the remaining 6 tablespoons walnut oil. Season with salt and pepper.

7. Cut each duck breast crosswise into 8 slices, and lay them between the asparagus spokes. Drizzle 3 to 4 tablespoons of the dressing over asparagus and duck. Divide blackberries between plates, sprinkle on cracklings in center, and serve. Pass remaining dressing at table, if desired.

◄ Pekin Duck Breast Salad
with Blackberries, Asparagus, and Cracklings (page 35)

pan-seared cod
with duck confit

SERVES 4

Are you among the culinarily adventurous? Good! When delicate sautéed cod is teamed with crisped duck confit, you will be rewarded with a spectacularly "meaty" meal. It's like cod meunière with moxie. Drink a white Graves, such as a 1994 Château Carbonnieux.

4 (7-ounce) skinless cod fillets, 1¼ inches thick

Salt and freshly ground black pepper to taste

All-purpose flour

2 tablespoons rendered duck fat

1 duck leg confit, boned, skin and meat finely diced (page 291)

⅓ cup minced shallots

½ cup dry white wine

GRIMAUD FARMS OF CALIFORNIA

In 1984 Groupe Grimaud, a French-based world leader in the duck industry, looked at the United States with the intention of increasing its presence in the American duck market. At that time, there were no significant growers of the Muscovy duck, long the favorite of European chefs and diners.

After researching the U.S. domestic duck industry, Joseph Grimaud and Claude Bigo decided to enter the market and started a venture in Stockton, California, where Grimaud Farms of California operates today. Claude Bigo is president of the American company.

CLAUDE BIGO: Two hard years later, I decided that the only way to really control the growth and direction of operations was to move to California permanently with my family. From that time, our business has grown from under $1 million in annual revenues in 1987 to more than $8 million today.

Prior to Grimaud's presence, Muscovys, either fresh or frozen, were virtually unavailable. To produce this exceptional breed of duck takes a lot of work. Every 18 months, our farm imports over 3,000 eggs from France to insure the genetic superiority of our breeding stock. This, along with the natural feed we give

them — corn, wheat, and soybeans — guarantees consistency of size and taste of the duck. It's an expensive purchase, but by going the extra yard we are sure of our product's quality.

In 1986, when we were barely getting started, Bob Shipley, of Squab Producers of California (page 125), introduced me to George Faison. Bob lives twenty miles down the road and had already hooked up with D'Artagnan. I flew to New Jersey and tried to find their office at 399 St. Paul Avenue, in Jersey City. After asking around, finally I found George and Ariane in this tiny cubbyhole. Happily, they liked our ducks, moved on to larger quarters, and we've grown together.

Today Grimaud Farms of California has eighty employees. There is a state-of-the-art headquarters and processing facility, five duck farms, and a 120-acre hatchery and breeding facility. Our newest achievement is our guinea fowl. They're raised naturally under close supervision and without antibiotics until they reach about 11 weeks. Their unique flavor is a cross between that of a pheasant and a free-range chicken.

1 tablespoon unsalted butter

1 tablespoon finely chopped flat-leaf parsley

1. Preheat oven to 375°F.

2. Season cod on both sides with salt and pepper, then dust with flour. Melt duck fat in a large nonstick skillet over high heat. Add cod, skinned side up, and cook until golden on the bottom, about 4 minutes. Carefully transfer fish to a baking sheet, browned side up, and bake until opaque throughout, about 5 minutes.

3. Meanwhile, pour off half the fat from the skillet. Add confit to skillet and cook over medium heat, stirring, until skin is crisp and meat is hot, 3 to 5 minutes. Transfer confit to a plate. Add shallots to skillet and cook over low heat, stirring until softened, about 2 minutes, then add to confit. Add wine to skillet and cook over medium-high heat until reduced by half. Off the heat, swirl in butter and stir in parsley.

4. Transfer fillets to 4 warmed dinner plates. Spoon wine sauce over fish, top with confit and shallots, and serve.

Adapted from Arnaud Daguin, chef-owner, Les Platanes, Biarritz, France

dixie duck confit
on corn and baby butterbean succotash with smoked tomato ketchup

SERVES 4

When classic confit meets good ole Southern hospitality, the results are eye-opening and sure to please y'all. In this recipe traditional French seasonings have been changed to reflect a personal style. All the elements in this "best of Dixie" dish are easily made ahead and reheated. (Allow at least a day or two for the duck legs to rest after confiting; if time is limited, substitute D'Artagnan's prepared duck confit.) Succotash, a traditional American vegetable dish usually made with corn kernels and lima beans, is popular in Southern cooking. The name is derived from *msickquatash*, a Narraganset Indian word for stewed kernels of corn.

4 whole Moulard duck legs

2 tablespoons coarse salt

2 tablespoons fresh thyme leaves, plus 4 small thyme sprigs, to garnish

2 tablespoons coarsely chopped garlic

2 tablespoons coarsely chopped shallots

1 tablespoon cracked black pepper

1 tablespoon sweet paprika

1 teaspoon mustard seeds, crushed

1 teaspoon ground cumin

½ teaspoon cayenne pepper

4 cups rendered duck fat (see Note)

Smoked Tomato Ketchup (recipe follows)

Corn and Baby Butterbean Succotash (recipe follows)

1. Rub flesh side of legs with salt. Combine thyme leaves, garlic, shallots, black pepper, paprika, mustard seeds, cumin, and cayenne, and rub on flesh, using all of the mixture. Pack legs, seasoned sides together, into a glass or plastic container, cover, and refrigerate for 24 hours.

2. Preheat oven to 250°F.

3. Remove legs from refrigerator, wipe off marinade, and blot dry. Melt duck fat in an oven-safe casserole large enough to hold all of the legs. Slip legs into fat, making sure they are covered by at least an inch of fat. Heat on stovetop over low heat until fat registers 180°F on an instant-read thermometer. Cover with foil and bake until legs can be easily pierced with a toothpick at the joint, 1½ to 2 hours.

4. Remove casserole from oven and let legs and fat cool at room temperature. Remove legs to a clean container and strain fat over them, making certain they are completely submerged. Cover and refrigerate. *Recipe may be prepared up to 2 weeks ahead to this point.*

5. While duck legs are resting, make Smoked Tomato Ketchup. On serving day, or up to 2 days before, make Corn and Baby Butterbean Succotash.

6. To serve, remove confit from refrigerator and place in a warm spot to melt fat. Heat a nonstick skillet over medium heat. Add 1 to 2 tablespoons of duck fat and the duck legs, skin side down. Adjust heat to medium-low, cover pan, and cook until skin is crisp and deep golden brown, about 10 minutes. Carefully remove cover so moisture does not fall into pan. Turn legs and cook flesh side 2 minutes longer.

7. Spoon a mound of hot succotash into the center of each of 4 plates. Top succotash with duck. Dribble Smoked Tomato Ketchup around, and garnish with thyme sprigs.

NOTE:
Use duck fat that you have rendered and saved in the freezer (it keeps up to 6 months), or order from D'Artagnan or from a local purveyor of fine meats and poultry.

corn and baby butterbean succotash

1 tablespoon rendered duck fat or peanut oil

½ cup finely diced Vidalia or other sweet onion, such as Walla Walla or Maui

½ cup *each* finely diced celery, red bell pepper, and green bell pepper

1½ tablespoons minced garlic

½ teaspoon ground coriander

¼ teaspoon crushed red pepper flakes

¼ teaspoon ground cumin

½ small bay leaf

½ tablespoon molasses

2 cups fresh or defrosted frozen baby lima beans

1¼ cups chicken stock

Kernels cut from 3 ears Silver Queen or Summersweet white corn, or 3 cups defrosted frozen corn

Salt and freshly ground black pepper to taste

¼ to ½ cup finely chopped, peeled, and seeded tomatoes or drained canned tomatoes

1 tablespoon fresh thyme leaves

1 tablespoon apple cider vinegar

1 tablespoon unsalted butter

1. Heat duck fat in a large skillet over medium heat. Add onion, celery, and bell

Dixie Duck Confit on Corn and Baby Butterbean Succotash ❯ with Smoked Tomato Ketchup (page 39)

peppers, and sauté until softened but still bright in color, about 4 minutes. Add garlic, coriander, red pepper flakes, cumin, and bay leaf, and cook 1 minute. Stir in molasses, lima beans, and chicken stock, bring to a simmer, and cook until beans are done but still firm. Stir in corn, cook for 2 minutes, then season with salt and pepper. If not using immediately, cool quickly over ice to avoid overcooking. Cover and refrigerate until needed. *Recipe may be prepared up to 2 days ahead to this point.*

2. Reheat over low heat. Stir in tomatoes, adjusting amount to your taste. Add thyme leaves, vinegar, and butter. Taste for seasonings and keep warm.

smoked tomato ketchup

MAKES ABOUT 1¼ CUPS

¾ cup smoked tomato purée (see Note 1)

2 tablespoons tomato ketchup

2 tablespoons apple cider vinegar

2 tablespoons olive oil

1 tablespoon mustard seeds, lightly toasted and ground, or ½ tablespoon dry mustard

2 teaspoons tamarind concentrate dissolved in ¼ cup warm water

½ tablespoon roasted garlic purée (see Note 2)

½ tablespoon Asian garlic chili paste (available at supermarkets and Asian groceries)

1 teaspoon Tabasco

1 teaspoon Worcestershire sauce

Salt to taste

Combine tomato purée, ketchup, vinegar, oil, mustard seeds, dissolved tamarind and water, garlic purée, garlic chili paste, Tabasco, and Worcestershire sauce in an electric blender, and pulse until blended. Season with salt, scrape into a clean container, cover, and refrigerate until needed. Keeps for up to 1 month in refrigerator.

NOTES:

1. Heat canned tomato purée in a small skillet until slightly reduced; add a little chopped chipotle pepper. (Chipotles are dried, smoked jalapeños. They are usually sold canned in adobo sauce, and are available in Latin American markets.)

2. Roasted garlic purée is sold in some markets and specialty food stores. Or try this shortcut: thinly slice 3 large cloves garlic and slowly sauté them in the 2 tablespoons of olive oil over low heat until lightly caramelized, 4 to 5 minutes. Use oil and garlic when you purée mixture.

Adapted from Ben Barker, chef-owner, Magnolia Grill, Durham, North Carolina

seared breast of moulard duck à la d'artagnan
on potato galette

SERVES 8

A classic dish from the southwest of France. Note that 3 glasses of Madiran wine are listed in the ingredients but only 2 are used in the sauce. That's because a good cook must always verify the quality of the ingredients. So drink the third glass and enjoy! These seared duck breasts are served with an addictive Potato Galette, which you can make ahead and keep warm. It's a wonderful dish on which to splurge with a truffle. But you can make it without the truffle for everyday dining. Serve the same Madiran you used for the sauce to accompany the meal.

Potato Galette (recipe follows)

2 whole boneless Moulard duck breasts, about 4 pounds, excess fat removed, skin and fat scored diagonally into small squares, patted dry

Salt and freshly ground black pepper to taste

2 shallots, minced

3 (5-ounce) glasses Madiran wine

2 tablespoons duck and veal demi-glace (see page 33)

5 ounces heavy cream

1. Prepare Potato Galette.

2. Season both sides of duck breasts with salt and pepper.

3. Heat 2 heavy skillets until medium hot, over medium-high heat. Put duck breasts in pans, skin side down, without any butter or fat. Cook for 8 minutes, checking to avoid burning. Remove fat as it accumulates. Flip breasts over, lower heat to medium, and cook 4 minutes longer. Remove duck from heat and keep warm in one of the skillets.

4. Discard almost all of the fat and any burned particles from the other skillet. Still at medium heat, add shallots, and when they become translucent but not yet brown, about 1 minute, pour in 2 glasses (1¼ cups) of the wine. Raise heat to high, reduce liquid by half. Add demi-glace and again reduce by half. Pour in cream, but do not move the pan or stir the liquid. When the cream has blended itself into the sauce, it is ready.

5. Cut duck breasts in half, then cut them across the grain into ¼-inch slices. Divide the slices among 8 warmed plates, placing them in a fan shape. Pour sauce over the duck, add a slice of Potato Galette, and serve at once.

HOW A LOCAL CONTEST BECAME INTERNATIONAL

In the Gascon town of Nogaro, there is a competition each July called Le Concours de Demoiselles — in English, it's the less romantic-sounding Carcass Eaters Competition. This local spectacle draws hundreds of visitors to see who can clean the most duck carcasses in the fastest time. Winners get their weight in wine and Armagnac. Every morsel of meat — the little oysters, the fillets, anything left — has to be whittled or nibbled off, so the bones are totally clean. Only a pocketknife is allowed to help.

As you can imagine, in rustic areas like this, local champions have emerged over the years. Thus, when a petite, slender American entered the race about six years ago, no one paid much attention. What locals didn't know was that George Faison's wife, Carol, is a world-class chicken-bone gnawer. Here, in Nogaro, she'd finally met a contest that suited her just right. With fifty contestants in the fray, our Carol carried the day, becoming the first *championne américaine*. And now the competition is known as the International Carcass Eaters Competition.

potato galette

2 pounds red potatoes, scrubbed and cut into
   $1/16$-inch slices (see Note)

1 medium-small onion, cut in half and thinly
   sliced

Salt and freshly ground black pepper to taste

3 tablespoons rendered duck fat

1 small black truffle, shaved paper thin
   (optional)

1 tablespoon finely chopped flat-leaf parsley

1 teaspoon minced garlic

1. Blot potatoes dry on paper towels.
Combine in a large bowl with onions and
a liberal amount of salt and pepper, and
mix well.
2. Heat fat until hot in a 10-inch nonstick
skillet, over medium-high heat. Add potatoes, shaking the pan and turning them

to cover evenly with fat. Once a few slices
begin to brown, press potatoes with a
spatula to flatten into a disk. Adjust heat
to medium low, cover tightly, and cook
until several slices are golden brown on
the bottom, about 5 to 7 minutes.
Carefully lift off cover so condensation
does not fall on potatoes, and wipe it dry.
Mix cooked slices into other potatoes,
then add shaved truffles, if desired.
Replace cover, and cook until bottom
of galette is golden brown, about 5 minutes longer. Shake pan to loosen if
potatoes are stuck.
3. Slide galette onto a plate, cover with a
second plate of the same size, invert,
then slide galette back into pan. Do not
worry if some slices need rearranging.
Flatten potatoes again, and cover. Cook
10 to 12 minutes longer, removing lid after
5 minutes, or until potatoes are golden
brown, turning heat up slightly if needed

THE FIRST SMOKED MAGRETS

The first smoked magrets officially made by
D'Artagnan were a disaster! They were being
smoked for a 1985 Chaîne des Rôtisseurs dinner
at the Hotel Pierre in New York.

The most suitable place to smoke magrets
at that time was George's eleventh-floor apart-
ment on West End Avenue. George went jog-
ging, and Ariane was reading, while the magrets
were gently smoking on top of the stove, in a
homemade smoker.

The smoke was thick, so Ariane set up a fan
to create a draft and opened the kitchen window
to clear the air. The fan made quite a racket, and
Ariane was at first unaware that someone had
begun knocking at the door. When she realized

what the noise was and rushed to open the
door, there stood eight firemen, looking somewhat like astronauts, preparing to break the
door down.

To make a long story short, the firemen ate
the whole batch! George and Ariane had to buy
more fans and smoke a fresh supply of magrets
a few at a time. They worked all night, while
George's girlfriend and now wife, Carol, made
margaritas to relieve the stress of being caught
again smoking lots of ducks in a residential area.

to color potatoes. Turn galette again, if necessary, and cook uncovered for a few minutes longer, or until golden brown. *Galette may be loosely tented with aluminum foil and kept warm in the oven or on top of the stove.*

4. Slide galette onto a flat plate. Season with salt and pepper. Combine parsley with garlic, and sprinkle over potatoes. Cut into 8 wedges and serve.

NOTE:
Slicing potatoes into $\frac{1}{16}$-inch slices is easily done with a food processor using a 2 x 2-mm slicing blade.

molasses-roasted muscovy duck breast

with cornbread–venison sausage dressing

SERVES 4

In this contemporary, Southern-style dish, lusty, spirited molasses-glazed duck is set off with creamy, cool buttermilk sauce. Don't be fooled by the traditional "stuffing and bird" format. A seductive mixture of spices and hot chilies lurks just below the surface, adding all kinds of taste experiences that you'll keep on discovering. We know the list of ingredients looks long, but the recipe is actually quite simple, and much of the work can be done ahead. Also, you could substitute good-quality purchased cornbread or cornbread mix to save time.

$\frac{1}{3}$ cup *each* buttermilk and mayonnaise

$\frac{1}{2}$ teaspoon lemon juice

$\frac{1}{2}$ teaspoon plus 1 tablespoon molasses, plus 1 tablespoon, to garnish

$\frac{1}{4}$ teaspoon *each* Tabasco and salt

Cornbread–Venison Sausage Dressing (recipe follows)

1 tablespoon olive oil, plus a little olive oil to sauté ducks

1 teaspoon *each* lime juice and chili powder

$\frac{1}{2}$ teaspoon salt

2 whole boneless Muscovy hen breasts, about 2 pounds, excess fat removed, skin and fat scored diagonally into small squares

4 watercress sprigs, to garnish

Pecan halves, lightly toasted, to garnish

1. Combine buttermilk, mayonnaise, lemon juice, the $\frac{1}{2}$ teaspoon of molasses, Tabasco, and $\frac{1}{4}$ teaspoon salt together in a small bowl. Stir to blend, cover, and refrigerate until needed. *Sauce may be prepared a day ahead.*

2. Prepare Cornbread–Venison Sausage Dressing.

3. Combine 1 tablespoon molasses, 1 tablespoon olive oil, lime juice, chili powder, and $\frac{1}{2}$ teaspoon salt together in a small bowl and mix well. Brush duck breasts with mixture.

4. Heat remaining olive oil in a large ovenproof skillet over medium-high heat until hot. Add breasts, skin side down, adjust heat to medium low, and slowly sauté skin to render as much fat as possible and to brown the skin well, 5 to 10 minutes. When skin is browned, turn breasts over, raise heat to medium high, and sear flesh side for about 1 minute.

5. Set skillet aside in a warm spot, and allow breasts to rest for 5 minutes, for juices to settle.

6. Divide the whole breasts into individual breast halves, then cut each half crosswise into thin slices. Spoon a tight mound of the Cornbread–Venison Sausage Dressing into the center of each of 4 dinner plates. Shingle duck slices over dressing. Finely drizzle the plates with the remaining 1 tablespoon molasses and the reserved buttermilk dressing. Garnish with watercress sprigs and toasted pecans, and serve.

cornbread–venison sausage dressing

12 tablespoons (1½ sticks) unsalted butter, plus butter to grease pan

1 cup *each* all-purpose flour and yellow cornmeal

1 tablespoon sugar

1½ teaspoons *each* baking powder and salt

1 egg

1 cup milk

1 small onion, finely chopped

½ pound venison or pork sausage, casing removed, broken into small pieces

2 serrano chilies, stemmed, seeded, and chopped

1 poblano chili, stemmed, seeded, and chopped

1 rib celery, chopped

½ medium carrot, chopped

2 teaspoons dried oregano

Salt and freshly ground black pepper to taste

1. Preheat oven to 350°F. Lightly grease an 8 x 8-inch square baking pan.

2. Melt 8 tablespoons (1 stick) of the butter and set aside. Sift flour, cornmeal, sugar, baking powder, and salt together into a large bowl. Lightly beat egg with milk in another bowl. Add egg mixture and melted butter to dry ingredients, and mix until just combined. Do not overmix. Scrape into prepared pan and bake until a toothpick inserted into center of cornbread comes out clean, 20 to 25 minutes. Remove from oven, set pan on a rack, and cool to room temperature. *Cornbread may be prepared several days ahead of time. Cover and store in a cool spot.*

3. Melt 3 tablespoons of the remaining butter in a skillet, over medium heat. Add onion and sausage, and sauté until onions are translucent, 5 minutes. Add both kinds of chilies, the celery, and carrot, and sauté until tender, 5 to 6 minutes.

4. Break cornbread into small pieces and add to skillet with vegetables, stirring to blend ingredients. Add oregano, salt, pepper, and remaining tablespoon of butter, and stir again. Transfer to a serving dish and keep warm.

Adapted from Robert Del Grande, chef-owner, Café Annie, Houston

breast of pekin duck with creamy polenta, olives, raisins, and dried tomatoes

SERVES 4

The blend of golden raisins, green olives, dried tomatoes, and small roasted onions — spiked with orange zest in this dish — recalls medieval flavors and Sicilian caponata. The polenta is irresistibly creamy, while rosemary-infused Chianti is reduced to a lush sauce. Serve with Sautéed Swiss Chard (page 213) and a Chianti wine.

2 whole Pekin duck breasts, about 2 pounds, excess fat removed, skin and fat scored diagonally into small squares, blotted dry

Salt and freshly ground black pepper to taste

4 to 5 tablespoons olive oil

2½ cups low-fat milk

½ cup polenta

¼ cup grated imported Parmesan cheese

3 tablespoons unsalted butter

⅓ cup golden raisins

1 tablespoon tawny port

4 white onions, about 1½ inches in diameter

4 cloves garlic

1½ cups Chianti wine

1½ cups duck and veal demi-glace (see page 33)

2 large sprigs rosemary, plus small sprigs, to garnish

1 small eggplant (about ¾ pound), peeled and cut into ½-inch dice

Zest of 1 orange, minced

½ cup pitted and sliced imported green olives

⅓ cup julienned oven-dried or sun-dried tomatoes (not in oil)

1. Season both sides of duck with salt and pepper. Pour about 1 tablespoon of the olive oil into a large skillet, and heat over medium heat until hot. Place duck breasts, skin side down, in pan and cook until fat is rendered, 8 to 9 minutes. Set aside. *Duck may be prepared a couple of hours ahead to this point.*
2. Pour milk into a heavy saucepan and bring to a boil over medium heat. Add polenta in a slow stream, stirring continuously to avoid lumps. Continue cooking and stirring until thick, smooth, and soft, about 20 minutes. Stir in Parmesan cheese and 2 tablespoons of the butter, season with salt and pepper to taste, cover, and keep warm.
3. Combine raisins with port in a small bowl and set aside. (If raisins are very dry,

A SUMMER SALAD

When the barbecue is hot and summer fruit is at its peak, grill magrets along with halves of peaches and nectarines. Slice both the duck and the fruit, season with salt and pepper, some chopped herbs if you like, and toss with vinaigrette.

heat mixture briefly in a microwave oven or over medium-low heat to soften.)

4. Preheat oven to 350°F.

5. Slice ends from onions. Toss onions and garlic cloves with 1 tablespoon of the olive oil in a small skillet or pan, and bake until tender and lightly browned, turning occasionally, 10 to 15 minutes. Watch that garlic doesn't burn.

6. Remove garlic and combine with Chianti, demi-glace, and large sprigs rosemary in a nonreactive saucepan. Bring to a gentle boil and reduce by two-thirds to sauce consistency. Strain into a clean pan, season to taste, and keep warm. Before serving, whisk in remaining tablespoon of butter.

7. Turn breasts skin side up and finish in 350°F oven until medium rare, 5 to 10 minutes, depending on how cool they are before placing in oven. Remove skillet from oven and let stand in a warm spot for at least 5 minutes.

8. Meanwhile, season eggplant dice with salt and pepper, and toss with another tablespoon or two of the olive oil. Heat a large skillet over medium-high heat. Add eggplant and cook until lightly brown on all sides and just cooked through, 2 to 3 minutes, turning often. Add orange zest, raisins and port, olives, tomatoes, and glazed onions, and heat over medium-low heat until just warmed through. Season with salt and pepper.

9. To serve, spoon ½ cup of the polenta at about 10 o'clock on each of 4 warm dinner plates. Just to the right, place a dollop of Swiss chard, if serving, and at 2 o'clock, a glazed onion. Cut whole duck breasts into 2 cutlets, then crosswise into thin slices. Fan 1 breast across the front of each plate. Top with olive-raisin-tomato mixture near center of plate, and ladle on Chianti sauce. Add a rosemary sprig before serving.

Adapted from Ris Lacoste, executive chef, 1789 Restaurant, Washington, D.C.

crispy pan-fried duck

SERVES 4

Do you want a crisp duck with almost no fat in under an hour? It's possible with this skillet method, originally described in *Paula Peck's Art of Good Cooking* (1961) and revived by Mark Bittman in his *New York Times* column. The bird is first cut into serving pieces and cooked initially in a covered skillet on top of the stove. This serves two purposes: it renders the fat, and the steaming tenderizes the meat. When the duck is almost cooked, the pan is uncovered and the bird crisps in its own fat. The cooking time has been shortened from the original 60 minutes suggested by Ms. Peck, so you have just enough time to stir-fry some greens on which to serve the duck.

1 Pekin duck, 5 to 6 pounds

Salt and freshly ground black pepper to taste

1 tablespoon soy sauce

1 tablespoon dry sherry

Minced fresh gingerroot or cilantro leaves, to garnish

1. Cut the duck into 6 or 8 serving pieces, reserving wing tips, back, and neck for stock. (Cut gizzard into ⅛-inch slices and fry it along with the duck if you like; reserve liver for another use.) Rub duck with salt, pepper, soy sauce, and sherry. Place duck pieces, skin side down, in a heavy 12-inch skillet, and turn heat to medium high. When duck begins to sizzle, cover skillet, and lower heat to medium.

2. After 15 minutes, turn duck, cover, and cook for 15 minutes more. Uncover skillet and turn heat back to medium high. Cook duck, turning pieces as necessary, so that they brown nicely on both sides, about 15 minutes more.

3. Serve hot or at room temperature, garnished with ginger or cilantro.

Adapted from Mark Bittman, New York Times *food columnist and cookbook author, Woodbridge, Connecticut*

duck à l'orange

SERVES 2 TO 4

Whole roasted duck with orange sauce is a traditional favorite. Having instructed several hundred customers how to make a moist, juicy bird with this citrus sauce, master butcher Loic Jaffres shares his foolproof method with you. Adjust the marmalade according to your own taste from

sweet to bitter. To serve 4, carve the duck into slices or cut it into quarters. Serve it with long-grain or wild rice. A Gamay or Merlot goes well with this.

1 quart orange juice, preferably freshly squeezed

1 (12-ounce) jar bitter or sweet orange marmalade, or a combination of the two

½ cup honey

1 Pekin duck, 5 to 6 pounds, giblets and excess fat removed and discarded, wing tips turned under

Salt and freshly ground black pepper to taste

1 large onion, thinly sliced

2 tablespoons all-purpose flour

1 thin-skinned orange, washed and cut into thin slices

½ cup Cointreau or triple sec

Cooked long-grain or wild rice (optional)

2 to 4 sprigs watercress, to garnish

1. Combine orange juice, marmalade, and honey in a bowl deep enough to hold duck. Add duck, cover, and refrigerate for 8 hours or overnight, turning duck once or twice if marinade doesn't cover it.

2. Preheat oven to 375°F.

3. Remove duck from marinade, reserving marinade. Prick duck skin all over with a fork (do not pierce the flesh), and season inside and out with salt and pepper. Place breast side up on a rack in a roasting pan and transfer to oven. After 10 minutes, turn heat down to 350°F and roast for 1½ hours. (It may also be cooked on a rotisserie for 1½ hours in a 350°F oven.)

NO RACK? NO PROBLEM

If you don't have a poultry rack, you can improvise by using the metal screw tops of two jars. Position them under the bird's front and rear end, with the flat (closed) side resting on the roasting pan.

4. Once duck has rendered some fat, spoon 2 tablespoons of it into a saucepan. Heat over medium-high heat, add onion, and sauté until tender and light brown, 5 to 6 minutes. Sprinkle on flour and cook for 1 minute to lightly color, stirring occasionally. Pour in reserved marinade and bring to a boil over high heat, stirring up any browned bits. Adjust heat to medium and reduce liquid until thickened, 20 to 25 minutes. Scrape sauce into an electric blender or food processor and purée until smooth. Pour through a strainer into a pan and set aside.

5. When duck has roasted for 1½ hours, remove pan from oven and turn heat down to 325°F. Discard all but a little fat from roasting pan, and lay orange slices over bottom of pan. Return to oven and cook until slices begin to brown, about 10 minutes. Remove orange slices and duck from pan, and let stand for 10 minutes while finishing sauce.

6. On top of stove, pour Cointreau into roasting pan and carefully ignite, stirring up all browned particles. When flames subside, pour in reduced orange sauce and stir to blend. Keep warm.

7. *To serve for 2:* Cut duck in half using sharp scissors or poultry shears. Remove backbone by cutting along one side and then the other, then cut along breastbone. *For 4:* Cut each half into breast and leg sections.

8. Place each duck portion on a warm plate. Spoon a generous mound of rice next to it, lay orange slices around it, add watercress sprig, and ladle on sauce.

Adapted from Loic Jaffres, master butcher and meat manager,
Sutton Place Gourmet, Bethesda, Maryland

lavender honey–glazed roast duck

SERVES 4

This moist, lavender-infused duckling, with a crisp lavender honey glaze countered by oil-cured olives, brings a generous bite of Provence to your table. Dried lavender flowers are available anywhere sachets are sold. It's worth looking for the floral honey for this intoxicating flavor. In southern France this kind of dish would traditionally be served with baby artichokes braised with herbs in white wine. Serve with a rosé from Provence, such as Tavel, or a full-bodied Médoc.

1 female Muscovy duck, about 3½ pounds, giblets, excess fat, and 2 wing joints removed, skin pricked, patted dry

Salt and freshly ground black pepper to taste

½ cup niçoise (oil-cured black) olives

2 tablespoons dried lavender

2 tablespoons olive oil

4 tablespoons lavender honey

1. Preheat oven to 350°F.
2. Season duck inside and out with salt and pepper. Put olives and lavender inside duck and truss or close with a skewer.

A FISHY DUCK

If you see "Bombay duck" on an Indian menu, be aware that it is not a bird but a fish, often salted and dried, that is used as a flavoring.

Heat 1 tablespoon of olive oil in a large skillet over medium-high heat until hot. Add duck and sauté on all sides until skin is golden brown. Transfer to a rack in a roasting pan.

3. Mix 2 tablespoons of the honey with the remaining 1 tablespoon olive oil. Brush over duck and roast until juices run clear when duck is pricked deep in thigh, about 45 minutes. About halfway through the roasting time, combine 1 tablespoon of pan drippings with the remaining 2 tablespoons of honey, and brush over duck.

4. When duck is cooked, remove it from oven and let rest for 15 minutes in a warm place before carving and serving.

Adapted from Dominique Tougne, chef-partner, Bistro 110, Chicago

slowly roasted mallard apicius
with roasted quince

SERVES 2

Using honey and spices as a glaze hails back to ancient times. In Imperial Rome, Apicius was regarded not only as a great gastronome, but as a gourmand as well, for the luxury of his feasts. He was the author of *Apicius De Re Coquinaria,* the first known cookbook in existence. Although the work was directed at professional cooks, many of his principles and recipe ideas — including sweet-and-sour sauces made with honey and vinegar — are still used by today's home cooks. Here acidic quince takes on the vinegar role,

and you savor each bite of the fruit with the lacquered duck. Slow, slow cooking brings this oft-firm duck to tenderness. Serve over barley or wild rice pilaf.

1 quince, or 1 firm, barely ripe Bartlett pear plus 1 teaspoon apple cider vinegar

1 small sprig rosemary

1 tablespoon plus ½ cup honey

1 tablespoon unsalted butter

Salt and freshly ground black pepper to taste

1 teaspoon *each* ground coriander and ground cumin

½ teaspoon *each* white and black peppercorns (or 1 teaspoon black peppercorns), coarsely ground

Pinch dried lavender

1 Mallard duck, 2 wing joints removed, patted dry

1 tablespoon olive oil or canola oil

1. Preheat oven to 300°F.

2. Place quince, rosemary, 1 tablespoon honey, butter, and salt and pepper to taste inside a square of aluminum foil. Wrap securely and bake until just tender, 1 to 2 hours, depending on size (a pear will cook in about half the time).

3. Bring remaining ½ cup honey to soft ball stage, 230°F on a candy thermometer, over medium heat. Remove from heat, stir in coriander, cumin, ground peppercorns, and lavender, and let mixture cool until slightly thickened. *Recipe may be done 1 day ahead to this point. Refrigerate quince in its foil wrapper, and cover honey glaze.*

4. Season duck with salt and pepper. Heat oil in a heavy skillet over medium heat. Add duck and slowly sauté until crisp on all sides, about 25 minutes. Turn heat down to medium low if skin browns too quickly.

5. Roast duck in a preheated 300°F oven, breast side up, until tender, 15 to 20 minutes for rare to medium rare. (If quince was made the day before, reheat it briefly in the oven, and warm the honey glaze over hot water.)

6. Remove duck from oven and let cool to room temperature. Cut off legs and brush some of the warm honey glaze on them. Set aside and let glaze soak in.

7. Peel, core, and finely dice quince. Keep warm. Preheat broiler. Cut breasts from the bone, brush with more of the glaze, and broil along with legs until skin is crisp and brown, 2 to 3 minutes. Watch carefully that they don't burn. Serve a breast and leg on each plate, along with 2 small spoonfuls of quince.

Adapted from Craig Shelton, chef-owner, The Ryland Inn, Whitehouse, New Jersey

roasted breast of mallard with legs in salmis sauce

SERVES 4

A whole Mallard needs long slow cooking to tenderize the legs and thighs. Yet game fanciers prefer the breast rare. The answer? Cook the parts separately, starting with the legs. A *salmis* is a richly flavored sauce made from the roasted bones and small pieces of game meat or birds, wine, and an ample amount of seasonings. Truffles and wild mushrooms are frequent additions. Often, as here, the sauce is used over pasta. Serve a red wine, such as a Côte-Rôtie.

2 Mallard ducks, 1½ to 2 pounds each

2 tablespoons rendered duck fat

1 onion, chopped

1 carrot, chopped

1 head of garlic, cut in half crosswise

1 bouquet garni: 8 parsley stems, 4 to 6 sprigs thyme, chopped green part of 1 leek, and 1 bay leaf, tied in cheesecloth

2 quarts water

Salt and freshly ground black pepper to taste

8 shallots, fairly finely chopped

4 cups dry white wine

1 pound fresh linguini

⅓ cup heavy or light cream

1. Remove drumstick-thigh sections and breasts from ducks; keep breasts on the bone. Set legs and breasts aside.

2. Chop all remaining bones with a sharp knife or cleaver into 2-inch pieces. Heat 1 tablespoon of the duck fat in a large, heavy pan over medium-high heat. Add bones and any bits of meat and sear until light brown, about 20 minutes. Add onion, carrot, and garlic, and cook until richly browned but not burned, stirring often. Add bouquet garni. Pour in 2 quarts water, bring to a slow boil, and reduce liquid for 1½ hours. Pour stock through a fine strainer and season with salt and pepper.

You should have 2½ to 3 cups liquid. *Recipe may be done 1 day ahead to this point. Stock may be frozen for 3 months.*

3. Heat ½ tablespoon of duck fat in a large heavy skillet over medium-high heat. Season duck legs with salt and pepper, and add them skin side down to pan. Sauté until golden brown on both sides. Remove and set aside. Add shallots to pan and cook over medium heat until they are translucent and lightly colored, 2 to 3 minutes.

4. Pour in wine, stirring up any browned cooking bits, bring to a boil, and reduce by two-thirds. Stir in reduced stock, return legs to pan, and simmer uncovered, turning in liquid every 15 minutes, until legs are very tender when pierced with a fork, 45 minutes. Keep warm.

5. Preheat oven to 400°F. Bring a large pot of salted water to a boil.

6. Brush duck breasts with remaining ½ tablespoon fat. Season with salt and pepper, place in a roasting pan, and roast until rare or medium rare, 12 to 15 minutes. While breasts cook, boil pasta in salted water until al dente. Drain and toss with cream. Divide among 4 plates and keep warm. Let breasts rest for 5 minutes when cooked.

7. Cut breasts from the bone and slice each into 3 pieces lengthwise. Place on plates with pasta. Add a leg to each plate and spoon on salmis sauce. Serve at once.

Adapted from Jean-Louis Dumonet, chef-owner, Trois Jean, New York City

---

MERCI, JULIA, OR PIERRE'S TASSE DE CAFÉ EXTRAORDINAIRE

ARIANE: Michel Richard decided to honor Julia Child on her eightieth birthday for raising the level of cooking in the United States. He invited many prominent chefs and 500 guests to his Los Angeles restaurant, Citrus, for the feast. With so many meals to prepare, the *mise en place* (prep work) was being done all over town. I was supposed to work at the hot foie gras station. I had also brought foie gras mousse and pitted prunes in Armagnac with me from New Jersey, so I could prepare our French Kisses (see page 297) once I arrived.

That morning the kitchen was a mess. Celebrated chefs such as Jean-Louis Palladin, Vincent Guerithault, and Thomas Keller were working like maniacs to get their dishes organized. TV reporters and journalists followed them around, asking questions, trying to get a sound bite or quote. Cameras flashed.

I found a little corner to work in the hallway, and started by draining the Armagnac from the soaked prunes into Styrofoam cups, which were the only thing I could find to use. As Laurent Manrique and I piped the mousse into the drained prunes, the smell of foie gras and Armagnac filled the air. Daniel Boulud, standing nearby, got a whiff of the Armagnac-prune juice and took a judicious sip from one of the cups.

Just then the late Pierre Franey came ambling down the hall and asked Daniel what he was drinking. "Coffee," he said with an obvious wink, and offered the cup to Franey. Without thinking, Franey knocked back the whole cup of fruity Armagnac — at 10 A.M., a true French Kiss.

pomegranate koresh with duck (fesenjan)

with saffron basmati rice (chelow)

SERVES 6 GENEROUSLY

The affinity between the pomegranate and duck goes back to ancient Persia. One of the finest Persian meals of the fourth century was duck in pomegranate sauce. In this *koresh* — a refined Persian stew that combines meats (lamb, beef, poultry, or fish), vegetables, fresh or dried fruits, and beans, grains, or sometimes nuts with fresh herbs and spices — the long, slow simmering achieves a magical fusion of flavors. As flavorful as this dish is, it needs a colorful garnish. Beyond pomegranate seeds, thinly sliced scallions or chopped cilantro would be appropriate. Golden-crusted Saffron Basmati Rice, or *chelow,* is another Persian specialty.

1 Pekin duck, 4 to 5 pounds, excess fat, neck, and giblets removed, patted dry

Salt and freshly ground black pepper to taste

3 scallions

3 cloves garlic

Julienned zest of 1 large orange

2 tablespoons vegetable oil

2 large onions, thinly sliced

1 pound shelled walnuts, finely ground

1 cup finely diced carrots

¾ cup sugar

1 teaspoon cinnamon

½ teaspoon ground saffron dissolved in 2 tablespoons hot water

1 cup pomegranate concentrate diluted with 5 cups water, or 6 cups freshly squeezed pomegranate juice (see Note)

Saffron Basmati Rice (recipe follows)

DUCK SOUP (A FAMOUS PERSIAN STORY)

A relative came to see Mullah Nasruddin from the country, and brought a duck. The Mullah was grateful and had the bird cooked, and shared it with his guest.

Presently, another visitor arrived. He was a friend, as he said, "of the man who gave you the duck." The Mullah fed him as well.

This happened several times. The Mullah's home had become like a restaurant for out-of-town visitors. Everyone was a more and more distantly removed friend of the original donor of the duck.

Finally, the Mullah was exasperated. One day there was a knock at the door, and a stranger appeared. "I am the friend of the friend of the friend of the man who brought you the duck from the country," he said.

"Come in," said Mullah Nasruddin.

They seated themselves at the table, and Nasruddin asked his wife to bring the soup.

When the guest tasted it, it seemed to be nothing more than warm water.

"What sort of soup is this?" he asked the Mullah.

"That," said Mullah Nasruddin, "is the soup of the soup of the soup of the duck."

—As repeated by Najmieh Batmanglij

Pomegranate seeds, to garnish

1 scallion including green part, thinly sliced, or 3 to 4 tablespoons chopped cilantro, to garnish

1. Preheat oven to 350°F.

2. Generously season duck all over with salt and pepper. Fill cavity with scallions, garlic, 1 tablespoon salt, and ½ teaspoon black pepper. Put duck on a rack in a large roasting pan. Roast in middle of oven until meat easily separates from the bone and duck is brown and crispy, 2¾ to 3 hours, basting occasionally with pan drippings.

3. Meanwhile, combine orange zest with enough water to cover in a small saucepan. Bring to a boil, drain, and rinse under cold water. Blot dry.

4. Heat oil in a large Dutch oven or heavy casserole over medium-high heat. Add onions and sauté until limp, 5 minutes. Stir in walnuts and cook for 2 minutes, stirring constantly, then add carrots, orange zest, and sugar. Keep stirring until sugar has completely dissolved, then add cinnamon, 1 teaspoon salt, saffron water, and diluted pomegranate concentrate or juice. Reduce heat and simmer over low heat for 40 minutes, stirring occasionally with a wooden spoon to prevent nuts from burning. Taste koresh and adjust seasonings if necessary. It should taste sweet and sour. Add sugar to sweeten, pomegranate concentrate to sour. If too thick, add pomegranate juice or water to thin it. Keep warm.

5. Prepare Saffron Basmati Rice.

6. Fifteen minutes before serving, transfer koresh from Dutch oven to a deep, oven-proof serving dish. Cut up roasted duck.

For less fat, remove skin; for easier eating, remove bones. Arrange pieces over koresh in serving dish, cover, and keep in warm oven until ready to serve. Sprinkle on pomegranate seeds and scallion or cilantro, and serve with rice.

NOTE:
Pomegranate concentrate is available in specialty groceries. There are two kinds. The Persian kind is very sweet, and the Arab kind is very sour. For this recipe, use the Arab kind. For fresh pomegranate juice, seed pomegranates and run the seeds through a juicer. You can also buy bottled pomegranate juice at specialty groceries.

saffron basmati rice (chelow)

3 cups long-grain basmati rice

10½ cups water

3 tablespoons salt

2 tablespoons plain yogurt

½ teaspoon ground saffron dissolved in ¼ cup hot water

¾ cup butter or ghee (clarified butter)

1. Pick over rice and wash in a large container filled with lukewarm water. Agitate gently, drain, and repeat five times, until rice is completely clean and water runs clear. Drain well.

2. Bring 10 cups water with salt to a boil in a large nonstick pot. Add rice and boil briskly until rice rises to the top, about 10 minutes. Drain rice in a fine-mesh colander and rinse in 2 or 3 cups warm water. Drain again.

3. Mix 2 large spoonfuls of the rice in a bowl with the yogurt, ½ cup water, and a few drops of the saffron water. Melt ½ cup of the butter in a large heavy pot or skillet, then spread the yogurt-rice mixture over the bottom of it. Gently place 1 spoonful of rice at a time on top of the yogurt mixture, gradually shaping the rice into a mound. Cover tightly and cook rice over medium-low to medium heat until it forms a golden crust, about 30 minutes. Reduce heat to very low until ready to serve.

4. Dissolve remaining ¼ cup butter in ½ cup hot water and pour over the mound of rice. Pour remaining saffron water over the top and replace cover. Remove pot from heat and allow to cool on a damp surface for 5 minutes. This helps to free the crust from the bottom of the pot. Remove lid and invert a serving dish over pot. Hold dish and pot together and flip to unmold rice. The rice will be cakelike and can be cut into wedges for serving.

Adapted from Najmieh Batmanglij, consultant, teacher, and cookbook author, Washington, D.C.

goose

If your goose is *well* cooked, it has succulent, tender dark meat that is rich tasting but free of fat. A fine roasted goose can be a feast for king and peasant alike, suggested the French writer Honoré de Balzac.

Although plentiful and relatively inexpensive for the common man throughout history, these long-necked, web-footed birds are a rich source of legend and folktales. Egyptian mythology tells that a goose laid the primal egg from which the sun god, Ra, sprang. Brahma, the Hindu personification of divine reality and spiritual purity, rides a great gander. Until the Romans conquered the Gauls, who taught them how to feed and cook their geese, the Romans considered the birds sacred.

Charlemagne was so fond of eating goose he mandated that his lands be kept supplied with them. Queen Elizabeth I was another fan. One tradition says that when she was told about the destruction of the Spanish Armada, it was September 29, the Feast of Saint Michael, or Michaelmas, and she was dining on roast goose with sage and onion stuffing. She decreed that thereafter goose was to be served on this day in celebration.

Yet, for all of these colorful tales, goose seems to elicit scowls or shrugs of frustration from home cooks. "It's fine to let someone else fuss," is a popular sentiment about geese. The perception of a fatty bird with a large frame and poor ratio of meat to bone is accurate, particularly when speaking about domestic geese. Incidentally, *goose* refers to a male or female. A *gander* is male; a *gosling* is a young goose under 4 months of age.

ARIANE: The bird raised for the table in America is the white Embden goose from Germany. It is pure white with an orange bill and orange legs and feet. The average dressed weight is 10 to 12 pounds. In France, there are Toulouse geese that are roasted,

and a subspecies, the Masseube, a gray goose with a big thoracic capacity where the liver expands for foie gras. Masseube geese can be very heavy. But once the liver is taken, they are quite fatty, and good to eat only when made into confit. Domesticated Chinese geese are smaller, brown-and-white birds.

Wild geese, of which the principal varieties are the Canada goose, snow goose, blue goose, and brant (black), are extremely lean and generally smaller than their domesticated cousins. However, in the thirteenth century, Marco Polo reported that the wild geese he saw in Fuchow weighed up to 24 pounds. The report was accurate; they are still the largest wild geese.

These waterfowl spend their lives flying and grazing on foods in their environment. If their principal diet is fish, beware; the bird may be very pungent. However, if they eat mostly grains, they are divine. The best wild geese to roast or grill are young birds, weighing about 5 pounds. They should be barded to protect their flesh from drying out.

Geese lay their eggs in the spring. Therefore, by Christmas a young goose is at its optimum weight. And that's when most people think of having a goose. When buying, look for a young bird, one that is about 6 to 8 months, and between 8 and 12 pounds. In estimating serving size, you should allow 1½ to 2 pounds of goose (raw weight) per person. Fresh geese are not available during February and March because the older birds are stringy and tough. If you have a mature bird, more than 12 pounds, you should braise, stew, or confit it in pieces, as you would a duck.

To prepare a goose, cut off the excess fat from the neck and from the inside cavities. The fat may be rendered like duck fat and made into cracklings, or used to cook potatoes,

⌃ A flock of geese

croutons, or omelets. Prick the skin of the back, breast, and legs well to let the fat escape as the bird cooks. There will be a lot of fat — up to a quart — so it needs to be removed at least every 30 minutes during cooking. A bulb baster or large spoon will work. Take care; that fat is very hot!

As with most poultry, the problem with geese is that if they are cooked whole, the breast gets done first and can dry out while the legs are finishing. Either remove the breast and keep it warm, or tent it with aluminum foil. Either way, continue to baste the legs often to keep them moist.

The bird is cooked when the meat measures 165° to 170°F on an instant-read thermometer and the breast juices run pale pink (not rose-colored, like a duck's) when pricked. As a rule of thumb, calculate between 13 and 15 minutes per pound unstuffed, and 18 to 22 minutes per pound stuffed. When the goose is done, remove it from the oven and let stand for at least 20 to 25 minutes before carving.

To reheat a goose, cover the bird with aluminum foil and put it back in a moderate oven (350°F) until heated through. Alternately, reheat in a sauce to keep moist.

One more thing about those "dumb" geese: They are actually pretty clever. The birds are also notoriously territorial. On farms, if geese are not fed by the same person every day they stage a hunger strike. If someone unknown tries to enter their domain, they are likely to attack. This characteristic has been appreciated through the ages. Romans kept geese at their villas as pets to protect their children and properties, and NASA has a flock to guard its launch pads.

gala goose

SERVES AT LEAST 6

Forget your fear of flabby, greasy goose! This do-ahead method produces a succulent, flavorful bird with crispy skin. After poaching, only a half hour of high-heat roasting is needed before serving. Potatoes sautéed in goose fat are a sublime accompaniment for this festive offering. By placing a small piece of parchment paper on the rack under the goose breast when you start poaching it, you will keep the skin from sticking and tearing when the bird is turned. Discard parchment after turning.

1 goose, 9 to 11 pounds

3 tablespoons rendered goose fat

1½ cups *each* coarsely chopped carrots, onions, and celery

6 tablespoons all-purpose flour

4 cups chicken stock

2 cups dry white wine

4 sprigs flat-leaf parsley

Peelings from 1 green apple (optional)

6 whole cloves

1 large bay leaf

1 ounce dried porcini mushrooms, soaked, cleaned, and coarsely chopped, liquid strained and reserved

½ cup dried cherries

2 tablespoons Armagnac

1 tablespoon red currant jelly

Salt and freshly ground black pepper to taste

1. Remove giblets and neck from cavity, pull off any loose fat, and cut off first 2 wing joints, if still attached; reserve all. Wash goose, pat dry, tie legs together, prick skin all over, and set aside.

2. Put goose fat in a large sauté pan over medium-high heat, and render about 3 tablespoons of fat. Remove and discard remaining fat (or save for another use). Add giblets, wing pieces, neck, and chopped vegetables to pan. Sauté until vegetables are browned, 7 to 8 minutes, turning frequently. Sprinkle on flour, adjust heat to medium, and continue cooking until flour is lightly browned, 6 to 7 minutes, stirring often.

3. Pour chicken stock and white wine into a covered roasting pan large enough to hold the goose, and bring to a boil. Place goose breast side down on a rack covered with parchment and lower into stock. Add browned giblets and vegetables, parsley, apple peelings, cloves, and bay leaf. Pour in enough water to cover goose by about two-thirds, and bring to a simmer. Whisk a cup of the simmering liquid into the sauté pan used in Step 2 and deglaze pan. Scrape the thickened liquid back into the roasting pan. Cover pan and cook very gently, regulating heat if necessary, to keep it just simmering.

4. After an hour, turn goose over, being careful not to break the skin. (A pair of rubber gloves is helpful when doing this.) Poach goose a total of 2 to 3 hours, or until meat is tender when pierced with a fork. Turn off heat and finish immediately, later in the day, or the next day. *Recipe may be done ahead to this point (see Note).*

5. To finish immediately, preheat oven to 450°F.

6. Remove goose from liquid, drain, and place on a rack breast side up in a shallow roasting pan. Roast until skin is brown and crispy, about 30 minutes. Remove from oven, and allow to stand for about 15 to 20 minutes before carving.

7. Meanwhile, skim grease from poaching liquid and strain liquid to remove pieces of goose, vegetables, and seasonings. Discard pieces of goose and seasonings. Purée vegetables in an electric blender or food processor, and add back to pan along with the strained liquid. Boil quickly to reduce liquid by about half.

8. Add porcini and their strained soaking liquid, cherries, Armagnac, and red currant jelly. Season sauce to taste with salt and pepper, and keep warm until needed.

NOTE:

To finish later or the next day, let cool briefly uncovered, then cover pan and set in refrigerator. When ready to resume preparation, remove layer of congealed fat from liquid. Lift out goose and bring liquid to a boil over high heat. Reduce heat to a simmer, then reheat goose in stock for about 10 minutes while preheating oven. Proceed with recipe as above.

Adapted from Sally Kofke, cooking teacher and consultant, Montclair, New Jersey

roasted holiday goose breast and braised legs with cassis sauce

SERVES 8

Are you looking for a perfect centerpiece to celebrate the holidays? With this combination of marinated goose breast roasted until moist and succulent, and legs that are braised and shredded, your search is over. Both are sauced with a black currant–

flavored cassis sauce. Serve with candied sweet potatoes and roasted pearl onions.

1 goose, 10 to 12 pounds, excess fat removed

Salt and freshly ground black pepper to taste

1 tablespoon *each* crushed juniper berries and grated fresh gingerroot

1 orange, zest removed in thin strips, fruit peeled and diced

1 rib celery, diced

1 onion, quartered

1 leek, white part only, split lengthwise

4 cups diced mirepoix: mixed carrots, onions, celery, and leeks

1 bouquet garni: 4 bay leaves, 2 tablespoons dried thyme, 1 tablespoon black peppercorns, and 4 whole cloves, tied in cheesecloth

1 quart poaching liquid reserved from legs, or chicken stock

1 cup cassis (black currant liqueur)

2 shallots, minced

½ cup dried red currants

1 tablespoon unsalted butter, at room temperature

1. One day before serving, remove legs from goose at thigh joint, leaving breast on carcass. Rub breast and carcass inside and out with salt, pepper, juniper berries, ginger, and orange zest. Place diced orange, celery, onion, and leek inside cavity. Prick skin all over, place carcass on a rack, and refrigerate uncovered for 24 hours.

2. While breast is marinating, place legs in a casserole with mirepoix and bouquet garni. Add enough water to cover and

QUATTRO'S GAME FARMS

A stop at Quattro's Game Farms store on Route 44 in the Hudson River Valley is like a step back in time. The simple stucco market is filled with fresh poultry, meats, cold cuts, institutional-size bottles of spices and condiments, and Italian baked goods, along with piles of homegrown fruits and vegetables, frozen novelty ice creams, and assorted sundries. Friends and customers stop in for a sub, a chicken, or homemade meatballs, and a snatch of friendly chat.

There's a quiet purposefulness to Carmella Quattrociocchi, the matriarch of the large extended clan that raises geese and wild turkeys for D'Artagnan, along with other birds and animals to sell at the Union Square Greenmarket. (The family goes by the shortened "Quattro" for convenience.) Carmella and her sons, Sal and Frank, Jr., take the birds from breeding to butchering, while her husband, Frank, runs the store. Everything at Quattro's is done simply but "just so." It's easy to see where the farm's high standards come from. Carmella has been around poultry her whole life.

During the 1930s, Carmella Fanelli's mother owned a successful fresh poultry and fish market in Yonkers. But the air was supposed to be healthier in the country, so in 1944 she and her husband moved little Carmella and her seven brothers to Pleasant Valley. Since the early 1800s, the land had been a self-sufficient farm. The Fanellis bought a hundred acres and raised Leghorn chickens, known for their prolific egg production. Carmella married Frank Quattrociocchi, and they had two sons and a daughter. She never left the farm.

SAL QUATTROCIOCCHI: Ever since I can remember, we've raised geese. But it was George Faison constantly asking me at the Union Square Greenmarket for wild turkey that got us involved with that. You know how persistent he can be.

We raise white Embden geese, letting them roam in wide pens. On this farm, my brother, Frank, Jr., is really master of the geese — you know how they like to be fed by only one person. He lets Mom and me nurture the goslings only until they are "feathered out" at about 6 to 7 weeks. We give them high-protein feed, plus different vitamins and minerals so their bones develop properly. Then, when they are hearty enough to be released outdoors, they are his — absolutely his — until they're grown.

Frank free-ranges them, and feeds them on alfalfa and pasture, with corn and oat supplements. Most of our birds average 10 to 11 pounds, but they can go up to 15. They hatch in April, and then it takes 8 or 9 months for them to mature, so it's just in time for Thanksgiving or Christmas. It's a slow process that doesn't improve with shortcuts.

Geese are still considered holiday food, and many people think they are too fatty. It's true that they have a thick layer of fat, but when it's properly rendered, the meat is juicy and the fat's gone. I've seen some commercially raised geese, and our birds are leaner. Plus, by growing them out and giving them the right diet, there are no pin feathers. They are real clean.

Joan Fanelli, Carmella's sister-in-law, has been removing feathers for twenty-plus years. She explains the process. "Once the birds have been scalded in warm water, they are put into a drum for about fifty seconds. The majority of feathers are removed. At that point, I take a strawberry huller and methodically go to work pinching out any stragglers. We don't wax the geese." When they are finally chilled in cold water, the birds are again examined to be sure each one is perfect.

bring to a boil over high heat. Reduce heat so liquid just simmers, cover pot, and cook until legs are tender and meat easily pulls away from the bones, at least 2 hours. Remove from heat and let cool. When legs are cool enough to handle, remove skin and bones, and discard. Skim fat from top of poaching liquid; strain liquid and reserve. Shred leg meat and reserve. *Legs may be cooked 1 day ahead, covered, and refrigerated.*

3. Remove breast from refrigerator and allow to stand for 30 minutes at room temperature. Preheat oven to 475°F.

4. Place goose, breast side up, on a rack in a large roasting pan, and roast for 30 minutes. Turn heat down to 400°F, and continue roasting until skin is golden brown and juices run pale pink when meat is pricked deep in breast, about 35 minutes longer, basting periodically with pan juices. Remove from oven and transfer to a platter. Tent with aluminum foil and let rest.

5. Discard fat from roasting pan and empty contents of carcass and any juices into pan. Pour in 1 quart of the reserved poaching liquid, the cassis, shallots, and currants, and deglaze pan, stirring up all browned particles. Pour into a saucepan and bring sauce to a boil over high heat. Cook until reduced by two-thirds. Strain sauce, season with salt and pepper, and stir in butter. Keep warm.

6. Warm leg meat, and moisten with a little cassis sauce. Place a large spoonful of leg meat in the center of each warmed dinner plate. Remove breast from goose carcass and carve across grain into long angular slices. Drape 3 to 4 slices over leg meat, spoon sauce over, and serve.

Adapted from Peter Kelly, chef-owner, Xavier's Restaurant, Garrison, New York

alsatian roasted christmas goose with foie gras and chestnuts
over braised red cabbage

SERVES 6

This luxurious Alsatian-style goose is stuffed with ground veal and pork, and foie gras. It is the perfect main course to serve for dinner on Christmas Eve. It's presented on a bed of claret-red cabbage. Add roasted potatoes and serve with an Alsace Gewürztraminer Vendages Tardives, or a Pinot Rouge from Alsace.

1 pound chestnuts

½ pound sliced white bread

⅓ cup milk

1 teaspoon plus 2 tablespoons unsalted butter

1 large shallot, chopped

½ pound *each* pork shoulder and veal shoulder

2 teaspoons ruby port

1 teaspoon Cognac

2 teaspoons chopped flat-leaf parsley

½ teaspoon quatre épices, or ⅛ teaspoon *each* ground cloves, nutmeg, cinnamon, and black pepper

Salt and freshly ground black pepper to taste

1 goose, 8 to 10 pounds, 2 wing joints, giblets, neck, and excess fat and skin removed, skin pricked

1 medium-size Grade A foie gras, about 1 pound, cleaned (see page 255)

Braised Red Cabbage (recipe follows)

1 *each* onion and carrot, coarsely chopped

1 cup Alsace Riesling wine

½ cup cold water

1. Score each chestnut with an X on the flat side with a sharp knife. Put in a saucepan, cover with water, and bring to a boil. Reduce heat to medium, and cook for 10 minutes. Remove chestnuts from the hot water a few at a time, peeling off shell and inner skin as soon as they are cool enough to handle.

2. Preheat oven to 325°F.

3. Cut chestnuts into quarters, place on a flat baking pan, and bake until light brown, about 15 minutes. Remove from oven and set aside to cool.

4. Soak bread in milk. Heat the 1 teaspoon butter in a small skillet over medium heat, add shallots, cover, and sweat until tender, 3 to 4 minutes.

5. Squeeze milk from bread. Combine bread, pork, and veal in a food processor, and pulse until chopped medium fine. Do not overprocess. Scrape mixture into a bowl, and add shallots, chestnuts, port, Cognac, parsley, quatre épices, and salt and pepper, and mix just to blend.

6. Season inside of goose cavity with salt and pepper. Gently pack stuffing into goose, placing foie gras in the center of the stuffing. Truss goose with butcher's twine, season outside with salt and pepper, and place on a rack in a roasting pan large enough to hold it comfortably. Melt the remaining 2 tablespoons of butter, and brush over goose.

7. Turn goose on its side and roast for 1 hour. Turn bird to other side and roast another hour. While goose is roasting, prepare Braised Red Cabbage.

8. After goose has roasted 2 hours, scatter onion and carrot in roasting pan, and turn bird on its back, breast up. Roast for 30 minutes longer, basting with pan juices two or three times. Goose should be golden brown, and juices should run pale pink when bird is deeply pricked in the breast.

9. Remove goose from pan to a warm platter, tent with foil, and keep warm. Discard all fat from roasting pan and set pan on top of stove. Pour in wine and, over medium-high heat, deglaze pan, stirring up all browned cooking bits. Reduce liquid to a glaze, then stir in the cold water and simmer for 5 minutes. Strain sauce and keep warm.

10. Present whole roasted goose on a bed of red cabbage. Slice at the table, and serve with stuffing and sauce.

braised red cabbage

1 large head red cabbage

1 cup red wine

2 teaspoons red wine vinegar

1 bay leaf

2 teaspoons rendered goose or duck fat

1 medium onion, sliced

2 Jonathan apples, peeled, cored, and diced

Salt and freshly ground black pepper to taste

1 teaspoon red gooseberry jam or red currant jelly

1. Remove and discard any damaged cabbage leaves. Core and quarter cabbage, then cut into ¼-inch shreds. Combine wine, vinegar, and bay leaf in a bowl.

2. Heat goose fat in a large, deep casserole over medium-high heat. Stir in onion and sauté until lightly browned, 5 minutes, stirring occasionally. Add cabbage, apples, and wine-vinegar mixture, and season with salt and pepper. Cover, and cook slowly for 45 minutes, stirring occasionally. Just before serving, stir in jam or jelly.

Adapted from Jean Joho, chef-owner, Everest and Brasserie Jo, Chicago

risotto of goose giblets

SERVES 6 AS A MAIN COURSE

When slowly simmered, goose giblets impart an extremely mild, even delicate taste to this risotto-like dish. It's very simple, since the hot liquid is added all at once, rather than by half cupfuls, and there is no constant stirring involved. The result is a dish that is rich but not overwhelming, filling but not leaden. Serve with a crisp green salad, and either red or white wine, according to your own preference.

Gizzard, heart, and neck from 1 goose, washed

1 large leek, including an inch of green, cleaned

2 carrots

6 cups cold water

1 teaspoon salt

6 black peppercorns

7 tablespoons rendered goose or duck fat

1 medium onion, finely chopped

2 cups arborio rice

½ pound white mushrooms, wiped clean, trimmed, and sliced

¾ cup frozen petite peas, defrosted

Salt and freshly ground black pepper to taste

Chopped flat-leaf parsley, to garnish

1. Combine gizzard, heart, neck, leek, carrots, and cold water in a saucepan. Add 1 teaspoon salt and peppercorns, and bring to a boil over high heat. Turn heat down and simmer, partially covered, until meats are tender, about 1 hour. Keep piping hot.
2. Heat 5 tablespoons of the goose fat in a heavy medium-size saucepan over medium heat. Add onion and gently sauté until translucent. Stir in rice, turning to coat all kernels, and cook until they turn opaque and begin to swell. Pour all but ¼ cup of the hot stock through a strainer into rice, stir once, cover pan tightly, and simmer until liquid is absorbed and rice is tender, about 20 minutes.
3. Meanwhile, heat the remaining 2 tablespoons goose fat in a skillet over medium-high heat. Stir in mushrooms and sauté until just limp. Chop gizzard and heart into small pieces, and remove meat from neck. Keep meats warm in a little of the stock.
4. Stir peas, giblets, and mushrooms into risotto. Season with salt and pepper. Sprinkle with parsley, and serve at once.

Adapted from Susan Derecskey, cookbook author, food writer, and editor, Washington, D.C.

Ere I would say, I would drowne my selfe
for the love of a Gynney Hen,
I would change my Humanity with a Baboone.

—William Shakespeare,
Othello, 1604

 # guinea hen

The name guinea correctly identifies this fowl's West African origins. In early Rome and Greece, the birds were imported and served as a great favorite of the nobles. When the Roman Empire collapsed, however, the bird's popularity vanished along with it.

It wasn't until the sixteenth century that the Portuguese, who by then had conquered Guinea, introduced *pintada* to France. The Portuguese name, meaning painted or spotted bird, became *pintade* in French, where the birds are still highly esteemed. Today they are also known as *Perlhuhn* in Germany and *faraona* in Italy. In Europe, annual consumption of guinea hens is about 100 million birds. In the New World, guinea hens first appeared in Haiti. It's believed that they were transported alive, in cages, on board ships carrying African slaves.

The bird's name has always been confusing, since the terms "guinea fowl" and "guinea hen" are used interchangeably, and refer to either female or male birds of the species. In plumage the sexes are indistinguishable, but the males are larger.

Guinea hens are similar in size to chickens and pheasants. Because these birds have never been totally domesticated, their flesh is darker and more flavorful or gamy tasting, like a pheasant's. Unlike a pheasant's, the guinea hen's legs do not have tough tendons, so they are more usable.

Guinea hens have 50 percent less fat than chicken, and a 50-50 ratio of meat to bone. Because the bird is lean, the flesh can become dry and stringy, so many recipes call for moist cooking methods. If you roast a guinea hen, it should be generously covered with fat, such as bacon, duck fat, or butter, and slowly roasted. Additionally, you can cook the parts of the bird separately: braise the breast, and roast, braise, or confit the legs. A fresh bird should be refrigerated and used within 2 days. Frozen guinea hens should be defrosted in the refrigerator, on a plate, for a day, then used within 1 to 2 days.

GEORGE: The guinea hens we sell at D'Artagnan are raised for us by Grimaud Farms (see page 38). The birds consistently weigh between 2½ and 3 pounds. They are grain-fed for 12 weeks, without any steroids or hormones.

Guinea hens are easily recognized by the distinct white dotted pattern of their pearly gray plumage, as well as their bald, vulturelike head. Even without seeing a guinea hen, once you hear its unique screech — described as sounding like a rusty windmill — it is easily distinguished.

Although guinea hens are found on farms, they are independent and unsocial and have never been totally domesticated. They like to perch on the highest branches of the tallest trees. If they sense that the grain being offered is a lure or trap, they go off and forage for themselves. Put them in cages to try to mate them, and they won't lay eggs. Leave them in the open, and they bury their eggs where it's difficult to find them. They are undaunted by larger birds, and have no problem bossing turkeys around.

One famous New York chef, celebrated far and wide for his roast hen and mashed potatoes, was constantly being asked where he got his fantastic birds. His reply: "I have them raised for me on a private farm."

Well, those "hens" were actually guinea hens. I know, because he got them from D'Artagnan.

breast of guinea hen
with porcini mushrooms

SERVES 6

Gently sautéed guinea hen breasts are an elegant way to showcase the pure taste of the birds. The shower of porcini mushrooms, along with the reduced essence of guinea hen and porcini, all add layers of rich flavors. Serve over Yukon Gold mashed potatoes.

3 guinea hens, 3 pounds each

2 tablespoons olive oil or rendered duck fat

1 quart veal stock, or 2 cups duck and veal demi-glace (see page 33)

1 bouquet garni: 1 bay leaf, 2 sprigs thyme or 1 teaspoon dried leaves, and several parsley stems, tied in cheesecloth

2 ounces dried porcini mushrooms

2 cups warm water

3 tablespoons unsalted butter

2 shallots, minced

2 tablespoons minced garlic

1 cup dry white wine

2 tablespoons heavy cream

Salt and freshly ground black pepper to taste

2 tablespoons chopped flat-leaf parsley

1. Bone breast cutlets from each hen. You should have 6 breasts, about 6 ounces each. Remove all skin and fat from breasts. Remove legs from birds and reserve for another use (such as the fricassee on page 70 or the Braised Guinea Hen on page 71). Chop carcass into ¾-inch pieces. Discard giblets or save for another use.

2. Heat olive oil or duck fat in a skillet over medium-high heat. Add chopped bones and cook until golden brown, turning to color all sides. Drain off all fat, then add 1 cup of the veal stock and the bouquet garni to pan. Slowly reduce to a glaze. Do this until all stock is used, and 1 cup of glaze remains. (Alternatively, instead of roasting bones and reducing veal stock, use prepared demi-glace, add bouquet garni, and slowly reduce quantity by half.) Strain and reserve essence. *Recipe may be done 1 day ahead to this point and refrigerated.*
3. Soak porcini in the 2 cups warm water until soft, about 20 minutes. Lift mushrooms from water, then strain liquid through a fine strainer lined with paper towels, to remove dirt and sand. Reserve the liquid. Clean mushrooms and set aside.
4. Melt 2 tablespoons of the butter in a skillet over medium heat. Add shallots and sauté until translucent, 3 to 5 minutes. Stir in mushrooms, garlic, and wine, and cook until reduced to a glaze. Pour in mushroom soaking liquid and, over high heat, reduce by two-thirds. Stir in reserved guinea hen essence, and simmer for 5 minutes. Add heavy cream and continue to simmer for 1 minute. Season to taste with salt and pepper.
5. Melt the remaining 1 tablespoon butter. Brush guinea hen breasts with butter and arrange in a 12-inch skillet (or 2 medium skillets). Cover, place over medium-low heat, and cook gently for 4 minutes per side. They should not color. Season both sides with salt and pepper. Remove breasts from skillet to a cutting board, tent with aluminum foil, and let rest for 5 minutes.
6. Pour essence into skillet, and taste to adjust seasonings. Stir in parsley. Slice

breasts across the grain, and arrange over mashed potatoes, if serving, on 6 plates. Drizzle sauce and mushrooms over breasts, and serve.

Adapted from Gary Danko, chef-owner, Gary Danko, San Francisco

breast of guinea hen
with corn salad and truffle-mushroom sauce

SERVES 2

When guinea hen breasts are sauced with a reduced mushroom stock, with a touch of white truffle oil and crème fraîche, the taste is intoxicating. If you buy a whole bird, you can add the legs to the fricassee of guinea hen that follows. It will then feed at least 4. Serve a light burgundy, like a Côte-Rôtie.

2 boned breast halves of guinea hen with skin on, about 6 ounces each, patted dry

Salt and freshly ground black pepper to taste

6 tablespoons olive oil

½ teaspoon fresh thyme leaves

Pinch fresh rosemary leaves

2 slices smoked bacon, cut into thin strips

2 ears of corn, kernels cut from cob

2 tablespoons minced red onion

12 to 14 thin green beans, tipped, cut cross-wise in half, and blanched

½ cup very well reduced mushroom stock (see sidebar)

2 tablespoons crème fraîche or sour cream

1 tablespoon white truffle oil

1. Preheat oven to 375°F.
2. Generously season guinea hen breasts with salt and pepper. Heat a skillet over high heat, add 4 tablespoons of the olive oil, and place breasts skin side down in pan. Immediately lower heat to medium, slowly rendering fat from the skin while it becomes golden brown and crispy, about 6 to 8 minutes.
3. Raise heat to high, turn breasts over, and season with a pinch of the thyme and all the rosemary. Transfer to oven and roast until juices run clear when pricked, about 2 to 3 minutes, basting with pan drippings. Remove and let rest.
4. While breasts roast, sauté bacon in a medium skillet until crisp, remove and blot on paper towels. Discard all but 2 table-spoons of fat from the pan, and heat over medium-high heat. Stir in corn and sauté for 1 minute, add bacon, onion, green

MUSHROOM ESSENCE

Every time you reconstitute dried wild mush-rooms, strain the liquid through paper towels or a fine sieve, reduce it in a small saucepan or in the microwave by at least half, and freeze. You can add layer upon layer to the jar; just boil the essence before you reuse it. You'll be amazed at how the smallest amount can per-fume a sauce, soup, or stew. Alternatively, soak 1 ounce dried mushrooms in 2 cups warm water, then reduce the strained soaking liquid to ½ cup. Cover and refrigerate the mushrooms for use in another recipe; they will keep for at least a couple of days.

beans, remaining thyme, and salt and pepper, and heat through. Set aside. Heat mushroom stock in a small saucepan and add crème fraîche. Season with salt and pepper. Remove from heat, and whisk in truffle oil just before serving.

5. Spoon corn salad in center of 2 warmed plates. Lay breasts over corn salad. Spoon truffle emulsion around plate and serve.

Adapted from Michael Schlow, chef-owner, Radius, Boston

fricassee of guinea hen
with shallots

SERVES 2 TO 3

A French-style dinner that plays to anyone's love of comfort foods. Prepared as a traditional fricassee, the bird, along with a healthy handful of shallots, is first sautéed in butter. It is then simmered with wine, cream, and lemon juice to devastating deliciousness, and served over pasta.

14 shallots

9 scallions

1 guinea hen, 2½ pounds, giblets and neck removed

Salt and freshly ground black pepper to taste

8 tablespoons unsalted butter

1 cup dry white wine

1 cup plus 2 tablespoons water

1 cup heavy cream

Juice of ½ lemon

1 teaspoon sugar

½ pound fresh pasta

1. Blanch 12 of the shallots in boiling salted water for 3 minutes, then drain, peel, and set aside. Finely slice remaining shallots. Remove root ends from scallions. Cut off about 2 inches of white part, and blanch in salted water for 3 minutes, shock under cold water, and blot dry. Reserve green parts of 4 scallions; wash, finely slice, and set aside.

2. Cut guinea hen into 8 pieces, removing backbone from thighs and breastbone from breast. Reserve bones. Season guinea hen with salt and pepper. Melt 2 tablespoons of the butter in a large heavy skillet over medium heat. Put pieces in pan, skin side down, and sauté until brown, about 3 to 4 minutes, then turn and cook second side until brown. Remove with a slotted spoon and set aside.

3. Add reserved bones to skillet and sauté until light brown, about 6 minutes. Add 2 sliced shallots and sauté 1 minute longer. Pour in wine and 1 cup water, stirring up any browned bits, and simmer for 15 minutes. Add cream, lemon juice, and guinea hen. Cover, and cook over medium heat for 10 minutes.

4. Heat 4 tablespoons of the butter in a heavy skillet over high heat. Add blanched shallots and sprinkle with salt, pepper, and sugar. Add the 2 tablespoons of water and cook, shaking pan continuously, until shallots are caramel-colored all over, about 8 minutes. Stir in blanched scallions and sauté for 2 more minutes.

5. Bring a large pot of salted water to a boil. Add pasta and cook until al dente. Drain, return to pot with remaining 2 tablespoons of butter, and season with salt and pepper. Serve pasta in center of a platter. Place guinea hen pieces around pasta.

6. Bring sauce to a boil over high heat and reduce by one-third. Taste for seasoning, then strain over guinea hen. Add caramelized shallots and scallions, sprinkle on chopped scallions, and serve.

Adapted from André Soltner, former chef-owner, Lutèce, and master chef and senior lecturer, French Culinary Institute, New York City

braised guinea hen
with morbier cheese polenta

SERVES 6

Fork-tender morsels of delicately seasoned guinea hen ragout take a sassy partner in creamy polenta with Morbier cheese. This semisoft cow's-milk cheese from France has a characteristic thin line of ash between the two layers of the wheel. It has a mild, nutty flavor. In this cool-weather dish, you'll discover that poultry simmered on the bone retains a maximum of flavor.

2 guinea hens, 3 pounds each, giblets and neck removed

Salt and freshly ground black pepper to taste

All-purpose flour for dredging

Olive oil for sautéing

2 large carrots, cut on the bias into ¼-inch-thick slices

10 ounces pearl onions, peeled, with an X cut in the root end of each onion

¾ pound small white mushrooms, trimmed and wiped clean

12 cloves garlic

⅓ cup dry white wine

3 cups chicken stock

2 ounces fresh thyme sprigs, leaves stripped from half and chopped, the rest reserved for garnish

Morbier Cheese Polenta (recipe follows)

2 pounds thin fresh asparagus, woody ends removed, sliced diagonally into 1-inch pieces

1 to 2 tablespoons unsalted butter (optional)

1. Remove first 2 wing joints and backbones from guinea hens (discard or save for stock), then cut birds into breast and leg quarters and pat dry. Heat a large, deep, heavy skillet over medium-high heat. Season guinea hen pieces with salt and pepper, then dredge in flour. Pour 2 tablespoons of olive oil into skillet, add birds skin side down, and brown, 3 to 4 minutes. Remove with a slotted spoon to a plate and reserve. Do this in batches if necessary. Add more oil as needed.

2. Add carrots and onions to pan, and cook for 5 minutes, stirring often. Add mushrooms, cook for 2 minutes, then add garlic cloves and cook 1 minute longer, stirring. Pour in wine, stirring to incorporate all the vegetables. Bring to a boil, and reduce until wine has almost completely evaporated. Add stock and chopped thyme.

3. Return guinea hens to pan and adjust heat so liquid simmers. Cover pan and cook until meat is tender, 30 minutes. Remove pieces from pan and spread out on a baking sheet to cool. When guinea hens are cool enough to handle, remove meat from bone in bite-size pieces, not shredded, and return to pan. *Recipe may be prepared ahead to this point, covered, and refrigerated for up to 2 days. Reheat gently in sauce before serving.*

4. Prepare Morbier Cheese Polenta.

5. Bring a large pot of salted water to a boil. Add asparagus and cook until tender, 4 to 5 minutes. Drain, shock under cold water, and blot dry. Stir asparagus into guinea hens. Taste to adjust seasonings of broth, adding butter if desired. Spoon polenta onto 6 warmed dinner plates. Serve guinea hen ragout over polenta, spooning sauce over hens and vegetables. Garnish with remaining thyme sprigs and serve.

morbier cheese polenta

1 quart low-fat milk

1 teaspoon salt

1½ cups instant polenta

½ pound Morbier or Gruyère cheese, rind removed, diced into ¼-inch pieces

Bring milk and salt to a boil in a saucepan over medium-high heat. Add polenta, stirring constantly until creamy, 3 to 5 minutes. Stir in Morbier cheese, and continue stirring until melted. Taste to adjust seasonings if necessary, and serve at once.

Adapted from Charles Dale, chef-owner, Renaissance Restaurant, Aspen, Colorado

"sro" guinea hen

SERVES 2 TO 4

In the case of a guinea fowl done SRO style, the letters are slightly removed from the common usage referring to standing room only. Taking advantage of a vertical roaster, the bird is cooked in a standing position to juicy, crunchy perfection. Ariane calls it a "standing room oven" bird. It's a treat for everyday meals. Serve with Sautéed Parsleyed Potatoes and a Côtes de Gascogne red.

1 guinea hen, 2½ to 3 pounds, giblets and neck removed, patted dry

2 to 3 tablespoons rendered duck fat or unsalted butter

Salt and freshly ground black pepper to taste

8 cloves garlic

Sautéed Parsleyed Potatoes (page 7)

1. Preheat oven to 475°F.

2. Rub guinea hen all over with duck fat. Season liberally, inside and out, with salt and pepper.

3. Slice garlic cloves, removing the green germ if present. Using your fingers, gently loosen breast and thigh skin. Slip some garlic slices under skin and around the neck. Place bird on vertical roaster. Turn wing tips under and wedge more garlic slices under wings.

4. Roast bird for 15 minutes, then adjust heat to 350°F and continue roasting for 15 minutes more. While bird roasts, prepare Sautéed Parsleyed Potatoes. Remove guinea hen from oven and let rest for 10 minutes, then carve and serve with potatoes.

roast guinea hen breasts and leg roulades
in black truffle sauce

SERVES 4

Roasted guinea hen breast, served with rolled and stuffed thighs filled with a truffle-scented forcemeat, is dining at its most refined. The birds are simply glazed with a reduced sauce. But what a glaze it is: sliced truffles and butter are added to the rich stock. Asparagus and morels add another luxurious touch.

2 guinea hens, 2½ to 3 pounds each, giblets and neck removed

½ cup Reduced Guinea Hen Stock (recipe follows), or ½ cup duck and veal demi-glace (see page 33)

2 tablespoons cold heavy cream

2 tablespoons truffle oil

1 tablespoon olive oil

1 pound fresh morels, cleaned in cold water until all dirt is removed, blotted dry

Salt and freshly ground black pepper to taste

1 bunch asparagus, woody ends removed, stalks trimmed to 2½ inches and peeled

3 tablespoons unsalted butter

1 black truffle, about 1 ounce

4 small sprigs thyme, to garnish

1. Remove breasts with skin intact from carcasses, and trim away excess fat. Remove tenderloin from breasts and set aside. Cut legs from carcasses and remove thigh bones, reserving bones. Place legs skin side down on cutting board. Cover boned thighs with plastic wrap and gently pound with your palm or a wooden spoon to flatten, keeping meat intact. Cover and refrigerate breasts and legs.

2. Prepare Reduced Guinea Hen Stock.

3. While stock is simmering, place breast tenderloins in a food processor. Pulse to chop, then add heavy cream and truffle oil, and blend just until mixture is smooth. Remove, cover, and refrigerate.

4. Heat olive oil in a large skillet, add morels, and sauté until tender, then season with salt and pepper and set aside. Bring a pot of salted water to a boil, add asparagus, and boil until just tender, then shock in ice water. Remove and blot dry. Set aside.

5. Lay guinea hen legs skin side down on counter. Season with salt and pepper. Divide puréed tenderloin mixture among the boneless thighs, top with morels, then fold the edges of the meat over to enclose the mix, creating a roulade with each thigh. Tie roulades evenly with butcher's twine in several places.

6. Preheat oven to 350°F. Lightly oil a large roasting pan and heat over high heat.

7. Season breasts and legs with salt and pepper, place in hot pan skin side up, and roast in oven until skin is golden brown, about 25 minutes. Remove from oven and let rest in pan. Reheat asparagus in a skillet with a little water and 1 tablespoon of the butter. Place a breast cutlet and a leg on each of 4 warmed dinner plates and lay asparagus on top of hen. Heat Reduced Guinea Hen Stock over medium-high heat. Slice truffles and stir into sauce. Off the heat, stir in remaining 2 tablespoons butter, taste to adjust seasonings, and spoon over hen. Garnish with thyme sprigs.

reduced guinea hen stock

You may substitute about 2 pounds of bones from other game birds or chickens in this stock, and make it several weeks ahead and freeze.

Reserved carcasses and bones from Step 1 above, or 2 pounds bones from other game birds

1 tablespoon vegetable oil

1 carrot, chopped

2 ribs celery, chopped

1 onion, chopped

5 cloves garlic, split in half

1 tablespoon tomato paste

1 tomato, chopped

½ cup dry white wine

2 quarts water

2 bay leaves

5 sprigs flat-leaf parsley

4 sprigs thyme

Salt and freshly ground black pepper to taste

Chop reserved carcasses and thigh bones into 1½-inch pieces. Heat oil in a large deep skillet, add bones, and cook over medium-high heat until golden brown, turning occasionally. Add carrot, celery, onion, and garlic to pan, and cook until vegetables are golden brown, 7 to 8 minutes. Stir in tomato paste and tomato, cook 5 minutes. Then add white wine and cook 2 minutes longer. Add water, bay leaves, parsley, and thyme sprigs. Simmer for 1 hour, skimming surface from time to time. Pour through a fine strainer into a clean pot. Bring to a boil and reduce to about ½ cup liquid. Season to taste with salt and pepper.

Adapted from Kevin O'Kane, chef, Fifty-Seven Fifty-Seven Restaurant at the Four Seasons Hotel, New York City

guinea hen
two ways with garlic and lemon sauces

SERVES 4 TO 6

The two garlic-rich sauces of this dish — one with slowly reduced lemon slices, the other with garlic confit and port wine reduction — provide a maximum of flavor with a minimum amount of effort. Garlic slowly boiled or cooked in duck fat loses its bite and turns sweet and mild. Peeled cloves of garlic sold in many markets are a real convenience here. Serve with fresh pasta and light red wine, slightly chilled.

3 lemons, thinly sliced crosswise, seeds removed

1 pound peeled garlic cloves, plus 2 cloves garlic, chopped

2 quarts of water with 2 tablespoons of salt added

1¼ cup heavy cream

2 guinea hens, 2½ pounds each, giblets and neck removed, patted dry

Salt and pepper

1 tablespoon plus ½ cup rendered duck fat (see Note)

1 carrot, chopped

1 onion, chopped

5 ounces ruby port

1. Combine lemons and half the peeled garlic with the salted water in a saucepan. Bring to a boil over high heat and let water evaporate completely. Pour in 1 cup of the cream and let mixture cook gently over medium-low heat. Reserve.

2. Preheat oven to 400°F.

3. Season guinea hens with salt and pepper, then put in a roasting pan, and spread about 1 tablespoon duck fat over each bird. Turn birds on one side and roast for 20 minutes. Add carrot, onion, and the 2 cloves chopped garlic, and turn birds to other side, and roast 15 minutes longer. Remove birds from pan. Remove legs from birds. Lightly tent breast portions (still on the bone) with aluminum foil and keep warm.

4. While birds are roasting, make garlic confit: Combine remaining garlic cloves with ½ cup duck fat in a saucepan, and slowly cook until completely tender, about 20 minutes. Remove garlic with a slotted spoon.

5. After birds have been removed from roasting pan, heat about a teaspoon of the duck fat in the pan over medium-high heat. Add legs and sauté until golden brown on both sides, 4 to 5 minutes, turning once. Remove legs to a platter and keep warm. Deglaze pan with port, then pour in the remaining ¼ cup cream. Transfer mixture to an electric blender or food processor along with the garlic confit (reserving a few cloves as a garnish) and purée until smooth. Strain into a clean pan, season with salt and pepper, and keep warm.

6. Gently reheat the garlic-lemon sauce if necessary, then spoon it over one half of serving platter and lay legs on top of it. Cut breasts off the bone, then cut crosswise into slices, and place them on the other side of the platter. Spoon the port wine sauce over them, and serve garnished with reserved garlic confit.

NOTE:

Use duck fat that you have rendered and saved in the freezer (it keeps up to 6 months), or order from D'Artagnan or from a local purveyor of fine meats and poultry.

Adapted from André Daguin, former chef-owner, Hôtel de France, Auch, and president, Fédération Nationale de l'Industrie Hôtelière, Paris

ostrich

Ostrich is making a comeback. "When was it in?" you may ask. If you are racking your brain to recall the last time the large flightless bird had any culinary cachet, you'd have to look back to ancient Rome. That was when the noted gastronome Apicius created a special sauce for boiled ostrich, an expensive delicacy. It included pepper, mint, cumin, celery seeds, dates, honey, vinegar, *garum* (fish sauce), and *passum* (a sweet wine pressed from grapes dried on the vine).

Apicius's feasts were extravagant by any measure, even when compared with those that followed in the Middle Ages. Any bird that can grow to 7 feet tall and weigh up to 400 pounds has to be quite an undertaking to prepare. However, don't start custom-building an oven to roast the whole bird, since from the cook's point of view, ostrich is nothing but two huge legs.

In present-day ostrich farming, the ideal age for processing birds for their meat is between 12 and 16 months, when they weigh between 250 and 300 pounds. The yield is between 85 and 100 pounds of meat, as well as about 14 square feet of ostrich leather. Hens lay between 30 and 60 eggs a season, and as many as 100. The birds can live up to 80 years, and produce for 50 of those. For gargantuan appetites, try an ostrich drumstick; each one weighs a hefty 30 to 40 pounds.

The growth in the ostrich industry can be attributed to the bird's beefy red meat, which has less fat than turkey, making it healthful yet satisfying. Ostrich meat comes from the thigh and leg. Its flavor is similar to that of beef fillet and top sirloin steak; and the delicate texture is somewhat like that of venison or flank steak. The birds we sell don't receive hormones and are free of antibiotics.

Ostrich is easily adaptable to all dry-cooking techniques, from stir-fry and barbecue to roasting and sautéing. It also takes well to marinades. For optimum results, slice the meat into medallions and cook quickly over high heat to rare or medium rare, about 140° to 150°F on an instant-read thermometer. Because it's so lean, there is almost no shrinkage. To prevent sticking, add a little oil (especially a flavored one) to the pan, or brush the meat with it. Even a short amount of overcooking can make ostrich dry and unappealing. If you stew or braise ostrich, do so over very low heat. (For more guidelines on cooking ostrich, see page 168).

ostrich fajitas
with tomato-avocado pico de gallo

SERVES 4 TO 6

Fajitas are meal pleasers for all ages. The marinated, sliced ostrich and thick slices of portobello mushrooms, grilled peppers, and onions are wrapped, burrito-style, in large, warm tortillas. Half the fun is eating the slurpy, juicy meal. Look for some of the newer flavored tortillas, like chili or sun-dried tomato. Instead of making guacamole, which is sometimes served with fajitas, we've added diced avocado to the pico de gallo, the finely chopped raw tomato salsa.

4 to 5 tablespoons olive oil

2 tablespoons fresh lime juice

1½ tablespoons minced garlic

1 tablespoon chili powder

½ tablespoon ground cumin

1 teaspoon salt

¼ teaspoon Tabasco

1 piece ostrich meat, 1½ pounds, cut in half
    horizontally to be about 1 inch thick

Tomato-Avocado Pico de Gallo (recipe follows)

8 to 12 (8-inch) tortillas

2 *each* red and yellow bell peppers, cored,
    seeded, and cut into ¼-inch strips

2 large portobello mushroom caps, wiped
    clean, and cut into ½-inch slices

1 large red onion, cut into thin wedges

Freshly ground black pepper to taste

1. Combine 2 tablespoons of the oil, the lime juice, garlic, chili powder, cumin, salt, and Tabasco in a large resealable plastic bag. Add ostrich, seal bag, and turn several times to coat well. Refrigerate for at least 3 hours or overnight.

2. Prepare Tomato-Avocado Pico de Gallo.

3. Wrap tortillas in foil and warm in a slow oven.

4. Heat a large cast iron or heavy skillet over high heat. Remove ostrich from marinade and cook until rare or medium rare, 6½ to 8 minutes per side. Remove to a cutting board, cover lightly with foil, and let rest for 10 minutes.

5. Meanwhile, heat 2 tablespoons of the remaining oil in the skillet. When hot, add peppers, mushrooms, and onions, and sauté until crisp-tender, about 5 minutes, stirring occasionally. Add more oil if necessary. Season with salt and pepper.

6. Slice ostrich across the grain into thin slices, and transfer to a warm platter. Place sautéed vegetables alongside, and serve with warmed tortillas and pico de gallo.

tomato-avocado pico de gallo

2 cups seeded, cored, and diced ripe tomatoes

½ cup thinly sliced scallions, mostly white
    parts

1 to 1½ tablespoons minced fresh jalapeño
    pepper

1 firm, ripe avocado

2 tablespoons fresh lime juice

1 tablespoon extra-virgin olive oil

Salt and freshly ground black pepper to taste

¼ cup chopped cilantro

Combine tomatoes, scallions, and jalapeños in a bowl. Peel avocado, and cut flesh into ¼-inch dice. Add it to tomatoes, along with lime juice, oil, salt, and pepper, and set aside. Just before serving, stir in cilantro, and taste to adjust flavors.

mustard-glazed ostrich fillet with berry marmalade sauce
and sweet potato croquettes

SERVES 4

The meaty taste of ostrich — best served rare, since it is so lean — takes well to the crunchy, flavorful Sweet Potato Croquettes. *Panko,* irregularly shaped Japanese bread crumbs, give the croquettes an extra-crispy crust. Layers of mustard and berry flavors blend into a mouthwatering sauce. Serve with thinly sliced red cabbage sautéed until tender in a mixture of olive and hazelnut oils, seasoned with cumin seeds, salt, and pepper.

Sweet Potato Croquettes (recipe follows)

4 teaspoons olive oil

1 large shallot, thinly sliced

2 tablespoons berry marmalade (available at specialty food stores) or berry preserves

1 tablespoon cracked black pepper

¼ cup red wine vinegar

1 cup duck or chicken stock

¼ cup fruit mustard (available at specialty food stores)

4 ostrich fillets, 5 ounces each, blotted dry

Salt and freshly ground black pepper to taste

2 teaspoons unsalted butter, at room temperature

1. Prepare Sweet Potato Croquettes through Step 1.

2. Heat 1 teaspoon of the oil in a skillet over medium heat. Add shallot and cook until wilted, 2 to 3 minutes. Stir in marmalade and cracked pepper. Pour in vinegar, turn up heat, and boil until liquid has almost evaporated. Stir in stock, then the mustard, and gently boil until reduced to the consistency of a thin sauce. Keep warm.

3. Season ostrich with salt and pepper. Heat remaining 3 teaspoons oil in a large skillet over high heat until hot. Add ostrich and cook quickly on both sides until browned and rare or medium rare, turning once. Remove from pan and keep warm. Finish croquettes.

4. Place croquettes on 4 warmed plates. Lay ostrich fillets on top. Strain berry sauce into a clean pan, stir in butter, and season with salt and pepper. Pour over ostrich and serve at once.

sweet potato croquettes

2 medium sweet potatoes, baked until tender

2 tablespoons chopped hazelnuts, toasted

1 tablespoon chopped fresh sage leaves

Salt and freshly ground black pepper to taste

All-purpose flour

2 eggs beaten with 1 tablespoon milk

Mustard-Glazed Ostrich Fillet with Berry Marmalade Sauce ❯
and Sweet Potato Croquettes

½ to 1 cup Japanese bread crumbs (*Panko,* available at Japanese or Asian markets)

Olive oil, to sauté croquettes

1. When potatoes are cool enough to handle, scoop out flesh and transfer to a nonstick skillet. Heat skillet over medium heat and cook potatoes until very dry, turning occasionally, and breaking up with a wooden spatula. Let cool, then stir in hazelnuts, sage, and salt and pepper. Form into 4 round cakes, about 1 inch thick. Dust with flour, drop into egg wash, then cover with bread crumbs. Set aside on a rack.

2. Pour enough oil into a skillet to measure about ½ inch deep, and heat over medium-high heat until hot. Add croquettes and cook until golden brown on one side, turn with a spatula, and cook second side until brown. Remove, blot dry on paper towels, and keep warm.

Adapted from Jean-Robert de Cavel, chef, Maisonette, Cincinnati

grilled ostrich fillet with chili-honey glaze

SERVES 4

The marriage of heat and sweet from the chili-honey glaze gives new meaning to simple pleasures. You'll be tempted to serve the meaty fillets often. Add a basic salad and, perhaps, baked yams. Cascabel chilies have a rich, nutty taste, and are of medium-intensity heat. They are dried and dark brick colored. If no cascabels are available, substitute 2 jalapeños.

4 cascabel chilies, or 2 fresh jalapeños, seeded

1 cup honey

½ cup chicken stock

3 tablespoons tomato purée

1 teaspoon sweet paprika

1 teaspoon ground cumin

4 ostrich fillets, 4 ounces each, blotted dry

2 tablespoons olive oil

Salt and freshly ground black pepper to taste

1. Soak chilies in warm water for about 2 hours prior to using. (If using jalapeños, soaking is not necessary.) Drain and combine with honey, stock, tomato purée, paprika, and cumin in a saucepan. Bring mixture to a boil, then simmer over medium heat for 10 minutes, stirring occasionally. Scrape mixture into an electric blender, and purée until smooth.

2. Heat a charcoal or gas grill. Or light a broiler. Rub ostrich with oil, and season with salt and pepper. When hot, place ostrich on grill and cook 3 minutes. Brush with chili-honey glaze and cook each side

SLOW GO

Ostrich farming had a tough time getting started in France. Grimaud Farms, already raising some of the finest Muscovy ducks, decided to diversify and farm ostrich. They ordered a pair, a male and female, from South Africa, at a very high premium. When the large flightless birds had been around for almost a year without so much as a single egg appearing, closer examination revealed that this particular male was missing an important part.

2 minutes longer. Remove meat from grill and allow to rest for 5 minutes, then cut each fillet on the bias into 4 slices. Transfer to warmed plates, drizzle remaining glaze over ostrich, and serve at once.

Adapted from Vincent Guerithault, chef-owner,

Vincent's on Camelback, Phoenix

ranch ostrich with honey-malt glaze

on yellow tomato–pozole stew

SERVES 4

In Mexican cooking, *pozole* refers both to what is known as hominy in the United States — dried corn kernels boiled with pickling lime — as well as to a thick soup/stew made with pork and the corn (hominy) kernels. It is a beloved staple of rich and poor homes alike, and there are many variations, including red, white, and green pozoles, the colors of the country's flag. Our version is a stew that also uses cooked pozole. Typically, lots of garnishes are added. In this case, one of the garnishes — the lacquered ostrich steak — is actually the star. It makes all of the other ingredients shine more brightly. This is a deep, soul-satisfying dish.

Yellow Tomato–Pozole Stew (recipe follows)

3 tablespoons canola oil

4 red bell peppers, cored, seeded, and chopped

2 tablespoons *each* chopped onion and chopped garlic

2 cups honey

1 cup malt vinegar

Salt and freshly ground black pepper to taste

4 ostrich fillets, 6 ounces each, about ¾ inch thick

Avocado slices and cilantro sprigs, to garnish

1. Prepare Yellow Tomato–Pozole Stew.

2. Heat 2 tablespoons of the oil in a large saucepan over medium-high heat. Add bell peppers, onion, and garlic, and cook until golden. Add honey and reduce over high heat by one-third. Stir in vinegar, reduce by one-third, strain, and taste to adjust seasonings.

3. Season ostrich with salt and pepper. Heat remaining 1 tablespoon oil in a large skillet over medium-high heat. Sauté ostrich for 1 minute, brush liberally with glaze and cook until glaze thickens, 1 minute more. Turn and cook second side 1 minute, again brush with glaze, and cook until meat is medium rare, about 1 minute. Cook only as many fillets as will comfortably fit in pan without crowding. Repeat until all fillets are cooked.

4. To serve, spoon some pozole onto 4 warmed plates and place ostrich fillets on top. Garnish with avocado slices and cilantro sprigs, and serve.

yellow tomato–pozole stew

4 large yellow or red tomatoes, cut in half crosswise, cored, and seeded

5 tablespoons canola oil

10 corn tortillas

2 tablespoons chopped onion, plus ½ cup diced onion

2 tablespoons chopped garlic

1 poblano chili, seeded and chopped

1 cup chopped celery, plus ½ cup diced celery

1 teaspoon *each* ground cumin, ground white pepper, and fennel seeds

½ cup *each* gold tequila and beer

4 cups chicken stock

Salt and freshly ground black pepper to taste

Lime juice to taste

1 cup diced ham

½ cup diced, seeded jalapeños

1 cup *each* corn kernels and cooked pozole (hominy)

½ cup *each* diced red and yellow tomato

1. Preheat oven to 350°F.
2. Place tomatoes cut side down on a flat nonstick baking pan and roast until partially dried, about 45 minutes. Set aside.
3. Heat 2 tablespoons of the oil in a large skillet and quickly fry tortillas for 30 seconds on each side. Drain on paper towels.

When all the tortillas have been fried, tear into 2-inch pieces. Heat 2 more tablespoons of the oil over medium-high heat. Stir in the 2 tablespoons of chopped onion and the garlic, and sauté until translucent, 3 minutes. Add poblano chili and 1 cup celery, cook 3 to 4 minutes, then add cumin, white pepper, fennel seeds, and tortillas. Cook for 2 minutes, then deglaze pan with tequila and beer. Add stock and roasted tomatoes, bring to a simmer, and cook 4 to 5 minutes. Purée the mixture in an electric blender or food processor, and strain. Season with salt, pepper, and lime juice. Set yellow tomato sauce aside.

4. Sauté ham in the remaining 1 tablespoon oil over medium-high heat. Add the remaining ½ cup onion and celery, and the diced jalapeños, and cook over medium heat for 3 to 4 minutes. Add corn and pozole, cook for 7 to 8 minutes, then add diced tomatoes and simmer until heated through, 1 to 2 minutes. Stir mixture into reserved yellow tomato sauce and keep warm.

Adapted from Dean Fearing, executive chef,
The Mansion on Turtle Creek, Dallas

If the partridge had the woodcock's thigh
It would be the best bird that ever did fly.

— John Ray, British naturalist and philologist,
   1627–1705, *English Proverbs*

partridge ⤳

The partridge is a medium-size, plump-bodied Old World game bird with tender white flesh. Of the four major species, the two most common are the red-legged partridge, a bird that originated in Spain and southern France, and nests in woodland trees; and the gray-legged partridge, from Great Britain, which is about 12 inches long and nests on ground cover, like open fields and moors. Neither is indigenous to the United States. A third species of partridge, the chukar, was imported from Asia into North America for hunting in 1927, and has been farm-raised ever since. Unfortunately, the birds don't take well to domestication, and the results are pale in comparison to the real thing. To confuse matters even more, what is called a partridge in the United States is often really a ruffed grouse or bobwhite quail, and in the American South they are sometimes mistakenly called pheasants.

Partridges are one of the mildest-tasting game birds. They average 10 to 12 ounces dressed, or perhaps 14 ounces for a fat gray-legged bird. Chukars can weigh still more.

ARIANE: When hunting partridge, a *perdreau* — a bird of the current year — is the prize catch. In France, a young bird that makes it past October 1, St. Rémi's Day, is said to be mature. The unmistakable sign of a young bird is the tiny white spot at the end of the long wing feather. The talent of the hunter is to recognize surroundings that could be enticing to partridges, and to find a bird that has just gotten its adult colors: earthy tints with rusty tans and, sometimes, a rusty-brown horseshoe line of feathers on the breast. Far more tender than a *perdrix,* or old partridge, the young bird is rarely hung. (See page 93 for a discussion of hanging.) It's usually cooked for just 15 minutes, and is served with a mild sauce. Often the breast is first covered with a grape leaf and then the bird is encircled with a layer of ventrèche (pancetta). It is roasted on top of a thick slice of country bread to trap the best part: the juice. Older birds require hanging, slow cooking, and a strong sauce to compete with the gamy taste. Traditionally, a perdrix is slowly braised with cabbage.

partridge, pear, and wild mushroom strudel
with pear-onion chutney

SERVES 4 AS A FIRST COURSE

Partridges are small and, admittedly, pricey . . . unless you shoot them yourself. (But that takes time and, often, a plane ticket.) Usually, you need 1 bird for 2 diners. This thyme-scented pear-and-mushroom-flavored strudel is a glamorous way to serve 4 guests graciously from 1 bird. Tangy chutney mirrors the strudel's flavors, and lightly dressed mixed greens finish the plate. Use firm pears so the fruit does not fall apart. Assemble the strudels ahead of time, then bake just before you serve them for maximum crispness.

1 partridge, 10 to 12 ounces, giblets and neck removed

4 to 5 tablespoons unsalted butter

1 tablespoon minced onion

⅔ cup chopped fresh chanterelles, hedgehogs, or other flavorful wild mushrooms, plus a few mushrooms, to garnish

1 large firm green Bartlett pear, peeled, cored, and cut into ¼-inch dice (about ⅔ cup dice)

2 teaspoons chopped fresh thyme leaves

Pinch cayenne

1 teaspoon salt or to taste

Freshly ground black pepper to taste

4 sheets phyllo pastry, defrosted according to package directions, if frozen

Pear-Onion Chutney (recipe follows)

½ cup Quick Game Bird Demi-Glace (see page 88)

2 to 3 ounces mixed field greens

1 tablespoon extra-virgin olive oil

1 teaspoon raspberry vinegar

1. Bone partridge without skinning meat, but removing tendons from the legs. Reserve bones for stock. Chop meat and skin, either by hand or by pulsing in a food processor, until cut into ⅛-inch pieces. Do not overprocess into a smooth paste. Set aside.

2. Heat ½ teaspoon of the butter in a small skillet. Add minced onion and sauté over medium heat until lightly browned, 3 to 4 minutes, stirring occasionally. Add another 2 teaspoons of butter and the mushrooms, and sauté until mushrooms are wilted and have given off their liquid. Set aside to cool, then scrape into bowl with partridge.

3. Heat another teaspoon of butter in the skillet and sauté pears over medium-high heat until lightly browned, 2 to 3 minutes, shaking pan often. Scrape into bowl with partridge. Stir in 1½ teaspoons of the thyme, the cayenne, salt, and pepper, mixing only enough to blend well. Cover, and refrigerate for 2 hours or overnight.

4. Remove mixture from refrigerator. Melt 3 tablespoons of the butter. Lay a piece of parchment paper larger than the phyllo on a workspace. Lay 1 sheet of the phyllo on it so the long edge is nearest you. Brush lightly with butter. Lay a second sheet over the first, brush lightly with butter, and sprinkle on remaining ½ teaspoon thyme. Add the third sheet of phyllo, brushing with butter, and then the last layer, without buttering it. Cut pile in half from top to bottom, including parchment paper. Turn each pile a quarter turn so long edge is close to you.

5. Divide stuffing into 2 equal parts. Form each part into a thin cylinder almost the length of one of the phyllo piles. Lay it about 1 inch from lower edge, and roll it up tightly in the pastry. You do not need to turn in the ends. Place the rolls seam side down on a flat dish, brush with butter, and chill for 15 to 20 minutes. *Recipe may be done 1 day ahead of time to this point.*

6. Prepare Pear-Onion Chutney.

7. Preheat oven to 425°F.

8. Bake strudels on a baking sheet in upper third of oven for 10 minutes, then turn pan back to front, and adjust heat to 400°F. Bake until golden brown, about 12 minutes longer. Remove and let rest for a few minutes.

9. Meanwhile, heat mushrooms reserved for garnish in a little butter. Heat Quick Game Bird Demi-Glace. Toss greens with oil and vinegar, and season with salt and pepper. Divide among 4 luncheon plates. Spoon a rounded tablespoon of chutney on each plate.

10. Cut each strudel roll into 2 portions with a sharp knife, then cut each portion into 2 pieces with a diagonal, sushi-style cut. Lay 1 piece of the strudel on its side; prop the second half up against it so filling shows. Sprinkle mushrooms around rim of plates, drizzle on demi-glace, and serve.

pear-onion chutney

MAKES ABOUT 2½ CUPS

1 cup sliced onions

½ cup white wine vinegar

⅓ cup firmly packed light brown sugar

2 teaspoons minced fresh gingerroot

⅛ teaspoon *each* cinnamon and white pepper

Pinch *each* cayenne, ground allspice, ground clove

1 bay leaf

2 to 3 large firm green Bartlett pears, peeled, cored, and cut into ½-inch dice (about 2 cups dice)

Combine onions, vinegar, brown sugar, ginger, cinnamon, white pepper, cayenne, allspice, clove, and bay leaf in a saucepan, and bring to a boil. Reduce heat and boil gently until onions are translucent and liquid is reduced to a syrup, about 15 minutes. Stir in pears, turning to coat all pieces, and cook until fruit is just tender, 7 to 10 minutes. *Recipe may be made several weeks ahead and stored in a covered container in the refrigerator.*

Adapted from Brendan Walsh, chef-owner, The Elms Restaurant & Tavern, Ridgefield, Connecticut

---

QUICK GAME BIRD DEMI-GLACE

Chef Brendan Walsh suggests that once you debone any game bird, you chop the bones and roast them on a flat baking pan in a hot (400°F) oven until lightly browned. Then deglaze the pan with 2 cups good-quality, unsalty chicken stock. (Purchased stock, unless all-natural and low in sodium, produces a salty, chemical syrup.) Bring the mixture, bones and all, to a boil with a few sprigs of the herb of your choice — for his strudels he uses thyme — and reduce to ½ cup. Strain to remove bones and herbs.

partridge with bacon, cider-glazed cabbage, and sautéed apples

SERVES 6

In France, braised cabbage is a classic partner for partridge. Here, young partridges are steamed over bacon and apple cider–scented cabbage. The simple cooking process yields a mouthwatering meal for any chilly evening. Serve with spaetzle or mashed potatoes. A chilled Alsatian Riesling will complement the dish well. If partridges are unavailable, pheasants or ruffed grouse may be substituted.

¾ pound slab bacon, cut into ½-inch cubes

2 small heads green cabbage, cored, quartered, and shredded (about 8 cups)

1 cup apple cider

1 to 2 cups chicken or duck stock

6 red-legged partridges, 10 to 12 ounces each, giblets and neck removed, patted dry

Salt and freshly ground black pepper to taste

2 tablespoons rendered duck fat or unsalted butter

3 to 4 large Granny Smith apples, peeled, cored, and cut into eighths

2 tablespoons sugar

Few drops lemon juice

1. Place bacon in a large deep skillet or casserole and, over medium heat, slowly render the fat, but don't brown the cubes. Remove bacon with a slotted spoon and drain on paper towels. Discard all but 2 tablespoons of the fat.

2. Heat bacon fat. Add cabbage and sauté over medium-high heat until it starts to wilt and cook down, turning often. Pour in cider and enough stock to come halfway up the cabbage, and bring to a boil for 2 minutes. Stir in reserved bacon, season partridges with salt and pepper, and place over cabbage. Turn heat down so liquid just simmers, cover pan, and cook gently for 20 minutes. Turn off heat, and let skillet sit covered for 10 minutes more.

3. Meanwhile, heat duck fat in a large skillet over medium-high heat. Add apples and sauté until beginning to brown. Sprinkle on sugar, turning to coat evenly, and continue cooking over low heat until lightly caramelized. Squeeze on lemon juice, turn again, and keep warm.

4. Uncover partridges and slice breasts and legs from carcasses. Serve partridge with cabbage and cooking juices. Garnish with sautéed apples and serve with spaetzle or mashed potatoes, if desired.

ON THE FIRST DAY OF CHRISTMAS

On the first day of Christmas my true love sent to me a partridge in a pear tree. . . . If the traditional day for determining when a young partridge becomes mature, and thus of little culinary interest, is October 1, what does it say about the ardor of the lover referred to in this old English folk song? What a mixed message! The bird would be stringy and the pear tree, out of season, would bear no fruit.

partridge cacciatore

SERVES 6 TO 8

Close your eyes and let the luscious smells wafting from your oven transport you to a rustic Tuscan hunting lodge. The sweet aroma of roasting garlic mixed with herbs and tomatoes fills the room. You're there with a crackling fire, a well-worn wooden trestle table, and comfortably cushioned chairs. Soon, a large platter of linguine with juicy pieces of partridge nestled on top tempts your every sense. Alongside, perhaps a green salad or stewed baby artichokes. A bottle of Chianti to go with dinner, a slice of fresh cheese and ripe pears to follow. It's easy and so rewarding.

3 partridges, 10 to 12 ounces each

½ cup all-purpose flour, seasoned with salt and freshly ground black pepper, for dredging

½ cup canola oil

1 *each* large onion and green bell pepper, coarsely chopped

2 cloves garlic, finely chopped

1 cup small white mushroom caps, wiped clean and trimmed

4 large ripe tomatoes, quartered, or 2 cups canned plum tomatoes, quartered

1 cup medium Madeira

1 tablespoon *each* chopped fresh oregano, basil, and tarragon, or 1 teaspoon *each* dried

1 to 1½ pounds dry linguine, cooked al dente

Sprigs of fresh basil, to garnish

1. Preheat oven to 350°F.

2. Remove first 2 wing joints from partridges, then cut birds into breasts, drumsticks, and thighs. Dredge pieces in seasoned flour, patting to remove excess. Heat oil in a large heavy skillet over medium-high heat. Sauté partridges until skin is crisp and golden brown, turning once. Do this in batches, if necessary, so pieces do not steam. Remove pieces with tongs or a slotted spoon and transfer to a large oven-safe casserole or roasting pan.

3. In the same skillet, sauté onion, green pepper, garlic, and mushrooms until onions are golden brown, about 7 minutes, stirring occasionally. Stir in tomatoes, Madeira, oregano, basil, and tarragon, and season with salt and pepper. Pour mixture over partridge, cover pot, and bake for 1 hour. Serve over linguine, garnished with fresh basil sprigs.

Adapted from Loic Jaffres, master butcher and meat manager, Sutton Place Gourmet, Bethesda, Maryland

partridge
with marsala and brandy

SERVES 4

Another simple and pleasurable Italian-style partridge that's easy to prepare. Here the blend of dry Marsala — a fortified wine originally from Sicily — a touch of brandy, and porcini mushrooms enhances the mild-flavored birds. Serve with orzo and sautéed spinach.

1 ounce dried porcini or mixed wild mushrooms

2 partridges, 10 to 12 ounces each

½ cup all-purpose flour, seasoned with salt and
freshly ground black pepper, for dredging

2 tablespoons olive oil

2 tablespoons unsalted butter

2 cloves garlic

2 bay leaves

Salt and freshly ground black pepper to taste

¾ cup imported dry Marsala

1 teaspoon dried thyme

¼ cup brandy

1. Cover porcini with hot water and soak until soft, 15 to 20 minutes. Drain, scraping away any dirt, and set aside. Discard soaking liquid or strain and save for another use.

2. Remove first 2 wing joints and giblets from partridges, and discard or save for making stock. Cut birds into breasts, drumsticks, and thighs. Dredge partridge pieces in seasoned flour, patting to remove excess. Heat oil and butter in a large heavy skillet over medium-high heat. Sauté partridges until skin is crisp and golden brown, turning several times. Do this in batches, if necessary, so pieces do not steam. Add garlic, bay leaves, and salt and pepper to taste. Cook until liquid from bird evaporates, stirring constantly.

3. Reduce heat to medium low, add ½ cup of the Marsala, the mushrooms, and thyme. Cover and simmer for 5 minutes, then raise heat to medium. Cook, stirring occasionally, until partridge is almost tender, 35 to 45 minutes. Add the remaining ¼ cup Marsala and cook for 10 minutes. Adjust heat to high, add the brandy, and cook 3 to 4 minutes longer. Transfer pieces to a platter, discard garlic, and serve with mushroom sauce.

Adapted from Ed Giobbi, artist, sculptor, and cookbook author, Katonah, New York

One past makes up the prince and peasan,
Though one eats roots, the other feasan.

— Howell, *Letters,* 1650

pheasant

To the pheasant goes the honor of being the most widely consumed feathered game in the world. The medium-size native Asian bird, of which there are many species, has been a prized addition to royal banquets and feasts for centuries.

Pheasants inspire fantasies in the kitchen, wrote British food expert Elizabeth David, and more than a few legends. Ancient Romans, renowned for their culinary acrobatics, carefully skinned the birds, cooked the meat, and then reassembled them in plumage before serving. Our modern interpretation, a pheasant pâté *sur les plumes,* is on page 299. During the Middle Ages, pheasants were even elaborately decorated and presented with gilded legs and beaks. At one monumental feast, medieval knights swore an oath to pheasants before going to battle against the Saracens.

ARIANE: The pheasant is the bird responsible for the biggest controversy in meat aging: To *faisander,* or not to *faisander,* or hang, is the question. Once you make the choice, there follows a second question: For how long? My father says you can only *faisander* a game bird if it came with its death certificate — that is, if you know exactly when and where it was shot.

Influential food writers and gastronomes have long debated the subject. In eighteenth-century France, Grimod de la Reynière advocated that a bird shot on Ash Wednesday should hang until Easter before cooking. Jean Anthelme Brillat-Savarin more judiciously suggested pheasants were best just as decomposition began and the aroma of the bird's oil smelled slightly fermented.

This preference for hanging birds didn't cross the Atlantic. In Eliza Leslie's *Directions for Cookery in Its Various Branches* (1848 ed.), the American food writer observed that "it is not the custom in America, as in some parts of Europe, to keep game till it begins to taint; all food when inclining to decomposition being regarded by us with disgust." Today the custom is dying out even in Parisian haute cuisine restaurants.

GEORGE: If the bird is brought down with a clean shot, the pheasant will indeed gain some more flavor if hung by the head, not plucked or eviscerated, for 3 or 4 days. (Not cutting the bird open prevents cross-contamination with bacteria from the outside.) Alternatively, if you have room in the refrigerator, and a sympathetic housemate, you can let it sit in there for a couple of days. To let it hang more than a few days will impart a strong off or "high" flavor to the bird, which may have been desired by kings, but doesn't appeal to commoners today. Practically speaking, unless you yourself hunt, you won't have to deal with this dilemma. A reliable butcher or game purveyor is all you need.

During hunting season (October to February), ask for wild Scottish pheasants when available. The meat is much more flavorful than that of any farm-raised pheasants. A female wild Scottish pheasant, weighing about 1 pound, serves one person and is superb for a quick roast. Of the two sexes, they are the more tender. A male 2-pounder should be cut up, cooked more slowly, and divided between you and a guest. They have larger breasts, but their legs are virtually useless for eating. The legs do, however, make great sauces.

From the end of September to mid-April, you can buy farm-raised, free-range cocks (males) that average 3 to 3½ pounds. Like the wild Scottish male pheasant's, their legs have many tendons and can be tough, needing longer, slower cooking. Therefore, the breast is often removed and cooked separately. When preparing the legs, make a cut at the joint between drumstick and thigh, so the tendons don't pull the meat up as they cook.

Farm-raised hens of about 2½ to 3 pounds are available all year. As with wild birds, the domesticated hens are more tender than cocks; they're also slightly plumper. Serve a half bird per person. Baby pheasant is a true delicacy. Each weighs about 1¼ pounds and is a single portion.

ARIANE: Some people complain that pheasant can become tough or dry. The ways to avoid this are to bard the breast with unsmoked bacon, ventrèche, or pancetta before cooking, or to slip some duck fat between the breast meat and skin. Cook the bird slowly in moist heat, or quickly sauté the breasts. Don't overcook; the meat should still be slightly pink. Another suggestion: roast pheasant with the breast down, or on its side, so the juices keep the breast from drying out. It is worth repeating — game birds are very lean and cannot stand overcooking.

GEORGE: Which brings us to what breed of bird to choose. Ring-necked pheasants are commonly found in Europe and the United States. They have a distinctive taste and better texture than commercially raised Milan white pheasants. For our purposes, although they are harder and more expensive to raise, there is no question which breed we prefer.

According to George Rude of Griggstown Farm, who supplies D'Artagnan's domestic pheasants, basically there are two ways to raise these birds. One is outside, under nets, in a natural environment of bushes and grass. The other is inside an overcrowded coop, like commercial chickens, where they eat feed pellets. If a pheasant is raised like a chicken, it will look as pale and taste as bland as a commercially raised chicken.

Birds that range freely can eat foods in their surroundings. They are fed as little supplemental food as possible. What additional food they get is corn and high-protein soy. The birds move around, even during the winter, and they grow slowly and naturally. Guess which pheasants we think are better?

sautéed pheasant breasts
with wild mushrooms

SERVES 4

Here you have a few choices about how to prepare these succulent pheasant breasts with wild mushrooms and Madeira sauce. Bone the pheasants the first day and make a well-reduced stock, then cook them the following day. Or rely on the "rollover" method: use game bird stock from your freezer for this dish, saving these bones for the next batch of stock. Or substitute diluted demi-glace for stock, deglaze the roasted bones with it, and even add some essence of pheasant if you want. Serve over wild rice. Pour a rich Chardonnay or Pinot Noir.

2 pheasants, 2½ to 3 pounds each

2 tablespoons olive oil

1 pound mixed wild mushrooms, such as shiitakes, chanterelles, and pleurottes, wiped clean, trimmed, and sliced

Salt and freshly ground black pepper to taste

½ cup minced flat-leaf parsley

2 teaspoons minced garlic

2 tablespoons unsalted butter

1 large shallot, minced

1 cup dry Madeira

1 cup reduced pheasant or game bird stock, or ⅔ cup duck and veal demi-glace plus ⅓ cup water (see page 33)

¼ cup minced fresh tarragon

1. DAY 1: Remove breasts from pheasants with skin, bones, and wings attached.

Split each breast into 2 half breasts. Cut off first 2 joints of wings, leaving drummettes attached. Use carcass, legs, and wing tips to prepare a rich, well-reduced stock. Cover breasts and refrigerate overnight.

2. DAY 2: Heat oil in a large heavy skillet over medium heat. Add mushrooms, season with salt and pepper, and cook until they have given off their water, 6 to 7 minutes. Stir in parsley and garlic, and keep warm.

3. Preheat oven to 250°F.

4. Blot breasts dry with paper towels. Heat butter in a heavy skillet over medium-high heat until hot. Add breasts and sauté each side for 4 minutes. Wrap breasts in aluminum foil and keep warm in oven.

5. Add shallots to pan, adjust heat to medium, and cook until lightly browned, 1½ to 2 minutes, then deglaze pan with Madeira. Turn heat to high and reduce liquid by half. Pour in stock and again

ESSENCE OF PHEASANT

Americans don't traditionally hang pheasants to develop their gamy taste, and farm-raised birds admittedly have a milder flavor than their wild cousins. To intensify the pheasant flavor, make a stock from the roasted game bird bones, then reduce this liquid down to a concentrated essence. Freeze in a small airtight container. Stir into pâtés, soups, sauces, or anywhere you want a stronger taste.

reduce by half. Add tarragon and season with salt and pepper.

6. Carve breasts from the bone, slice on the diagonal, and fan out on 4 dinner plates. Spoon on mushrooms, and ladle sauce over pheasant breasts. Serve at once.

roast pheasant breasts
with oyster, pancetta, and fresh sage dressing

SERVES 6

This would make a splendid holiday dish as a surprise replacement for the Thanksgiving turkey or to create an elegant New Year's Eve supper. Serve with a light Cabernet to balance the flavors without overwhelming the dish. Since only the breasts are used in this recipe, you might sauté the legs and save them for D & D Game Bird Pâté (page 307).

3 pheasants, 2½ to 3 pounds each, giblets removed

3 tablespoons vegetable oil, plus additional oil to grease casserole

2 cups mixed finely chopped carrot, celery, and onion

5½ cups chicken stock

2 cups veal stock

1 bouquet garni: 1 small bunch parsley stems, 10 peppercorns, 1 teaspoon dried thyme, and 2 bay leaves, tied in cheesecloth

4 cups stale cubes of French bread, lightly toasted

2 tablespoons chopped flat-leaf parsley

2 tablespoons chopped fresh sage, plus 12 sage leaves and 6 sprigs sage, to garnish

½ teaspoon poultry seasoning

1 egg, lightly beaten

¼ pound pancetta, cut into ¼-inch dice

1 cup *each* finely diced onion and celery

3½ tablespoons unsalted butter

12 freshly shucked oysters, including liquor

Coarse salt and freshly ground black pepper to taste

¼ cup finely diced shallots

½ cup brandy

1. Remove breasts from pheasants, with skin and bones attached. Split breasts along breastbone and refrigerate. Cut off legs and save for another use. Chop wings and remaining carcass into 2-inch pieces.

2. Heat 2 tablespoons of the oil in a heavy saucepan over medium-high heat. Add bones and sauté until lightly browned, about 10 minutes. Add chopped carrot, celery, and onion, and sauté until rich brown, about 10 minutes, stirring occasionally. Add 4 cups of the chicken stock, the veal stock, and the bouquet garni. Bring to a boil, then turn heat down and gently boil, skimming occasionally, until reduced by two-thirds, at least 30 minutes. Strain through a fine strainer, and discard solids. You will have about 2 cups of sauce. If you have more, boil strained liquid to reduce further, then set sauce aside.

3. Preheat oven to 350°F. Grease a 2-quart gratin dish or casserole and set aside.

4. Combine bread cubes, parsley, chopped sage, and poultry seasoning in a large mixing bowl. Stir in beaten egg and set aside.

5. Heat a large sauté pan over medium heat. Add pancetta and sauté until all fat has been rendered and pancetta is crisp, about 10 minutes. Stir in diced onion and celery and cook until translucent, about 5 minutes. Add remaining 1½ cups chicken stock and 1½ tablespoons of butter and bring to a boil. Add oysters with their liquor and immediately remove pan from heat. Carefully scrape contents of pan into bread mixture. Toss together, being careful not to mash bread down. Season with salt and pepper as you toss ingredients together. Transfer stuffing to prepared casserole, gently tapping down to even top. *Dressing may be made early in the day. Bake and finish just before serving.* Bake in oven until golden, about 20 minutes.

6. While dressing is baking, heat the remaining tablespoon of oil in a large skillet over medium heat. Season pheasant breasts with salt and pepper. When oil is hot, place breasts, skin side down, in pan. Sear until a crisp golden crust forms, about 7 minutes. Turn and sear second side for 5 minutes.

STEMS AND ALL

While we often think of chopped parsley leaves for flavor or garnish, it's the stems that have the stronger taste. Herbs like thyme or rosemary have woody stems that are removed before the leaves are chopped, but with parsley you can use the whole bunch. If you have parsley stems left over, they are a great addition to a bouquet garni or a stock where the solids will be puréed or strained out.

Transfer breasts to a warm platter, lightly cover with aluminum foil, and keep warm.

7. Drain fat from pan. Return to medium heat, add shallots, and sauté for 2 minutes. Stir in brandy, remove from heat, and carefully ignite liquor. Allow flames to die, then return to heat, add reserved sauce, and cook for 2 minutes. Stir in sage leaves and remaining 2 tablespoons butter. Taste to adjust seasonings.

8. Remove dressing from oven and spoon equal portions in the center of 6 warmed dinner plates. Rest a breast on top of each portion, spoon sauce over, and garnish with a sprig of fresh sage. Serve immediately.

Adapted from Charles Palmer, chef-owner, Aureole Restaurant, New York City, and other restaurants

seared breast and confit of baby pheasant with zinfandel reduction sauce

SERVES 4

The first steps for both the legs and the breasts of these pheasants start the day before you serve them. You begin by marinating the breasts and making confit of the legs. When you eat the two types of meat, you will discover a theme and variation of tastes that play off each other. The same sweet spices are used in both preparations. Note that 1 thyme sprig and 1 bay leaf are used in each of the marinades, as well as in the wine reduction. Serve with the Potato Galette on page 44, adding 1 tablespoon fresh savory or thyme, and the black truffle. Zinfandel is the obvious wine choice.

4 baby pheasants, 1¼ pounds each, necks, giblets, and 2 wing joints removed and reserved

¼ cup olive oil

5 whole cloves

1 cinnamon stick, broken into pieces

3 sprigs thyme, plus 4 sprigs, to garnish

3 small bay leaves

3 cloves garlic

1½ tablespoons coarse salt

1 teaspoon freshly ground black pepper

3 cups plus 1 tablespoon rendered duck fat (see Note)

1 tablespoon olive oil

1 cup sliced shallots

½ tablespoon black peppercorns

1 bottle (750 ml) good-quality Zinfandel

3 cups pheasant or game stock, reduced to ¾ cup, or ¾ cup duck and veal demi-glace (see page 33)

Salt and freshly ground black pepper to taste

1 tablespoon unsalted butter

Potato Galette (see page 44)

1. Remove breasts (rib cage and drummettes attached) and legs from birds. You can use the bones and trimmings to prepare the stock called for in Step 5 below. Combine breasts with olive oil, 2 of the cloves, the cinnamon, 1 sprig of thyme, and 1 bay leaf in a resealable plastic bag or bowl. Seal or cover, and marinate overnight in the refrigerator.

2. Combine legs with garlic, coarse salt, the teaspoon of black pepper, 1 sprig

thyme, 1 bay leaf, and the remaining 3 cloves in a resealable plastic bag or bowl. Seal or cover, and refrigerate overnight.

3. The next day, preheat oven to 275°F.

4. Wipe off salt mixture from legs, reserving the garlic, cloves, thyme sprig, and bay leaf, if possible. Place legs and gizzards in a large heavy pot along with the garlic, thyme, cloves, bay leaf, and duck fat. Set pan in oven and cook slowly until meat pulls easily from bone, about 2 hours. Remove legs from fat and blot on paper towels. *Legs may be made several days ahead, covered, and refrigerated. Reheat before serving.*

5. While confit cooks, heat olive oil in a nonreactive saucepan over medium heat. Add shallots and peppercorns, and sauté until shallots are caramelized, 5 to 8 minutes, shaking pan often. Add wine and reduce mixture until approximately 1 cup of syrupy liquid remains, 30 to 40 minutes. Add 1 sprig of thyme, last bay leaf, and the reduced stock or demi-glace. Bring to a boil and then strain. Season with salt and pepper. *Wine reduction may be made several days ahead, covered, and refrigerated. Reheat before serving.* Stir in butter.

6. Prepare Potato Galette.

7. Adjust oven temperature to 400°F, place legs on a flat baking sheet, and cook until crisp, 15 to 20 minutes.

8. While legs crisp, heat the 1 tablespoon duck fat in a medium skillet over medium-high heat. Wipe marinade from breasts, season with salt and pepper, and sear skin side until skin is crisp and rich golden brown, 3 to 5 minutes. Turn and sauté second side for the same amount of time.

9. Serve confit legs and seared breasts on wedges of Potato Galette. Ladle some Zinfandel sauce around pheasant. If desired, sauté pheasant livers until still pink in center, and add some as a garnish to each plate along with a thyme sprig. Serve at once.

NOTE:

Use duck fat that you have rendered and saved in the freezer (it keeps up to 6 months), or order from D'Artagnan or from a local purveyor of fine meats and poultry.

Adapted from Debbie Gold and Michael Smith, co–executive chefs, American Restaurant, Kansas City, Missouri

braised baby pheasants spanish style

SERVES 4

When young pheasants are gently braised, the delicate-tasting meat becomes fall-off-the-bone tender. The pan juices are blended with a sprinkle of unsweetened chocolate — a reminder that chocolate was first brought to the Spanish court by Cortés — and minced parsley. You won't taste chocolate per se, but the flavors of the sauce deepen and become richer. Be sure to squeeze lemon juice over the birds to complete the complex flavor spectrum. A spicy Zinfandel or Merlot would be an excellent choice. Serve over barley or rice pilaf.

4 baby pheasants, 1¼ pounds each, wing tips folded under, giblets and neck removed, patted dry

Salt and freshly ground black pepper to taste

Flour for dredging, plus 1 tablespoon flour

3 to 4 tablespoons olive oil

20 pearl onions, peeled, with an X cut in each root end

2 cloves garlic, thinly sliced

¼ cup dry white wine

1 cup chicken stock

2 teaspoons finely grated unsweetened chocolate

2 tablespoons finely chopped flat-leaf parsley

1 lemon, ends sliced off, cut lengthwise into 8 wedges

1. Season pheasants inside and out with salt and pepper. Lightly dust with flour, patting to remove any excess. Heat 3 tablespoons of the oil in a large heavy casserole with a tight-fitting lid over medium-high heat until hot but not smoking. Add birds and brown on all sides, carefully turning with wooden spatulas or tongs. This will take about 5 to 6 minutes. If necessary, do this in batches so birds aren't crowded. Remove to a plate.

2. Add onions to pot with a little more oil, if needed, and sauté until lightly browned on all sides, shaking often. Remove with a slotted spoon to plate with pheasants. There should be about 1 tablespoon of oil left in pan.

3. Adjust heat to medium. Stir in garlic and cook just until golden, about 30 seconds to 1 minute. Sprinkle on 1 tablespoon flour, and when it is light brown, whisk in wine and stock until smooth. Bring to a boil, stirring constantly. Mixture will thicken.

4. Return pheasants, breast side up, to pan, baste with sauce, and cover pan. Simmer

GRIGGSTOWN FARM

Whenever he's cautioned about putting all of his (pheasant) eggs in one basket, George Rude, the managing partner of Griggstown Farm, near Princeton, New Jersey, gives the answer he's given for years: "That's the only basket out there." As D'Artagnan's sole purveyor of domestic pheasant, and one of its first suppliers, George Rude has watched his business grow to tenfold of what he anticipated at the beginning.

Today, an average of 35,000 naturally fed Chinese ring-necked pheasants — a heavy, meaty breed — roam freely on the farm under large nets suspended 20 to 30 feet above the ground. Over the years, observes Rude, game has come a long way from the frozen pheasants commonly delivered to America's finest restaurants.

In 1973 Rude, then an ex–construction manager and Vietnam vet, was living on an eighty-acre farm owned by Peter Josten, an investor, and the late Stephen Spector, a restaurateur. He was raising about 1,500 birds a year to train hunting dogs. One day Josten took a pheasant to a friend of his, the celebrated food expert James Beard. Beard, savoring every morsel, said he hadn't had a fresh bird for years, and "could use a lot of them" in his restaurant consulting business.

GEORGE RUDE: He wasn't exaggerating. Beard and I went to see André Soltner at Lutèce, in New York City, and the chef immediately committed to 36 to 50 per week. Next thing, the Four Seasons was regularly taking 200. From there the business swelled.

Those were the old days. I'd drive in to New York to make a delivery and get the next week's order. No one asked about the price or weight of the birds. Paul Kovi, a partner of the Four

Seasons at that time, once quipped: "It's not the cost of the pheasants as long as you can sell them Cognac afterward."

Linking up with D'Artagnan in 1984 changed Griggstown's business and put an end to my trucking birds to the city. I had spoken to George Faison on the phone and agreed to sell them pheasants. At our first meeting, George pulled into the parking lot of the Holiday Inn just before the entrance to the Holland Tunnel in New Jersey. He was driving a beat-up red van. I handed him this large box of fresh-dressed pheasants. He threw it into his rattle-trap and drove off to make his rounds. He and Ariane were doing everything themselves at that time.

When D'Artagnan went into this business, game was only being bought by white-table-cloth restaurants. They were unique, and with a lot of hard work, their volume grew dramatically. Meanwhile, over the years, customers of these restaurants were becoming interested in making some of the dishes at home.

Ultimately, D'Artagnan's willingness to stick its neck out and do whatever it took — the enthusiastic "jump in full-fisted" style, and exploration of all possible avenues — created a new market, selling game to home cooks. George and Ariane personally go to gourmet stores and markets to introduce people to their products.

And you know what? George still jumps in the car at a second's notice to make a delivery. Only the car's better.

over low heat until birds are tender and juices run pale yellow when thigh is pricked in thickest part, 30 to 35 minutes. About 15 minutes before birds are done, add pearl onions to pan to finish cooking.

5. Remove pheasants and onions with a slotted spoon to a heated platter. Skim fat from casserole. Add chocolate to sauce, stirring constantly. Cook over medium-low heat for 2 to 3 minutes. Add parsley and taste to adjust flavors. Spoon sauce over pheasants and serve each bird with 2 lemon wedges.

Adapted from the late Stephen Spector of Griggstown Farm, Griggstown, New Jersey

pheasant with dates, quince, and pinot noir sauce

SERVES 6

You're in for a double treat of taste and texture with this pheasant dish: the legs are braised in an aromatic broth and then shredded; the breasts are seared and then fanned with vanilla-infused quince slices and dates. Serve with brussels sprouts and baby carrots. For a red wine, pour a Pinot Noir or Beaujolais Cru; a rich Chardonnay works for white wine. Most of the preparation can be done at least a day ahead. The simple syrup in this recipe is made by boiling sugar and water together until sugar dissolves.

3 pheasants, 2½ pounds each

Salt and freshly ground black pepper to taste

3 tablespoons olive oil

1 large onion, finely chopped

2 carrots, finely chopped

2 ribs celery, finely chopped

1½ cups Pinot Noir

1 quart chicken stock

1 bouquet garni: 6 sprigs parsley, 1 teaspoon dried thyme, 2 bay leaves, and ½ tablespoon black peppercorns, tied in cheesecloth

2 quinces, chopped, plus 2 quinces, peeled, cored, and thinly sliced (or use 4 firm Bartlett pears plus 1 teaspoon lemon juice)

½ cup chopped dates, plus 9 dates, halved and pitted

3 cups simple syrup (made from 2⅔ cups water and 1⅓ cups sugar), cooled

1 vanilla bean, split in half lengthwise

1 teaspoon unsalted butter

1. Preheat oven to 375°F.

2. Bone pheasant breasts, leaving skin intact, and remove first 2 wing joints. Set breasts aside. Remove leg sections in one piece on the bone. Blot dry and season lightly with salt and pepper. Chop carcasses into 2-inch pieces. Heat 2 tablespoons of the oil in a large heavy casserole with a tight-fitting lid over high heat. Add legs plus carcass bones and brown very well, 10 to 12 minutes, turning to color all sides. Remove legs from pan.

3. Add onion, carrots, and celery, adjust heat to medium high, and sauté until browned and caramelized, 6 to 8 minutes, stirring often. Add wine and stock to pan, scraping up all browned particles. Return legs to pan along with bouquet garni, the 2 chopped quinces, and ½ cup chopped dates. Cover pan, place in preheated oven, and roast until meat is very tender, about 1½ to 2 hours. Remove meat from pot and refrigerate. When cooled, pull it into small strips.

4. Strain liquid from casserole into a clean saucepan and gently boil until reduced by two-thirds, at least 30 minutes. Keep warm.

5. Meanwhile, poach the 2 sliced quinces in simple syrup with vanilla bean until tender but still firm, about 1 hour. (If using pears, this will take only 10 minutes or less. Don't overcook.) Strain, cool fruit and liquid separately, then store quince in liquid in refrigerator. *Recipe may be prepared 1 day ahead to this point. Reheat wine sauce before continuing.*

6. Preheat oven to 225°F.

7. Melt butter in a saucepan, add halved dates, and cook until warmed through, then stir in quince slices and transfer to oven to keep warm.

8. Combine shredded leg meat with a little of the wine sauce in a pan and reheat. Pour remaining tablespoon of oil into a large skillet and heat over medium-high heat until hot but not smoking. Place breasts, skin side down, in skillet and cook until skin is golden brown and crisp, 4 to 5 minutes; turn and cook second side for 4 minutes. Transfer skillet to oven to allow breasts to finish cooking, 2 to 3 minutes. Meat should be slightly pink.

9. To serve, make 3 lengthwise cuts into each breast and place each on the bottom half of a warmed dinner plate. Fan slices and tuck 1 piece of quince and 1 date half into each cut. Place vegetables, if serving, on top half of plate, add a mound of shredded thigh meat near breasts, spoon wine sauce over breasts, and serve.

Adapted from David Walford, executive chef, Splendido at the Chateau, Beaver Creek, Colorado

jack daniel's pheasant
braised under cabbage

SERVES 4

The earthy, complex flavors of bourbon do magic for a lot of game meats. In this slowly braised pheasant casserole, we use Jack Daniel's, but any fine-quality bourbon will do. It marries elegantly with the cream and mustard in the sauce. Partnered with cabbage that is sautéed until its natural sugar caramelizes and turns sweet, this is a dish to savor on a cold winter night. The renewed popularity of this American spirit makes it especially appealing. Serve with sautéed spinach or green beans.

3 tablespoons unsalted butter

1½ tablespoons canola oil

2 large onions, chopped, plus 1 medium onion stuck with 6 whole cloves

1 large green cabbage (about 2½ pounds), tough ribs cut off, cored and shredded

Salt and freshly ground black pepper to taste

7 to 8 juniper berries, crushed

1 pheasant, 3 to 3½ pounds, giblets and neck removed, patted dry

2 tablespoons Dijon mustard

All-purpose flour for dredging

2 thick slices unsmoked bacon, ventrèche, or pancetta

½ cup Jack Daniel's or other bourbon

1 cup heavy cream

1. Heat 2 tablespoons of the butter with 1 tablespoon of the oil in a large heavy casserole over medium-high heat. Add chopped onions and sauté until lightly colored, 6 to 8 minutes. Add cabbage and continue cooking until cabbage is caramelized and medium brown in color, 35 to 40 minutes, stirring occasionally. Use a combination of uncovered and covered cooking, and lower heat if cabbage browns too quickly. As moisture evaporates and cabbage browns, cover pan to prevent burning. As moisture collects on cover and drops onto cabbage, lift cover, stir cabbage to incorporate liquid, and continue cooking. Repeat as necessary. Season generously with salt and pepper, and stir in juniper berries. Set aside. *Cabbage may be cooked a couple of days ahead, covered, and refrigerated. Reheat when ready to continue.*

2. Preheat oven to 350°F.

3. Season cavity of bird with salt, pepper, and mustard, then insert the whole onion. Tie legs together with string and turn wing tips under. Dredge bird all over with flour. Heat remaining tablespoon of butter and ½ tablespoon oil in a large skillet over medium-high heat. Quickly brown pheasant on all sides, 6 to 8 minutes.

4. Transfer pheasant, breast side up, to casserole with cabbage. Lay slices of bacon on breast, pack cabbage around and over the bird, cover, and bake in the middle of the oven until juices are pale pink when bird is pricked deep in thigh, 35 to 45 minutes. Baste with pan juices a couple of times as it cooks.

5. Remove pan from oven, push cabbage off pheasant, discard bacon, then cover pan and return to oven. Cook until juices run clear and thigh moves easily in its socket, about 10 minutes.

6. Remove pan from oven, untie legs, discard whole onion, and drain juice from cavity into the casserole. Transfer pheasant to a heated platter, lightly tent with aluminum foil, and keep warm in turned-off oven. On top of stove, add bourbon to pot, adjust heat to high, and boil liquid for 2 to 3 minutes, stirring often to prevent cabbage from burning. Add cream, lower heat, and simmer for 3 to 4 minutes. Taste to adjust seasoning. Present pheasant whole and carve at table, or cut it into pieces and serve on the cabbage bed.

roast wild scottish pheasant
with swiss chard and wild mushrooms
with sweet potato–vanilla purée

SERVES 4

If you're fortunate enough to have a pheasant that has lived its life in the woods, this enticing dish will showcase the wild bird's taste, which is gamier than that of a farm-raised pheasant. It plays well against the robust flavors of Swiss chard, wild mushrooms, and sweet potato perfumed with orange and vanilla.

Sweet Potato–Vanilla Purée (recipe follows)

2 teaspoons juniper berries, finely ground

2 male wild Scottish pheasants, 1¾ pounds each, giblets removed, rinsed and patted dry, wing tips turned under (see Note)

Salt and freshly ground black pepper to taste

2 medium bunches fresh sage

5 tablespoons unsalted butter, at room
temperature

1 tablespoon grapeseed oil

¾ pound red Swiss chard

1 cup assorted wild mushrooms, trimmed,
wiped clean, and sliced

¼ cup dry white wine

¾ cup diced onion

1 ounce smoked slab bacon, sliced into thin
pieces

1 cup chicken stock

1. Prepare Sweet Potato–Vanilla Purée.
Preheat oven to 350°F.

2. Rub ½ teaspoon ground juniper berries
into upper cavity and on breast and sides
of each pheasant. Season with salt and
pepper. Place 1 bunch of sage in cavity of
each bird, and truss birds with kitchen
string. Using 1½ tablespoons of the butter
for each bird, rub entire bird with butter.

3. Heat a 12-inch ovenproof skillet or
roasting pan over medium-high heat. Add
oil, then birds, and sear, turning to lightly
brown all sides. Transfer skillet to oven
with birds breast side up. Roast until an
instant-read thermometer inserted into
thickest part of breast reads 135°F for
medium, about 15 minutes. Transfer birds
to a platter, keep warm, and allow to rest
for 10 to 12 minutes. Reserve pan and
drippings.

4. Remove stems from Swiss chard leaves,
and cut stems into 1½-inch pieces; chop
leaves into medium pieces and reserve.
Melt 1 tablespoon of the butter in a small
skillet, add mushrooms, and sauté quickly

until mushrooms are lightly browned and
begin to soften; set aside.

5. Bring white wine to a boil in a small
nonreactive saucepan over high heat, and
reduce by three-quarters. Add it to pan the
birds were roasted in and, over medium-
high heat, scrape the bottom of the pan
with a spatula or wooden spoon to deglaze.
Add onions and bacon, and lower heat to
medium. Stir until onions are transparent,
3 to 4 minutes. Add Swiss chard stems,
and sauté until barely tender, about 4 minutes. Add chard leaves and chicken stock.
Reduce chicken stock by half. Add sautéed
mushrooms and cook an additional 2
minutes. Remove from heat and whisk in
the remaining tablespoon butter until
emulsified. Season with salt and pepper.
Cover and keep warm.

6. To serve, carve pheasants, removing
the breast meat, drumsticks, and thighs.
Debone drumsticks and thighs. Divide
mushrooms, Swiss chard, and sauce
among 4 warmed dinner plates. Top with
a breast, drumstick, and thigh, and serve
with Sweet Potato–Vanilla Purée.

NOTE:
Wild game may contain tiny pieces of shot
that can't be removed before cooking.
It's not harmful to the meat, but caution
should be taken when eating it.

sweet potato–vanilla purée

1¾ pounds sweet potatoes

½ cup heavy cream

1 teaspoon firmly packed grated orange zest

1 vanilla bean

Sea salt and freshly ground black pepper
to taste

1. Preheat oven to 350°F.

2. Place whole potatoes on a baking sheet. Bake, turning two or three times during cooking, until a fork can pierce them without any resistance, about 45 minutes. Allow potatoes to cool enough to be handled. Split in half lengthwise. With a spoon, scoop pulp into a food processor; avoid including any skin.

3. Combine heavy cream and orange zest in a small saucepan. Split vanilla bean lengthwise, and scrape pulp into pan; reserve pod for another use. Place pan over high heat, and bring to a boil. Immediately remove from heat. Let stand for 20 minutes to blend flavors.

4. Add cream mixture to sweet potatoes and purée until very smooth, scraping down sides as needed. Season with salt and pepper. If necessary, cover and reheat in a preheated 300°F oven, or transfer to a microwave-safe dish and reheat until hot.

Adapted from Terrance Brennan, chef-owner, Picholine, New York City

The people asked, and he brought quails,
and satisfied them with the bread of heaven.

— Psalm 105:40

quail

ARIANE: Few game birds are as versatile, simple to cook, and easy to enjoy as quail. In fact, these plump, juicy birds should be the basis for "Game 101," because they make everyone — from novices to professionals — look like a champion. Grilled, broiled, or sautéed, they're almost impossible to ruin. The medium-dark flesh has a mildly gamy taste that readily takes to being marinated, stuffed, or highly seasoned.

GEORGE: I love quail just off the fire; they're so succulent and crunchy. Don't be surprised, once people taste them, how fast they'll reach for another. A perfect example is our grilled quail appetizer (page 109). Although 1 quail is usually enough for an hors d'oeuvre or, when stuffed, as an entrée, 2 birds are essential when served as the main course. Just remember that because quail are lean and low in fat, they need to be cooked quickly over high heat, and served medium rare to retain their moisture and flavor.

To make handling and turning easier, Manchester Farms (page 113), our sole supplier, created these nifty V-pins to use for semiboneless quail. They also have perfected the process of sleeve-boning, or glove-boning, the bird — removing the entire rib cage and backbone — without tearing the flesh. Anyone who has tried this procedure knows it's pretty labor intense.

ARIANE: Today there are lots of quail available in the marketplace, of which 100 percent are farm-raised. At D'Artagnan we sell pharaoh quail, *Coturnix coturnix,* which are from Eurasian stock, because we believe they are tastier and moister.

Today's ready supply is a huge change from when we started. At that time, quail was perceived as a white-tablecloth restaurant delicacy. Now, with millions of quail regularly available, we have a year-round supply of birds that are about 6 to 8 weeks old and weigh 4 to 5 ounces.

Pharaoh, or Eurasian, quail are migratory upland birds that travel in large bevies of up to a hundred. The small birds are physically unable to fly long distances. Instead, they shoot forth in a straight line at low altitudes, leaping from one stopping point to the next, crossing arid wastelands, rivers, or swamps. Often, they exhaust themselves in the process, dropping to the ground virtually unable to move. From a hunter's perspective, their straight flight and easy fatigue make them simple prey.

This behavior gives rise to the belief that it was hordes of the common quail (*Coturnix coturnix Japonica*), called *selav*, or "plump one," in Hebrew, that saved the Israelites wandering in the wilderness after leaving Egypt. Was this the God-sent miracle or manna mentioned in Exodus and Numbers? The birds certainly could have been traveling in their annual migration. As late as the turn of this century, Egyptian bird catchers still exported more than 2 million quail a year to European chefs.

European, Japanese, and rain quail of southern Asia belong to the same family, Phasianidae, of the order Galliformes. They are classified as *Coturnix*. Wild quail are not the same breed, although they are Galliformes.

When early settlers arrived in what is now the northeastern United States, they encountered birds about the same size and coloring as the quail they had known in the Old World, and misnamed them. To complicate matters, the bobwhite quail (so called for the male's loud whistle) was known as a partridge in the South. Among quail found in America are the bobwhite, Gambel's quail, mountain quail, blue quail, and Montezuma quail.

HOW TO GLOVE-BONE POULTRY

Glove-boning a bird requires that you remove the backbone, rib cage, shoulder bones, wishbone, and thigh bones *without* tearing the skin or detaching it from the meat. The wings are left attached. It is important to use a *sharp* boning knife. Reserve all bones for stock or sauce.

First, cut off wing tips and then open neck area and cut along wishbone to pull it free. Work knife blade around to free the meat from around backbone. Make sure to keep meat attached to skin. Next, use your knife to loosen the shoulder meat from the inside. Place thumbs on either side of shoulders and start paring back meat from bones to the point where you can see or feel the wing sockets. Cut through them to separate from carcass. Start turning the meat and skin inside out like a glove. With the point of your knife, cut meat away from breast bones, scraping the blade against the bone to keep from cutting meat.

Turn bird breast side down. Complete separating meat from bones by exposing the backbone, taking care not to break the skin. Continue gently to coax meat and skin from skeleton until all interior bones are exposed to the thigh joint. Grab drumstick and pull thighbone out of hip socket. Cut thighbone free, making sure to leave meat attached to skin. Finish pulling meat off the skeleton to the tailbone and cut with knife. Reassemble bird, keeping skin taut as you bring it back over meat.

grecian quail
on the grill

SERVES 4 AS AN APPETIZER

Simple and satisfying, while providing almost instant gratification, these birds lend a touch of class to any meal. Use this same technique with poussin, squab, baby pheasant, or partridge. The birds are "spatchcocked": after the backbone and 2 end joints from each wing are removed, leaving only the drummettes, the bird is opened out and flattened. Serve a Tavel or Bandol rosé, or chilled Beaujolais Villages to drink.

4 whole quail, backbone and 2 wing joints removed, opened flat

2 tablespoons olive oil

1 tablespoon lemon juice

1 teaspoon minced garlic

1 to 2 tablespoons fresh rosemary leaves

Salt and freshly ground black pepper to taste

Sliced lemon, to garnish

1. Rub quail with olive oil, lemon juice, and garlic. Sprinkle lightly with rosemary, salt, and pepper.
2. Heat a gas or charcoal grill until hot. Place quail skin side down and grill just until skin is nicely browned, 1 to 1½ minutes, then turn, close lid, and continue grilling until cooked through, 2½ to 3 minutes. Remove and serve with lemon slices.

greek-style
quail salad

SERVES 4 AS A LIGHT LUNCH

Use the savory little Grecian quail from the preceding recipe as the centerpiece for a handsome salad. Double all the ingredients for a perfect summer dinner. Serve with a chilled dry white wine or a chilled rosé.

1 large bunch arugula, coarse stems discarded, trimmed to uniform length

4 Grecian Quail on the Grill (preceding recipe)

1 small cucumber, sliced

8 cherry tomatoes, split

4 thin slices red onion, separated into rings

4 ounces feta cheese, crumbled

8 to 12 Greek oil-cured olives

½ cup extra-virgin olive oil

2 to 3 tablespoons lemon juice

½ teaspoon dried oregano

Salt and freshly ground black pepper to taste

1. Divide arugula among 4 plates, laying it like spokes radiating out from the center of the plate.
2. Grill quail, then split them along breastbone. Place 2 quail halves in the center of each plate. Add cucumber slices, cherry tomatoes, and onion rings. Sprinkle on feta and add olives.
3. Whisk olive oil, lemon juice, oregano, salt, and pepper together in a small bowl. Dribble dressing over salad and serve.

southern fried quail salad
with ranch dressing

SERVES 4

Grilled or broiled quail are juicy morsels of heaven. When fried to golden perfection, as in this salad, they are nearly impossible to resist. Prop them atop some mesclun, potatoes, and sliced mushrooms for one terrific salad, especially with our Ranch Dressing.

Ranch Dressing (recipe follows)

8 whole quail, backbone and 2 wing joints removed

1 cup buttermilk

Peanut oil, for frying

1 cup flour

Salt and freshly ground black pepper to taste

Pinch of cayenne

6 ounces mesclun

12 ounces yellow fingerling potatoes, boiled until tender and cut into ½-inch slices

4 ounces small white mushrooms, trimmed, wiped clean, and sliced

1. Prepare Ranch Dressing.
2. Split quail along breastbone and marinate in buttermilk for ½ hour, turning to coat all sides. A resealable plastic bag works well.
3. Add enough oil to a large skillet to measure about 1 inch deep. Begin heating oil over medium-high heat. Season flour with salt, pepper, and cayenne. Lift quail from buttermilk, allowing excess to drain off, and dredge in flour, patting to remove excess. When oil is hot, add quail in batches and cook until golden brown, about 4 minutes. Drain for 5 minutes.
4. Divide mesclun among 4 plates and scatter potatoes and mushrooms around it. Add 4 quail halves to each plate, drizzle on Ranch Dressing, and serve.

ranch dressing

MAKES ABOUT 2 CUPS

This recipe for creamy garlic dressing makes more than you need here. But it's so good you'll find plenty of uses. It's great with raw vegetables and on baked potatoes. Just keep it covered in the refrigerator. It will last for at least a couple of weeks.

1½ cups buttermilk

½ to ⅔ cup mayonnaise

4 teaspoons Dijon mustard

2 teaspoons minced garlic

VERSATILE BUTTERMILK

The main ingredient of ranch dressing is buttermilk, once upon a time the by-product of making butter. Today buttermilk is made from skim or low-fat milk with enzymes added to thicken it and give it a tangy taste. The enzymes are useful in marinades for tenderizing meats. The low-fat liquid makes delicious, creamy salad dressings, soups, and dips.

Greek-Style Quail Salad (page 109) ❯

2 teaspoons green peppercorns packed in brine, drained and minced

3 to 4 tablespoons finely chopped cilantro

Freshly ground black pepper to taste

Blend buttermilk, mayonnaise, mustard, garlic, and green peppercorns together in a bowl until smooth. Stir in cilantro and season with pepper. Cover and refrigerate for at least 1 hour before using.

grilled quail wrapped in grape leaves on white bean salad

SERVES 2

Inspired by Turkish cuisine, these marinated quail wrapped in grape leaves and grilled are a succulent counterpart to the fresh bean, onion, and tomato salad. Once you discover the tangy, mildly salty-lemon taste of sumac used in the salad, you'll want to add it to marinades for meat and to yogurt sauces. Sumac is a familiar spice in Middle Eastern cuisines, especially Lebanese and Turkish dishes. It was used as a souring agent in early Rome before lemons were available. It grows on bushes that bear small round berries. When dried, they are a dark brick-red color. In the United States, sumac is generally sold as a coarsely ground powder in Middle Eastern groceries.

(2 bamboo skewers, 7 to 8 inches long, soaked in water overnight)

1 cup vegetable oil

1 large onion, thinly sliced

1 teaspoon soy sauce

6 bay leaves

10 black peppercorns

4 semiboneless quail, 2 wing joints removed, split in half lengthwise

4 ounces (⅔ cup) dried Great Northern beans, soaked overnight

1 red onion, thinly sliced

1 medium tomato, coarsely chopped

2 tablespoons fruity olive oil

1 tablespoon lemon juice

¼ teaspoon ground sumac

Salt to taste

2 tablespoons torn mint leaves, plus 2 mint sprigs, to garnish

8 large untorn grape leaves, blotted dry

1 large red bell pepper, cored, seeded, and cut into 1-inch squares

1. Combine oil, onion, soy sauce, bay leaves, and peppercorns together in a resealable plastic bag or nonreactive dish just large enough to hold quail in a single layer. Add quail, turning to coat with marinade. Seal or cover and refrigerate for 8 hours or overnight. Baste once during this time.

2. Bring a large pot of water to a boil. Add beans and cook until just tender, 35 to 45 minutes. Drain and, while beans are still warm, add red onion, tomato, olive oil, lemon juice, sumac, salt, and torn mint leaves. Toss gently to mix.

3. While beans are cooking, heat a gas or charcoal grill or a broiler. Remove quail from marinade and drain. Spread grape leaves out flat. Place a half quail on the lower edge of a leaf. Roll the bird up in the leaf, turning in the sides as you roll. Repeat with remaining leaves and quail halves. Run a skewer crosswise through a roll, then add a piece of red pepper.

Repeat until you have 4 rolls and 4 pieces of pepper per skewer.

4. Once salad is made and charcoal is hot, put skewers on grill, and cook quail for 5 minutes, then turn and cook second side for 5 more minutes.

5. Divide beans between 2 large plates and lay skewered quail rolls on top. Garnish with mint sprigs and serve.

MANCHESTER FARMS

In 1971 Bill Odom, then a poultry specialist with the Campbell Soup Company in Sumter, South Carolina, decided to raise quail as a hobby for hunting purposes. Bill soon discovered that pharaoh quail were too migratory to be released in South Carolina. However, during the off-season Bill started freezing his excess quail and selling them to his friends and neighbors. As the demand grew, so did the market for "farm-raised quail," which Bill produced in converted poultry houses in Dalzell, South Carolina. By 1974, the company, named Manchester Farms, was in full-time production, processing more than 23,000 quail per year.

Bill and his customers realized that the all-medium-dark-meat pharaoh quail were tastier and moister than the native North American bobwhite quail, which have a combination of dark and white meat. From a production standpoint, pharaoh quail were naturally more disease resistant, and they matured in about 6 weeks, compared to about 16 weeks for the bobwhite. In almost thirty years, through selective breeding, Manchester Farms has virtually doubled the size of its quail.

JANET ODOM: One major advance we developed in the early seventies is a process we call European sleeve-boning. That's removing the entire rib cage, including breastbone and backbone, but leaving the wings and legs intact, so the bird can be stuffed.

Thinking about the task, we asked the ladies in our plant to help us figure out how to do it most efficiently. Fact is, it's done entirely by hand using kitchen shears. Some do it from the top, others from the bottom. A fast boner does fifteen in an hour, that's one every four minutes! For most people — professionals and home cooks alike — sleeve-boning can be a time-consuming and sometimes frustrating job.

Early on we committed to selling only the very best quality semiboneless birds and to absorb the cost of downgraded quails — we sell seconds at our farm office. It's an expensive process, but well worth maintaining our reputation in the marketplace. Today, 60 percent of the quail we sell to D'Artagnan are semiboneless. Our food-services customers — restaurants, airlines, and so forth — buy an even higher percentage of semiboned quail.

Manchester Farms is the largest producer of farm-raised quail in the United States. It is truly a family-owned business, including Bill and Janet, their son, Steven, and daughter, Brittney. The company employs more than 180 people. Currently they raise close to 10 million quail a year.

marinated grilled quail
with beet, jicama, and orange salad

SERVES 4 AS AN APPETIZER;
2 AS A MAIN COURSE SALAD

Crunchy quail make this colorful, warm-cool salad of orange, jicama, and beet into an elegant first course. It's very easy, especially since the walnut oil and orange juice do double duty as a marinade and as a vinaigrette for the salad. Jicama is a crunchy, mildly sweet tuber also known as a Mexican potato. Once you peel off the brown skin and fibrous underlayer, the flesh is ivory. When cut up into wedges or batons, jicama makes a refreshing crudité for dips. Cubed, it can be used in salads, salsas, or stir-fry dishes. It is very low in calories. Serve a chilled Sauvignon Blanc.

⅔ cup fresh orange juice

⅔ cup walnut oil

1 teaspoon ground cardamom

½ teaspoon ground coriander

½ teaspoon Tabasco

Zest of 1 orange, minced

4 semiboneless quail, 2 wing joints removed

1 tablespoon balsamic vinegar

Salt and coarsely ground black pepper to taste

2 beets, leaves trimmed, rubbed with canola oil

2 large navel oranges

4 ounces jicama

6 to 8 ounces mixed field greens

2 teaspoons torn chervil leaves, to garnish

1. Whisk orange juice, walnut oil, cardamom, coriander, Tabasco, and orange zest together in a small bowl. Put quail in a small resealable plastic bag or flat dish. Pour in about half the vinaigrette. Seal bag or cover bowl and marinate quail in refrigerator for 6 hours or overnight, turning once or twice. Whisk balsamic vinegar into remaining vinaigrette, season with salt and pepper, and set aside.

2. Preheat oven to 375°F. Wrap beets in foil or place in a covered dish and bake until easily pierced with a knife, about 1¼ hours. Remove from oven and let cool. Trim off ends, peel, and cut crosswise into ¼-inch slices. Meanwhile, peel oranges, removing all pith, then cut crosswise into ¾-inch slices. Peel and finely julienne jicama. A 2 x 2-mm food processor blade works well. Blot dry with paper towels. Set aside.

3. Preheat broiler, positioning rack 4 to 5 inches from heat.

4. Remove quail from marinade and season with salt and pepper. Place them breast side down on a flat baking pan. Broil until skin is brown and crunchy, 2½ to 3½ minutes; turn and broil second side until brown, 2½ to 3 minutes. Set quail aside.

5. Toss field greens with half the remaining vinaigrette, and divide among 4 large plates. Alternate 3 orange and 3 beet slices over field greens. Add a mound of jicama in center, place a quail, breast side up, on jicama, and spoon remaining vinaigrette over salad. Season with black pepper and sprinkle on chervil leaves before serving.

pomegranate-mint marinated quail with figs, arugula, and crispy potato croutons

SERVES 6

A mouthful of these pomegranate-and-mint-spiced birds atop citrus-laced figs and arugula will transport you to the Aegean as if by magic carpet. The perfumed birds are sheer bliss. A light red Bordeaux wine would be appropriate to serve.

1 cup fresh mint leaves

½ cup pomegranate juice (available at specialty food stores)

8 cloves garlic

12 semiboneless quail, 2 wing joints removed

6 medium baking potatoes

Peanut oil for deep-frying

7 tablespoons extra-virgin olive oil

6 tablespoons lemon juice

4 tablespoons orange juice

1 tablespoon honey

Salt and freshly ground black pepper to taste

12 fresh figs, preferably Black Mission

3 cups arugula leaves

1. Combine mint, pomegranate juice, and garlic in a food processor or electric blender and purée into a smooth paste. Scrape into a large resealable plastic bag, add quail, seal bag, and turn several times to coat birds evenly. Refrigerate 8 hours or overnight.
2. Preheat oven to 450°F.
3. Bake potatoes until just barely cooked through, about 30 minutes. Remove from oven, and when cool enough to handle, peel and cut roughly into large cubes. Adjust oven to warm. Fill a large deep skillet halfway with peanut oil. Heat to 375°F. Add potato pieces and cook until crispy and golden. Fat should cover pieces as they cook. Remove with a slotted spoon and blot on paper towels. Do this in batches if necessary. Keep warm in oven.
4. Whisk 6 tablespoons of the olive oil with the lemon juice, orange juice, and honey. Season with salt and pepper. Quarter figs, then combine with arugula leaves and toss with vinaigrette.
5. Heat 1 very large or 2 medium skillets over medium-high heat. Add the remaining tablespoon of olive oil (a little extra if using 2 pans). Remove quail from marinade, season with salt and pepper, and sauté breast side down until skin is crisp and a rich brown, 2½ to 3½ minutes. Turn and cook second side until browned, 2½ to 3 minutes.
6. Arrange arugula and figs in center of each plate, lay 2 quail on top, scatter potato croutons around, and serve.

Adapted from Anne Rosenzweig, chef-owner, The Lobster Club, New York City

barbecued quail
over silver queen corn and vidalia onion risotto

SERVES 4

There are numerous outrageous barbecue sauces on the market. We suggest you find your personal favorite — be sure it's thick and rich — and invest your time in making this unique risotto. Wait till you taste these grilled, slathered quail over the creamy Marsala-laced rice. Yum. You'll be wanting a beer or two with these.

8 semiboneless quail, 2 wing joints removed

2 cups prepared spicy barbecue sauce

Silver Queen Corn and Vidalia Onion Risotto (recipe follows)

Salt and freshly ground black pepper to taste

2 tablespoons unsalted butter

1. Combine quail and barbecue sauce in a large resealable plastic bag. Close, and refrigerate quail for 1 to 2 days, turning occasionally.
2. Begin preparing Silver Queen Corn and Vidalia Onion Risotto. When risotto is about halfway done, heat a large cast iron skillet over medium heat until hot. Lift quail from barbecue sauce, scraping off sauce. Season with salt and pepper. Add butter to skillet, and when it browns, put in quail, breast side down. Cook until crisp and browned, 2½ to 3 minutes per side, turning once.
3. Divide risotto among 4 plates. Place 2 quail on each plate of risotto, and serve.

silver queen corn and vidalia onion risotto

1 teaspoon plus 2 tablespoons olive oil

2 Vidalia onions, thinly sliced

⅔ cup dry Marsala

3 ears Silver Queen or other sweet white corn

4 to 5 cups chicken stock

1 cup mixed finely chopped carrots, onions, and celery

1 cup arborio rice

1 cup dry white wine

Salt and freshly ground black pepper to taste

4 tablespoons unsalted butter

½ cup freshly grated Parmigiano-Reggiano

1. Heat 1 teaspoon of oil in a heavy skillet over medium heat. Add onions, cover, and sweat until just past translucent and beginning to caramelize. Uncover, stir in Marsala, and cook over medium heat until wine is absorbed. Scrape onions into a food processor or electric blender and purée until smooth. Spread purée on a sheet pan to cool.
2. Remove corn kernels from cob and sweat in a skillet until cooked, 3 to 4 minutes; set aside. Combine corn cobs with chicken stock in a saucepan and simmer together. Keep stock hot while making risotto.
3. Heat 2 tablespoons of oil in a large saucepan over medium heat. Stir in carrots, onions, and celery, and sauté until wilted, 3 to 4 minutes.
4. Add rice, stirring to coat with oil, then pour in wine and over medium-high heat continue stirring until liquid has almost evaporated. Add 1 cup of hot stock, stirring until it is absorbed before adding the next cup. Once the rice is creamy, with only a small white dot in the center of a grain, it is done. (The amount of stock needed can vary.) The process should take about 20 minutes.
5. A few minutes before rice is tender, stir in corn and puréed onions. Once it is done, add butter and Parmigiano-Reggiano. Season with salt and pepper and serve.

Adapted from Scott Howell, chef-owner, Nana's Restaurant and Pop's Trattoria, Durham, North Carolina

chinese red soy-braised quail
on chinese long beans

SERVES 4

In Chinese cuisine, red-cooked foods are braised in a mixture of soy sauce, sugar, sherry, and a wide range of seasonings. These semiboneless quail — filled with sautéed napa cabbage to keep them plump — are simmered with a spice sachet (or bouquet garni) in tangerine-scented liquid while they develop the style's characteristic red-brown glaze. You'll savor every morsel. This same method may be used with squab by increasing the braising time to 20 minutes. Chinese long beans look like green beans gone to dramatic lengths (up to 3 feet). They taste similar (although they are actually related to black-eyed peas) but are not as sweet, and they are more pliable. Look for them in Asian markets.

1 to 2 slices thick-cut bacon, cut into thin strips

4 cups shredded Chinese (napa) cabbage

8 semiboneless quail, 2 wing joints removed

2 tablespoons vegetable oil

5 small dried hot red peppers

2 scallions, including green parts, cut into 2-inch lengths

1 tablespoon minced fresh gingerroot

1 tablespoon dried tangerine or orange peel, or 2 large strips fresh orange zest

½ cup dry sherry

3 tablespoons dark soy sauce

2 tablespoons dark brown sugar

1½ cups water

Spice sachet of 1 star anise, 1 cinnamon stick broken into 2 or 3 pieces, 6 whole cloves, and ½ teaspoon fennel seeds, tied in cheesecloth

Chinese Long Beans (recipe follows)

1. Heat bacon in a large wok until it renders about a tablespoon of fat. Add cabbage and sauté over medium-high heat until wilted and light brown, 3 to 4 minutes, turning often. Remove and let cool. Spoon into quail, closing cavity with a skewer or toothpick.
2. Heat a wok over high heat. Add oil, rotate to cover pan, then put in red peppers, scallions, ginger, and tangerine zest, and stir-fry for a few seconds. Stir in sherry, soy sauce, and sugar, and bring to a boil. Add water and spice sachet, return to a boil, and reduce liquid by half. Add quail, turning to cover with liquid, and cook over medium-high heat until quail are glazed and almost all of the liquid has evaporated, 12 to 15 minutes.
3. Meanwhile, prepare Chinese Long Beans. When quail are cooked, remove skewers, divide beans among 4 plates, place quail over beans, and serve.

chinese long beans

1 pound Chinese long beans or green beans, tips removed

2 teaspoons sesame oil

2 teaspoons black sesame seeds, lightly toasted

Salt to taste

Bring a pot of salted water to a boil. Add beans and cook just until crisp-tender, 3 to

4 minutes. Drain. Turn into a hot wok or skillet and toss with sesame oil and sesame seeds. Season to taste with salt and keep warm.

Adapted from Rosa Lo San Ross, chef-owner, Wok on Wheels Catering, East Marion, New York

roasted gascon quail
with grapes, foie gras, and armagnac

SERVES 4 AS A FIRST COURSE

A pair of Gascon specialties — foie gras and Armagnac — transform these quail into a singularly lavish prelude to a grand dinner. The birds are incredibly simple to prepare. Serve a mature Bordeaux, such as 1988 Château Gruaud-Larose or 1985 Château Ducru-Beaucaillou, or a California Cabernet Sauvignon.

4 ounces mousse of foie gras, purchased or homemade (see page 262)

½ cup Armagnac

2 tablespoons golden raisins

4 semiboneless quail, 2 wing joints removed

Salt and freshly ground black pepper to taste

1 tablespoon rendered duck fat or unsalted butter

1 pound seedless green grapes, stemmed (split if large)

½ cup duck or chicken stock

1. Allow the foie gras mousse to soften, then thoroughly combine it with 1 teaspoon of the Armagnac and the raisins in a bowl. Refrigerate until firm, about 10 minutes. Spoon foie gras filling into quail cavities. Flatten birds slightly and, using toothpicks, close cavities. Season with salt and pepper.
2. Preheat broiler with rack about 8 inches from heat.
3. Melt duck fat in a skillet over high heat. Add quail and half the grapes, and brown quail, about 2 minutes per side. Transfer birds to a broiler pan, breasts up.
4. Add remaining Armagnac and stock to skillet, and cook over high heat until liquid is slightly reduced and grapes are soft, about 3 minutes. Transfer contents of skillet to an electric blender and purée. Return sauce to skillet, add remaining grapes, and cook over high heat until sauce is reduced by half, about 3 minutes.
5. Meanwhile, broil quail until just pink at the bone, about 4 minutes. Transfer quail to a warm platter and remove toothpicks. Add any accumulated quail juices to sauce, and pour sauce and grapes over quail. Serve at once.

◄ Roasted Gascon Quail with Grapes, Foie Gras, and Armagnac

squab (pigeon) and wood pigeon

ARIANE: Squab are young pigeons that have never flown. For thousands of years, they have been a favorite meal for every stratum of society throughout the world. They were unequivocally the first domesticated poultry, even preempting chicken.

This may surprise twentieth-century Americans. More often we think of pigeons as annoying denizens of city monuments and buildings. In fact, these are rock doves, a relative of pigeons, and far less edible. Yet squab is considered a most exquisite ingredient in cuisines as distinct as Cantonese, Moroccan, and French. The simple reason for squab's universal appeal is the delicate, succulent flesh, truly unlike that of any other bird. Squab is a dark-meat bird, like duck and goose, yet the meat is not nearly as fibrous, rendering it far more tender. Its flavor, when properly cooked, is a lush, rich essence, reminiscent of sautéed foie gras, albeit with more texture.

Historically, squab were a reliable and inexpensive source of animal protein. Documents detailing aristocratic banquets frequently show squab used in one or several important courses. B'stilla, a splendid Moroccan phyllo-crusted pie that is sweet, salty, crispy, and juicy at the same time, is traditionally made with the bird. It dates from around the fifteenth century, when the Moors were kicked out of Andalusia and migrated to North Africa. (See our updated version of b'stilla on page 122.) Huge molded timbales of pasta, and molded domes of rice made with squab and rich accompaniments, were fashionable sixteenth- and seventeenth-century Italian culinary showpieces. Our Squab Game Torte on page 302 was inspired by these glamorous predecessors, but isn't nearly as complicated to make.

Early on, wide circular structures with tapered tops, or dovecotes, were built in fields to attract wild pigeons to roost. Numerous cubbyholes lined the interior, accommodat-

ing several breeding pairs. Adult birds forage independently and, being monogamous, return every evening to the same roost throughout their adult life. Other than constructing the residence facility, the squab farmer was required to do little or no maintenance except to harvest the young squab. Using a revolving ladder, one simply plucked them from the nest.

In the United States squab are raised primarily in central California and South Carolina. The birds weigh about 1 pound each. Large covered pens are used for up to a dozen breeding pairs. They are capable of producing up to 24 offspring a year. Parents share in all activities required to raise the squab. They build their nest together, incubate the eggs, and feed the young. The male participates willingly so long as the female accommodates him sexually on demand. When she refuses, he pecks her in the middle of the head. As a result, farmers can separate the sexes far more easily than might otherwise be the case. They just look for the bald birds, which are females.

GEORGE: Sorting young squab from mature pigeons is also an easy activity. The farmer gathers his squab in a crate. When the crate is opened and shaken vigorously, any birds that fly away are not squab but adult pigeons.

No one farms squab to make a fortune. The birds' notorious sensitivity prevents using modern poultry techniques, like those sometimes employed in the mass farming of chickens, to produce enormous flocks at minimal costs. They respond poorly to artificial insemination and inferior-quality feeds laced with animal by-products.

Farm-raised pigeons must have the same food year-round. Their nesting cubbies must never be disturbed. For this reason the cost of squab, which has remained constant for decades, is expensive relative to mass-marketed chickens. It's a whole lot of bother to raise good squab. But as you will discover on the following pages, these succulent birds make a feast fit for royalty.

Besides farm-raised squab, we also sell wood pigeons, which are wild birds that we import from northern Scotland. They weigh about 8 ounces apiece when dressed, and their flavor is substantially more intense than that of domesticated birds.

▲ A *pigeonnier,* or dovecote, in Gascony

moroccan squab pie (b'stilla)

SERVES 6 TO 8

A traditional Moroccan feast dish, b'stilla is often served at weddings. Under its sugar-and-cinnamon-dusted phyllo crust it brings together a remarkable combination of sweet and savory tastes plus crunchy and smooth textures. Although domestic squab are milder than wild birds, their juicy meat lends an authentic touch to this fabled dish. Karen Berk, who coedits the Zagat Los Angeles restaurant and marketplace surveys, visited Morocco in search of b'stilla. She discovered the centuries-old dish has many variations. One version was entirely deep-fat-fried — pastry and all. Another had entire birds inside (including bones and everything else). The following recipe is adapted from one of Karen's.

6 tablespoons unsalted butter

3 squab, cut into quarters, rinsed and patted dry

2 cups chopped onions

½ cup chopped flat-leaf parsley

½ cup chopped cilantro

2 teaspoons paprika

1 teaspoon ground ginger

¼ teaspoon turmeric

¾ teaspoon cinnamon

1 teaspoon salt or to taste

Freshly ground black pepper to taste

1 cup water

8 eggs

1½ tablespoons peanut oil

10 ounces blanched almonds

¾ cup sugar

1 tablespoon clarified butter

8 to 10 sheets phyllo pastry, defrosted according to package directions

Confectioners' sugar, whole blanched almonds, and cinnamon, to garnish

1. Melt 2 tablespoons of the butter in a large skillet or casserole over medium-high heat. Add squab and brown on all sides, 10 to 12 minutes, doing this in batches if necessary, so birds do not steam. Remove squab with a slotted spoon to a bowl.

2. Add onion and sauté until soft and transparent, 5 to 6 minutes, stirring often. Stir in parsley, cilantro, paprika, ginger, turmeric, ¼ teaspoon of the cinnamon, salt, pepper, and 1 cup water. Mix well. Bring to a boil over high heat.

3. Return squab to pan along with any juices that may have accumulated. Reduce heat, cover, and simmer until squab are tender, 25 to 30 minutes. Remove squab and cool. Reserve broth. Remove skin and bones from squab and shred meat. *Recipe may be made ahead to this point.*

4. Measure ¾ cup of the reserved broth into the skillet and bring to a boil. Whisk eggs in a bowl until well blended, then pour into broth. Cook over medium heat, whisking continuously, until eggs are set and look like dry scrambled eggs. Season with salt and set aside.

5. Heat peanut oil in a skillet over medium-high heat. Stir in almonds and cook until deep golden brown, shaking and turning often. Set aside to cool, then combine with sugar and remaining ½ teaspoon of cinnamon in a food processor. Process until finely chopped. Set aside.

6. Preheat oven to 375°F.

7. Pour clarified butter into a 12- or 14-inch skillet or cake pan. Lay 4 or 5 sheets of phyllo across bottom of skillet, alternating directions so excess phyllo hangs over different parts of pan. Spread three-quarters of the egg mixture on dough, followed by half the ground almonds and half the squab. Repeat with remaining eggs, squab, and almonds.

8. Fold overhanging parts of phyllo over to enclose filling. Place an additional 5 sheets on top of filling, tucking the excess under the edges of the pie. Melt remaining 4 tablespoons unsalted butter and brush over dough. *Recipe may be made 1 night ahead to this point and refrigerated. It may also be frozen at this point. If frozen, defrost overnight in refrigerator.*

9. Bake in 375°F oven until top is golden, 30 to 35 minutes. Remove pan from oven and invert pie onto a large serving platter. Sprinkle confectioners' sugar heavily across top (about ¼ inch thick), and decorate with a crisscross pattern of cinnamon and whole almonds.

Adapted from Karen Berk, co-owner, The Seasonal Table School, Los Angeles, and coeditor, Zagat Los Angeles restaurant and marketplace surveys

pan-roasted squab
with savoy cabbage and smoked bacon
on potato purée

SERVES 4

A hearty dish that is unchallenging to make and comforting to eat, and at the same time boasts exquisitely complex flavor. Pan-roasted squabs are napped with a sauce that uses every last shard of the squab bones (even the ribs from the cooked birds are added to the pot), infusing layer upon layer of richness. These tastes are balanced by braised Savoy cabbage, enhanced with smoky bacon and a touch of cream. Sure, you can make the satiny mashed potatoes with less butter, but the results won't be as glorious. These birds deserve a rich red wine.

2 ounces smoked slab bacon, rind removed, cut into 4 pieces

⅓ cup chopped onion

1 tablespoon crushed garlic

1½ cups chicken stock

1 small carrot, cut in ¼-inch dice

1 head Savoy cabbage, 1 pound, outer leaves discarded, cut into ½-inch-wide shreds

¼ cup heavy cream

3 tablespoons unsalted butter

Coarse salt and freshly ground white pepper to taste

Potato Purée (recipe follows)

4 squab, excess fat and skin removed and discarded, 2 wing joints, neck, giblets, and backbones removed and reserved

2 tablespoons canola oil

2 shallots, finely minced

½ cup dry red wine

¾ cup duck and veal stock, or 6 tablespoons duck and veal demi-glace (see page 33) diluted with 6 tablespoons water

1. Heat a medium saucepan over medium-high heat. Add bacon and cook until very lightly browned, about 5 minutes. Add onion and garlic, reduce heat to medium low, cover, and cook until onion softens, about 7 minutes. Drain off any fat. Add chicken stock and bring to a boil over high heat. Cook until reduced to 1 cup, about 10 minutes. Remove pan from heat and let stand for 20 minutes. Strain stock into a medium bowl. Dice and reserve bacon. Discard onion and garlic.

2. Meanwhile, cook carrot in salted boiling water until barely tender, about 2 minutes. Drain and set aside. Cook cabbage in boiling salted water over high heat until barely tender, 3 to 4 minutes. Drain and shock in ice water. Squeeze out all excess moisture from cabbage with your hands.

3. Bring chicken-bacon stock and cream to a boil in a medium saucepan over high heat. Add cabbage, reserved bacon, and carrot. Reduce heat to low and simmer for 10 minutes. Gently stir in 2 tablespoons of the butter and season with salt and pepper. Set aside.

4. Begin preparing Potato Purée.

5. Place squab, breast side up, on work surface. Press down on breast with the heel of your hand to crack the breast keel bone. Coarsely chop reserved bones, gizzards, and hearts (not livers), and set aside. Rinse birds and blot dry.

6. Heat oil in a 12-inch skillet over medium-high heat. Season squab with salt and pepper and place in pan, skin side down. Add the remaining tablespoon butter and cook, basting occasionally, until squab are browned, about 8 minutes. Turn and continue cooking, basting occasionally, until other side is browned and breasts are medium rare, about 4 minutes. Remove to a plate, pull out remaining rib bones, and add them to reserved bones. Cover squab loosely with aluminum foil to keep warm.

7. Pour off all but 1 tablespoon of fat from skillet. Add reserved bones and giblets and cook over medium-high heat, stirring occasionally, until browned, about 10 minutes. Add shallots and stir until they soften, about 1 minute. Add wine and bring to a boil, scraping up any browned bits in the bottom of the pan with a wooden spoon. Cook until wine is reduced to ¼ cup, about 5 minutes.

8. Add stock and collected juices from squab, and bring to a simmer. Reduce heat to low and simmer to concentrate flavors, 3 minutes. Strain sauce through a fine strainer, pressing hard on the solids. Season with salt and pepper.

9. Spoon Potato Purée just off center on 4 warmed plates. Place squab next to potatoes, and spoon cabbage next to it. Spoon sauce around plate and serve.

potato purée

2¼ pounds Idaho or russet potatoes, peeled and quartered

8 to 10 tablespoons unsalted butter, cut up

½ cup sour cream, at room temperature

Coarse salt and freshly ground white pepper to taste

1. Place potatoes in a saucepan, cover with water, bring to a boil, and cook partially covered until tender, 15 to 20 minutes. Drain well.

2. Return potatoes to saucepan and cook over medium heat, stirring often, until excess moisture evaporates and they begin to stick slightly to bottom of pan, about 3 minutes. Pass potatoes through a ricer or food mill into a larger bowl, or mash them in the bowl with a potato masher. Combine with the butter and sour cream, and season with salt and pepper. If necessary, keep warm in the top of a double boiler set over simmering water.

Adapted from Alfred Portale, executive chef–owner, Gotham Bar & Grill, New York City

SQUAB PRODUCERS OF CALIFORNIA

At the core of American agriculture during most of this country's history has been the farmer cooperative. That concept has worked particularly well for the Squab Producers of California. Since 1943 members have been working together to improve their lot and better the quality of their birds.

Early members — all of whom raised pigeons within an 85-mile radius of San Francisco — merely hauled live birds to the city's markets, especially Chinatown. Today, says Bob Shipley, the group's president, the cooperative operates a dual USDA and California Department of Food and Agriculture inspected processing plant in the Central Valley. The number of farmers has grown from 22 to 78.

BOB SHIPLEY: The cooperative's advantage is that we have the best of both worlds. The farms are generally of a manageable size and are run by a husband-wife team. Small farmers are better caregivers — they can offer TLC. The flip side is that because we combine resources, we have bigger production facilities than any of us could hope to have on our own — more modern, cleaner, and state-of-the-art. There is an economy of scale that benefits everyone. Additionally, in California we take great pride in the genetics of our squab.

Pigeons do better in a natural environment, and that's what we emphasize.

In 1963 the association became politically active and began a lobbying effort to get state and federal officials to disallow the term "squab chicken" in marketing and packaging poultry. This term was being used in advertising and on labels for Cornish game hens. We felt it was misleading consumers into thinking they were actually getting squab. The effort succeeded, and in June 1964 the USDA recognized the difference between the two birds and no longer approved the use of the term "squab chicken."

Today we produce three times more squab annually than the next largest producer in the country. The birds are processed efficiently and are served in many eating establishments throughout the country.

Squab in a dovecote ▲

roasted squab with szechuan peppercorn marinade

over sweet rice, taro, and pineapple with fresh mango chutney

SERVES 4

The beauty of this dish is that each component maintains its integrity, yet when combined all the textures and tastes come together in splendid harmony. The simple preparation and direct flavors produce a mouthwatering Chinese meal. Serve with Chinese beer or a glass of Banyuls. Taro is a starchy tuber used in Caribbean, Asian, and African cuisines. Look for it at ethnic markets. It is always served cooked.

Sweet Rice, Taro, and Pineapple (recipe follows)

4 squab, 2 wing joints, giblets, and neck removed, rinsed and patted dry

1 tablespoon coarse sea salt

2 tablespoons Szechuan peppercorns

1 tablespoon vegetable oil

3 shallots, minced

1½ cups ruby port

Fresh Mango Chutney (recipe follows)

¼ cup honey

3 tablespoons white wine vinegar

Rosemary sprigs, to garnish

1. Prepare Sweet Rice, Taro, and Pineapple through Step 1.
2. Cut away and discard excess neck skin and back fat from squab with scissors or a sharp knife. Heat a small heavy skillet over medium-low heat. Add salt and peppercorns, and roast until peppercorns turn dark brown, shaking pan occasionally. Transfer to a bowl, let cool, then rub squab inside and out with mixture. Place birds in a resealable plastic bag, seal, and refrigerate 4 to 6 hours or overnight.
3. Heat oil in a medium saucepan over medium heat. Add shallots and cook until shallots are soft, about 2 minutes. Pour in port and cook until sauce thickens and reduces by about two-thirds, about 15 minutes. Set aside. *Recipe may be done ahead to this point.*
4. Preheat oven to 400°F. Finish sweet rice and prepare Fresh Mango Chutney.
5. Whisk honey and vinegar together in a small bowl. Place squab on their side on the rack of a broiler pan. Brush generously with honey mixture and roast for 6 minutes. Turn birds to other side, brush again, and roast for 6 minutes. Brush one more time, and roast breast side up until squab are nicely browned, about 6 more minutes.
6. Use poultry shears to split birds down the middle; remove backbones. Place squab halves on a platter. Reheat port sauce if necessary and spoon it around birds. Garnish with rosemary sprigs. Serve with sweet rice and Fresh Mango Chutney.

sweet rice, taro, and pineapple

2 cups short- or medium-grain white sweet (glutinous) rice (available at Oriental markets)

1 cup peeled taro root cut into ⅛-inch dice

½ cup peeled, cored, and chopped fresh pineapple, or ½ cup canned chopped pineapple in juice

1 tablespoon unsalted butter

½ cup unsweetened coconut milk

1 tablespoon sugar

½ teaspoon coarse salt

1. Place rice in a large bowl and cover with 6 cups warm water. Soak for 4 hours or refrigerate overnight. Drain.

2. Prepare a steamer by placing a layer of cheesecloth in the bottom of a rack (see Note). Spread rice and taro in an even layer over cheesecloth. Set rack aside while you fill bottom of steamer with water close to, but not touching, the level where the rack will rest and bring to a boil. Place rack on top, cover steamer, and steam rice and taro until tender, about 30 minutes. Transfer mixture to a large bowl.

3. Combine pineapple, butter, coconut milk, sugar, and salt in a small saucepan. Bring to a boil over high heat, stirring until sugar dissolves, about 2 minutes. Remove from heat, stir into rice mixture, and serve. Leftover rice can be stored, covered, in refrigerator for up to 2 days. Do not freeze. Warm either by steaming or by heating in microwave.

> **NOTE:**
> If you don't have a steamer but do have a large wok, a round cake rack, and a lid for the wok, cover the rack with cheesecloth and steam rice as indicated above.

fresh mango chutney

2 large ripe mangoes, peeled and diced

2 tablespoons unsalted butter

1 jalapeño, seeded and minced

1 tablespoon minced fresh gingerroot

1 tablespoon honey

Combine mangoes, butter, jalapeño, ginger, and honey in a saucepan. Bring to a boil over medium heat. Cook for 2 minutes, stirring often. Remove from heat and serve with squab.

Adapted from Suzanna Foo, chef-owner, Suzanna Foo, Philadelphia

spice-roasted squab with porcini and foie gras

SERVES 4

The seeds and peppercorns for this lush, heady dish are readily available at supermarkets or spice stores. Licorice root might entail a trip to a Chinatown herbalist. It's worth the effort. However, you may omit it. The subtle bitterness in the sweet chestnut honey adds an exotic dimension to the taste that's hard to forget. Serve with porcini and foie gras for a luxurious meal, or simply pair with sautéed bitter greens. Pour a French Côte-Rôtie or American Zinfandel.

¾ cup duck and veal demi-glace (see page 33)

12 ounces licorice root

1 large bunch thyme

Salt and freshly ground black pepper to taste

¼ cup *each* coriander seeds, cardamom pods, mustard seeds, fennel seeds, aniseed, white peppercorns, and red peppercorns

3 star anise, broken into pieces

4 squab, 2 wing joints, giblets, neck, and excess fat and skin removed

1 tablespoon unsalted butter or canola oil

½ cup chestnut honey (available at specialty
food stores)

½ pound porcini mushrooms, sliced ¼ inch
thick

2 ounces Grade B foie gras, cut into cubes
(see page 255)

4 teaspoons olive oil

1. Bring demi-glace to a gentle boil in a
small saucepan and reduce to about ½ cup.
Stir in 4 ounces of the licorice root and
4 sprigs of thyme, and steep for 5 minutes.
Season with salt and pepper, strain, and
keep warm.
2. Preheat oven to 350°F. Tear 4 (12 x 12-
inch) squares of aluminum foil.
3. Place coriander seeds, cardamom pods,
mustard seeds, fennel seeds, aniseed, white
peppercorns, red peppercorns, and star
anise in a flat pan and warm in the oven
for 1 to 2 minutes. Remove, pour into
spice grinder or clean coffee grinder, and
grind until fairly fine. Spread on a flat plate.
4. Season birds inside and out with salt
and pepper. Stuff each squab with 2
ounces of the licorice root and a few
sprigs of thyme. Truss and tie squab, and
blot dry. Heat butter in a large skillet over
medium-high heat and quickly brown
squab on all sides. Put them in the oven in
the same pan to roast. After 10 minutes,
remove pan, brush squab with honey, and
roll them in spice mixture. Return to oven
and roast until squab are medium rare,
3 minutes longer. Remove and let rest in
a warm place.
5. While birds roast, divide mushrooms,
foie gras, olive oil, 4 sprigs of thyme, and
salt and pepper among the 4 foil squares.

Gather up corners of foil and twist into
small bundles. Increase oven temperature
to 400°F and roast bundles for 15 minutes.
6. Place 1 squab on each of 4 warm
plates. Open mushroom bundles and
spoon contents onto plates. Spoon about
2 tablespoons of licorice sauce onto each
plate and garnish with a thyme sprig.

Adapted from Tom Colicchio, executive chef–owner,
Gramercy Tavern, New York City

mint and garlic–marinated grilled squab
over rice tabbouleh with smoked tomato vinaigrette

SERVES 4

Smoked tomato vinaigrette and fresh mint
make these grilled birds satisfying warm-
weather dining. The flavors are tangy and
refreshing. The chilled tabbouleh is made
with basmati rice rather than bulgur. It's a
perfect garnish to the squabs. If you'd like
a more generous serving, double the rice
recipe. Add a green salad and some crusty
bread, and summer living couldn't be easier. A Belgian or French country ale, such
as St. Amand, affords a change of pace, or
choose a Bandol rosé or Tavel.

4 semiboneless squab, 2 wing joints, giblets,
neck, and excess fat and skin removed

⅓ cup plus 1 tablespoon olive oil

Juice of ½ lemon

½ bunch mint leaves, chopped

3 cloves garlic, thinly sliced

2 shallots, thinly sliced

1 teaspoon ground black pepper

Rice Tabbouleh and Smoked Tomato
 Vinaigrette (recipes follow)

Salt to taste

2 tablespoons mixed chopped fresh chives and
 julienned mint leaves, to garnish

1. Combine squab with ⅓ cup olive oil,
lemon juice, mint, garlic, shallots, and pepper in a resealable plastic bag and marinate
in refrigerator for 6 hours or overnight.
2. Prepare Rice Tabbouleh and Smoked
Tomato Vinaigrette.
3. Heat a gas or charcoal grill. Season
squab with salt and grill (or sauté in a skillet in 1 tablespoon olive oil) until golden
brown on both sides and medium rare, 3
to 4 minutes per side. Divide tabbouleh
among 4 plates. Place squab on tabbouleh
and spoon vinaigrette over. Sprinkle on
chive-mint mixture.

rice tabbouleh

MAKES 1½ TO 2 CUPS

1½ tablespoons olive oil

2 tablespoons finely diced onion

¼ cup basmati rice

⅓ cup chicken stock, heated

¼ bay leaf

2 plum tomatoes, peeled, seeded, and finely
 diced

1 cup loosely packed flat-leaf parsley leaves,
 coarsely chopped

1 scallion, including green part, finely diced

2 tablespoons extra-virgin olive oil

1 tablespoon lemon juice

¼ teaspoon ground coriander

Salt and freshly ground black pepper to taste

1. Preheat oven to 350°F.
2. Heat 1½ tablespoons olive oil in a skillet over medium heat. Add onions and
sauté until transparent, 2 to 3 minutes.
Add rice and sauté for 30 seconds. Add
hot stock and bay leaf and bring to a boil.
Cover pan with buttered parchment or
wax paper and bake in oven until all liquid
is absorbed, 5 to 7 minutes. Fluff with fork
to separate. Rice will not be tender.
3. Transfer rice to a bowl and refrigerate
until cool. Stir in tomatoes, parsley, scallion, extra-virgin olive oil, lemon juice, and
coriander. Season to taste with salt and
pepper, and let sit for at least 2 hours to
soften. Taste again before serving.

smoked tomato vinaigrette

8 plum tomatoes, cut in half crosswise and
 seeded

3 tablespoons extra-virgin olive oil

Coarse salt and freshly ground black pepper to
 taste

1 teaspoon chipotle peppers in adobo sauce,
 finely chopped

½ cup olive oil

3 tablespoons rice wine vinegar

1. Preheat oven to 250°F.
2. Toss tomatoes with extra-virgin olive
oil, salt, and pepper. Bake them on a rack
in a shallow baking pan until they are about
half size but still juicy, 2½ to 3 hours.

3. Remove tomatoes to a cutting board, add chipotle pepper, and finely chop. Combine tomatoes with ½ cup olive oil and vinegar, and season with salt to taste.

Adapted from Sandy D'Amato, chef-owner, Sanford and Coquette Café, Milwaukee

braised squab stuffed with black truffles, foie gras, chestnuts, and rice on root vegetables

SERVES 6

An extravagant main course that pulls out all the stops: foie gras, truffle, and chestnut stuffing roasted inside the squab, more truffles under the breast skin, and Cognac-scented pan juices. The birds are carved and served over layered root vegetables with the stuffing on the side. Wow!

3 black truffles, 1½ ounces

3 squab, 2 wing joints and neck removed, rinsed and patted dry

3 tablespoons unsalted butter

3 tablespoons Cognac or brandy

1 shallot, minced

1 cup cooked arborio rice

3 ounces Grade B foie gras, diced into ½-inch pieces (see page 255)

6 cooked chestnuts, coarsely crumbled

Coarse salt and freshly ground black pepper to taste

1 small onion, thinly sliced

1 medium turnip, thinly sliced

1 medium parsnip, thinly sliced

1 small celery root, thinly sliced

1 cup white vermouth

1 cup chicken stock

2 tablespoons chopped fresh herbs, such as parsley, thyme, and marjoram

1. From each truffle, cut 2 slices ¼ inch think. Chop remainder of truffles and set aside.

2. Remove giblets from squabs and discard all but the livers. Heat a small saucepan over medium-high heat. Add 1 tablespoon of the butter and the livers, and quickly sear. Remove livers and set aside to cool. Deglaze pan with Cognac, then add shallots and cook until softened, 1½ to 2 minutes. Meanwhile, mince cooled livers. Add them to the pan along with the rice, foie gras, chestnuts, and reserved minced truffles. Stir just to mix well, season with salt and pepper, and remove from heat.

3. Loosen skin over squab breasts by gently slipping your fingers under it. Slip 1 slice of truffle under skin on each breast half. Season birds inside and out with salt and pepper. Stuff squab with rice mixture both in the body cavity and under the neck skin flap. Truss birds or skewer closed.

4. Heat a saucepan or deep skillet just large enough to hold the birds snugly. Melt remaining 2 tablespoons butter over medium-high heat, and brown birds on each side and back. Do not brown breasts. Remove birds and set aside.

5. Add onion to the same pan. Layer turnip, parsnip, and celery root on top. Place birds, breast up, on vegetables. Pour in vermouth and stock, cover pan, and braise squab over low heat until done, about 30 minutes. Breast should be uniformly pink and legs well done. Let birds rest on a warm platter for 10 minutes before serving.

6. Remove root vegetables from pan and keep warm. Skim off any fat from pan juices, then bring to a boil over high heat and reduce by half. Keep warm.

7. To serve: Carve each breast half in a single piece from squab. Cut off legs, and cut between the joint to separate pieces. Scoop out all stuffing. Spoon some cooked vegetables in the center of 6 warmed dinner plates. Top with a spoonful of stuffing. Arrange a leg, a thigh, and a whole breast half on top. Spoon some reduced sauce around meat and sprinkle with chopped herbs. Serve at once.

Adapted from Wayne Nish, chef-owner, March Restaurant, New York City

grilled squab and sherry vinegar sauce
with bean ragout
and celery root cakes

SERVES 4

Tender grilled squab are matched with robustly flavored potato and celery root cakes. They're crunchy on the outside and creamy inside. Crisp mixed beans sautéed together at the last minute add color and texture to the plate. Serve a Graves or a lighter Côtes du Rhône.

Celery Root Cakes (recipe follows)

1 cup duck stock

½ cup dry white wine

¼ cup sherry vinegar

4 semiboneless squab, 2 wing joints, giblets, neck, and excess fat and skin removed, rinsed and patted dry

1 tablespoon olive oil

Salt and freshly ground black pepper to taste

1 to 1½ pounds mixed green, Italian flat, and wax beans (or all of 1 kind), tips removed

1 tablespoon unsalted butter

1 tablespoon chopped flat-leaf parsley

1 teaspoon minced garlic

1. Prepare Celery Root Cakes through Step 1. Combine stock with white wine and vinegar, and reduce to 1 cup. Set aside and keep warm. Light gas or charcoal grill or broiler. Brush squab with olive oil and season inside and out with salt and pepper.

2. Bring a large pot of salted water to a boil. Drop each kind of bean in separately, and cook until crisp-tender. Remove with a strainer, spread on a sheet pan, and refrigerate. Continue with remaining beans. *Beans may be blanched several hours ahead of time.*

3. When grill is medium hot, place squab, breast side down, on grill and cook until richly browned, about 6 minutes. Move aside to a cooler spot if the skin burns and they cook too fast. Turn and cook second side for the same length of time. Breasts should be medium rare and legs cooked through. Remove to a platter and keep warm.

4. While squab cook, finish Celery Root Cakes. Reheat sauce and reduce slightly. Drain any juices from squab into sauce.

Taste to adjust flavors, adding a splash of vinegar and salt or pepper, as needed. Sauté beans with butter and a little water until warmed. Stir in parsley and garlic.

5. Cut breasts from each squab, slice crosswise into thin slices, and arrange on 4 plates. Add 2 legs, a celery root cake, and some of the beans to each plate. Pour hot sauce over squab and serve at once.

celery root cakes

2 small baking potatoes, peeled and quartered

1 small celery root, peeled and cut into chunks

¼ cup milk

3 to 4 tablespoons unsalted butter, softened

2 tablespoons all-purpose flour

1 egg plus 1 egg white

Salt and freshly ground black pepper to taste

2 tablespoons clarified butter

1. Combine potatoes and celery root in salted water, bring to a boil, and cook until tender, about 20 minutes. Drain well, then pass through a food mill. Stir in milk, unsalted butter, and the flour, then add egg and egg white. Mixture should be the consistency of a thick batter. Season with salt and pepper.

2. Heat 1 tablespoon of the clarified butter in a large nonstick skillet over medium-high heat. Add batter by large spoonfuls, forming 3-inch pancakes. Flatten slightly and cook until pancakes are golden brown, 3 to 4 minutes. Carefully turn with a wide spatula and cook second side for the same length of time. Keep warm. Repeat with remaining batter, adding more butter if needed.

Adapted from Jean-Pierre Moullé, executive chef, Chez Panisse, Berkeley, California

---

FATHER MEETS MOTHER

ARIANE: One day in San Francisco my friend Denise Lurton said she wanted me to meet her fiancé, Jean-Pierre Moullé, so we drove to a restaurant. When we arrived, the reservation was for only two people. Seeing my confusion, Denise explained that Moullé was the chef; the restaurant was Chez Panisse in Berkeley.

Several years later Jean-Pierre, who loves everything from the southwest of France, and in particular his wife, Denise, convinced the owner of Chez Panisse, Alice Waters, to organize a special dinner with my father, our old friend Zizou Duffour, and me as guest chefs. Until then my father had looked at the American food business with a somewhat condescending eye.

On that day, December 9, 1993, my father met Alice Waters, the acknowledged mother of California cuisine. She showed him hams in the walk-in that were drying in the same manner as in Bayonne. Most impressive was that at nine in the morning, aside from the hams, the refrigerator was empty! Alice and Jean-Pierre had no idea what the daily menu would be until local farmers began lining up outside the kitchen. From those small suppliers, they would carefully choose the best they had to offer.

At that point my father realized how much American restaurants had improved over the last decades and that they now catered to serious eaters. At least one of them, Chez Panisse, was taking freshness and the intrinsic quality of the ingredients to a level rarely seen, even in France.

boneless sautéed squab and foie gras on green lentils
with lentil sprout salad

SERVES 4

It's hard to imagine French lentils ever being more desirably situated than they are here. As a cushion for the quickly cooked squab and foie gras, they absorb every last nuance of taste that drips onto them. The crunchy, lemony Lentil Sprout Salad is so right as a counterpoint to the other flavors and textures. The mixture of peppercorns may surprise you with the variation in heat and taste. The combination is more aromatic than hot. If the particular ones named here are unavailable, substitute other kinds of peppercorns or all black ones. Enjoy a fine Bordeaux with this.

6 ounces small green French lentils, soaked overnight in cold water

1 carrot

1 onion, cut in half

2 cloves garlic

5 cups chicken stock

12 sage leaves

1 cup squab stock, or ½ cup duck and veal demi-glace (see page 33) diluted with ½ cup water

4 small sprigs thyme

2 tablespoons sherry vinegar

Salt and freshly ground black pepper to taste

Lentil Sprout Salad (recipe follows)

3 tablespoons extra-virgin olive oil

16 thin scallions, trimmed to about 4 inches

4 teaspoons Indonesian peppercorns

2 teaspoons *each* Szechuan, Jamaican, and black peppercorns

4 semiboneless squab, 2 wing joints, giblets, neck, and excess fat and skin removed, cut in half lengthwise

2 tablespoons rendered duck fat or unsalted butter

8 ounces Grade B foie gras (see page 255), cut into 1½-inch cubes

1. After lentils have soaked, rinse in a strainer under cold water. Combine in a saucepan with carrot, onion, garlic, and chicken stock. Bring to a gentle boil and cook until lentils are soft, 20 to 25 minutes, skimming surface from time to time. Turn off heat, stir in 6 of the sage leaves and 2 of the thyme sprigs. Let infuse for 5 minutes, then remove vegetables, garlic, and herbs, and discard. Put the lentils and a bit of their cooking liquid in a food processor or electric blender and purée until almost smooth, adding only enough liquid to facilitate the purée. Set aside.

2. Combine squab stock or diluted demi-glace, remaining 2 sprigs thyme, and 4 sage leaves in a small saucepan, and bring to a boil over medium-high heat. Cook until liquid is reduced to ¾ cup, then strain. Stir vinegar and half of the liquid into lentil purée. Chop remaining 2 sage leaves and mix into lentil purée. Season mixture with salt and pepper. Spoon in the center of 4 plates.

3. Prepare Lentil Sprout Salad and place it at the top of each plate.

4. Heat olive oil in a skillet over medium-high heat. Add scallions and sauté until lightly colored and just wilted, 3 to 4 minutes. Set aside in warm place.

5. Process peppercorns to a medium-coarse grind in a spice mill or clean coffee mill. Blot squab halves dry and season with salt and plenty of the ground peppercorns. Heat duck fat in a large heavy skillet over medium-high heat. Add squab, skin side down, and sauté until skin is crisp and rich brown, 4 to 5 minutes. Turn and cook second side for 1 to 2 minutes to brown. Birds should be medium rare. Place 2 squab halves on lentil purée on each plate. Arrange scallions around squab.

6. Discard all fat from pan and reheat until hot. Season foie gras with salt and pepper, and sauté until browned on all sides, turning often, about 1½ minutes. Spoon over squab and serve.

lentil sprout salad

2 ounces lentil or other sprouts

2 teaspoons small capers, drained

¼ cup extra-virgin olive oil

1 tablespoon lemon juice

Salt and white pepper to taste

3 sage leaves, thinly sliced

Place sprouts and capers in a bowl. Mix together the ¼ cup oil, lemon juice, salt, pepper, and sage leaves. Add enough of this vinaigrette to sprouts to lightly coat. Taste to adjust seasonings.

Adapted from Laurent Gras, chef, Peacock Alley at the Waldorf Astoria Hotel, New York City

boneless stuffed squab with mole sauce
on grilled polenta with corn kernels and thyme

SERVES 8

These moist little birds, stuffed with a spicy mixture of cornbread, pumpkin seeds, and sausage, are slathered with one of Mexico's culinary gifts — dark mole sauce. The mixture of roasted ground seeds, spices, and unsweetened chocolate is complex, with only a whisper of sweetness, a perfect complement to the dark meat of the bird. Be sure to pass extra sauce at table to ladle over the circles of grilled polenta. Leftover birds may be served at room temperature or even reheated, if tightly wrapped in aluminum foil. A spicy red Zinfandel would pair well with the birds and sauce.

2 cups finely crumbled cornbread

½ cup plus 2 tablespoons pumpkin seeds, lightly roasted

4 ounces mild or spicy cooked chicken sausages, chopped (see Note)

½ cup finely chopped red bell pepper

1 jalapeño, seeded and minced

½ cup lightly packed chopped cilantro, plus extra leaves for garnish

4 teaspoons olive or vegetable oil

1 cup finely chopped onion

Salt and freshly ground black pepper to taste

8 semiboneless squab, wings, giblets, neck, and excess fat removed

8 slices bacon

Grilled Polenta with Corn Kernels and Thyme
   (recipe follows)

1 (8-ounce) jar purchased mole paste, oil
   drained

1½ cups crushed or ground canned tomatoes

1 cup chicken stock

1. Combine cornbread, ½ cup of the
pumpkin seeds, the chicken sausage, red
bell pepper, jalapeño, and chopped cilantro in a bowl. Heat 2 teaspoons of the oil
in a skillet over medium-high heat. Add
onion and sauté until limp and lightly colored, 5 minutes. Add to cornbread mixture,
season with salt and pepper, and toss just
to mix. Set aside. *Stuffing may be prepared
1 day in advance, covered, and refrigerated.*
2. Preheat oven to 400°F.
3. Rinse squab and pat dry. Season inside
with salt and pepper. Fill each squab with
about ¾ cup of the cornbread mixture.
Roll up birds from the tail end, wrapping
neck flap around the stuffed birds to form
a neat cylinder. Secure neck flap with a
skewer. Heat the remaining 2 teaspoons
oil in a large skillet over medium-high
heat. Brown the birds, turning to color
evenly. Wrap a slice of bacon around each
bird to cover the breast.
4. Transfer squab to a roasting pan large
enough so they are not crowded. Roast for
28 minutes. Remove from oven and let
stand at least 10 minutes before serving.
While squab are roasting, prepare Grilled
Polenta with Corn Kernels and Thyme.
5. Meanwhile, combine mole paste, tomatoes, and chicken stock in a saucepan. Stir
until well blended. Bring mixture to a boil
over medium-high heat, then reduce heat,

cover, and simmer until needed, stirring
occasionally.
6. Remove skewers and cut birds in half
across each cylinder. Place halves cut side
down on circles of polenta. Spoon on
some mole sauce and sprinkle on cilantro
leaves and remaining 2 tablespoons pumpkin seeds. Serve 1 to 2 halves per person.
   NOTE:
If precooked sausages are unavailable,
substitute about 1 pound of uncooked
spicy sausage. Remove from casing, crum-
ble, and sauté until browned before draining and using.

grilled polenta with corn kernels and thyme

8 cups water

2 to 3 teaspoons salt, or to taste

2 cups instant polenta

1 cup fresh or defrosted frozen corn kernels

2 tablespoons fresh thyme leaves, or
   2 teaspoons dried thyme

Olive oil

1. Line a large jelly roll pan with wax paper
or lightly oiled parchment.
2. Bring water to a boil over high heat in
a large pan. Add salt, then add polenta
in a slow, steady stream, stirring constantly.
Continue stirring for 5 minutes. Remove
from heat, stir in corn and thyme. Spread
mixture in prepared jelly roll pan. Cover
with another piece of paper and allow to
cool.
3. Position oven rack close to heat. Turn
oven to broil.
4. Remove top paper. Using a 3-inch
cookie cutter or clean can, cut out circles

of polenta. Transfer them to a lightly oiled baking sheet and broil until lightly colored, 3 to 4 minutes, then serve. *Polenta circles may be done ahead of time and once lightly colored, left in a warm oven.*

casserole of scottish wood pigeon and root vegetables

SERVES 4

Seductive, earthy aromas permeate this robust one-dish meal. If no imported Scottish wood pigeons are to be found, farm-raised domestic squab are plenty satisfying. Squab are about twice the size of the wood pigeons, though, so you'll need to double the roasting time. Enjoy a Châteauneuf-du-Pape or Bordeaux to drink.

3 tablespoons rendered duck fat or unsalted butter

2 carrots, cut into ½-inch dice

2 medium potatoes, peeled and cut into ½-inch dice

1 large, crisp red apple, cored, peeled, and cut into ½-inch dice

1 small celery root, peeled and cut into ½-inch dice

1 small rutabaga, peeled and cut into ½-inch dice

1 head garlic, broken into cloves but not peeled

1 cup medium Madeira

1 cup duck and veal demi-glace (see page 33)

6 sprigs thyme

2 bay leaves

4 wood pigeons, about 8 ounces each

Salt and freshly ground black pepper to taste

1. Preheat oven to 500°F.

2. Heat 2 tablespoons of the duck fat in a skillet over medium-high heat. Add carrots, potatoes, apple, celery root, and rutabaga, and sweat until almost tender, about 9 minutes. Transfer to a shallow ovenproof casserole large enough to hold vegetables in a layer about 1 inch deep.

3. Combine Madeira and demi-glace in a small pan and bring to a boil. Reduce by one-third, then pour into casserole with vegetables. Add garlic, 2 of the thyme sprigs, bay leaves, and just enough water to cover vegetables. Roast in oven for 10 minutes. Remove pan and baste vegetables.

4. Rinse wood pigeons and pat dry. Rub with remaining tablespoon of duck fat, season with salt and pepper, and place on top of vegetables. Return pot to oven and roast for 10 minutes.

5. Reduce oven temperature to 350°F.

6. Remove birds and let rest for 5 to 7 minutes on a platter. Meanwhile, if vegetables are not tender, return casserole to oven.

7. Remove backbones from wood pigeons with scissors or poultry shears. Slice breast and leg together in one piece from carcass. Lay wood pigeon halves on vegetables and return to oven for 5 minutes longer. Divide vegetables among 4 plates. Place 2 wood pigeon halves on each serving of vegetables, garnish with remaining thyme sprigs, and serve.

BAIN OF TARVES

For more than 10 years, D'Artagnan has relied on Bain of Tarves, in Aberdeenshire, Scotland, to send prime-quality wild game. To understand how this 40-year-old family business works, you should know a little about the history of Scotland and hunting.

JOHN BAIN: In Scotland, wild birds and animals have been freely hunted for sustenance since after the Ice Age. But the feudal system, developed in tenth-century Europe, introduced controls to restrict game hunting to the king, his noblemen, and the other great landowners. In the Scottish Highlands, however, the clan system ensured that the land belonged to the entire tribe, not to any individual, so great communal hunts provided food for all. This practice continued until the clan system was broken up after the Battle of Culloden in 1746.

By the mid-nineteenth century, the Industrial Revolution created a new moneyed class eager to become landowners. At just this time, Queen Victoria purchased the Balmoral estate in Aberdeenshire. Her passion for everything Scottish made it very fashionable to own an estate in the Highlands. The extension of the railway system also accelerated the purchase of old clan lands by industrial wealth from England. This resulted in the establishment of sporting estates and the building of shooting lodges and residences, which ranged from mansions to palaces. Sport shooting reached its high point

Two world wars saw the decline of the landed classes as well as venison stock. However, from the 1950s, deer numbers rebounded, and the meat started to be commercially handled. In 1955 my father, John, founded Bain of Tarves, in Aberdeenshire, when a local trapper could

find nowhere to sell his rabbits and hares and brought them to him.

Then as now, our game is mainly obtained by personal contact with the successors to some 2,000 great estates from earlier times. They range in size from about 2,000 acres to great tracts of over 100,000 acres. Many of the old clans and lowland gentry are still among the largest of the estate owners. The financial input of game is now a very important part of an estate's budget, and in turn the estates are becoming more and more professional in marketing their sporting facilities. Sportsmen are brought in from all over the world to stalk deer and to shoot birds, hares, and other small game. Catering and accommodations are often provided in the great houses. It is a rare experience that commands a commensurate price.

Once the stalk or the shoot is completed, the game is brought back to the estate larder and prepared, then collected by Bain of Tarves. One of our fleet of refrigerated vans then sets out on what can be a long and difficult journey over twisting roads in all kinds of weather. Thus, a chain of events starts that will shortly result in a satisfying meal somewhere in the world.

Wild game from Scotland

pan-roasted wood pigeon
over george's curried orzo

SERVES 4

Simply roasted wood pigeons share the limelight with George's outrageously well seasoned curried orzo, a rice-shaped pasta. You could substitute purchased curry powder, but George says making your own is infinitely better. In any case, be sure to add the saffron. There's a lot of it, but don't stint. The results justify the indulgence. This orzo is a spectacular partner for any full-flavored red meat or poultry, from magret of duck to venison or wild hare. Rub the spice mixture on the meat too, if you want.

George's Curried Orzo (recipe follows)

4 wood pigeons, about 8 ounces each, rinsed and patted dry

2 tablespoons olive oil

Salt and freshly ground black pepper to taste

1 shallot, finely chopped

1 cup tawny port

¼ cup good-quality balsamic vinegar

1 cup duck and veal demi-glace (see page 33)

1 teaspoon saffron threads

1 tablespoon unsalted butter, at room temperature

1 tablespoon minced flat-leaf parsley

1. Prepare George's Curried Orzo and keep warm.
2. Remove backbone, 2 wing joints, and extra skin from wood pigeons with sharp scissors. Split in half along breastbone.

Brush with 1 tablespoon of the oil and season with salt and pepper.
3. Heat a large cast iron or other heavy skillet over medium-high heat until hot. Add wood pigeons, skin side down, and cook until skin is crisp and brown, about 2 minutes. Turn birds, place a cover smaller than diameter of skillet on birds and some weights, like a couple of 1-pound cans, on top. Cook until breasts are medium rare, about 4 minutes longer. Remove to a warm platter.
4. Heat remaining tablespoon of oil in a small saucepan over medium heat. Add shallot and sauté until translucent, 1 to 1½ minutes. Pour in port and balsamic vinegar, bring to a boil over high heat, and reduce to 1 cup. Stir in demi-glace and saffron and reduce to ½ cup. Whisk in butter and season to taste with salt and pepper. Spoon a generous amount of orzo on each plate. Add 2 wood pigeon halves, a spoonful of sauce, and a sprinkle of parsley to each plate, and serve.

george's curried orzo

1 pound dried orzo

2 tablespoons olive oil, or more

1 tablespoon ground cumin

½ tablespoon *each* ground cardamom and ground coriander

1 teaspoon saffron threads

¼ teaspoon *each* cayenne, cinnamon, white pepper, turmeric, and nutmeg

1 cup golden raisins

1 cup slivered almonds, lightly toasted

½ cup chopped flat-leaf parsley

Salt to taste

Bring a large pot of salted water to a boil. Add orzo and cook until al dente, drain, and toss with 2 tablespoons olive oil. Combine cumin, cardamom, coriander, saffron, cayenne, cinnamon, white pepper, turmeric, and nutmeg, and mix together thoroughly. When orzo is done, toss it with the spice mixture. Add raisins, almonds, and parsley. Toss to blend, adding more olive oil to taste. Season with salt to taste and serve.

salmis of wood pigeon with peas

SERVES 4

Wood pigeons make a salmis of the highest order. The birds are exquisitely flavorful on their own. The reduced sauce made from the bones and trimmings is an elegant magnification of that taste enhanced with aromatic vegetables and wild mushrooms. Don't stint on the quality of wine. As it reduces, imperfections are intensified. Rather than making a demi-glace, however, use ours. That's not cheating, it's an intelligent use of your time. If you want to make this dish even more spectacular, debone it after removing from oven and serve on a thin slice of seared foie gras with some shaved black truffles on top.

½ ounce dried sliced cèpes or porcini

1 cup hot water

4 wood pigeons, about 8 ounces each, rinsed and patted dry

Salt and freshly ground black pepper to taste

2 tablespoons rendered duck fat, plus fat to grease pan

¼ cup *each* finely chopped onion, carrot, and celery

3 tablespoons Armagnac

1¼ cups full-bodied red wine, such as Madiran or Côtes de Gascogne

¾ cup duck and veal demi-glace (see page 33)

2 tablespoons unsalted butter, plus extra to toss with peas

4 slices firm white sandwich bread, crusts removed

1 cup shelled young peas or defrosted frozen petite peas

1. Preheat oven to 475°F.

2. Cover cèpes with hot water and let soak until soft, about 20 minutes. Strain liquid through 2 layers of paper towels to remove all grit. Set liquid aside. Remove sandy parts from mushrooms.

3. Remove giblets and necks from wood pigeons and reserve all but the livers. Season birds inside and out with salt and pepper, rub with 1 tablespoon of the duck fat, truss, and place in a shallow baking pan greased with a little duck fat. Roast until skin is crisp and rich brown and birds are quite rare, about 10 minutes. Remove from oven. Using poultry shears or scissors, cut whole breasts with rib cage from backbones. Split lengthwise along breastbone, then tent lightly with aluminum foil and keep warm.

4. Chop legs, wings, backbones, necks, and reserved giblets into small pieces. Heat remaining tablespoon of duck fat in a heavy saucepan over medium-high heat.

Stir in bones and chopped onion, carrot, and celery, and cook until bones and vegetables are browned.

5. Pour in Armagnac and carefully ignite. When flames subside, pour in wine, scraping to incorporate all browned cooking bits, and reduce by half over medium-high heat. Add demi-glace and reserved mushroom soaking liquid, and cook for 6 minutes longer over medium heat. Pour sauce through a fine strainer, pressing with the back of a wooden spoon to extract as much flavor as possible. Off the heat, stir in reserved mushrooms and 1 tablespoon of the butter, and season with salt and pepper. Salmis should be a relatively thin sauce. Keep hot.

6. Melt remaining tablespoon of butter and lightly brush bread slices. Toast them on both sides in a skillet until golden brown, then cut diagonally into 2 triangles. Heat peas and toss with a little butter.

7. Place 2 toast triangles on each plate. Carve breast from bone and put a breast half on each toast. Spoon sauce over breasts, add a mound of peas between the breasts, and serve.

Adapted from Roger "Zizou" Duffour, founding chef-owner of
Le Relais de l'Armagnac, Luppé-Violles, Gascony

LA PALOMBITE, A SERIOUS SEASONAL DISEASE

ARIANE: Gascons are frank, straight, and loyal, like their hero D'Artagnan. There are only two times a year when a Gascon won't look you in the eye. The first is during elections. The second is in October, when they're all looking up at the sky at the wood pigeons on their annual migration to Africa. That's when that serious disease we call *la Palombite* strikes. Absenteeism reaches record levels as unused vacation days are claimed and mysterious maladies keep untold others away from the workplace. It happens every year.

Where is everyone? Hidden away in the forests, among the pines or oaks, in *palombières*, fern-covered wooden cabins with a vantage point of the treetops and sky. Some of these are quite grandiose; they have stood for years and are extravagantly outfitted. It is a matter of pride for the whole team of hunters to have the most comfortable and efficient palombière.

On the first day of the season, what the hunters share is total silence and concentration on the birds. Tensions mount, and nerves are on edge. But mistakes happen. I know of one case where two guys haven't spoken to each other for 20 years. Why? Because one sneezed just as the birds arrived.

Although the spirit is friendly among the groups of hunters, it's also pretty competitive. Sometimes two palombières are too close to each other. If group B notices that the birds are attracted toward the palombière of group A, they might "accidentally" fire a wild shot to be sure that the birds scatter. In that case, no one wins, but no one loses either.

By the second day, the mood relaxes. Discussions of what to eat, which wine to drink, and past hunting stories begin to unroll. This is Gascony, after all. By the evening, a salmis of wood pigeon or some other game dish invites hunters to unwind and enjoy their temporary lodgings for a little while longer.

When the vine-grower or ploughman wants a treat on some long winter evening, what do we see roasting over a bright fire in the kitchen where the table is laid? A turkey. . . . And in high places of gastronomy, at those select gatherings where politics are forced to give way to dissertations on taste, what do the guests hope for and long for as the second course? A truffled turkey!

— Jean Anthelme Brillat-Savarin,
La Physiologie du goût, 1825
(translated by M.F.K. Fisher)

domestic and wild turkey

Few foods are more closely associated with an American holiday than turkey. From the Pilgrims' first feast in Plymouth, with Governor Bradford and Chief Massasoit in attendance (where some sources say turkey wasn't on the menu), to the preferred main course served annually on the fourth Thursday in November, this native North American bird invariably signals Thanksgiving. Whether you buy a tom (male), the larger bird, and considered to have the best meat-to-bone ratio, or a hen (female), thought to be more tender, is up to your personal preference.

GEORGE: The single most important step to attaining a juicy and moist bird, no matter what kind of turkey you buy — farm-raised or wild — is to baste it constantly and, if cooking the bird whole, to shield the breast with aluminum foil or a well-basted cheesecloth so it doesn't dry out while the legs finish cooking. Turkeys, especially wild birds, don't have a lot of fat, so you can even braise them. Follow this advice and I think you'll enjoy my wild turkey recipe on page 148.

ARIANE: And what about my favorite turkey recipe, on page 155? Actually, if you want a really good, meaty-tasting turkey, I think it's just as important to start with a bird that feeds naturally on wholesome grain and fresh spring water, and wanders about. Protein supplements and chemicals injected to taste like butter and make the bird fatter are just ruining a good bird. Eberly Poultry supplies us both free-range and free-range organic turkeys that meet these requirements. Hens are 14 to 20 weeks old and weigh from 8 to 22 pounds. Toms weigh 22 to 34 pounds.

GEORGE: Here's one more bit of advice that we agree on: Don't rely on plastic pop-up devices to let you know when the turkey is cooked. Sometimes they don't work at all; more often they are inaccurate. As we've said before, an instant-read thermometer is essential. It should be inserted deep into the thigh meat (unless the recipe says otherwise) and should not touch the bone.

Even though wild turkeys are more readily available than in past years, the turkeys you buy at supermarkets are generally domesticated. That's not surprising, since by the time the Pilgrims landed on Plymouth Rock in 1620, turkeys had already been imported into Spain and domesticated by priests who had traveled with Cortés's conquistadors in Mexico. From Spain they were exported back to America. Early accounts described them as large hens and cocks that were more tender than peacocks.

Europeans took readily to turkeys, and quickly made them the favored fowl of noble and peasant alike. Charles IX of France chose roasted turkey to celebrate his nuptials in 1570, for by that time turkey had spread from Spain into France.

Meanwhile, pre-Columbian Native Americans of the Southwest had already domesticated this native Mexican bird and made it an important staple. Indians attached to the soil found they would have a ready food source if they fed corn to the birds. The birds ended up decimating the crops and ultimately were enclosed in pens to protect the grain. Tribes of the Plains and East hunted turkey with bow and arrow.

GEORGE: When the first settlers arrived here, there were an estimated 7 million to 10 million birds that roamed the forests and fields of what are today thirty-nine states. As the pioneers moved westward, and huge numbers of trees were felled for homes and farms, the flocks were nearly wiped out. By the 1930s there were fewer than 30,000 wild turkeys left.

Remarkably, the 1937 Federal Aid in Wildlife Restoration Act, and money from hunting licenses, along with the National Wild Turkey Federation, have all played a role in conserving the wild birds. Today there are more than 4 million birds in forty-nine states.

maple-pepper roasted turkey

SERVES 8

It's almost impossible to have both the breast and leg meat of a whole turkey cooked perfectly. The problem is that the breast reaches its juicy best at 165°F, while the leg needs to go to 180°F to be cooked through. Removing the breast from the whole bird when it's done, and returning the legs to the oven to finish cooking and to take on crisp, caramel skin, is the best way to perfect the process. If cooking a turkey whole, roast until legs are done.

Use only pure maple syrup to glaze and flavor this turkey. For the best quality, choose mild-tasting Fancy or Grade A pale amber syrup. Grades B and C are progressively darker in color and stronger in taste.

Maple-Pepper Butter and Glaze (recipe follows)

1 cup lemon juice

¾ cup pure maple syrup

½ cup corn oil

6 medium shallots, thickly sliced

6 large cloves garlic, thinly sliced

4 sprigs thyme

3 bay leaves

2 teaspoons finely grated lemon zest

1 teaspoon freshly ground black pepper

1 turkey, 10 to 12 pounds, giblets, neck, and neck skin removed and reserved, rinsed and patted dry

3 medium onions, cut into 1-inch dice

3 medium ribs celery, cut into 1-inch pieces

1 tablespoon all-purpose flour

2 cups chicken stock

Salt and freshly ground black pepper to taste

1. Make Maple-Pepper Butter and Glaze.
2. Combine lemon juice, maple syrup, oil, shallots, garlic, thyme, bay leaves, lemon zest, and 1 teaspoon pepper in a sturdy 2-gallon plastic bag. Add turkey, squeeze out as much air as possible, and seal bag. Distribute marinade evenly over and inside turkey. Set turkey, breast side down, in a bowl in refrigerator and marinate for 24 hours, turning occasionally.
3. Preheat oven to 450°F. Position oven rack near bottom of oven.
4. Remove turkey from marinade. Wipe off any shallots and garlic that are clinging to it and pat bird dry. Strain marinade into a bowl; skim off oil and reserve the rest. Set herbs, garlic, and shallots aside separately.
5. Carefully loosen turkey skin over breast and thighs with your fingers. Put all but 3 tablespoons of the softened Maple-Pepper Butter in a pastry bag fitted with a small round tip, and pipe it under the breast and thigh skin, patting gently to spread butter. Alternatively, spread it evenly with your fingers.
6. Put one-third each of the diced onions and celery in the cavity. Tie legs together with kitchen string and set turkey, breast side up, on a rack in a large roasting pan. Rub remaining maple butter over the turkey and roast for 30 minutes, basting twice with pan juices. The skin may appear dark in patches because the maple syrup in

the marinade and butter caramelize as the turkey cooks. Cover bird loosely with foil to keep skin from burning.

7. Reduce oven temperature to 350°F. Spread the remaining onions and celery around turkey, and roast until an instant-read thermometer inserted in thickest part of breast just above wing joint measures 165°F and juices run clear, about 1½ hours. During last 30 minutes, add reserved shallots, garlic, and herbs to pan, then remove foil from turkey and brush twice with Maple-Pepper Glaze. When breast is done, transfer bird to a carving board. Remove whole legs from turkey, cutting them off at the hip joint. Cut off wings from breast. Loosely cover breast with aluminum foil, and let rest until ready to carve.

8. Return legs and wings to pan and roast until an instant-read thermometer measures 180°F when inserted in thickest part of thigh and juices run clear, about 30 minutes longer. Transfer legs and wings to carving board, cover with foil, and let stand 15 minutes before carving.

9. Meanwhile, make gravy: Set roasting pan over 2 burners over high heat and cook vegetables remaining in pan until golden brown, stirring constantly. Carefully pour off all but 2 tablespoons of the fat. Add flour and whisk for 1 minute. Add reserved marinade and the chicken stock, and bring to a boil, scraping up any browned bits. Simmer, whisking constantly, for 3 minutes. Strain gravy into a saucepan and boil over high heat until reduced by half, about 10 minutes. Season with salt and pepper, pour into a sauceboat, and serve alongside turkey.

maple-pepper butter and glaze

Butter and glaze may be made 1 day ahead, then covered and refrigerated. Return to room temperature before using.

MAPLE-PEPPER BUTTER:

2 sticks (½ pound) unsalted butter, softened

6 tablespoons pure maple syrup

3 tablespoons lemon juice

2 teaspoons finely grated lemon zest

1 tablespoon coarsely ground black pepper

2 teaspoons coarse salt

MAPLE-PEPPER GLAZE:

4 tablespoons pure maple syrup

1 tablespoon lemon juice

½ teaspoon finely ground black pepper

1. FOR BUTTER: Combine all ingredients in a food processor or electric blender, and process until blended, then scrape into a bowl.

2. FOR GLAZE: In another bowl, combine maple syrup, lemon juice, and the finely ground pepper. Cover until ready to use.

Adapted from Sandy D'Amato, chef-owner, Sanford and Coquette Café, Milwaukee

bacon-wrapped turkey breast and turkey leg burrito
with green chili–almond sauce and whole wheat dressing

SERVES 10

Are you bored with the same roast turkey? Why not shake up the traditional Thanksgiving scenario? This grand production with mildly spicy burritos, herb dressing, and bacon-wrapped slices of breast meat will energize any fiesta. The best part is that you can do almost all of the preparation the day before. Never again will you think turkey mundane. How about sangria for your holiday drink?

1 turkey, 15 pounds, giblets, wings, and neck removed and discarded, skinned

1 onion, diced

1 large carrot, diced

5 ribs celery, diced

4 cloves garlic, sliced

1 sprig rosemary

5 sprigs thyme

2 quarts chicken stock

1½ cups bourbon

1 teaspoon black peppercorns

½ cup roasted garlic purée (see Note)

2 tablespoons lemon juice

Salt and freshly ground black pepper to taste

30 slices smoked bacon

Green Chili–Almond Sauce (recipe follows)

Whole Wheat Dressing (recipe follows)

4 shallots, minced

2 poblano chilies, roasted, peeled, seeded, and diced

1 carrot, finely diced

1 bunch cilantro, chopped

10 (8-inch) flour tortillas

2 eggs plus 2 tablespoons water, beaten

Canola oil for sautéeing

1. Remove turkey leg quarters from carcass. Combine onion, carrot, celery, sliced garlic, rosemary sprig, 1 sprig of thyme, the chicken stock, bourbon, and black peppercorns in a large pot and bring to a simmer. Add leg quarters and braise until tender, about 2 hours. Remove meat from liquid and let cool. Strain liquid into a bowl and reserve.

2. Bone breasts from carcass. Cut each breast half into 5 equal portions, slicing the meat lengthwise. Remove the leaves from 2 sprigs of thyme and chop. Combine thyme with garlic purée and lemon juice in a large bowl. Add breast pieces, season with salt and pepper, and mix.

3. Lay 3 slices of bacon side by side on counter, place 1 portion of breast on bacon, and roll. Repeat with remaining bacon and breast portions. Set aside.

4. Prepare Green Chili–Almond Sauce and Whole Wheat Dressing.

5. MAKE BURRITO FILLING: Remove meat from turkey legs and shred. You should have about 2 pounds of turkey. Combine with 1 cup of the reserved braising liquid, the shallots, chilies, carrots, leaves from remaining 2 thyme sprigs, and the cilantro, season with salt and pepper, and blend well. *Recipe may be done 1 day ahead to this point. Wrap bacon-rolled breasts with plastic wrap, cover burrito filling, and refrigerate until ready to continue.*

6. Divide filling into 10 portions. Put 1 tortilla on workspace, add 1 portion of filling, brush edges of tortilla with egg wash, and roll tightly. Continue with remaining tortillas and filling.

7. Pour 1 tablespoon oil in the bottom of each of 2 large skillets, and heat both over medium heat until hot. Sauté burritos in 1 skillet over medium-low heat until brown, 12 to 15 minutes, turning frequently, and adding more oil if needed. Remove and blot on paper towels. Sauté turkey breasts in other skillet over medium-low heat until bacon is crisp and turkey is cooked through, 12 to 15 minutes, turning frequently. Remove and let stand.

8. Spoon Green Chili–Almond Sauce on 10 warm plates. Cut each turkey breast roll into 3 equal portions, and place at the front of plate. Spoon a portion of Whole Wheat Dressing just behind breast. Trim ends from each burrito, then cut into 2 pieces on the bias sushi style. Place behind dressing and serve.

NOTE:

Roasted garlic purée is sold in some markets and specialty food stores. It is easy to make. Cut a head of garlic in half crosswise, place on a square of aluminum foil, and drizzle with olive oil. Wrap tightly and bake in a 375°F oven until soft, about 40 minutes. When it is cool enough to handle, squeeze pulp from cloves and purée in a blender or food processor.

green chili–almond sauce

2 teaspoons canola oil

1 large onion, diced

4 cloves garlic, sliced

3 poblano chilies, seeded and diced

1 green bell pepper, seeded and diced

1 quart chicken stock

1½ cups sliced almonds, toasted

1 bunch cilantro, chopped

Salt and freshly ground black pepper to taste

Heat oil in a medium saucepan over medium heat. Add onion, garlic, chilies, and bell pepper, partially cover, and sweat until soft. Add stock, bring to a boil over high heat, and reduce by one-third. Remove from heat and let cool. When cool, transfer to a food processor or electric blender and purée, adding almonds and cilantro, until smooth. Season with salt and pepper, and serve warm. *Sauce may be made 2 days ahead and refrigerated.*

whole wheat dressing

Butter to grease casserole, plus ½ cup unsalted butter, melted

4 pounds whole wheat bread, cut into large dice

6 ribs celery, shredded

1 large carrot, shredded

1 tablespoon chopped fresh sage

1 tablespoon fresh thyme leaves

1 cup braising liquid (reserved from turkey legs)

Salt and freshly ground black pepper to taste

1. Preheat oven to 350°F. Butter a large ovenproof casserole.

2. Combine bread, celery, carrot, sage, and thyme in a large bowl, and toss to blend. Dribble on the ½ cup melted butter, toss to blend, then add braising liquid, salt, and pepper and toss lightly just to blend. Put stuffing into greased casserole and bake until top is golden brown and crusty, 35 to 40 minutes. Remove from oven and keep warm.

Adapted from David Walzog, chef, Tapika and Michael Jordan's Steak House, New York City

george's fantastic wild turkey in two courses

SERVES 4 TO 6

The multilayered flavors of fork-tender turkey meat in a rich reduced wine and port sauce served over pasta are haunting and so satisfying. Prepare the ragù first, even a day or two before, then the breast and vegetables. Wild turkey breast is succulent and moist when frequently basted with chicken stock, as it is here. The root vegetables absorb the taste of the pan juices. We like a spoonful of Cranberry-Apple Chutney (page 302) with the turkey. Serve the same red wine, such as a Côte-Rôtie or Madiran, with both courses.

part 1 — braised wild turkey leg sauce over pasta

1 cup red wine

1 cup ruby port

1 tablespoon dried thyme

1 cup duck and veal demi-glace (see page 33)

1½ cups chicken stock

4 bay leaves

12 black peppercorns

6 cloves garlic

5 sprigs flat-leaf parsley, plus small sprigs, to garnish

3 carrots, cut into 1-inch lengths

2 ribs celery, cut into 1-inch lengths

1 onion, quartered

Legs and wings from 1 (6- to 8-pound or larger) wild turkey, legs skinned

Salt and freshly ground black pepper to taste

2 tablespoons unsalted butter, optional

8 to 12 ounces dried pasta, such as fettuccine, penne, or rigatoni

1. Combine wine, port, and thyme in a large pot and reduce by half over high heat. Add demi-glace, chicken stock, bay leaves, peppercorns, garlic, 5 sprigs parsley, carrots, celery, and onion, and bring to a boil. Reduce heat so liquid is simmering, add turkey legs whole, with feet if still attached, and wings.

2. Cover and cook gently until meat easily separates from bone when pricked with a fork, about 2 hours for a young bird. Older birds can take up to 4 or 5 hours. Check every half hour. If pan juices get lower than 1 inch in the pot, add stock or water to bring level back up. When meat is cooked, remove from pan, let cool, and shred.

3. Strain cooking liquid into a saucepan, pressing solids with a wooden spoon or spatula to extract all juices. Bring to a boil over high heat and reduce until slightly syrupy. Season to taste with salt and pepper, add the shredded meat, and stir in butter, if using. Keep hot, *or refrigerate for up to 2 days, then reheat.*

4. Bring a large pot of salted water to a boil. Add pasta and cook until al dente. Drain and divide among 4 or 6 plates.

5. Spoon on sauce, garnish plates with parsley sprigs, and serve at once.

part 2 — wild turkey breast roasted on diced vegetables

Bone-in breast from 1 (6- to 8-pound or larger) wild turkey, wings removed

1½ tablespoons vegetable oil

Salt and freshly ground black pepper to taste

1 tablespoon dried thyme

GOBBLE, GOBBLE, GOBBLE, GOBBLE: HUNTING THE WILD TURKEY

GEORGE: The sound of an amorous male wild turkey blasting out his song of love to every female turkey within earshot on an early spring morning is a prelude to one of nature's most extraordinary mating rituals. Pursuing the gobbler is an amusing as well as enervating hunt. I say amusing because the tom turkey behaves in a hilarious manner, gobbling to attract hens, then strutting, puffing up his feathers, and fanning his tail to convince the hens that *he* is the one. The hunt is enervating because turkeys are so unpredictable in their behavior and therefore very difficult to get a bead on.

Boss gobblers (3- to 4-year-old birds) round up as many hens as possible each morning and drive off any advances from younger *jakes*. Raucous fights are common.

As the hunter, I arrive in the woods an hour before sunrise to be in position to convince the gobbler that I am the hen of his dreams. This is accomplished by dressing completely in camouflage, remaining perfectly still, and using a mouth call to mimic the hen in heat. When all works according to plan (about 5 percent of the time), I get to shoot one delicious bird. However, more often than not something goes awry.

Reason number 1: The gobbler is already with a hen. The expression "a bird in the hand

is worth two in the bush" applies to turkeys specifically.

Reason number 2: Another hen steals the gobbler. My entreaties are hardly private, and frequently other hens will intercept the gobbler on his way to me. He's happy. In fact, for all he knows, she is me.

Reason number 3: Making an unusual noise before I can take a shot alerts every bird that something is amiss. Sometimes the disturbance comes from another bird letting out an alarm call. This leads to shooting the bird in a more figurative manner.

Reason number 4: After all this frustration, the hunter still has to shoot straight. Believe it or not, this is the cause for more missed turkeys than any of the previous three reasons combined.

George with his dog, Mike ⌃

2 to 3 *each* baking potatoes, carrots, and turnips, cut into 1-inch cubes

6 cloves garlic, unpeeled

1½ to 2 cups chicken stock

1. Preheat oven to 400°F.

2. Rub turkey breast with a bit of the oil. Season generously with salt, pepper, and thyme. Pour remaining oil into a gratin dish or shallow baking dish large enough to hold turkey. Scatter potatoes, carrots, turnips, and garlic in pan, then put turkey, skin side up, on top of vegetables.

3. Transfer pan to oven. After 7 to 10 minutes, pour about ½ cup of the chicken stock over breast. Continue basting every 7 to 10 minutes, adding the remaining stock by ½ cupfuls. If liquid evaporates, add more stock or water. Bake in oven until skin is golden brown and an instant-read thermometer registers 168° to 170°F. A small breast requires about 1 hour. Remove from pan and let stand 10 to 15 minutes before cutting into slices. If vegetables are not tender, return pan to oven while turkey rests. Spoon some roasted vegetables and pan juices onto each plate, and serve.

roasted wild turkey with bourbon-pecan stuffing

SERVES 6

A tried and true recipe with guaranteed wonderful results. Turning the wild turkey from side to side and letting it rest breast side down keeps the meat moist. The sausage stuffing with a hint of herbs and bourbon is sure to please. A little bourbon is used in the sauce and as part of the basting liquid as well. Yams are a traditional accompaniment.

½ tablespoon olive oil, plus oil to brush on aluminum foil

1 cup sweet Italian sausage meat, removed from casing and crumbled

1 small onion, finely chopped

1 rib celery, finely chopped

1½ teaspoons chopped fresh rosemary leaves, or ½ teaspoon dried rosemary, crumbled

1½ teaspoons chopped fresh thyme leaves, or ½ teaspoon dried thyme

¾ cup bourbon

¼ cup pecan halves, coarsely chopped

1 egg, beaten

6 slices stale Italian bread, crumbled, about 6 cups

4½ to 5½ cups turkey or chicken stock

Salt and freshly ground black pepper to taste

1 wild turkey, 7 to 8 pounds, giblets and neck removed, rinsed and patted dry

2 tablespoons all-purpose flour

1. Preheat oven to 450°F. Brush a piece of aluminum foil with oil and place it on a rack in a roasting pan.

2. Heat ½ tablespoon oil in a large heavy skillet over medium-high heat. Add sausage and cook until browned and no pink remains, 5 to 6 minutes, stirring and breaking it up as it cooks. Pour off all but 2 tablespoons of fat. Add onion, celery, rosemary, and thyme, and cook until onion is soft. Add ¼ cup of the bourbon and bring to a boil. Remove from heat and let cool.

3. Combine sausage mixture with pecans and egg. Add bread, ½ cup of the stock, salt and pepper, and gently toss to blend. Stuffing should be a little dry. Set aside to cool.

4. Stuff turkey loosely with stuffing, truss, and set it breast side down on foil-covered rack in roasting pan. Add 2 to 3 cups of the stock and ¼ cup bourbon to bottom of pan and place in oven. After 10 minutes turn heat down to 325°F and roast for 20 minutes more, basting with pan juices every 10 minutes.

5. Turn turkey on one side and roast 30 minutes. Turn to other side and roast 30 minutes more. Turn turkey breast side up and roast 15 minutes longer. Continue to baste every 10 minutes. Turkey is done when meat is soft to the touch, leg moves easily in the joint, and an instant-read thermometer measures 180° to 185°F when inserted into deepest part of thigh. Remove turkey from pan and set aside, breast side down.

6. Pour pan juices into a bowl or fat separator and skim off as much fat as possible. Reserve about 2 tablespoons of fat. Add enough of the remaining stock to pan juices to make 1½ cups liquid. On top of stove, add fat to roasting pan and sprinkle on flour. Stir over medium heat until flour begins to brown. Whisk in pan juices and remaining ¼ cup bourbon, and bring to a boil for 5 minutes. Season with salt and pepper to taste.

Adapted from Carmella Quattrociocchi, owner, Quattro's Game Farms, Pleasant Valley, New York

roasted wild turkey
with apple-sausage dressing

SERVES 6

Because wild turkeys are leaner, with denser flesh than their domesticated relatives, rub plenty of butter into the flesh before roasting, and then baste it often. Leaving the turkey uncovered in the refrigerator causes the skin to tighten and become very crisp when roasted. The bird roasts directly on the vegetables. The caramelized vegetables and cider then become a savory sauce. Because the apple-sausage mixture is not stuffed inside the bird, it's a dressing.

1 wild turkey, 6 to 8 pounds, giblets and neck removed, rinsed and patted dry

Coarse salt and freshly ground black pepper to taste

2 carrots, sliced

2 ribs celery, sliced

1 medium onion, sliced

1 small parsnip, chopped

1 bay leaf

6 cloves garlic

1 teaspoon black peppercorns

3 juniper berries

3½ tablespoons unsalted butter, at room temperature

2 cups sweet apple cider

Apple-Sausage Dressing (recipe follows)

2 tablespoons all-purpose flour

2 cups chicken stock

Roasted Wild Turkey with Apple-Sausage Dressing ❯

1. The day before roasting, season turkey inside and out with salt and pepper. Truss turkey with kitchen twine and refrigerate uncovered overnight.

2. When ready to cook, preheat oven to 500°F.

3. Put carrots, celery, onion, parsnip, bay leaf, garlic, peppercorns, and juniper berries in a heavy roasting pan large enough to hold turkey. Rub turkey all over with 1½ tablespoons of the butter, then place on top of vegetables.

4. Put turkey in oven, reduce heat to 325°F, and roast uncovered for 45 minutes, basting frequently with remaining 2 tablespoons of butter. Pour apple cider into pan and cover turkey loosely with aluminum foil. Continue roasting for 45 minutes more, basting every 15 minutes. While turkey roasts, prepare Apple-Sausage Dressing, and about 40 minutes before turkey is done roasting, put dressing in oven.

5. Uncover turkey and roast 10 to 15 minutes to brown skin further. Drumsticks should move easily in the sockets, and meat should measure 180° to 185°F when an instant-read thermometer is inserted into deepest part of thigh. Do not overcook. Transfer turkey to serving platter and cover with foil.

6. Pour off excess fat from roasting pan, leaving cider and pan drippings. Place pan over medium heat and stir in flour. Cook flour 3 to 4 minutes, stirring constantly. Pour in stock and bring to a boil. Lower heat and simmer until gravy is thickened, about 10 to 15 minutes. Season to taste with salt and pepper, then strain into a bowl, and serve with turkey and dressing.

apple-sausage dressing

¾ cup dark raisins

3 cups sweet apple cider

1 tablespoon unsalted butter

1 cup sliced celery

1 cup diced onion

1 pound fresh fennel-spiced pork sausage, casing removed

2 crisp, tart apples, such as Gala or Granny Smith, peeled and diced

4 fresh sage leaves, finely chopped, or 1 teaspoon dried sage leaves

4 cups cubes day-old sourdough bread

½ teaspoon coarse salt

¼ teaspoon freshly ground black pepper

1. Preheat oven to 325°F.

2. Combine raisins and apple cider in a small saucepan and bring to a boil. Remove from heat and set aside to plump.

3. Melt butter in a large ovenproof saucepan or Dutch oven over medium heat. Add celery and onion and cook until vegetables have softened, 5 to 7 minutes. Add sausage to vegetables. Sauté until meat is well browned, about 5 minutes, using a

TRAVELING TURKEYS

In the olden days, when big flocks of turkeys were "walked" into London — a journey often taking a week or more — the birds were protected from "cold feet" by being shod, their feet being tied up in sacking and provided with leather boots.

— E. G. Boulenger, *A Naturalist at the Dinner Table*, 1927

wooden spoon to break up meat into small pieces. Stir in apples and sage, and sauté 5 minutes.

4. Stir in bread cubes. Season with salt and pepper, then add cider and raisins. Bring liquid to a boil, cover, and bake for 25 minutes, stirring once halfway through. Remove cover, stir, and bake uncovered for 10 minutes more. Liquid should be absorbed and stuffing still moist.

Adapted from Michael Romano, chef-partner, Union Square Café, New York City

ariane's poached-roasted christmas turkey in the style of bresse

This 2-day turkey recipe is prepared in a favorite style of cooking capon in the poultry capital of France, Bresse. On the first day, the bird is poached in a rich broth. The following day, it's roasted. You are guaranteed a juicy bird with crackling brown skin, as well as a no-fuss dinner party. The black truffles under the skin elevate this turkey to a spectacular level.

6 quarts heavily seasoned chicken or duck stock (there should be slightly too much salt and pepper to be used as a soup)

3 medium carrots, cut in cubes

3 onions, thickly sliced

1 head of garlic, papery skin removed

1 cup rendered duck fat (see Note)

As many fresh black truffles as you can afford (1 to 3), thinly sliced

1 turkey, 10 to 12 pounds

1. Combine stock, carrots, onions, and garlic in a stockpot large enough to hold the turkey. Make sure it is filled no more than halfway. Bring to a boil over medium-high heat.
2. While stock heats, rinse turkey and, starting at the neck, carefully separate the skin from the breast and upper thighs with your fingers, taking care not to tear the skin. Rub duck fat all over between skin and flesh, and then distribute truffle slices. Truss turkey. (Trussing is not mandatory but makes it easier to handle the bird later.)
3. When stock is boiling, add turkey, turn heat down so stock simmers, and cover pot with a lid if the entire turkey is not submerged. Simmer 40 minutes, then remove pot from heat, and let it slowly cool to room temperature, up to 4 hours. Store in a cool spot (about 40°F) outside during the night (a garage, deck, or balcony), or refrigerate.
4. The next day, before your guests arrive, carefully take bird out of pot, place it on a rack in a roasting pan, and preheat oven to 475°F. Put turkey in the oven, then 30 minutes later turn oven off, leaving the bird inside.
5. When you are ready to eat the main course, the bird will be perfectly cooked and nicely rested. The leftover stock can be strained and used as a wonderful base for soups. (The turkey and vegetables will have reduced the saltiness of the stock, but taste before seasoning further.)

NOTE:
Use duck fat that you have rendered and saved in the freezer (it keeps up to 6 months), or order from D'Artagnan or from a local purveyor of fine meats and poultry.

The distinctive flavour of grouse is not easily abated by other subtleties, so that, however you dress your bird, whether as soup or braise or pie, . . . and short of violence with a clove of garlic or a curry that would make coke palatable, it is impossible to cover it.

— Maj. Hugh Pollard,
The Sportsman's Cookery Book, 1926

The meat of the woodcock is the only terrestrial food of the Gods.

— Alexandre Dumas,
quoting the cook Elzéar Blaze

grouse and woodcock

GEORGE: Speak to serious bird hunters about grouse and they practically become ecstatic even thinking about the subject. The bird, indigenous to the Scottish moors, the famous sandy lands covered with sedges, heather, and bracken, is the focus of the "Glorious Twelfth." The twelfth of August is the annual opening of the grouse-shooting season, when traditionally there is a race among British hunters and gourmets to be the first to shoot and eat a grouse of the season. France's Beaujolais Nouveau race pales in comparison to the energy and money hunters expend in this adventure.

Grouse, which are only available as wild birds, never farm-raised, have a distinctive resin flavor derived from a unique diet of young heather sprigs. An examination of the craw yields nothing but tiny purple flowers. To improve the wild bird's habitats, controlled burns are conducted across Scotland to facilitate the growth of new heather, since older shrubs don't flower as frequently. This in turn has provided more feed, resulting in more grouse on the Scottish Highlands than there were at the turn of the century. Unfortunately, attempts to introduce grouse elsewhere in Europe and even America have failed.

Grouse average 10 to 12 ounces dressed weight. They are an acquired taste. But like most things exotic or unique, they're well worth trying. Potatoes or root vegetables are frequently served as an accompaniment to the bird.

ARIANE: There are two small birds that are protected by law in France. One is woodcock, the other is the ortolan. Although they are rarely if ever available in the United States, we discuss them here simply because of their importance to French game con-

noisseurs. In France as well as in the United States, woodcock may be hunted and eaten, but not sold. Although it is a favorite of gourmets, emotions don't run as high about hunting this small woodland bird as they do about ortolans.

In the United States, the bird goes by several names, including bog sucker, mud bat, timberdoodle, Labrador twister, American woodcock, and *Scolopax minor*. In France its scientific name is *Scolopax rusticola*.

Woodcocks migrate from the Nordic countries, or eastern North America, to warmer climates as winter approaches. Characteristically, their flight pattern is a nocturnal zigzag, making them a hard bird to hunt. The distinctive long bill, the tip of which stays open while the rest of the beak is closed, is useful for catching earthworms, its principal diet. Among the bird's russet plumage is a feather in the wing joint that is highly sought after by European and Asian painters because it is supple and strong, yet very fine.

These fat, juicy birds weigh about 6 to 8 ounces dressed. Their preparation should be very simple: roasted to a pale rose color in a ramekin with a piece of bacon to help it brown; or done on a spit, where the juices can drop onto a thick slice of farmer's bread, deliciously flavoring it. The giblets are sautéed, mixed with a drop of Armagnac and an ounce of foie gras, then spread on the toast.

The very name ortolan is synonymous with one of the greatest food delicacies and ritualized culinary feasts in France.

This small bunting, or songbird, weighs no more than an ounce and a quarter. Although the birds are technically not endangered, since 1979 they have been protected by a law that forbids hunting, selling, or eating them. The violation carries a fine of from $85 upward. Until 1999, the exception to the rule was in the Landes region of Gascony, where they could be captured alive in nets and eaten, but not sold. Actually, it doesn't matter what the law says. Gascons will eat ortolans as long as they migrate south to North Africa every fall. It's part of our patrimony. Try to stop the locals and you'll have a riot on your hands.

Before being eaten, the little birds are fattened up on millet to three times their normal weight. Then they drink a fatal drop of Armagnac. They're delicately plucked, and prepared extremely simply: just roasted in a small earthenware ramekin for 5 to 7 minutes in a very hot oven.

∧ Ortolan, a great delicacy in France

Connoisseurs of fine food savor the birds whole, served hot. Each diner's head and face are covered by a large white napkin, in gustatory isolation and the grandest contemplation. It's part of the mystique. In Gascony we say there are three reasons for the napkin. One, to capture the aroma. Two, to cover an open mouth while eating a large and very hot mouthful. Three, to hide yourself from God while eating such a small and succulent bird. *Larousse Gastronomique* says that a priest-friend of the nineteenth-century gastronome Brillat-Savarin started the practice. Who knows? The ritual heightens the expectation and the experience.

A FRIEND IN DEED

ARIANE: Roger "Zizou" Duffour is many things to many people. He is the founder of the Gascon roundtable where local chefs come together to advance local products; he is one of the best chefs in the region; he's a fierce hunter; and he is my daughter Alix's godfather. Those last two categories merged a few years ago, when Alix was seven.

It was the day of Zizou's annual ortolan and woodcock ritual. The foods, the wines and Armagnac, the camaraderie, are all legendary, and I was enthusiastically anticipating the meal. Sadly, Alix had a serious horseback riding accident that afternoon, and was taken to the closest hospital, in Mont de Marsan. Instead of enjoying a feast, we both spent the night in the hospital room.

The next morning, as I nervously waited while Alix had surgery, in walked Zizou with packets of all the foods I'd missed the previous night. Within minutes, the plates of insipid food on the hospital tray were scraped, rinsed, and filled with Zizou's treats. As Alix began to wake up, I gave her little bites of ortolan, while savoring every morsel of the meal myself. All that remained was the long beak of the woodcock.

When the doctor came in to check on his patient, he kept staring at the plate. Everyone in the region knows what a woodcock's beak looks like. Finally I said: "You have really good food in this hospital." To which the doctor replied that he could certify that Alix would be back on her feet, good as new, if we could find him that same kind of hospital food.

roasted scottish grouse
with braised savoy cabbage and chanterelles

SERVES 6

Hail the Glorious Twelfth — the August day when grouse season begins in Scotland. Should you be lucky enough to have a brace or two of these fat little birds, this classic dish will do them and your appetite justice. To drink, a hearty red, like a Madiran, would be ideal.

1 quart milk

20 juniper berries, crushed

6 black peppercorns

4 bay leaves

9 sprigs thyme

1 sprig rosemary

1 tablespoon coarse salt

6 grouse, 1 pound each, cleaned, neck and giblets removed, rinsed and patted dry

1 teaspoon crushed garlic

3 tablespoons extra-virgin olive oil

Salt and freshly ground black pepper to taste

6 slices bacon

½ carrot, sliced

½ onion, sliced

1 rib celery, sliced

3 shallots, sliced

2 cups good red wine, such as Madiran or Syrah

2 cups game bird or chicken stock

Braised Savoy Cabbage and Chanterelles (recipe follows)

2 tablespoons unsalted butter, at room temperature

1. Combine milk, 12 of the juniper berries, the peppercorns, 3 of the bay leaves, 5 sprigs of the thyme, the rosemary, and the coarse salt in a medium pot and bring to a boil over high heat. Reduce heat and simmer for 5 minutes, remove from heat, and let infuse for 30 minutes. Strain, refrigerate until cool, then add grouse and marinate overnight.

2. Preheat oven to 450°F.

3. Remove leaves from the remaining 4 thyme sprigs. Break remaining bay leaf into 6 pieces. Pat grouse dry with paper towels, and season each bird inside with some of the garlic, thyme leaves, the remaining 9 juniper berries, and crumbled bay leaf.

4. Brush birds lightly with olive oil, using about 1 tablespoon. Season with salt and pepper. Wrap each bird with a slice of bacon and tie closed with kitchen string. Place grouse in a roasting pan and roast in oven for 10 minutes. Remove birds from pan and let rest for 5 minutes. Discard bacon, remove string, and debone birds completely. Cover breast and leg meat lightly with foil and set aside.

5. Chop up carcass bones. Heat the remaining 2 tablespoons of oil in a large deep skillet over high heat. Add bones and brown evenly, shaking and turning often. Lower heat and add carrot, onion, celery, and shallots. Cover and sweat for 5 minutes, then deglaze pan with red wine, stirring to incorporate any browned bits.

Stir in stock and reduce liquid over medium-high heat down to 1¾ cups. Strain and reserve.

6. Prepare Braised Savoy Cabbage and Chanterelles. *Recipe may be done ahead to this point. If more than 2 hours ahead, refrigerate, then bring back to room temperature before continuing.*

7. Reheat grouse, cabbage, and chanterelles in a low-temperature oven. Bring grouse sauce to a simmer, remove from heat, and whisk in butter. Taste to adjust seasonings.

8. Arrange cabbage in the center of 6 warmed dinner plates. Place grouse on top with chanterelles around. Spoon sauce over grouse and serve.

braised savoy cabbage and chanterelles

2 pounds Savoy cabbage, outer leaves removed, cored and julienned

2 ounces bacon, cut into thin strips

5 tablespoons unsalted butter

1 cup chicken stock

Salt and freshly ground black pepper to taste

1 pound chanterelles

1 tablespoon olive oil

2 shallots, finely chopped

1 sprig thyme

1. Bring a pot of salted water to a boil, add cabbage, and blanch for 2 minutes. Drain, then shock cabbage in ice water to stop cooking. When cabbage is cool, drain well. Heat a large skillet over medium heat. Add cabbage, bacon, 4 tablespoons of the butter, and ½ cup of the chicken

stock. Bring liquid to a boil, then reduce heat and braise until almost all of the liquid has evaporated and cabbage is glazed. Season with salt and pepper, remove from heat, and reserve.

2. Wash chanterelles 3 times in cool water to remove all grit and dirt. Blot until very dry on paper towels. Set aside.

3. Heat oil and the remaining tablespoon of butter in a skillet over medium heat. Add shallots, cover, and sweat for 1 minute. Add chanterelles, thyme, salt, and pepper, and sauté until wilted. Pour in the remaining ½ cup stock and cook until liquid is reduced and syrupy. Remove from heat and set aside. When ready to serve, reheat gently.

Adapted from Daniel Boulud, chef-owner, Restaurant Daniel and Café Boulud, and co-owner, Payard Pâtisserie & Bistro, New York City

A PASSIONATE GROUSE LOVER'S CHALLENGE

A couple of years ago, John Bain and his Bain of Tarves (page 138) team rose to a challenge made by Daniel Boulud, of Restaurant Daniel in New York City. The dare: to provide 12 of the new season's grouse to the restaurant on the same day as the season opened, August 12.

While the average first-day hunt yields fewer than 50 birds, John and his men had only 2 hours to bag all of the grouse in the bet, then send them flying. This they did, making a dash to meet a waiting British Airways direct flight from Glasgow to New York. Upon arrival at Kennedy Airport, the birds were quickly shuttled across town to the waiting arms and pans of chef Boulud.

grilled grouse
with warm potato salad

SERVES 4

For those who like their game birds simple and direct, these grouse are delicious right off the grill. Grilling showcases the distinctive flavor of the birds. Serve with crusty bread, Warm Potato Salad, and a green salad. What else could you need . . . except a good bottle of red wine.

Warm Potato Salad

4 grouse, 1 pound each, neck and giblets removed, rinsed and patted dry

Grapeseed or canola oil

Salt and freshly ground black pepper to taste

1 teaspoon dried thyme

1. Prepare Warm Potato Salad.
2. Spatchcock the grouse by removing backbone and wing tips, then spreading bird out, skin side up, and pressing on breastbone to flatten.
3. Light a gas or charcoal grill. Make sure grouse are flat. Brush liberally with oil and season with salt, pepper, and thyme. When grill is medium hot, add grouse and cook until nicely browned and cooked through, 10 to 12 minutes, turning once. Baste often with oil, and move away from fire if skin is burning. Remove from heat, tent lightly with aluminum foil, and let stand for a couple of minutes before serving with Warm Potato Salad.

warm potato salad

2 pounds red potatoes

Coarse salt

3 slices bacon, cut into thin strips, cooked crisp, cooled, and crumbled (optional)

¼ cup dry white wine

2 teaspoons Dijon mustard

2 teaspoons minced garlic

3 tablespoons minced flat-leaf parsley

3 tablespoons lemon juice

6 to 8 tablespoons mild olive oil

Salt and freshly ground black pepper to taste

1. Place potatoes in a pot, cover with cold water, add a generous sprinkle of salt, and bring to a boil. Cook until potatoes are almost tender when pierced with a knife. Drain, cover pot with a towel, and let cool. The potatoes will finish cooking. When cool enough to handle, peel, cut into medium-size cubes, and put in a bowl. Stir in bacon and wine.
2. Combine mustard, garlic, parsley, and lemon juice in a bowl. Slowly whisk in oil to form an emulsion. Pour over potatoes, tossing to blend wine into sauce and cover potatoes. Season with salt and pepper, and serve.

COOKING WOODCOCKS

Some Epicures like the bird very much underdone, and direct that a Woodcock should just be introduced to the Cook, for her to shew it to the Fire, and then send it up to Table.

—Thomas Love Peacock, 1785–1866,
British novelist and poet

woodcock à la ficelle

SERVES 6 AS A MAIN COURSE

A classic recipe that assumes you have a fireplace with a mantel . . . or at least you can visit someone who does have one. Next, you'll need *ficelle,* or strong string, with which to tie the birds and hang them in front of the hot fire. The string is twisted so that it is constantly turning in front of the fire. Bring woodcock to true game lovers and you'll have several invitations to follow.

6 woodcocks, wing tips folded under, rinsed and patted dry

Salt and freshly ground black pepper to taste

2 tablespoons rendered duck fat

1 small lobe Grade B foie gras (see page 255)

6 slices country bread, about ¾ inch thick

½ cup Armagnac

2 tablespoons duck and veal demi-glace (see page 33)

1 cup tawny port

1 tablespoon unsalted butter (optional)

1. Get a steady hot fire going in your fireplace.
2. Season woodcocks with salt and pepper. Tie a piece of butcher's twine around the neck of each woodcock and attach it to a hook on the fireplace mantel, so that the woodcocks are hanging slightly above and in front of the hot fire. Twist string and let it unroll so that birds are constantly turning.
3. Place a fireproof tray greased with duck fat directly below birds. Baste often with drippings, and continue to keep birds turning. Cook until birds are richly browned, about 20 minutes. Remove woodcocks from twine and cut in half. Scoop out the birds' entrails and reserve; keep the woodcock halves warm in a pan on the side of the fireplace.
4. Discard gizzards and mash rest of reserved giblets and entrails with foie gras until well blended. Grill slices of bread on the drip tray on top of the fire (or put drippings in a large skillet and grill on stovetop), then spread them with foie gras mixture. Cut them in half, place on a serving plate, and keep warm.
5. On top of stove, pour Armagnac on woodcock and carefully ignite. Add demi-glace and port, and reduce liquid by half. Whisk in butter, if desired, and season with salt and pepper. Place each half woodcock on a foie gras–giblet canapé, spoon over sauce, and serve.

Adapted from Roger "Zizou" Duffour, founding chef-owner of Le Relais de l'Armagnac, Luppé-Violles, Gascony

braised woodcock pierre l'enfant

SERVES 4 AS AN APPETIZER

A simple recipe for this juicy king of game birds. Savor with a fine bottle of Puligny-Montrachet or other robust white wine.

4 woodcocks, giblets removed, wing tips folded under

Salt and freshly ground black pepper to taste

½ cup herb-seasoned sage-and-onion stuffing cubes, plus a small amount of stock or water, to moisten

4 tablespoons unsalted butter

1 tablespoon olive oil

1 cup dry white wine

2 chicken bouillon cubes

2 tablespoons minced flat-leaf parsley

1 small clove garlic, thinly sliced

1 teaspoon sweet paprika

1 to 2 teaspoons lemon juice

Dash *each* Worcestershire sauce and Tabasco, or to taste

4 slices whole wheat bread, crusts removed

1. Preheat oven to 350°F.

2. Rinse woodcocks, blot dry, and season inside and out with salt and pepper. Divide stuffing among birds and truss cavity. Heat 2 tablespoons of the butter and the oil in a heavy casserole over medium-

THE STORY OF WOODCOCK PIERRE L'ENFANT

"I had an outstanding woodcock last night, Bob."

"Yeah, I gather there are quite a few off Route 544 outside Chestertown. Or did you shoot it in the marshes south of Mount Vernon? Anyway, how did you cook it?" Bob asked.

"Actually, I got it outside the main entrance of COMSAT Corporation at 950 L'Enfant Place, in downtown Washington, D.C."

"That's an interesting shot. How did you manage it next to all those taxis?"

"It's a long story. I had just finished lunch and was ambling back with a colleague, when I spotted something brown and fluffy lying on the ground near the main entrance to COMSAT. From a distance the bird appeared to be a chukar or partridge, but I couldn't imagine how a game bird would collapse in the middle of the plaza. On closer inspection, it turned out to be a woodcock. The bird was cold and in near perfect condition, with no external wounds. It was colored a rich mottled brown, with a six-inch black bill, and long, delicate legs. Its neck was clearly broken.

"My friend grimaced when I picked it up. I explained that the bird had probably lost its bearings and hit a large window in the plaza. I told him I was going to have it for dinner. He was flabbergasted!

"I had a meeting to get to and not much time, so I popped the bird in a 'For Your Eyes Only' interoffice envelope, and stuck it in my briefcase. That night I hung the bird for a couple more days to enhance its flavor. My two teenage boys were incredulous. Both adamantly refused to taste my concoction. But I was not going to be diverted from preparing the ultimate Food of the Gods: Woodcock Pierre L'Enfant!

"I plucked the bird, turned the oven to 350°F, and prepared myself for the denouement. I seldom disclose recipes, and even more rarely commit them to paper. However, what followed was so delicious that I have been persuaded to grudgingly part with the recipe.

"In the English bible of cookbooks, Mrs. Beeton describes the very first action to be taken to cook a pheasant (or any game bird): 'First Catch Your Pheasant.' You will note Mrs. Beeton used the word 'catch' — not shoot, throttle, or dispatch. Although I had 'caught' my woodcock under rather questionable circumstances, nevertheless, it was, in my judgment, still 'caught.'"

—As told by Stephen Day

high heat. Add woodcocks and brown lightly on all sides. Season liberally with salt and pepper. Pour in wine, add bouillon cubes, parsley, garlic, paprika, lemon juice, Worcestershire sauce, and Tabasco, and stir to blend. Place in oven and bake until tender, about 20 minutes.

3. Meanwhile, melt remaining 2 tablespoons butter, brush over both sides of bread, and sauté until golden on both sides. Keep warm.

4. Serve woodcocks on toast, and pour sauce liberally over birds and bread.

Adapted from Stephen Day, avid hunter, bon vivant, and cook, Washington, D.C.

roasted woodcock with pancetta, armagnac, and cream

SERVES 4 AS A MAIN COURSE

A glorious entrée to a true game lover's feast. Fat roasted woodcocks are accompanied by a pair of game croutons, small toasts spread with the birds' chopped giblets, and a luxurious Armagnac and foie gras sauce. What a way to go! Woodcocks are traditionally served with their heads on. Here we follow that custom.

4 woodcocks

Salt and freshly ground black pepper to taste

12 slices French bread

1 Grade B foie gras, about 1 pound (see page 255), cut into ½-inch cubes

1 cup finely chopped onion

8 thin slices pancetta, finely chopped

½ cup Armagnac

1 cup heavy cream

1 cup duck and veal demi-glace (see page 33)

1. Preheat oven to 450°F.

2. If necessary, pluck birds and remove entrails (leave head on). Discard gizzards, set remaining giblets and entrails aside. Rinse birds and blot dry. Season woodcocks inside and out with salt and pepper, and stuff cavity of each with 1 slice of bread and a few cubes of foie gras. Truss cavity shut using the bird's beak. Set aside.

3. Heat a heavy skillet until hot over high heat. Add the remaining foie gras, ½ cup of the onion, and the pancetta to pan, and quickly sauté just until onions are lightly colored, about 2 minutes. Remove mixture from pan with a slotted spoon and reserve. Still over heat, add reserved giblets and entrails, and remaining ½ cup of onion, stirring until onions soften and a paste forms. Season with salt and pepper. Keep warm. Toast remaining 8 slices of bread, and spread with mixture.

4. Heat same skillet, and brown birds briefly on top of stove, then bake in oven for 7 to 8 minutes. Remove, transfer to a plate, untruss, tent with aluminum foil, and let rest. Return reserved foie gras, onion, and pancetta mixture to pan. Pour in Armagnac, scraping up any browned cooking bits, then add cream, demi-glace, and salt and pepper. Bring to a boil and cook until thickened. Serve 1 woodcock on each plate, garnished with 2 croutons.

Adapted from Kirk Avondoglio, executive chef–owner, Perona Farms, Andover, New Jersey

game meats 2

working with game meats

Fresh game meat is readily available in markets, butcher shops, and specialty stores. Whether you are buying venison, rabbit, hare, boar, or buffalo, the following guidelines apply.

BUYING AND STORING

Vacuum-packed meats can safely be refrigerated for up to 2 weeks. Opened packages or custom cuts of meat should be used within 4 or 5 days. You can now preorder any fresh meat you want from your butcher or by mail order 24 hours ahead. If there is *really* no fresh alternative, buy commercially frozen meat; you can store it in your freezer for up to 1 year. Home freezing is far less effective than commercial freezing at quickly lowering the temperature, so meat that has been frozen at home should be used within 3 to 4 months.

Opened packages of raw meat should be refrigerated on a covered plate — not in a plastic bag — to prevent the meat from sweating; or tightly wrap the meat in plastic wrap. When defrosting meats, do so slowly, in the refrigerator, so moisture and flavor loss are minimized. Make sure that the meat's juices do not drip on other foods.

Rabbit or hare keeps 4 to 5 days in its sealed package in the refrigerator. Once the package is opened, use it within 2 to 3 days.

COOKING AND SERVING

Before panfrying or grilling game meats, remove any fat, silver skin, or sinew from the meat. Before cooking a rabbit or hare, rinse, blot dry, and remove kidneys, liver, and fat.

❮ Rack of Venison Rubbed with Szechuan Pepper
with Spicy Fruit Chutney (page 236)

Remember, game meats are lean and low in fat. There are two ways of cooking such meats: quickly on high heat for tender cuts, or slowly over low heat in a braising liquid for tougher pieces. For maximum flavor and tenderness, serve steaks, medallions, and cutlets rare or medium rare at an internal temperature of no more than 125° to 130°F. An instant-read thermometer is an invaluable tool to determine doneness. Tender cuts of lean meats should be cooked at the last minute, just before you are ready to serve them. Everything else for the meal should be prepared before these tender cuts are cooked. After cooking, always let meat rest to allow juices to disperse evenly, then slice across the grain. Unless the meat is slowly braised or stewed, it won't reheat well.

SOME BROAD GUIDELINES FOR COOKING BOAR, BUFFALO, VENISON, AND OSTRICH

Steaks and medallions 1 to 1¼ inches thick: Blot dry. Brush pan or meat with a little oil. Heat pan to very hot. Sauté or grill them for 1½ to 2 minutes on each side over high heat for rare, or 2 to 2½ minutes for medium rare. Let stand 2 minutes before serving.

Stir-fry strips about ¼ inch thick: Add a little oil to skillet or wok. Heat pan to very hot. Stir-fry for 30 seconds on high heat.

Kebabs with ¾-inch to 1-inch cubes: Brush meat with oil. Panfry, barbecue, or grill for 1½ to 2 minutes on each side on high for rare, or 2 to 2½ minutes for medium rare.

Roasts and racks about 1 to 2 pounds, or 4- or 8-rib racks: Blot dry. Brush meat or pan with oil. Sear over high heat, then place in preheated 425°F oven for 3½ minutes for every ½ inch of thickness for rare, and 4½ minutes for medium rare. Let rest 5 to 10 minutes before serving.

Stews and pot roasts: Use meat from the shoulder, neck, or shank part of the hind leg. Blot dry. Sear meat in a little oil. Don't crowd. Add liquid and simmer very slowly until tender.

For basic information on cooking and cutting up rabbit or hare, see the introduction to the chapter "Rabbit and Hare."

wild boar

ARIANE: Remember Astérix and Obélix, those French cartoon characters depicting warriors in early Gaul? The lovable pair give us real clues about how man survived in early Gallo-Roman times. Every tale begins with a wild boar hunt and ends with a feast. To this day the mere mention of wild boar invariably evokes images of rustic hunts, colorful pageantry, and lusty banquets.

GEORGE: Pageantry? Mention boar hunting in Texas and it's more like a bunch of wild guys running around trying to save their hides while bagging one of these low-slung, hairy, muscular beasts with enormous upcurved tusks. With a body weight of between 100 and 400 pounds, and standing 3 to 4 feet high at the shoulder, they can be pretty mean when challenged. Truth is, boar catching is dangerous, especially when you're trying to make a living at selling the meat. The animals D'Artagnan sells come from South Texas and are definitely free-range, because they are wild. They roam on vast parcels of land and feed on wild greens, acorns, roots, and other vegetation. What a wild boar eats can dramatically affect how it tastes.

ARIANE: The very best tasting boars in the world come from Corsica, where they forage on chestnuts and acorns.

GEORGE: That's French turf, and people are used to full-flavored meats there. Getting people to try boar in the States is a different thing. It's a pity, because the meat is actually quite sweet and mild, and just a little nutty.

Those Texas boars are captured in the field by some pretty brave trappers, taken briefly to pens where they receive an identification tag, and then collected by trucks that take them to USDA-approved processing facilities. Each animal is tested for trichinosis (although there hasn't been a case reported for more than three decades), *E. coli,* and other harmful bacteria. They are free of steroids, growth hormones, and antibiotics.

The way these boars live preserves their distinct character. The idea of holding a boar in a pen to fatten him up is ludicrous. It is worth saying, however, that since these are really wild beasts, there can be big differences in taste and color from one animal to the next. Look for darker meat to be more flavorful. But don't try cooking an old boar; it will be inedible. The best meat comes from smaller animals that are less than a year old. Because boars are wild, they are muscular and lean. To retain the juiciness and flavor, they need to be cooked until still barely pink, an internal temperature of 125° to 130°F. Chops and loins can be grilled or broiled; roast or braise the leg; and slowly cook stew meat in a liquid

Another truth is that what is called wild boar in the United States, especially the Texas range wild boar, is a hybrid of razorback pigs, the feral offspring of domestic pigs brought from Europe, and Russian wild boars, brought to Texas for hunting. It is not to be confused with the javelina, or peccary, which is a small piglike animal with sharp tusks and porklike flesh native to the Americas, and an entirely different species. Javelinas are found in South and Central America and in the southwestern United States.

grilled creole wild boar tenderloins

with garlic-cheddar grits

SERVES 6

Here's an easy dish that will reward you with plenty of spice. Sear the boar either on a grill or in a cast iron skillet. Just don't overcook the lean meat. Serve it with creamy grits and the power-packing sauce. A rich ale or stout, or a young Rhone red, will round out the menu.

Garlic-Cheddar Grits (recipe follows)

2½ to 3 pounds wild boar tenderloin, well trimmed and silver skin removed, cut crosswise into 1½-inch-thick slices

3 tablespoons olive oil

3 medium onions, sliced in half moons

1 teaspoon minced garlic

½ teaspoon *each* dried thyme, dried basil, dried oregano, and dry mustard

¼ teaspoon cayenne

2 medium green bell peppers, cored, seeded, and julienned

KNOW YOUR OILS

When you are searing meat, as in this recipe, peanut oil is one of the best choices because it has the highest flame point. Next best options include canola oil, corn oil, and duck fat. Butter and delicate nut oils are likely to burn before the food is properly cooked.

2 medium red bell peppers, cored, seeded, and julienned

2 medium tomatoes, cut in wedges, or 1 cup canned diced tomatoes, drained

1¼ cups duck and veal demi-glace (see page 33)

4 tablespoons unsalted butter

Coarse salt and freshly ground black pepper to taste

2 to 3 tablespoons peanut oil

1. Prepare Garlic-Cheddar Grits.

2. Place pieces of boar between 2 layers of plastic wrap and gently pound to ½ inch thick.

3. In a large skillet, heat olive oil over medium-high heat. Sauté onions until browned. Add garlic and spices and cook 5 minutes longer. Add green and red peppers, cooking until tender. Add tomatoes, demi-glace, and butter. Season with salt and pepper, plus additional cayenne if desired, and keep warm.

4. Heat a grill (or a cast iron skillet) until hot. Brush tenderloin pieces with peanut oil, season with salt and pepper, and grill until done, 3 to 4 minutes, turning once. Remove and keep warm.

5. Place 2 pieces of wild boar on each plate and cover with sauce. Place a serving of grits next to meat.

garlic-cheddar grits

4 cups milk

1 cup stone-ground grits

3 tablespoons unsalted butter, plus butter to grease baking dish

2 teaspoons finely chopped garlic

2 cups grated sharp white Cheddar cheese

2 eggs, beaten

Coarse salt and white pepper to taste

1. Bring milk to a boil in a heavy saucepan. Slowly add grits while stirring to avoid lumps. Reduce heat to low and cook until thick and creamy, about 30 minutes, stirring frequently. If mixture becomes too tight before the end of the cooking time, add as much water as necessary in order to cook for a full 30 minutes.

2. Preheat oven to 350°F. Grease a 2½-quart baking dish.

3. While grits are cooking, melt 1 tablespoon of the butter in a small skillet over medium-low heat. Add garlic and sauté until soft, 1 to 1½ minutes. Add garlic, along with cheese, eggs, and the remaining 2 tablespoons butter, to cooked grits. Stir thoroughly, season with salt and pepper, and pour into baking dish. Bake until brown and crusty around the edges, approximately 30 to 35 minutes. Remove from oven and serve.

Adapted from Susan McCreight Lindeborg, chef, Morrison-Clark Inn, Washington, D.C.

yucatecan boar pot pie with jalapeño-corn crust

SERVES 4

A tongue-tingling blend of American — North, Central, and South — ingredients. Luscious and pleasing, these pot pies can be made a couple of hours ahead and heated when needed. Or prepare the stew and dough up to 2 days in advance.

They're cause for a fiesta. Celebrate the taste by serving a bold Mexican beer.

This recipe calls for tomatillos, a small green fruit covered with a tissue-thin husk. They are a common ingredient in Mexican cuisine. Although related to tomatoes, they taste more citrusy and acidic. Tomatillos never turn red. Generally, they are used while still green and firm. Yuca, also known as cassava or manioc, is a large brown root popular in Latin and Caribbean cuisines. When its thick skin is removed, the flesh is pale and fibrous. It is used to thicken stews, as here, or cut into wedges, boiled, drained, and deep-fried.

FOR THE BOAR STEW:

1 pound well-trimmed boneless boar stew meat from the shoulder, silver skin removed

Coarse salt and freshly ground black pepper to taste

2 tablespoons vegetable oil

1 cup *each* diced onions and diced, seeded poblano chilies

¼ to ⅓ cup minced garlic

2 cups peeled and diced yuca (cassava)

2 cups quartered tomatillos

2 cups orange juice

2 (12-ounce) bottles dark Mexican beer

1 teaspoon ground cumin, lightly toasted

½ cup chopped cilantro

FOR THE CRUST:

1¼ to 1½ cups all-purpose flour, plus additional flour for rolling dough

1 cup cornmeal

¼ cup sugar

1 tablespoon coarse salt, or 2 teaspoons
table salt

1 tablespoon chili powder

1 teaspoon baking powder

½ teaspoon baking soda

¾ cup (1½ sticks) unsalted butter

2 eggs

½ cup *each* corn kernels and grated Cheddar
or Monterey Jack cheese

1 tablespoon *each* minced seeded jalapeños
and minced red bell pepper

TO FINISH:

2 tablespoons milk

Sour cream, tomato salsa, and sprigs of
cilantro, to garnish

1. MAKE THE BOAR STEW: Cut the meat
into 1-inch cubes and blot dry. Season
with salt and pepper. Heat oil in a large
heavy pot with a tight-fitting lid over high
heat. Add boar and sear, turning to brown
all sides. Do not crowd or meat will steam.
Transfer meat with tongs or slotted spoon
to a bowl. Add onions and chilies to pot,
and cook over medium-high heat until
onions are caramelized and golden brown,
about 6 to 8 minutes, stirring frequently.
Add garlic and cook 2 minutes longer.
Stir in yuca, tomatillos, orange juice, beer,
cumin, and browned meat, and bring to
a boil.

2. Turn heat down so liquid simmers, and
cover pot. Cook slowly for 2 hours, stir-
ring and occasionally skimming off fat.
Stew may be made 2 days ahead to this point.
Cover and refrigerate. Reheat before continuing.
Add cilantro during the last 10 minutes.

Stew should be thick. Add a little water if
it gets too dry.

3. WHILE MEAT SIMMERS, MAKE
CRUSTS: Sift 1¼ cups of the flour with
remaining dry ingredients into a medium
bowl. Cream butter and eggs together in a
food processor. Add corn, cheese, and
peppers, and pulse just to blend. Add dry
ingredients and process just until well
blended, adding more flour if mixture is
very moist. It should be somewhat sticky.
Gather dough into a ball, cover with plastic wrap, and refrigerate for 20 minutes.
Dough may be made 1 to 2 days ahead of time,
then covered and refrigerated.

4. Preheat oven to 375°F. Divide hot stew
among 4 large ovenproof soup bowls.

5. Liberally dust a large workspace with
flour. Roll out dough to a thickness of ¼
inch. Cut out circles just large enough to
come to the edges of the bowls of stew.
Carefully top each bowl with a disk of
crust. Brush with milk and bake until gold-
en brown, 20 minutes. Top each pie with
a dollop of sour cream and some salsa,
and garnish with a few sprigs of cilantro.

Adapted from Joey Altman, chef-owner, Wild Hare Restaurant
and Bay Café Television Show, Menlo Park, California

drunken boar

SERVES 4

We've all known a few of the two-legged
species, but once boar of the four-legged
variety soaks in this martini-inspired
marinade, the meat of this beast is tamed,
tender, and flavorful. Mirin is a golden-
colored, sweetened Japanese rice wine
used exclusively for cooking. You can use

sherry as a substitute. For a beverage, try a Thai beer or, as George suggests, a martini.

⅔ cup mirin (available at Asian groceries and some supermarkets)

⅓ cup gin

12 juniper berries, bruised

2 teaspoons Chinese five-spice powder

1½ pounds lean boar, cut from leg, silver skin and fat removed, cut into ¾-inch-wide stir-fry strips

1 tablespoon peanut oil

1 medium onion, thinly sliced

½ pound shiitake mushrooms, wiped clean, stems removed, and cut into thick slices

¼ cup duck and veal demi-glace (see page 33)

1 cup coconut milk

1 tablespoon pomegranate molasses (available at specialty food stores)

1 (10-ounce) package wide rice noodles, cooked according to package directions and drained

Coarse salt and freshly ground black pepper to taste

¼ cup torn cilantro or basil leaves

1. Combine mirin, gin, juniper berries, and five-spice powder in a resealable plastic bag or bowl. Add boar, turn to coat, seal or cover, and refrigerate for at least 8 hours, or up to 2 days.
2. Lift meat from marinade and blot dry on paper towels. Strain and reserve marinade.
3. Heat a wok over high heat. Add about ½ tablespoon of the oil and rotate pan to cover with it. When oil is almost smoking, slowly add pieces of boar so that meat quickly browns rather than steams, 4 to 5 minutes, stirring often. Remove meat from wok with tongs or a slotted spoon and set aside.
4. Add remaining ½ tablespoon of oil and onion. Stir-fry until onion is light brown, 2 to 3 minutes, separating slices into rings. Add shiitake mushrooms and cook until wilted.
5. Pour marinade along with demi-glace into wok and bring to a boil. Cook until reduced by half, then stir in coconut milk and pomegranate molasses. Stir in meat and rice noodles, season with salt and pepper, and simmer until heated through. Sprinkle with cilantro and serve.

civet of wild boar

SERVES 4

At first glance this looks like a traditional stew in which boar meat is marinated and then slowly simmered with an abundance of seasonings until meltingly tender. But a jalapeño here and some paprika there impart a distinctive touch. This is a contemporary *civet* (traditionally, a stew that is thickened with the animal's blood). Here the sauce is thickened with bitter chocolate. Purists may use ½ cup blood instead of chocolate. Serve over polenta, spaetzle, or broad noodles. Pour a glass or two of a hearty Italian Barolo or French Burgundy.

Four pounds of boar shoulder may sound like a lot of meat for 4 servings. But once you remove the sinew, silver skin, and fat from the shoulder, you will end up with not much more than 2 or 2½ pounds of cubes.

3½ to 4 pounds wild boar shoulder, well
    trimmed and silver skin removed, cut into
    1-inch cubes

3 ribs celery, coarsely chopped

1 *each* onion and carrot, coarsely chopped

1 jalapeño, seeded and coarsely chopped

1 head garlic, cut crosswise in half

2 (750-ml) bottles hearty red wine

1 cup red wine vinegar

1 bouquet garni: ½ cup juniper berries,
    ⅓ cup black peppercorns, 5 whole cloves,
    2 bay leaves, and 2 sprigs rosemary, tied in
    cheesecloth

Peanut oil or corn oil for sautéing

2 tablespoons *each* all-purpose flour, tomato
    paste, and paprika

2 cups veal or chicken stock

STEVE TUMLINSON: HOG TRAPPER FOR SOUTHERN WILD GAME

"Hog trapping's no easy thing," says Steve Tumlinson, a wild boar supplier for Southern Wild Game, a wild game distributor headquartered in Devine, Texas. But it's a good, honest day's work that allows lots of free time to be with his wife, Joan.

"Waste of any kind is bad, especially when there are a lot of hungry people out there," says Tumlinson, of Dime Box, Texas (pop. 400), explaining why he switched from working in the oil fields. "Hunters used to come through with their dogs to shoot feral hogs. The dogs tore up the hogs so badly that they weren't worth anything. Then they'd leave them there to rot, with no respect for other people's property. I got to thinking that if we could get a price on them, we could feed a lot of people with this meat.

"Trapping only takes a couple of hours in the morning, from 6 o'clock to 8, then I get to be home with 'Mama,' plus I get a daily check," he adds in an easy Texas drawl that's punctuated now and again by a slow chuckle.

"Yeh! It's dangerous. You have to get them from the trap into your truck with a cage." Back at his ranch, the animals are weighed and get a numbered ear tag. (Trappers are paid by the pound; the number identifies the animal's source.) Next they're herded into a large pen in back of Tumlinson's single-story brick ranch house. "Keeping them in pens doesn't make them larger," says Tumlinson. "They grow on time, not feed.

"Wild boars are too treacherous to herd to market. So once a week, Southern Wild Game goes out in the field to the trappers to pick them up. The company's standards are very strict. They won't take any animals under 60 pounds." (Tumlinson sells smaller pigs on the side for barbecue meat.) "And most important, all of their animals are slaughtered in a USDA facility that guarantees the best quality and best-tasting meat."

Returning to the danger of dealing with hogs, Tumlinson adds, "There was this one time I had to go into the pen and get a real sick one out that wasn't moving. I was plenty scared. If a hog doesn't see you, he won't attack. So I crawled in with a sheet of plywood in front of me, got the boar, and got out fast."

Coarse salt and freshly ground black pepper
to taste

1 tablespoon grated bitter chocolate

Small sprigs rosemary, to garnish

1. Combine boar, celery, onion, carrot, jalapeño, and garlic in a deep nonreactive bowl. Pour in 1½ bottles of the red wine and the vinegar. Add bouquet garni. Cover and marinate in the refrigerator for 3 days or, preferably, 1 week. Mix and stir occasionally to marinate evenly.

2. Remove meat and chopped vegetables from marinade. Blot dry on paper towels. Discard bouquet garni. Pour marinade into a saucepan and bring to a boil. Strain through a fine strainer, then set aside.

3. Heat a large skillet over high heat. Pour in enough oil to cover bottom by ½ inch. When hot, add boar and vegetables, and sauté until browned, turning to cook all sides, 6 to 8 minutes. Do not crowd ingredients. Add flour, tomato paste, and paprika, and continue stirring and cooking until meat is well coated. Deglaze pan with the remaining ½ bottle of wine, stirring to incorporate all cooking bits.

4. Transfer mixture to a heavy casserole. Stir in stock and reserved marinade. Gently simmer until meat is tender, about 1 hour. Season with salt and pepper. Strain stew and let cool. Discard vegetables. *Recipe may be prepared up to this point 24 hours ahead of time.*

5. Return meat and sauce to pot. Stir in chocolate, bring to a boil, and cook until sauce is thickened. Spoon civet over noodles, polenta, or spaetzle, if serving, and garnish with small sprigs of rosemary.

Adapted from Christian Albin, chef, Four Seasons, New York City

boneless leg of wild boar
with golden raisins

SERVES 6 TO 8

A succulent wild boar roast with a delectable reduced wine-and-stock sauce perfumed with golden raisins. Serve with green beans and baby carrots that have been steamed and then sautéed together in a little butter. A light red wine will complement this dish.

2 tablespoons olive oil

1 *each* onion, carrot, and celery rib, diced

1 cup beef stock

3 bay leaves

1 sprig thyme

¼ bunch flat-leaf parsley

12 black peppercorns

8 juniper berries, bruised

2 cups full-bodied red wine, such as Cabernet
Sauvignon

1 small wild boar leg, about 6 pounds, silver
skin and fat removed, boned and tied

2 teaspoons finely chopped garlic

Coarse salt and freshly ground black pepper
to taste

1½ tablespoons all-purpose flour

3 tablespoons light brown sugar

3 tablespoons red wine vinegar

1¼ cups golden raisins

3 tablespoons pine nuts, lightly toasted,
to garnish

1. Heat 1 tablespoon of the oil in a large skillet over medium-high heat. Add onion, carrot, and celery, and sauté until lightly browned, 6 to 7 minutes. Pour in stock and simmer for 10 minutes. Pour mixture into a plastic container or glass bowl large enough to hold boar leg.

2. Tie bay leaves, thyme, and parsley in a cheesecloth, and add to marinade along with peppercorns, juniper berries, and red wine. Set aside to cool. When cold, add boar leg, cover, and refrigerate for 2 days, turning daily.

3. When ready to cook, preheat oven to 350°F.

4. Remove boar from marinade and pat dry. Strain marinade, reserving liquid and vegetables separately. Combine garlic with salt and pepper and rub over meat. Roast boar in a shallow pan for about 12 to 15 minutes per pound of boned meat, or until an instant-read thermometer registers between 155° and 160°F.

5. Meanwhile, boil marinade liquid to reduce by half.

6. Heat remaining tablespoon of oil in a skillet over medium-high heat. Add drained vegetables and brown, 2 to 3 minutes. Sprinkle on flour and cook 1 minute longer. Stir in reduced marinade and simmer for 10 minutes.

7. Combine brown sugar and vinegar in a small saucepan and bring to a boil over high heat. Cook until mixture begins to caramelize, then slowly strain sauce made from reduced marinade into saucepan, stirring continuously to dissolve the caramel. Add raisins and simmer slowly until plump, about 12 minutes. Keep warm until needed.

8. Remove roast from oven, allow to stand for 10 minutes, then cut across the grain of the meat into slices. Serve with raisin sauce and a few pine nuts sprinkled over each slice.

Adapted from Loic Jaffres, master butcher and meat manager, Sutton Place Gourmet, Bethesda, Maryland

wild mushroom–stuffed loin of boar
with sautéed sunchokes

SERVES 6 TO 8

When the boneless loin of boar is cut lengthwise into two parts that are then stacked with a thyme-infused wild mushroom stuffing sandwiched between, you have a dazzling main course. Japanese-style coarse bread crumbs, or *Panko,* have sharp, uneven shapes that keep ingredients separate for a lighter filling. The meat is napped with sauce made from the pan-roasted vegetables and pan juices, along with vermouth and Dijon mustard. Be fastidious about preparing the meat, and use a sharp knife when slicing, so the roast cuts easily and presents well. We like nutty-tasting Sautéed Sunchokes (Jerusalem artichokes, or *topinambour* in French) with this. Drink a lush Côte de Beaune.

1 whole boneless wild boar loin, about 3½ pounds

6 tablespoons olive oil

2 teaspoons dried thyme

2 bay leaves, broken into large pieces

1 tablespoon chopped garlic

1 teaspoon ground coriander

1 teaspoon coarsely ground black pepper

4 ounces shallots, finely chopped

8 ounces mixed wild mushrooms, such as shiitake, porcini, oyster, and chanterelle, wiped clean, trimmed, and cut into fine dice

¼ cup fresh thyme leaves, stems reserved, plus extra sprigs, to garnish

1⅔ cups Panko bread crumbs (available at Japanese markets) or stale firm white bread crumbs

2 eggs, lightly beaten

2 tablespoons milk

¼ cup grated imported Parmesan cheese

Coarse salt and freshly ground black pepper to taste

1 *each* large carrot, onion, celery rib, and parsnip, coarsely chopped

Sautéed Sunchokes (recipe follows)

¾ cup dry vermouth

1¼ cups duck and veal demi-glace (see page 33)

2 tablespoons Dijon mustard

2 tablespoons unsalted butter, at room temperature

3 tablespoons minced flat-leaf parsley

1. Pare away all silver skin and fat from loin using a sharp knife. At the point where the silver skin and muscles divide and the roast is no longer a single piece of meat (about 3 inches from the end), cut off meat and reserve end for another purpose. Cut loin lengthwise into 2 equal pieces. Combine 2 tablespoons of the oil, the dried thyme, bay leaves, garlic, coriander, and coarsely ground black pepper in a resealable plastic bag or bowl. Add boar, turning to coat evenly, and seal or cover. Marinate in refrigerator for 5 to 6 hours or overnight.

2. Heat 2 more tablespoons of the oil in a large heavy skillet over medium heat. Add shallots and sauté until translucent, 2 to 2½ minutes. Stir in mushrooms and continue cooking until mushrooms are wilted and cooked through, about 3 minutes longer. Stir in thyme leaves, Panko crumbs, eggs, milk, Parmesan cheese, salt, and a generous amount of black pepper.

3. Lift pieces of bay leaf, garlic, and pepper from boar. Spread mushroom mixture over one piece of the loin, patting lightly to make a uniform layer. Lay second piece on first, lining them up as evenly as possible, then tie pieces together about every inch with butcher's twine. Take care not to squeeze out filling. Season with salt and pepper.

4. Preheat oven to 450°F.

5. Heat the remaining 2 tablespoons oil in a large roasting pan or heavy oval gratin dish, on top of the stove over medium-high heat. When hot, scatter carrot, onion, celery, and parsnip in pan. Cook until vegetables start to soften, about 5 minutes, turning often. Place roast over vegetables, add reserved thyme stems, and transfer pan to oven. Roast 10 minutes, then reduce heat to 350°F. Continue cooking until meat is pink and an instant-read thermometer registers 125° to 130°F when inserted into meat. This will take about 12 to 15 minutes per pound.

6. Meanwhile, prepare Sautéed Sunchokes.

7. Remove pan from oven, transfer meat to a warm platter, and tent lightly with foil.

8. Pour vermouth into pan, bring to a boil over high heat, and stir up all browned particles. Reduce by half. Pour liquid through a strainer into a clean saucepan, pressing vegetables with the back of a wooden spoon to extract as much flavor as possible. Add demi-glace and reduce by one-third, skimming sauce as it cooks. Stir in mustard, then turn off heat and whisk in butter. Stir in parsley and season with salt and pepper.

9. Cut roast into 1-inch-thick slices with a sharp carving knife. Carefully cut string from each slice before placing it on a plate. Spoon a little sauce over the meat, add a serving of sunchokes, and garnish each plate with a small thyme sprig.

sautéed sunchokes

1 tablespoon unsalted butter

½ tablespoon canola oil

1 pound sunchokes (Jerusalem artichokes), scrubbed and thinly sliced

2 tablespoons chicken stock or water

1 teaspoon lemon juice

Coarse salt and freshly ground black pepper to taste

Melt butter and oil in a large skillet over high heat until hot. Stir in sunchokes and cook until lightly browned, about 2 minutes, stirring often. Add chicken stock, lower heat to medium, and continue cooking until just tender, about 3 minutes. Season with lemon juice, salt, and pepper, and serve.

Inspired by a prizewinning recipe by Andrew Nordby, executive sous-chef, Heathman Hotel, Portland, Oregon

buffalo

Once bison roamed the Great Plains in such large numbers that they blanketed the landscape. It is estimated that before Europeans arrived in North America there were more than 125 million of the massive, shaggy beasts. "Thicker and thicker in larger groups they come, until by the time the grass is well up, the whole vast land appears a mass of buffalo," wrote Col. Richard Irving Dodge in the early nineteenth century.

In 1521, when Hernán Cortés first saw a bison in Montezuma's private zoo, he called them "humpbacked cows." The sixteenth-century Spanish explorer Francisco Vásquez de Coronado wrote during his travels through the Southwest that Native Americans lived entirely on bison, "for they neither plant nor harvest maize." The skins, wool, sinew, bones, fat, and meat provided for every aspect of their life. Tribes moved their villages in accordance with the great herds.

Sadly, within a few decades in the nineteenth century, this oxlike animal, standing 6 feet at the hump and weighing more than 2,000 pounds, went from the most populous beast in North America to near extinction. They were victims of a mercenary desire for buffalo skin and tongue (a prized delicacy), the wars against Native Americans, and the callous sport of shooting bison from luxury train cars, which left the landscape littered with spoiling carcasses. Sitting Bull, the Lakota Sioux Indian chief, said: "A cold wind blew across the prairie when the last buffalo fell . . . a death wind for my people." By 1889 only 600 bison remained in a couple of preserves, including Yellowstone Park.

The bison's fortunes turned in 1894, when President Grover Cleveland signed a federal bill forbidding the slaughter of the animals. Soon after, the American Bison Society was created. Its honorary president was Theodore Roosevelt; under his aegis, Congress established wildlife preserves for bison.

GEORGE: Today the calamity of the last century is starting to reverse itself. Bison herds are increasing across America and Canada, especially in the northern Plains states. Incidentally, bison, not buffalo, is the proper name. The animal's relatives are the European bison and Canadian wood bison; they're not related to either water buffalo or Cape buffalo. But in America the names are used interchangeably.

One significant reason herds are growing is that raising buffalo has become commercially attractive. The meat is very tasty when you cook it right. But that's the rub. Buffalo has less fat than other red meats, so it can't stand up to intense heat. Fat is an insulator that melts before meat begins cooking. When that doesn't take place, the meat starts cooking immediately. Since the cuts of beef and buffalo look the same, except that buffalo is darker in color — a brownish red — people mistakenly overcook it.

Generally, when cooking buffalo, rub it with a little oil. It's important to moderate the heat. If you'd roast a piece of beef at 325°F, lower the temperature to 275°F for a similar cut of buffalo. For broiling, lower the broiler pan down a notch, at least 6 inches from the heat. And for grilling, use the cooler part of a gas or charcoal grill. The meat will then cook in about the same length of time as beef. To be sure of the degree of doneness, an instant-read thermometer is the best tool. The ideal internal temperature is 125° to 130°F, medium rare. Once you taste it, you'll be hooked on the sweet, rich meat.

Like the true native that it is, buffalo is a great partner with other indigenous American foods. In the recipes that follow, you'll find buffalo with corn, tomatoes, peppers, chilies, and bourbon. But, like America, buffalo easily accommodates the flavors of other nationalities. A minimum of flavoring and cooking is all that's needed to make buffalo shine.

ARIANE: All of the following recipes could actually be prepared without the suggested marinades. For purists, the sweet taste of the meat alone is total pleasure. However, for variety and a different taste experience, do try the marinades. If you prefer to add just a subtle flavor, without changing the texture of the meat, cook any wine- or vinegar-based marinades and let them cool before adding to the meat. Cooking diminishes the unwanted acidity in the marinade. It is a longer process, but worth the effort.

Aside from the taste, buffalo boasts some appealingly healthful eating statistics. It has between 25 and 30 percent more protein and 25 percent less cholesterol than beef. In a 3½-ounce serving of buffalo sirloin, there are only 3 grams of fat (compared with 14 grams in beef sirloin), and about half the calories (120 versus 210). The hardy animals graze on a simple grass diet without growth stimulants or hormones and require only a minimal amount of care and intervention. According to Kenneth Throlson, D.V.M., an acknowledged expert and industry leader, there hasn't been any evidence of bacteria, like salmonella, in any bison meat processed in American bison cooperatives.

barbecued buffalo sloppy joe sandwiches

SERVES 4 TO 6

When you're out in bison country on the Great Plains, the best dishes are simple meals that satisfy big, basic appetites. Here's one with rich, meaty taste, to feed a bunch of friends for an afternoon of football watching, homecoming events, or anytime you want earthy fare. Slowly cooked buffalo chuck roast is sliced, then blended with barbecue sauce you make or buy and piled onto sandwich rolls. We've gussied up the sauce a bit, adding some bourbon and chopped chipotle peppers.

2 tablespoons canola oil

1 buffalo chuck roast, 3 to 3½ pounds, well trimmed and blotted dry

¾ cup chopped onions

2 tablespoons plus ¼ cup firmly packed dark brown sugar

Salt and freshly ground black pepper to taste

2 cups prepared ketchup

½ cup water

3 tablespoons bourbon (optional)

2 tablespoons *each* Worcestershire sauce and white vinegar

1 tablespoon prepared mustard

1 to 2 tablespoons chopped chipotle peppers in adobo sauce (optional)

4 to 6 sandwich rolls, split and warmed

1 cup shredded sharp Cheddar cheese

1 to 2 scallions, including green parts, thinly sliced

1. Preheat oven to 250°F. Tear off a large piece of heavy-duty aluminum foil.
2. Heat 1 tablespoon of the oil in a large skillet over high heat. Add chuck roast and sear on all sides until golden brown. Transfer buffalo to center of foil. Sprinkle on ½ cup of the onions and 2 tablespoons of the brown sugar, and season with salt and pepper. Close foil tightly, place package in a roasting pan, and roast until tender, about 2 hours. Remove from oven and let cool in foil.
3. While meat roasts, heat remaining tablespoon of oil in the skillet over medium-high heat. Add the remaining ¼ cup of onions and brown, 6 to 7 minutes. Stir in ketchup, water, bourbon (if using), Worcestershire sauce, vinegar, mustard, and chipotle peppers. Season with salt and pepper, and simmer for 20 to 25 minutes, stirring occasionally.
4. When meat is cool, cut across grain into thin slices, place in skillet with barbecue sauce, mix well, and heat through. *Recipe may be made ahead, refrigerated or frozen, and reheated. The flavor improves with time.*
5. Ladle meat over half of each warmed roll. Sprinkle with cheese, add some scallions, cover, and serve.

Adapted from Gayle Dodds, owner-manager, Bison Country Inn, New Rockford, North Dakota

buffalo chili

SERVES 6

The flavors of chilies and other slowly simmered stews improve when these dishes are made ahead of time. That's the perfect thing to do with this hearty buffalo dish: prepare it 1 or 2 days ahead. Make it hot or mild according to personal preference. For more heat from each chili pepper, include some or all of the seeds and membranes. These are the hottest parts. Depending on how expansive you want to be with garnishes, use any or all of the suggestions below.

2 tablespoons olive oil

2 cups finely chopped onion

¼ cup finely chopped celery

1 tablespoon minced garlic

1 jalapeño (for moderate heat, 2 to 3 for a scorcher), seeded and deveined, minced

2 teaspoons ground cumin

½ teaspoon ground coriander

¼ teaspoon dried oregano

2 bay leaves

1 tablespoon dark brown sugar

2 cups canned crushed tomatoes

1½ cups chicken or beef stock

4 tablespoons ancho chili purée or 2½ tablespoons high-quality chili powder

1 tablespoon red wine vinegar

2 to 2¼ pounds lean buffalo stew meat, fat and silver skin removed, cut into ½-inch cubes, blotted dry

3 cups cooked white navy beans or drained canned beans

Salt and freshly ground black pepper to taste

Chopped cilantro, shredded Monterey Jack cheese, salsa, and sour cream, to garnish

Heat oil in a large pot over medium heat until just smoking. Add onion and celery and cook until lightly browned, 6 to 7 minutes, stirring often. Stir in garlic and jalapeño and cook for 1 minute. Stir in cumin, coriander, oregano, and bay leaves, and cook briefly just to toast a little, about a minute. Add brown sugar and tomatoes, and cook a few minutes to blend ingredients. Stir in stock, chili purée, and vinegar. Stir in buffalo and bring liquid to a boil. Reduce heat and simmer for 2½ to 3 hours, until fork tender. Add beans in the last ½ hour of cooking. Season with salt and pepper. Serve with any or all of the garnishes.

Adapted from Brendan Walsh, chef-owner, The Elms Restaurant & Tavern, Ridgefield, Connecticut

charred buffalo medallions
with black coffee barbecue sauce

SERVES 4

The full flavor and rich mouth feel of charred buffalo steaks, crunchy on the outside and silky inside, are intensified by a brawny, coffee-and-chili barbecue sauce. Serve with garlic mashed potatoes and a Cabernet Sauvignon with plenty of heft.

½ cup Black Coffee Barbecue Sauce (recipe follows)

1 tablespoon olive oil

1 tablespoon unsalted butter

1½ pounds buffalo tenderloin, cut into 4 (1-inch-thick) medallions, blotted dry

Salt and freshly ground black pepper to taste

1 small Vidalia onion, diced medium fine

¼ cup gold tequila

2 to 4 tablespoons lime juice, to taste

1 cup rich beef or veal stock, or ⅓ cup water
    mixed with ⅔ cup duck and veal demi-glace
    (see page 33)

1. Prepare Black Coffee Barbecue Sauce.
2. Heat olive oil and butter in a large skillet over medium heat. Season buffalo with salt and pepper, then add to pan. Adjust heat to high and sear both sides of meat, 1 to 2 minutes per side for rare, 2 to 3 minutes for medium rare. Remove medallions to warm platter, cover lightly with aluminum foil, and set aside.
3. Add onions to pan and sauté over medium-low heat until softened and caramelized, about 5 minutes. Standing back from stove, add tequila to pan. Adjust heat to low, and stir to deglaze.
4. When liquid in pan is reduced by half, add 2 or 3 tablespoons lime juice and simmer until pan is almost dry. Add stock and simmer until it is reduced by almost half. Strain, then add ½ cup Black Coffee Barbecue Sauce. Simmer gently for 2 minutes, then season with salt and pepper to taste, adding more lime juice if desired. Serve buffalo medallions in a pool of sauce.

black coffee barbecue sauce

MAKES 2½ CUPS

½ cup very strong coffee, preferably espresso

1 cup ketchup

½ cup red wine vinegar

½ cup firmly packed dark brown sugar

3 jalapeños, halved and seeded

1 onion, chopped (about 1 cup)

2 tablespoons *each* dark molasses,
    Worcestershire sauce, ground cumin, and
    ancho chili powder or regular chili powder

2 tablespoons hot dry mustard, mixed with
    1 tablespoon water

2 teaspoons crushed garlic

1. Combine all ingredients in a medium nonreactive saucepan. Bring to a boil over medium-high heat, then reduce heat to low and simmer for 20 minutes.
2. Allow mixture to cool, then purée in a food processor or electric blender until smooth. Strain. Sauce may be stored, covered and refrigerated, for up to 2 weeks.

Adapted from Michael Lomonaco, executive chef, Windows on the World and Wild Blue, New York City

seared buffalo skirt steaks
with basil mashed potatoes

SERVES 4

This simple-to-prepare dish tastes and looks great. Basil-scented potatoes are a winsome cushion for the juicy steak. The meat is topped with a crunchy tangle of onion strings. The final touch: a robust red wine like a Shiraz from Australia or California Syrah.

½ cup *each* chopped onion, carrot, and celery

2 sprigs *each* rosemary and thyme

4 bay leaves

1 cup white wine

1 cup canola oil, plus oil for frying onions

1¼ pounds buffalo skirt steaks, fat and silver
    skin removed

Basil Mashed Potatoes (recipe follows)

1 large onion, thinly sliced

All-purpose flour for dredging

Salt and freshly ground black pepper to taste

1 tablespoon unsalted butter

1 large shallot, finely chopped

1 cup duck and veal demi-glace (see page 33)

4 tablespoons chopped flat-leaf parsley

1. Combine chopped onion, carrot, and celery with rosemary, thyme, bay leaves, wine, and 1 cup of canola oil, in a large resealable plastic bag or nonreactive bowl. Add steaks, seal or cover, and marinate in refrigerator for 8 hours or overnight.

2. Prepare Basil Mashed Potatoes.

3. Pour enough oil into a wide pot to measure about 2 inches in depth. Heat to 300°F. Separate onion slices into rings, rinse under cold water, and blot dry. Toss rings in flour, then fry until crisp in hot oil. This will take only a few minutes. Remove to paper towels. (Oil may be strained and used for frying a second time; store covered in refrigerator.)

4. Remove steaks from marinade, blot dry, and season with salt and pepper. Heat a large heavy skillet over high heat. When hot, cook steaks for 1½ to 2 minutes on each side for rare to medium-rare meat. Transfer to a heated plate to keep warm.

5. Adjust heat to medium. Add the butter and shallots to the pan, sauté until wilted, 1 minute, then pour in demi-glace. Bring

to a boil and reduce until thickened. Stir in parsley and season to taste. Keep warm.

6. Spoon mashed potatoes in the center of 4 heated dinner plates. Cut steaks into ½-inch slices across the grain. Lay slices around mashed potatoes. Stir juices from the cut steak into sauce, then spoon sauce around plates. Decorate mashed potatoes with fried onions and serve at once.

basil mashed potatoes

2 large cloves garlic

2 pounds baking potatoes, peeled and cut into
    chunks

1 cup loosely packed basil leaves

2 tablespoons olive oil

½ to ⅔ cup hot milk

2 tablespoons unsalted butter

Salt and freshly ground black pepper to taste

A MASHED POTATO PRIMER

Mashed potatoes rank high on many diners' list of favorite foods. Although this dish is traditionally laden with heavy cream and mounds of butter, some of today's most satisfying versions are prepared with stocks, milk, buttermilk, or infused oils. Herbs, like basil and parsley, add color and flavor. The essential trick is to use a potato ricer or food mill to mash the potatoes. Or, for more rustic "smashed" potatoes, use a fork. Food processors generally make potatoes gluey and starchy. Purée liquids and herbs before adding them to the warmed, mashed potatoes. Jeffrey Steingarten, in *The Man Who Ate Everything,* researched the fine points of mashed potatoes. His chapter on this subject is a must for all mashed potato fanatics.

1. Boil garlic and potatoes in salted water until tender. Meanwhile, combine basil and olive oil in an electric blender, and purée until smooth. Drain potatoes and garlic and pass them through a food mill or potato ricer. Return to pot.

2. Pour hot milk into blender with basil, pulsing to mix well, then pour mixture into pan with potatoes. Add butter, salt, and pepper, and stir to blend. Keep partially covered over low heat until needed.

Adapted from Edward Gruters, chef, Pierre's Restaurant, Harding, New Jersey

mustard-glazed buffalo flank steak stuffed with roasted peppers and smoked gouda

SERVES 4

Grill this stuffed and rolled flank steak on the "barbie" for a colorful, mouthwatering main course. Once the roast is sliced, the roasted red peppers and smoked Gouda appear as attractive pinwheels. Plenty of garlic and fresh oregano along with Dijon mustard add up to abundant taste. Serve with fresh corn on the cob and a green salad.

1 buffalo flank steak, 1½ to 2 pounds

Salt and freshly ground black pepper to taste

3 tablespoons chopped fresh oregano

1 tablespoon finely chopped garlic

1 to 2 large red bell peppers, peeled and roasted (see Note), or 1 (7-ounce) jar roasted sweet peppers (packed in water), drained and blotted dry

3 ounces smoked Gouda or other soft cheese, such as Muenster or Swiss, thinly sliced

¼ cup Dijon mustard

1 tablespoon olive oil

1 teaspoon Worcestershire sauce

1. Cut off all silver skin and fat from meat, using a sharp knife. Lay flank steak on work surface with long edge perpendicular to you. Trim off ragged narrow edge to form a neat rectangle.

2. To butterfly steak, use a long, sharp slicing knife. Start on one long side and carefully begin slicing the meat in half horizontally. Try to avoid cutting through either top or bottom of meat. It will be easier to see what you are doing if you lift back the top portion as you cut. Continue cutting until about ¾ inch from the opposite side. Open steak out like a book and gently flatten with the palm of your hand. It should be about 12 inches wide.

3. Position meat so the grain runs horizontally in front of you. Season generously with salt and pepper. Combine oregano and garlic, and spread over entire surface. Cut roasted peppers into pieces that will lie flat, then lay them close together over bottom third of meat. Cover peppers with cheese slices, then roll meat up tightly, starting at bottom edge and rolling away from you. Pin roll closed with short metal skewers (you'll need about 5), or tie it with butcher's twine every 1½ inches. Turn ends under and secure. Season outside with salt and pepper.

4. Mix mustard, oil, and Worcestershire sauce together in a small bowl, and brush liberally over roast.

5. Heat a gas or charcoal grill to medium hot. Place roast on grill, cover, and cook until medium rare, 14 to 15 minutes, turning twice, and brushing with mustard each time. Let stand 5 minutes before removing skewers or strings and cutting across the roll into 1-inch slices. Serve at once.

NOTE:

Here's a quick way to peel and roast peppers. Preheat oven to 400°F. Core peppers and cut lengthwise into large pieces, cutting along the folds between the lobes. Remove seeds and membranes, then peel using a swivel-action vegetable peeler. Brush a nonstick pan with olive oil, lay pepper pieces in it skinned side up, drizzle peppers with more oil, and place in oven. Roast 20 to 30 minutes, turning once or twice, until peppers are soft and a bit browned around the edges.

pan-seared buffalo hanger steak
with horseradish pasta

SERVES 4

Suddenly hanger steak, or *onglet,* as it is known in French bistros, is the new darling of bistro steak and frites lovers. With good reason. This long, thin strip of meat is exquisitely juicy and silky. While plenty of loin and rib steaks come from each animal, buffalo (and steers) have only one dangling tender, called a "hanger" by butchers, making it highly prized by chefs and cognoscenti. If making pasta is not in your time schedule, french fries are the perfect partner.

Horseradish Pasta (recipe follows)

2 pounds buffalo hanger steak, cut lengthwise into 2 strips to remove silver skin, blotted dry

Sea salt and freshly ground black pepper to taste

Olive oil

1. Prepare Horseradish Pasta through Step 4.

2. Preheat oven to 500°F.

3. Heat a large cast iron skillet to medium hot over medium-high heat. Season steaks liberally with salt and pepper. Add just enough oil to coat bottom of pan. Gently lay steaks in skillet, and allow them to crust well on one side, 1 to 1½ minutes. Adjust heat to keep an active sizzle without burning meat.

4. Turn steaks, transfer skillet to oven, and roast steaks approximately 3 to 3½ minutes for rare to medium rare. Remove skillet from oven, and buffalo from pan. Allow steaks to rest in a warm place for 5 minutes, then slice meat across grain into thick strips, paying careful attention to the change of direction in the grain.

5. While meat rests, finish pasta. Divide pasta among plates, add sliced buffalo, and serve with juices from slicing.

horseradish pasta

(3 or 4 plastic coat hangers or another place to dry pasta)

1 cup all-purpose flour, plus additional flour to dust pasta

◄ Mustard-Glazed Buffalo Flank Steak
Stuffed with Roasted Peppers and Smoked Gouda (page 187)

1 cup semolina flour

4 egg yolks

Coarse salt and freshly ground black pepper
   to taste

3 tablespoons prepared white horseradish

Water, as needed

1 quart chicken stock

½ cup (1 stick) cold unsalted butter, cut into
   chunks

1. Put 1 cup all-purpose flour plus semolina flour in a food processor and pulse a
few times to aerate. Beat egg yolks, salt,
pepper, and horseradish together in a
bowl. With the motor running, add egg
mixture through feed tube, and process
until dough is smooth and pulls together
in a ball. It should have a fairly firm consistency and not be sticky to the touch.
Add more flour if sticky, or a little water,
by teaspoonfuls, if dry. Gather dough into
a ball, wrap with plastic wrap, and refrigerate for at least 1 hour. *Dough may be made
12 hours ahead to this point and refrigerated.
Otherwise, freeze for up to a week.*
2. Cut dough into 4 pieces and, one at a
time, roll them through the widest setting
of a pasta machine. Fold each piece over
and flour outside lightly. Continue rolling
it through machine, flouring lightly each
time. Do this 6 or 7 times, or until dough
is a neat, smooth rectangle with even
edges and a uniform color. Then, always
flouring dough, pass it through rollers several times without folding, setting rollers
to a thinner setting each time dough goes
through, until desired thinness is reached,
the last or next to last setting.

3. Dust sheets of pasta liberally with flour
on both sides. Dough shouldn't stick to
itself. Roll each sheet of dough loosely
into a long tube, then use a sharp knife
to cut crosswise into strips ¼ to ⅛ inch
wide. (Or cut dough by machine, following directions with pasta maker.) Pick up
strips, shake them out, and drape over
coat hangers. Let pasta dry briefly before
cooking.
4. Bring stock to a boil in a large saucepan.
5. Stir in pasta, cover pan briefly to return
to boil. Uncover and boil gently, tasting
almost continuously until just cooked
through. Times may vary from 30 seconds
for very fresh pasta to several minutes for
dried pasta.
6. When ready, lift pasta from stock with
a pasta fork into a wide pan, not draining
too thoroughly. You need a bit of liquid to
form sauce. Taste, correct seasoning, then
turn heat on to high. Add cold butter and
swirl pan around by its handle, tossing
pasta until butter emulsifies into a creamy
sauce. Serve immediately.

*Adapted from Jimmy Snead, chef-owner, The Frog and the Redneck,
Richmond, Virginia*

smoked buffalo tenderloin
with maker's mark glaze
with chipotle-onion potato cake

SERVES 6 TO 8

If you have a smoker, you'll be won over
by buffalo's sweetness permeated with a
smoky taste. Another option is to roast the
meat on an oak plank in a very hot oven
(planks for this purpose are available at

better barbecue departments). A covered kettle grill with soaked wood chips will also work. The simply seasoned meat is brought to life with the bourbon-and-adobo glaze. The crunchy-tender potato cake packs a fiery blast of its own. Cut back or add chipotles to your own heat tolerance.

(Uncured oak plank for oven smoking, soaked, optional)

Chipotle-Onion Potato Cake (recipe follows)

1 buffalo tenderloin, 3 to 4 pounds, trimmed, fat and silver skin removed, blotted dry

Salt and coarsely ground black pepper to taste

2 cups duck and veal demi-glace (see page 33)

½ cup Maker's Mark or other fine bourbon

¼ teaspoon adobo sauce, reserved from potato cake

¼ teaspoon minced fresh thyme leaves, plus 4 small sprigs, to garnish

2 teaspoons unsalted butter, at room temperature

SMOKY CHIPOTLES

Chipotles are dried, smoked jalapeño peppers. They have a smoky, hot, somewhat sweet taste, especially when canned with adobo sauce, made from ground chilies, spices, and vinegar. Add chipotles slowly at first, depending on your heat threshold. They are available at specialty food stores and Latin American markets.

1. Preheat smoker to 220°F, or preheat oven to 500°F. Prepare Chipotle-Onion Potato Cake.
2. Season buffalo with salt and pepper on both sides. Prick meat deeply all over with a sharp fork (about 15 times on each side). Either smoke meat about 1 hour, or place meat on oak plank and roast in oven until medium rare, about 25 minutes, or until internal temperature measures 120° to 125°F on an instant-read thermometer. Remove from smoker or oven and let rest 10 minutes, then cut across grain into ½-inch-thick slices.
3. While meat cooks, combine demi-glace, Maker's Mark, adobo sauce, and thyme leaves in a small saucepan and bring to a gentle boil. Let liquid reduce until it coats the back of a wooden spoon, 12 to 15 minutes. Remove from heat, season with salt and pepper, then whisk in butter.
4. Layer sliced meat over a wedge of potatoes. Spoon some of the glaze around meat, add a thyme sprig, and serve.

chipotle-onion potato cake

3 tablespoons unsalted butter

2 tablespoons peanut oil

3 medium onions, thinly sliced

1 to 2 teaspoons chipotle peppers in adobo sauce

Coarse salt and freshly ground black pepper to taste

5 baking potatoes (about 3 pounds), cut into ⅛-inch slices

1. Preheat oven to 425°F.
2. Melt 2 tablespoons of the butter with 1 tablespoon of the oil in a large (10-inch)

nonstick skillet over medium-high heat. Add onions and sauté until golden brown, turning often, 10 to 12 minutes.

3. Meanwhile, remove some chipotles from the sauce, and finely chop enough to measure 1 to 2 teaspoons, according to taste. Reserve adobo sauce for glaze (above). Scrape onions into a bowl, mix in chipotles, and season with salt and pepper.

4. Melt remaining tablespoon of butter in the hot skillet. Arrange potato slices in a circular pattern on the bottom of pan and against sides, alternating and overlapping side and bottom slices, so cake doesn't separate when you invert it. Season with salt and pepper. Add a thin layer of onions, then another layer of potatoes seasoned with salt and pepper. Continue until pan is full, pressing down slightly on pile of potatoes. Brush top layer with remaining tablespoon of oil. Bake in oven, as far from heat source as possible, until crunchy and rich golden brown on the bottom, and completely cooked through, 1 hour to 1 hour 15 minutes. Insert a knife to test for doneness. Loosen cake from pan around edges and underneath, then invert onto a plate, cut into wedges, and serve with a little Maker's Mark glaze. *Cake may be made ahead, partially covered, and kept warm.*

Adapted from Jack McDavid, chef-owner, Jack's Firehouse and Down Home Diner, Philadelphia

ROCCO VERELLI AND NORTHFORK RANCH

Rocco Verelli graduated with a bachelor of science degree from McGill University in Montreal, in 1985. His major was agricultural economics. For his research project, Verelli chose the economic feasibility of raising buffalo in Canada. The paper received mixed comments from fellow students and faculty members.

Thus, Rocco Verelli went into the restaurant business. Within a short time he owned a large chain of restaurants. He also acquired firsthand knowledge of the quality, pricing, and public reaction to various meats. Success enabled Verelli to realize his dream and passion: to raise buffalo. In 1990 he began Northfork Ranch in St.-Rémi, Quebec, as a sideline.

First results were disappointing. Rocco had a difficult time getting the quoted price for his slaughtered animals, and he struggled. With frustration came reflection. Once he analyzed his personal vision of buffalo ranching, he realized that to achieve his goals, his commitment had to be absolute. This meant full-time dedication to providing the finest-grade meat, fed with natural grain and top-quality hay. No restaurant business, no sidelines, no part-time jobs.

ROCCO VERELLI: Selecting superior animals from the beginning is essential. When I buy them — usually at about 850 pounds — they have to have good genetic background. You can tell by the look and the shape — kind of an eyeball approach — if they are healthy. Otherwise, no matter what you do for them, they won't develop properly and will be tough.

Ranchers know me and my standards, so subcontractors bring animals to me from across Canada. I can pick and choose. Additionally, we feed them top-quality hay for 60 days before going to slaughter. That way, when a buffalo reaches 1,000 pounds, by 24 to 29 months, you end up with tender meat.

Today Verelli's herd of 125 buffalo roams the wide-open plains on his two farms totaling about 300 acres in St.-Rémi.

barbecued buffalo steaks
with kickin' onions

SERVES 4

Buffalo steaks are so darn good on the grill, you don't need to do much to them in terms of marinating or cooking. The meat is full of flavor, yet lean and, well, meaty. You'll find each mouthful is pure satisfaction if you don't overcook it. The ancho chili–flavored onions slathered on top certainly liven up the meal. (Ancho chilies are dried poblano peppers, sold in specialty food stores and Latin American markets.) A California Zinfandel can admirably stand the heat of this dish.

12 ounces dark beer, preferably Mexican

¼ cup firmly packed dark brown sugar

2 tablespoons cider vinegar

1 clove garlic, split

1 bay leaf

1¼ to 1½ pounds boneless buffalo loin, about 3½ inches thick, fat and silver skin removed

2 tablespoons canola oil

6 cups thinly sliced onions, separated into rings

1 ancho chili, seeds and stem removed

Salt and freshly ground black pepper to taste

1. Combine beer, brown sugar, vinegar, garlic, and bay leaf with buffalo in a large resealable plastic bag or nonreactive bowl. Seal or cover, and marinate for at least 30 minutes, or refrigerate overnight.
2. Meanwhile, heat oil in a large skillet over medium-high heat. Stir in onions and, after 2 or 3 minutes, when they begin to wilt, turn heat down to medium or medium low. Sauté onions until tender and a pale golden color, 12 to 15 minutes, stirring frequently. While onions are cooking, cover chili with boiling water and let it stand until softened, 4 to 5 minutes. Drain and finely chop, then stir into onions. *Onions may be done ahead to this point.*
3. Light a gas or charcoal grill and heat until medium. Remove buffalo from marinade and blot dry. Reserve marinade. Cook meat 8 to 9 minutes on first side, then turn and cook another 8 minutes, or until internal temperature reads 120° to 125°F (do not overcook).
4. While buffalo cooks, pour about 1 cup of the marinade over the onions and reduce over high heat until marinade evaporates and glazes onions. Season to taste with salt and pepper.
5. When steak is done, transfer to a wooden cutting board and let rest for about 5 minutes. Cut across the grain into 1-inch slices. Top each serving with a large spoonful of Kickin' Onions.

jerk buffalo ribeye
with bell pepper and onion compote

SERVES 4

Jerk-spiced Caribbean foods range from intolerably hot (to many palates) to only fiery enough to tickle and tease the taste buds. Buffalo meat is sweet and flavorful on its own, so you want to enhance, not blast away, the taste. This wet rub does just that: it sinks in to add plenty of complex flavor, but it won't bite back. You don't need a sauce, but the sweet bell pepper compote is a tasty condiment to serve beside or on top of the steaks.

5 serrano or 3 jalapeño chilies, seeds and membranes removed and reserved, chopped

5 scallions, including 2 inches of green part, cut into ½-inch-long pieces

3 medium cloves garlic

2½ teaspoons ground allspice

1 teaspoon cinnamon

¼ teaspoon freshly grated nutmeg

2 teaspoons hot or sweet paprika

1½ teaspoons salt or to taste

Freshly ground black pepper to taste

3 tablespoons apple cider vinegar

1½ tablespoons peanut or canola oil

4 buffalo ribeye steaks, 7 to 9 ounces each, 1 to 1¼ inches thick

Bell Pepper and Onion Compote (recipe follows)

1. Combine chilies, scallions, garlic, allspice, cinnamon, nutmeg, paprika, salt, and pepper in an electric blender. Purée until smooth, scraping down sides once or twice. With blender running, pour in vinegar and oil, blending into a paste. For a hotter jerk flavor, add some of the reserved seeds and membranes from the chilies. Brush paste over steaks. Put them on a plate, cover with plastic wrap, and refrigerate for 2 to 4 hours.

2. Prepare Bell Pepper and Onion Compote.

3. Light a gas or charcoal grill, or turn on broiler, adjusting broiler rack to about 4 to 5 inches from heat. When hot, grill steaks until medium rare, about 7 minutes per side, turning once. Remove and let stand for a few minutes before serving with compote.

bell pepper and onion compote

1 medium onion, sliced

½ medium red or green bell pepper, seeded and sliced (about 2 ounces)

4 tablespoons olive oil

2 teaspoons capers

1 teaspoon dried oregano

Salt and freshly ground black pepper to taste

Cayenne pepper to taste

Pinch sugar

1 tablespoon balsamic vinegar

1. Sauté onion and pepper slices in 2 tablespoons of the olive oil over medium heat until very soft but not brown, 8 to 10 minutes. Add capers, oregano, salt, black and cayenne peppers, and sugar. Stir and heat for 1 minute.

2. Let onion mixture cool for several minutes, then transfer to a food processor or electric blender. Purée while adding remaining 2 tablespoons of oil and the balsamic vinegar through the feed tube. Taste and adjust seasonings.

3. Reheat in microwave for 1 to 2 minutes, or very gently in a saucepan, and serve.

Adapted from William Rice, cookbook author and columnist, Chicago Tribune

grilled ribeye of buffalo
with yorkshire pudding topped with carrots and morels

SERVES 4

Grilled buffalo ribeye is a hearty reminder of how satisfying a juicy piece of meat can be. It's traditional fare with today's style. This lightened version of an Old World classic, Yorkshire pudding, pairs well with the New World meat. Serve an earthy, full-bodied red wine.

4 buffalo ribeye steaks, 10 to 12 ounces each

4 cups full-bodied red wine, such as Cabernet Sauvignon

½ cup extra-virgin olive oil

4 cloves garlic, sliced

4 shallots, sliced

2 tablespoons cracked black pepper

1 bunch fresh thyme

Yorkshire Pudding Topped with Carrots and Morels (recipe follows)

Salt and freshly ground black pepper to taste

1. Combine steaks with wine, oil, garlic, shallots, pepper, and thyme in a large resealable plastic bag or bowl. Seal or cover, and marinate in refrigerator for 24 hours.
2. Prepare Yorkshire pudding through Step 1.
3. Remove steaks from marinade and pat dry. Light a gas or charcoal grill or turn on broiler, and heat until hot. Meanwhile, finish Yorkshire Pudding Topped with Carrots and Morels. While puddings are baking, grill meat to desired degree of doneness (optimally 125°F internal temperature), about 7 minutes per side. Season meat with salt and pepper, and let rest 5 minutes before serving.

yorkshire pudding topped with carrots and morels

1 scant cup all-purpose flour

Pinch salt

1 egg

1 cup low-fat milk

4 teaspoons plus 1 tablespoon unsalted butter

4 ounces morels, cleaned in several changes cold water

24 tiny carrots, blanched

1 teaspoon fines herbes or a mixture of finely chopped fresh herbs

Salt and freshly ground black pepper to taste

1. Sift flour and salt together into a bowl. Combine egg and milk, and slowly whisk into flour until smooth. Set aside for at least 30 minutes or refrigerate overnight to rest.
2. Preheat oven to 425°F. Place 4 custard cups on a baking sheet.
3. Melt 4 teaspoons butter and pour into cups, rotating to coat sides. Stir batter and pour into custard cups. Bake in oven until puddings are puffed and golden, 23 to 25 minutes.
4. Melt 1 tablespoon butter in a skillet over medium-high heat. Add morels and sauté until cooked and any water rendered has evaporated. Stir in carrots, fines herbes, and salt and pepper, and warm through. Unmold puddings and spoon morels and carrots over them.

Adapted from Robert Weland, chef, Privé, New York City

buffalo ribeye roast
baked in salt

SERVES 6 TO 8

Baking meat such as this buffalo ribeye in a salt crust tightly seals the juices inside. Not a drop of moisture seeps out. Taste the succulent meat — it's decidedly unsalty — and you'll agree that this traditional method of cooking is a winner.

3 tablespoons fresh thyme leaves

4 teaspoons crushed garlic

1 teaspoon freshly ground black pepper

1 piece boneless buffalo ribeye, 3 pounds, well trimmed and blotted dry

3 tablespoons olive oil

8 cups coarse salt

2 cups water

3 bay leaves

1. Preheat oven to 450°F. Line a roasting pan with a double layer of aluminum foil.
2. Blend thyme, garlic, and pepper, and rub into buffalo.
3. Heat oil in a large skillet over medium-high heat. Sear buffalo on all sides until crusty.
4. Meanwhile, stir salt and water together into a coarse paste. Spoon about one-third of the salt paste into roasting pan. Transfer meat to roasting pan, and press meat into the salt. Put bay leaves on top of meat, and spoon over remaining salt paste and pat into place. Make sure salt completely seals roast.
5. Bake roast in lower third of oven for 30 minutes, then turn temperature down to 400°F and roast for an additional 30 minutes for rare, 40 minutes for well done. Remove roast from oven and let rest for at least 5 minutes. Break away salt cover and brush off any remaining salt. Carve across grain of meat into ¼-inch slices. Serve on a platter with natural juices of roast.

Adapted from David Liederman, chef-owner, Restaurant Luna, Mount Kisco, New York, and Chez Louis, New York City

buffalo fillet croustillant
with wild mushrooms over braised mustard greens

SERVES 4

Croustillant is French for "crunchy." The crispy phyllo crust is only the first part of the enchantment. Inside hide enticing layers of buffalo, goat cheese, portobellos, and vegetables. These packets could well be the pièce de résistance for the most gala feast. Wilted greens and a reduced wine sauce complete the plate. If you want to go one step further, add the crunchy fried mustard greens and sweet potato strings to garnish. Most of the work can be done ahead of time. Be sure all ingredients are ready before starting to assemble the dish. Serve with a fine, full-bodied Cabernet Sauvignon.

1½ cups Cabernet Sauvignon or other full-bodied red wine

¼ cup plus 2 tablespoons chopped shallots

3 sprigs fresh thyme, plus ¼ teaspoon fresh thyme leaves

1 teaspoon sugar

2 cups duck and veal demi-glace (see page 33)

Salt and freshly ground black pepper to taste

1 tablespoon unsalted butter

4 buffalo tenderloin steaks, 5 ounces each, trimmed and blotted dry

8 tablespoons olive oil, plus oil for brushing sheet pan

4 portobello mushrooms, stems removed, wiped clean

1 teaspoon finely chopped garlic

2 tablespoons black truffle butter (see Note) or other herb butter

White part of 1 leek, finely julienned

1 *each* carrot and celery rib, finely julienned

4 sheets phyllo, defrosted according to package directions, cut widthwise into 2-inch-wide strips, and covered with a damp towel to prevent drying out

2-ounce log goat cheese, cut into 4 equal slices

¼ cup clarified butter

Peanut oil for frying (optional)

1 small sweet potato, peeled and julienned, plus 1 ounce stemmed mustard greens, cut into fine julienne, to garnish (optional)

8 ounces mustard greens, stemmed

4 ounces mousserons, chanterelles, or other wild mushrooms, stems removed, wiped clean

1. Combine wine, ¼ cup shallots, thyme sprigs, and sugar in a nonreactive pan and boil until liquid has almost completely evaporated. Add demi-glace and gently boil until sauce is reduced to about 1 cup when strained. Season with salt and pepper and, off the heat, whisk in butter. Keep warm. *Sauce may be made several days ahead of time and refrigerated.*

2. Season fillets with salt and pepper. Heat 1 tablespoon of the olive oil in a heavy skillet over high heat. Add buffalo and sear on both sides until outside is crusty and meat is rare, about 1 to 1½ minutes per side, turning once. Remove from skillet and set aside.

3. Brush portobello mushrooms with a tablespoon of oil, and season with salt and pepper. Heat another tablespoon of the oil in the skillet over medium-high heat, and sauté portobellos until limp, 2 to 3 minutes, turning and shaking to cook evenly. Add half the garlic and the ¼ teaspoon thyme leaves to inside of caps when almost done. Remove mushrooms from skillet and blot on paper towels. Heat truffle butter in skillet over medium-low heat. Add leek, carrot, and celery, and sweat until limp. Season with salt and pepper.

4. Preheat oven to 325°F. Lightly oil a sheet pan.

5. Lay 6 strips of phyllo on a table in the shape of a pinwheel, with strips crossing in the center. Place 1 portobello, gill side up, in center. Add a slice of goat cheese, a buffalo fillet, and one-quarter of the vegetable mixture. Brush phyllo tips with clarified butter and wrap ends over fillet into a round package, meeting in the center. Gently brush packet with butter and place on sheet pan. Repeat with remaining 3 fillets. *Recipe may be prepared to this point 1 day ahead, lightly covered, and refrigerated.* Bake until pastry is golden brown and buffalo medium rare to medium, 10 to 12 minutes (4 minutes longer if refrigerated). Remove from oven and keep warm.

6. While meat is cooking, prepare garnish, if using. Pour enough peanut oil into a deep skillet to come halfway up the sides. Heat to 375°F and drop sweet potato strings into hot fat. Oil should cover them. When crispy, remove with a slotted spoon or skimmer, and blot dry on paper towels. Repeat with mustard greens. (Oil may be strained and reused if not burned; store covered in refrigerator.)

7. Heat 3 tablespoons of the olive oil in a large skillet over medium-high heat. Add the remaining 2 tablespoons chopped shallots and the remaining garlic, and sauté just until shallots wilt, 1 to 1½ minutes. Add mustard greens and sauté until wilted, about 5 minutes, then season with salt and pepper. Divide among 4 large warmed plates. Ladle about ¼ cup of sauce from Step 1 around each plate.

8. Heat the remaining 2 tablespoons oil in skillet and quickly sauté wild mushrooms until wilted, then season with salt and pepper. Sprinkle around the plates. Place finished buffalo packets in the center, and top with fried sweet potato strings and crispy mustard greens.

NOTE:

D'Artagnan and some specialty food stores sell truffle butter. Otherwise, mix ¼ cup softened unsalted butter, 1 teaspoon truffle oil, and ¼ teaspoon minced black truffles (fresh or canned). You can substitute basil or another herb butter if you prefer.

Adapted from Scott Cohen, executive chef, Las Canarias Restaurant at La Mansión del Rio Hotel, San Antonio

That's really the difference — the hare is rich and gamy in flavor, the rabbit . . . fresh and succulent. The hare makes one think of port, burgundy, red currant jelly, spices and cream; the rabbit needs onions, mustard, white wine and thyme.

— Jane Grigson,
Good Things, 1971

rabbit and hare

ARIANE: Fifteen years ago I couldn't sell rabbit. No one wanted to serve them. I remember convincing one of our first clients, chef André Soltner at Lutèce, to buy 4. A couple of days later, he said he'd had to serve them to "the family," i.e., the staff. Now we sell at least 3,000 fresh rabbits a week.

Finally Americans are starting to order rabbit in restaurants and to cook it at home. It took sort of a backdoor approach to make it happen, but interest in the mild, fine-textured, pink-white meat is growing. Exposure to ethnic cuisines has been an important key. You see a food often enough and it's bound to sink in. Dishes like a *stifado,* rabbit and onions braised in a sweet, dark Greek wine, then covered with flaky phyllo (page 206); or a simple Provençal-style stew with sweet bell peppers, olives, and a splash of Pernod (page 205) invite experimentation.

Besides, there's the ever-increasing desire for healthful, easily prepared, high-quality protein. Rabbit has virtually no fat, is low in cholesterol, and is raised without growth hormones and antibiotics. Retail markets and butchers reflect this new attention by selling the meat fresh rather than frozen.

Today's domesticated animals are bred from a cross of California white and New Zealand white, the most tender of all rabbit breeds. They are far better eating than the tough, strong-flavored rabbits that early American pioneers existed on during their trek across the country. That's because the animals are raised in off-the-ground hutches in a controlled environment. Because diet largely determines flavor, domestic rabbits are fed on sweet alfalfa hay, oats, wheat, and barley. Strong-flavored greens, such as kale or cabbage, are forbidden, to preserve the animal's delicate flavor.

Generally, young (8- to 12-week-old) farm-raised rabbits that weigh between 2½ and 3 pounds are available. These whole *fryers,* like chicken, which they closely resemble in taste, can be prepared in numerous ways, from frying to roasting. If you are buying parts separately, the saddles and loins are the most tender, and can be quickly grilled or sautéed. Larger rabbits, 15 to 20 weeks old, are called *roasters.* They weigh 4½ to 5½ pounds and, like older birds, need slow, moist cooking, like braising.

Wild animals have a more pronounced flavor and are leaner. When cooking wild rabbit, there is an additional safety precaution to take beyond rinsing and blotting dry: you should wear rubber gloves. Even though the risk is minimal, occasionally wild rabbits carry tularemia, a bacterial infection that is killed once the animal is cooked.

If rabbit has a mild flavor on its side, hare appeals mostly to ardent game lovers. Along with grouse and woodcock, it is decidedly gamy tasting. Although both animals are from the same family, they are from different genera: hare is *Lepus* and rabbit is *Oryctolagus.* Hares are larger, weighing anywhere from 5 to 8 pounds. They have longer ears, and larger hind legs and feet. In spite of their names, American jackrabbits and snowshoe rabbits are both hares. The cottontail, however, is a rabbit.

The flesh of hare is darker, and the legs always need long, slow braising to become tender and less gamy. The saddles are best served rare. Because of its assertiveness, hare loves aggressive flavors — dried fruits, rich wines, wild mushrooms — as its partners. A slow bath in a hearty red wine and dried cherries, or full-bodied port wine with fresh thyme, does wonders to temper a hare.

Of all the ways to prepare hare, the most noble is surely Lièvre à la Royale, Ariane's favorite dish. In our version (page 219), chef Philippe Boulot, of the Heathman Hotel in Portland, Oregon, adds some striking contemporary garnishes to this Old World triumph. Without a doubt, this is fare for a lavish event. Yet when the work is done (and it will take a couple of days), you will experience a gustatory treat.

CUTTING UP RABBIT OR HARE

Cut a rabbit or hare into 6 to 8 pieces as follows: Using a sharp boning knife and cleaver, remove hind legs at socket joint, where legs join torso. If hind legs are large, chop them into 2 pieces at the leg joint. Next, gently slide flesh of front legs and upper rib cage forward to include as much meat as possible in front leg sections and remove shoulders from torso. Chop 1 inch off the ends of the torso, where the front and hind legs were removed, and reserve or discard; the remaining part of the torso is the saddle. Depending on what the recipe requires, either cut the saddle across the backbone into 2 or 4 pieces or bone it. The boned-out muscle from the saddle is the loin. If the recipe calls for rabbit loins, check to see if belly flap (the piece of meat extending beyond the rib cage) is left attached as part of the cooking method; if not, remove flaps and discard.

rabbit risotto with ramps and fiddlehead ferns

SERVES 6 AS A MAIN COURSE

This red-and-green-flecked risotto is a sensorially stimulating entrée. It's enticing to look at and both crunchy and creamy to the bite. Add a green salad and the meal is complete. A fiddlehead is not a species of fern, says produce expert Elizabeth Schneider, but a growth stage of any fern. When the tightly coiled new frond pokes through the soil but hasn't begun to uncurl, it is called a fiddlehead. The flavor is reminiscent of asparagus, artichokes, and green beans, with a hint of mushroom. The fiddlehead's crunchy texture is uniquely its own. If fiddleheads or asparagus are unavailable, use sliced green beans, spinach, or watercress.

3 tablespoons olive or canola oil

1 to 1½ pounds uncooked boneless rabbit loin, cut into ½-inch pieces, blotted dry

4 ramps (wild leeks) or 1 large leek, white and light green part, rinsed to remove sand, and drained, sliced ¼ inch thick

½ tablespoon finely chopped garlic

1 large red bell pepper, cored, seeded, and cut into ¼-inch dice

1 pound arborio rice

1 cup dry white wine

1½ quarts rabbit or chicken stock, heated

½ pound fiddlehead ferns or young asparagus, cleaned, trimmed, blanched and shocked (leave fiddleheads whole; cut asparagus on bias into ½-inch pieces)

4 ounces Manchego or Parmesan cheese, grated

2 ounces assorted fresh herbs (flat-leaf parsley, thyme, tarragon, chives), chopped

Salt and freshly ground black pepper to taste

6 small sprigs thyme, to garnish

1. Heat oil in a large heavy sauté pan over medium-high heat until hot. Add rabbit, stir to separate pieces, then add ramps, garlic, and red pepper. Sauté until vegetables are soft, about 3 minutes. Add rice and stir until well mixed and heated. Pour in wine and bring liquid to a boil.

2. Reduce heat and, stirring often, add heated stock by cupfuls, stirring until rice has nearly absorbed all of the liquid before adding the next cup. This will take about 20 minutes.

3. Add blanched fiddlehead ferns, cheese, and herbs. Mix and cook until heated

DO-AHEAD RISOTTO

A helpful suggestion from chef Nora Pouillon: It is possible to make this recipe in two stages; it saves time and is especially helpful when entertaining. Cook the arborio rice ahead of time, using all but 2 cups of the liquid, just until al dente, about 10 minutes. Then spread it on a sheet pan to cool quickly. When needed, bring the remaining stock and a little extra wine to a boil. Add the cooked rice, plus all the blanched vegetables and the cheese. Stir until heated through, for about 5 minutes. Taste for seasoning and serve.

through, 5 to 10 minutes. Rice grains should be al dente, but risotto should have a creamy consistency. Add more liquid if too dry. Season with salt and pepper. Divide among 6 warmed plates and serve garnished with a sprig of thyme.

Adapted from Nora Pouillon, chef-owner, Restaurant Nora and Asia Nora, Washington, D.C.

spiced rabbit legs with tomatoes, okra, and ginger
with scented basmati rice

SERVES 4

A generous and colorful mélange of rabbit and vegetables served over basmati rice. Both the rice and casserole are perfumed with an exotic blend of spices that imparts a haunting Indian or Creole flavor. Keep the spice mixture tightly capped and store in a dark cupboard or shelf. You can use it in several dishes, including Cranberry-Apple Chutney (page 302).

Regime Blend spice mixture (recipe follows)

4 rabbit hind legs, blotted dry

2 tablespoons olive oil

1 large onion, split lengthwise and cut into thin lengthwise strips

3 tablespoons chopped garlic

3 cups peeled, seeded, and chopped plum tomatoes (about 10 to 12), or chopped canned plum tomatoes

1 bay leaf

1 sprig thyme, or 1 teaspoon dried thyme

1 sprig rosemary, or 1 teaspoon dried rosemary

1 teaspoon grated orange zest

2-inch piece fresh gingerroot, julienned

1 cup vegetable or chicken stock

Scented Basmati Rice (recipe follows)

1 small cauliflower, core removed, florets thinly sliced

½ cup pitted imported black olives

½ pound okra

Salt and coarsely ground black pepper to taste

Tabasco to taste

½ cup coarsely chopped cilantro

1. Make Regime Blend spice mixture.
2. Season rabbit with 1 teaspoon Regime Blend. Heat a large heavy pot over medium-high heat. Add olive oil and rabbit legs, and brown 3 to 4 minutes on each side. Stir in onion and garlic, reduce heat to medium, and cook until onion begins to brown, 7 to 8 minutes.
3. Add tomatoes, bay leaf, thyme, rosemary, orange zest, ginger, and vegetable stock, and bring to a boil over high heat. Reduce heat so liquid is simmering. Partially cover pot, and cook until rabbit is fork tender, 45 minutes to 1 hour. *Dish may be prepared ahead to this point.*
4. While rabbit simmers, prepare Scented Basmati Rice.
5. Once rabbit is tender, return liquid to a boil, then adjust to a simmer. Remove bay leaf and, if using fresh sprigs, thyme and rosemary. Add cauliflower, olives, and okra. Partially cover, and cook just until vegetables are crisp-tender, 10 minutes. Season with salt, pepper, and Tabasco. Just

before serving, stir in half the cilantro. Use the remaining cilantro as garnish.

regime blend

3 tablespoons coriander seeds

2 star anise

1 tablespoon fennel seeds, half raw, half roasted

2 teaspoons mustard seeds

Seeds from 5 cardamom pods

1 teaspoon cumin seeds

1 teaspoon ground ginger

½ stick cinnamon, broken into pieces

1 teaspoon white peppercorns

1 teaspoon black peppercorns

3 bay leaves

¼ teaspoon ground mace

Combine all ingredients and grind finely in a spice mill or coffee grinder. Store in a covered jar.

scented basmati rice

1 tablespoon olive oil

2 shallots, minced

1 cup basmati rice

2 cups water

½ x 3-inch piece lemon zest

1 small sprig rosemary

1 bay leaf

1 teaspoon salt

¼ teaspoon Regime Blend spice mixture (recipe above)

Freshly ground black pepper to taste

1. Heat a large saucepan over medium-high heat. Add olive oil and shallots, and cook just until shallots are soft but not brown. Add rice and stir until it is lightly coated with oil, then add 2 cups water. Bring to a boil, add remaining ingredients, stir once, and cover. Reduce heat so liquid barely simmers, and cook for 15 minutes.

2. Remove pan from heat and set aside for 5 minutes. Fluff rice with a fork, and turn it into a shallow bowl to cool slightly.

Adapted from Daniel Orr, executive chef, La Grenouille, New York City

"floppy-eared chicken"— aka lapin à la moutarde
with orange-scented asparagus

SERVES 4

A bone-suckingly scrumptious rabbit dish that's appropriate for casual and fancy dinners alike. This classic dish is best served over steamed rice or potatoes, along with fresh asparagus and a Pinot Noir or Burgundy.

2 tablespoons rendered duck fat or unsalted butter

1 large onion, chopped fairly fine

1 young rabbit, about 3 pounds, cut into 6 to 8 pieces and blotted dry

All-purpose flour seasoned with salt and freshly ground black pepper, for dredging

¾ cup Dijon or Pommery mustard

½ cup or more light or heavy cream

1 tablespoon fresh tarragon leaves, chopped, or 1 teaspoon dried tarragon, plus 1 teaspoon chopped leaves, to garnish

4 ounces shiitake or white mushrooms, trimmed, wiped clean, and thinly sliced

Salt and freshly ground black pepper to taste

Orange-Scented Asparagus (recipe follows)

1. Preheat oven to 350°F.

2. Heat 1 tablespoon of the duck fat in a large heavy skillet over medium heat. Add onion and sauté until golden brown, 6 to 8 minutes, stirring occasionally. Remove onion with a slotted spoon to a bowl, leaving fat in the pan.

3. Dredge rabbit pieces in flour, patting to remove excess. Paint pieces liberally with mustard.

4. Add the remaining tablespoon of fat to pan and heat over medium-high heat. Add rabbit, flesh side down, and cook until browned, 3 to 4 minutes. Turn and cook second side until lightly browned, 3 to 4 minutes longer. Remove rabbit to a heatproof dish. Partially cover with foil, then bake in oven until legs are tender when pricked with a fork, 35 to 45 minutes.

5. Meanwhile, turn heat under skillet to high. Return onions to pan and stir in cream and tarragon, scraping up all browned cooking bits in the bottom of the pan. Once cream begins to thicken, reduce heat to medium, add mushrooms, and taste to adjust seasonings. Add more mustard and cream, if needed, and salt and pepper to taste.

6. Return rabbit and any pan juices to skillet. Turn once or twice to cover with sauce. Leave partially covered over low heat and prepare Orange-Scented Asparagus. *This dish may be made a few hours ahead of time and gently reheated.* Sprinkle 1 teaspoon chopped tarragon over rabbit and serve.

orange-scented asparagus

1 pound tender asparagus, woody ends removed

1 tablespoon unsalted butter

1 tablespoon orange juice

Salt and freshly ground black pepper to taste

Grated zest of 1 orange

Steam or boil asparagus until just tender. Blot dry. Combine butter and orange juice in a skillet and heat over medium heat. Stir together, add asparagus, and turn to coat. Season with salt and pepper. Scatter on orange zest, and serve.

FLOPPY-EARED CHICKEN

JOANNA: In the early 1980s, after dining at the home of some French friends in Montreal, my husband complimented the chef on "the most delectable chicken I've ever eaten." The hostess replied that the chicken had very floppy ears! The recipe was written down, and that's how many guests at our table have come to be seduced by the delectable flavor of rabbit. Originally the dish was made with smooth Dijon mustard and heavy cream, but we now prefer coarse-grained Pommery-style mustard and light cream or half-and-half. The choice is yours.

Three cheers that Americans are beginning to discover how delicious rabbit is!

pot de provence
with saffron-scented couscous

SERVES 4

This richly perfumed rabbit stew combines the bright colors and flavors that abound in Provence, the sun-drenched region of southern France. Rabbit, sweet peppers, fennel, tomatoes, and black olives gently marry in an aromatic anise-flavored broth. Serve the rabbit over Saffron-Scented Couscous to capture every last drop of the sauce. Pour a chilled rosé from Provence.

2 or more tablespoons olive oil

1 young rabbit, about 3 pounds, cut into 6 to 8 pieces and blotted dry

Coarse salt and coarsely ground black pepper to taste

1 large bulb fennel, trimmed and cut into strips (reserve fronds)

1 large onion, cut in half lengthwise and sliced

½ *each* red, orange, yellow, and green bell pepper, seeded and cut into strips (or use 1 red and 1 green pepper)

2 tablespoons chopped garlic

½ x 4-inch piece orange zest

1 cup chicken stock

¼ cup Pernod, Ricard, ouzo, or other anise-flavored liqueur

1 (14½-ounce) can diced tomatoes, drained

½ cup imported black olives, pitted

2 tablespoons reserved minced fennel fronds, plus fennel fronds, to garnish

Saffron-Scented Couscous (recipe follows)

1. Preheat oven to 350°F.

2. Heat 2 tablespoons oil in a large heavy casserole over medium-high heat until hot but not smoking. Add rabbit pieces and brown on both sides, about 4 minutes on each side. Do not crowd. If necessary sauté rabbit in batches. Remove pieces to a platter and season with salt and pepper.

3. Add fennel, onion, and peppers to casserole, along with a small amount of additional oil if needed. Sauté over medium-high heat until onion is lightly browned, 6 to 8 minutes, stirring often. Add garlic, cook for 30 seconds, then stir in orange zest, stock, Pernod, and tomatoes. Bring to a boil.

4. Return rabbit to casserole, cover with a tight-fitting lid, and transfer to oven. Cook until rabbit is almost tender, 35 to 45 minutes. Stir in olives and minced fennel fronds, season with salt and pepper, and cook 10 to 15 minutes longer.

5. Prepare Saffron-Scented Couscous. Serve each plate with a mound of couscous topped by rabbit and sauce, garnished with small fennel fronds.

saffron-scented couscous

¾ cup boiling water

¼ teaspoon saffron threads

¾ cup chicken stock

1 tablespoon extra-virgin olive oil

½ teaspoon salt or to taste

1½ cups couscous

2 teaspoons finely chopped flat-leaf parsley

Combine boiling water and saffron in a small saucepan and let stand until saffron is softened. Add stock, olive oil, and salt, and bring liquid just to a boil. Stir in couscous, cover pan, turn off heat, and allow to stand for 5 minutes. Uncover, stir in parsley, fluff with a fork, and serve.

stifado of rabbit in phyllo
with skordalia whipped potatoes

SERVES 4

A *stifado* is a traditional Greek rabbit or hare stew usually made with the sweet red local wine Mavrodaphne and plenty of pearl onions. In this version, the rabbit is first deboned and cut up, and the dish is covered with a thin layer of flaky phyllo — another Greek specialty — to make a festive pot pie. Serve it with whipped potatoes infused with fruity olive oil and plenty of garlic, inspired by skordalia, a favorite Greek hors d'oeuvre. Make this ahead, and add the phyllo just before cooking. Open a bottle of Mavrodaphne, Châteauneuf-du-Pape, or Madiran.

5 to 6 tablespoons olive oil

1 young rabbit, about 3 pounds, deboned, meat cut into large chunks, and blotted dry

Salt and freshly ground black pepper to taste

2 tablespoons chopped garlic

2 tablespoons dried currants

2 bay leaves

2 pounds pearl onions, peeled, with an X cut in each root end

1 teaspoon sugar

2 cups Mavrodaphne wine or ruby port

½ cup red wine vinegar

½ teaspoon ground allspice

8 whole cloves, or ⅛ teaspoon ground cloves

4 sheets phyllo, defrosted according to package directions if frozen

Skordalia Whipped Potatoes (recipe follows)

1. Heat 1½ tablespoons of the oil in a large heavy skillet over medium-high heat until almost smoking. Add rabbit pieces, in batches if necessary, and brown on all sides, 6 to 8 minutes. Add more oil as needed. Remove pieces with a slotted spoon to an oven-safe shallow casserole or gratin dish (rectangular if possible) just large enough to hold the rabbit and onions in a single layer. Season liberally with salt and pepper. Sprinkle on garlic, currants, and bay leaves. Set aside.

2. Add another tablespoon of the oil to the skillet and, when hot, add onions and sauté until starting to brown. Sprinkle on sugar and shake pan to cover onions. Continue cooking, adding a few drops of water so sugar does not burn, until onions are rich golden brown, about 4 minutes. Scrape onions into dish with rabbit.

3. Preheat oven to 375°F.

4. Pour wine and vinegar into skillet and bring to a boil over high heat, scraping bottom to incorporate any browned particles. Add allspice and cloves. Reduce liquid to ⅔ cup, then pour evenly over rabbit and onions.

5. Brush 1 phyllo sheet with olive oil and place it, oiled side up, over casserole. If casserole is too large to be easily covered by a single sheet, cover part of the pan at a time with each sheet, overlapping the sheets of phyllo as you lay them down. (If using an oval pan, trim or fold edges over to fit.) Continue with remaining phyllo, brushing the top of each sheet with oil. *Dish may be prepared ahead to this point and refrigerated for up to a day. Bring back to room temperature before continuing.*

6. Bake in oven until top is rich dark brown and juices are bubbling, 45 to 50 minutes. Leave in turned-off oven until ready to serve.

7. Meanwhile, prepare Skordalia Whipped Potatoes.

skordalia whipped potatoes

1 pound baking potatoes, peeled and roughly chopped

3 to 4 tablespoons extra-virgin olive oil

2 tablespoons minced garlic

Salt and freshly ground black pepper to taste

Put potatoes in a pot of cold water, bring to a boil, and cook until tender. Drain and pass potatoes through a food mill or a ricer. Whip in the olive oil, garlic, and salt and pepper.

CONEY ISLAND

Coney Island was named by early settlers to the New York island for the many rabbits there. "Cony" or "coney" is an early English word for rabbits. In Spanish, the word is *conejo.*

sicilian baked rabbit
with green olives, golden raisins, capers, and pine nuts

SERVES 4

Moorish, Greek, and Italian influences can all be tasted in this rustic dish, where sweet and sour flavors joust with salty olives and capers in the topping that is spooned over crunchy oven-baked rabbit. Serve over fettuccine noodles tossed with a fruity olive oil. Make the caponata topping ahead, if you prefer, and gently reheat before serving. Sauté sliced zucchini to serve with this. Add a bottle of full-bodied Italian red wine, such as Dolcetto d'Alba, Barbaresco, or Barolo, for the final touch.

4 to 5 tablespoons fruity olive oil

½ cup fresh bread crumbs seasoned with salt and freshly ground black pepper

1½ teaspoons dried oregano leaves

1 young rabbit, about 3 pounds, cut into 6 to 8 pieces and blotted dry

¾ pound onions, thinly sliced

1¼ cups celery cut in ½-inch dice

¾ cup dry white wine mixed with ¾ cup water

½ cup golden raisins

½ cup chopped Sicilian-style green olives

2 tablespoons tomato paste

2 tablespoons small capers, drained

⅓ cup chopped sun-dried tomatoes, softened in a little warm water if needed

¼ cup pine nuts, lightly toasted

Juice and grated zest of 1 orange

¼ cup chopped flat-leaf parsley

1. Preheat oven to 350°F. Lightly brush a roasting pan with a little oil.

2. Combine seasoned bread crumbs with ½ teaspoon of the oregano in a bowl. Coat rabbit pieces with crumbs, patting to cover all sides.

3. Heat 2 tablespoons of the oil in a large heavy skillet over medium-high heat until very hot but not smoking. Add rabbit pieces, flesh side down, and brown on both sides, about 4 minutes each side. Do not crowd. Work in batches if necessary, adding more oil as needed. Transfer rabbit with tongs to roasting pan and bake until tender, 35 to 45 minutes, turning once or twice during this time.

4. While rabbit is baking, make the caponata: Wipe out skillet and, still over medium-high heat, add 1½ tablespoons oil. When oil is hot, stir in onions, separating them into rings. Adjust heat to medium. Sauté onions until wilted, about 10 minutes, then add celery and continue cooking until onions are golden brown and very soft, about 5 minutes longer, stirring occasionally.

5. Pour in diluted wine and bring liquid to a boil over high heat, stirring up any browned bits. Add raisins, olives, tomato paste, and capers. Turn heat down so liquid gently boils. Reduce liquid until almost evaporated, 20 to 30 minutes, stirring occasionally. Stir in sun-dried tomatoes, pine nuts, zest and juice of orange, and parsley. Season generously with pepper and cook for 5 minutes more.

6. Serve warmed rabbit pieces on a platter or on individual plates, with a liberal amount of caponata mixture on top.

oven-roasted rabbit
with herbs

SERVES 4

This hassle-free, foolproof recipe requires only a good fresh rabbit and a pretty decent windowsill herb garden. Serve over boiled rice, pasta, or polenta. Pour a light red, such as a Côtes du Rhône Villages, Buzet, or Beaujolais.

1 young rabbit, about 3 pounds, cut into 6 to 8 pieces and blotted dry, or 4 rabbit hind legs, blotted dry

All-purpose flour for dredging

Salt and freshly ground black pepper to taste

2½ to 3 tablespoons duck fat or olive oil

1 *each* onion, carrot, celery rib, coarsely chopped

1½ tablespoons crushed garlic

1 cup water

½ cup duck and veal demi-glace (see page 33)

¼ cup chopped fresh herbs (choose from rosemary, thyme, sage, oregano, savory, chives, chervil)

1. Preheat oven to 350°F. Heat a large heavy skillet over high heat.

2. Lightly dust rabbit with flour, patting to remove excess. Season with salt and pepper. Add duck fat to hot skillet and sear rabbit on all sides until golden brown, about 4 minutes on each side. Do this in batches if the pieces are crowded. Remove meat and set aside.

3. Add onion, carrot, celery, and garlic, and sauté until lightly colored, 4 minutes, stirring occasionally. Pour in water and demi-glace, stirring up any browned particles. Add herbs and reserved rabbit to pan. Season with salt and pepper. Bring to a gentle boil, then cover and bake for 40 minutes (if using just legs, continue cooking for 20 minutes longer).

4. Serve sauce, vegetables, and rabbit over boiled rice, pasta, or polenta, if desired.

penang curried rabbit and spinach in broth

SERVES 4

Bold and exciting, this one-dish meal includes pale morsels of juicy rabbit, thin ribbons of spinach, and toothsome, dark japonica rice set against a spicy, pale rose-colored broth. The combination will electrify your taste buds.

1 tablespoon canola oil

1 young rabbit, about 3 pounds, cut into 6 to 8 pieces and blotted dry

Salt and freshly ground black pepper to taste

¾ cup chicken stock

1 (14-ounce) can coconut milk

2 tablespoons Penang-style curry paste (available at supermarkets or Asian markets)

2 tablespoons fish sauce (*nam pla* or *nuoc mam*)

1 stalk lemongrass, trimmed, center portion finely chopped

2 small hot red chilies, thinly sliced

½ cup black japonica or Thai rice (see Note)

¾ to 1 pound leaf spinach, washed, coarse stems removed, and cut into fine shreds

3 tablespoons chopped cilantro

1. Heat oil in a large deep skillet over medium-high heat. Add rabbit and brown lightly on both sides, about 1 to 2 minutes. Do not crowd. If necessary, do this in batches. Remove pieces to a bowl and season with salt and pepper.

2. Pour in chicken stock and bring to a boil, stirring up all browned bits. Add coconut milk, curry paste, fish sauce, lemongrass, and red chilies. Return rabbit to pan, cover, and simmer gently until rabbit is tender, about 1 hour. Remove rabbit and, when cool enough to handle, debone it and cut into bite-size pieces. Return meat to broth.

3. Meanwhile, bring 1⅛ cups of salted water to a boil. Stir in rice, cover, and lower heat so liquid slowly simmers. Cook until rice is firm but tender, 45 minutes.

4. Before serving, stir spinach into broth and simmer until just tender. Place a mound of rice in the center of each of 4 large flat soup bowls. Divide rabbit pieces among bowls, spoon on liquid with spinach, sprinkle with cilantro, and serve.

NOTE: Like polished small oval pebbles, grains of the California-grown black japonica rice become dark mahogany-colored and densely flavorful when cooked. It is available at some supermarkets, health food stores, and Asian groceries.

b & b: bunnies and bourbon sauce

with sautéed swiss chard and southern-style stewed tomatoes

SERVES 6

You'll enjoy a gracious sample of Southern hospitality with loads of contemporary pizzazz in this imaginative pairing of seared rabbit loins and individual rabbit strudels. They are served atop Swiss chard with stewed tomatoes ringing the plates. A sauce of reduced stock and bourbon is dribbled over the meat.

Although this preparation looks complicated, don't panic. Much of the work is done ahead of time and spread out over a couple of days. Instead of making the stock, you can substitute 2½ cups duck and veal demi-glace (see page 33). You could easily double this recipe, without much more work, and serve a dozen guests. Garlic-Cheddar Grits (page 171) would be excellent with the rabbit. For a little Southern comfort, sip a refreshing mint julep while preparing the dish, and serve with a simple, hearty red wine.

3 rabbits, about 3 pounds each, cut into 6 pieces (leave flaps attached)

FOR THE LOINS AND THIGHS:

½ cup peanut oil, plus extra for sautéing

1 tablespoon minced garlic

2 teaspoons dried thyme

1 teaspoon black peppercorns

3 bay leaves, broken into large pieces

FOR THE STOCK AND SAUCE:

4 tablespoons unsalted butter

1 onion, diced

1 carrot, diced

2 ribs celery, diced

3 quarts water

¼ cup plus 1 tablespoon Maker's Mark or other fine bourbon

FOR THE STRUDELS:

1 tablespoon salt or to taste

Freshly ground black pepper to taste

Pinch freshly grated nutmeg

½ to ¾ cup heavy cream, chilled

6 tablespoons chopped pecans, lightly toasted

3 tablespoons chopped fresh chives

3 tablespoons unsalted butter

6 sheets phyllo, defrosted according to package directions

Sautéed Swiss Chard (recipe follows)

Southern-Style Stewed Tomatoes (recipe follows)

1. Bone the rabbit loins (leaving flaps attached) and thighs, and set aside all remaining rabbit bones and trimmings for stock.

2. Combine oil, garlic, thyme, peppercorns, and bay leaves with loins and thighs in a resealable plastic bag or shallow bowl. Mix well to cover meat. Seal or cover, and marinate in refrigerator for up to 2 days.

3. Preheat oven to 375°F.

4. MAKE THE STOCK AND SAUCE:
Chop bones and trimmings into 2-to-3-inch pieces, spread on a flat baking pan, and roast until a rich brown color, 40 minutes to 1 hour. Meanwhile, melt 2 tablespoons of the butter in a large skillet and when hot, add onion, carrot, and celery, and sauté until light brown, about 10 minutes, stirring frequently.

5. Combine roasted bones, vegetables, and water in a stockpot and bring to a boil. Reduce heat to medium low and simmer 2 hours. Strain stock and degrease. Pour stock into a saucepan along with ¼ cup bourbon. Bring to a boil and reduce mixture to 2 cups. If making in advance, cool and refrigerate in a tightly covered container. *May be prepared 2 days ahead. Or, to eliminate Step 4 and most of Step 5, substitute 2½ cups of duck and veal demi-glace for the stock, add the ¼ cup bourbon, and reduce to 2 cups.*

6. PREPARE STRUDELS: Put 3 of the marinated thighs, salt, pepper, and nutmeg in a food processor and pulse until puréed and smooth. With motor running, slowly pour in ½ cup of the cream, and process just until mixture is a pale pinkish-white color and completely smooth, adding more cream if needed. Do not over-process. Add pecans and chives, and pulse to blend. Test seasoning by frying a small amount of the mixture in a skillet. Adjust seasoning if needed. *This will make filling for 6 strudels. Save remaining thighs for another use, or sauté and slice later to add to the finished plates* (see Step 13).

7. Melt 3 tablespoons butter. Layer 3 sheets of phyllo on a clean workspace, brushing each sheet with melted butter. Position the stack so the long edge runs horizontally in front of you, and trim the stack to about 14 inches in length. Now cut phyllo into 3 equal stacks, each measuring about 4½ inches wide. Spoon 2½ to 3 tablespoons of filling, in a line, on the lower (short) edge of each pile, leaving a ½-inch margin on both sides. Roll lower edge of phyllo over filling, turn in sides, then roll up into a log. Each strudel should measure about 3 to 3¼ inches in length. Place on a baking sheet and brush tops with melted butter. Repeat with remaining phyllo and filling to make 3 more strudels. *Strudels may be prepared up to this point 2 days ahead of time, then lightly covered and refrigerated. Chilled strudels may take a few minutes longer to brown.*

8. Prepare Sautéed Swiss Chard through Step 1 and keep warm; prepare Southern-Style Stewed Tomatoes through Step 2.

9. Preheat oven to 350°F.

10. Bake strudels until hot and golden brown, about 20 minutes. Keep warm until needed. *Or strudels may be baked a few hours ahead of time and reheated.*

11. Return bourbon sauce to stove and bring to a boil over high heat. Stir in remaining 1 tablespoon bourbon and 2 tablespoons butter. Season with salt and pepper, and keep warm. Sauce should be jus-like.

12. Remove loins from marinade, picking off bay leaves and peppercorns. Wrap belly flap around loin, trimming edge of flap so it is straight and just long enough to encircle the loin; attach with a toothpick. Make 2 little cuts about ¼ inch long across each loin so they do not curl when cooking.

13. Film bottom of a large skillet with oil and heat until almost smoking over high heat. Add rabbit loins and cook for about 2 minutes, shaking the pan to turn them and color all sides evenly. Do not crowd. If necessary, do this in batches. Transfer loins to a rack and finish in a 350°F oven, until loins feel firm when pressed, about 10 minutes. *If cooking extra thighs, do so here. Brown in a hot skillet 2 minutes per side, and finish in oven for 20 to 25 minutes.* Finish stewed tomatoes. Let loins (and thighs) rest while you finish Swiss chard.

14. Pull toothpicks from loins and slice meat on a slight angle. Make a bed of chard on each of 6 warmed dinner plates. Place sliced loin on chard. Cut strudels in half on a diagonal. Lay 1 half on plate with second half propped up so filling is seen (add sliced thigh meat). Spoon stewed tomatoes around plates, ladle bourbon sauce over loins, and serve.

sautéed swiss chard

3 tablespoons unsalted butter

2 medium onions, diced

1 teaspoon minced garlic

2 pounds Swiss chard (not red variety), cleaned, with stems trimmed at end and thinly sliced lengthwise and leaves cut into wide strips

Coarse salt and freshly ground black pepper to taste

1. Heat butter in a large skillet over medium heat. Add onions and sauté until soft, 4 to 5 minutes. Stir in garlic and cook 2 minutes longer. Add chard stems and sauté until tender, about 3 to 4 minutes. Set pan aside until ready to finish. *May be done several hours ahead and reheated.*

2. Return sautéed chard mixture to stovetop. Turn heat to medium high and add cut chard leaves. Sauté just until leaves are wilted, about 10 minutes, adding 1 to 2 tablespoons of water if necessary. Season with salt and pepper and serve.

southern-style stewed tomatoes

4 tablespoons olive oil

1 cup firm white bread cubes about ¼ inch square

Salt and freshly ground black pepper to taste

1 cup finely diced onion

3 cups good-quality canned diced tomatoes, drained, or fresh tomatoes, peeled, diced, and drained

Pinch of sugar, if needed

1. Preheat oven to 325°F.

2. Heat 2 tablespoons of the oil in a skillet over medium heat. Add croutons, stirring gently for 5 minutes. Season with salt and pepper. Transfer to a baking sheet and toast until crisp and golden brown, about 10 minutes. Set aside. *Dish may be done ahead to this point.* Turn heat up to 350°F.

3. Heat remaining 2 tablespoons oil over medium heat. Add onions and sauté until soft but not brown, 4 to 5 minutes. Add tomatoes (and sugar, if tomatoes are acidic), and salt and pepper to taste. Pour into a 1-quart flat baking dish, top with croutons, and heat until warm, about 15 minutes.

Adapted from Susan McCreight Lindeborg, chef, Morrison-Clark Inn, Washington, D.C.

braised legs of wild hare in thyme–port wine sauce

SERVES 4

Here's a robust winter dish for game aficionados. Hare's substantial flavor and aroma stand up to very bold sauces, while the meat needs to simmer gently to become fork tender. If you don't want to invest the 3 days it takes to make Lièvre à la Royale (page 219) — Ariane's favorite dish — here is a succulent and simple alternative. Enjoy an excellent Châteauneuf-du-Pape or a California Rhone varietal blend, like Bonny Doon's Le Cigare Volant, with this hearty dinner.

1½ cups tawny port

2 teaspoons minced garlic

12 black peppercorns

2 bay leaves

1 bunch fresh thyme

4 wild hare hind legs

1 tablespoon rendered duck fat or olive oil

1 large shallot, minced

¾ cup duck and veal demi-glace (see page 33)

Salt and freshly ground black pepper to taste

10 ounces pearl onions, peeled, with an X cut in the root end of each

½ pound small white mushrooms, wiped clean, trimmed, and split

2 medium carrots, cut into 1-inch dice

1 pound fresh fettuccine noodles

1. Combine port, garlic, peppercorns, 1 of the bay leaves, and a few sprigs of the thyme in a saucepan, and bring to a rolling boil over high heat. Boil for 2 minutes, then turn off heat and cool for 1 hour. Put hare legs in a bowl or resealable plastic bag, and pour cooled marinade over legs. Cover bowl or seal bag, and refrigerate for at least 8 hours, or overnight.
2. Remove hare from marinade and pat dry. Strain and reserve marinade. Heat

---

ALL EARS

For three years, Pascal Coudouy, now chef at Le Périgord in New York, was André Daguin's sous-chef at the Hôtel de France in Auch. One of his duties was to work with the interns from the local hotel school who came to work in Daguin's kitchen. After a while, the sous-chef had a sense about who would or wouldn't make it as a cook. One young student was, in Coudouy's eyes, hopeless, and he soon grew tired of his ways. One day he asked the boy to skin, cut up, and clean the rabbits that were just brought in.

After the task was done, the sous-chef inspected the work and looked at the young man in mock horror. "But where did you put the ears?" he asked. When the intern confessed he had thrown them in the garbage, Coudouy bellowed, "But they are chef Daguin's favorite dish!"

It took the student an entire day before he went to Daguin to apologize. Sweating and stammering, he admitted to the chef that, yes, he had thrown out the ears. Daguin fired a glance over at Coudouy, who was doing his best not to laugh, and said, "OK, just don't let it happen again."

duck fat in a large, deep cast iron or other heavy skillet over high heat. Sauté legs for 3 to 4 minutes per side, turning to brown on both sides.

3. Remove legs. Lower heat to medium, add shallot, and sauté until lightly browned, 1 to 2 minutes, stirring often. Pour in marinade, bring liquid to a boil over high heat, stirring to incorporate any browned cooking particles. Reduce liquid by one-third, about 2 minutes. Add demi-glace and season with salt and pepper.

4. Return hare legs to skillet and add onions, mushrooms, carrots, remaining bay leaf, and all but 4 sprigs of the thyme. Bring liquid to a boil, then reduce heat so it just simmers. Cover and cook slowly until legs are fork tender, 45 minutes to 1 hour 15 minutes. Keep warm.

5. Bring a large pot of salted water to a boil. Add fettuccine and cook until al dente, then drain well and divide among 4 warmed dinner plates. Spoon sauce over fettuccine. Divide vegetables among plates, then add the legs and garnish with sprigs of thyme.

stephen's jugged hare

SERVES 4 TO 6

Jugged hare is one of the oldest traditional English dishes. References to hare, vegetables, and red wine sealed in a tall crockery jug, slowly cooked inside another pot of water, appear before the Roman invasion. Although originally considered fare of poor country folk, this richly seasoned dish will please the most urbane diner. Stephen Day, a transplanted Englishman residing in Washington, D.C., learned to make jugged hare from his mother and from his grandfather and uncles, who hunted. Here the jug is replaced by a heavy casserole, and the hare is braised in a slow oven. Making it a day or two ahead and then slowly reheating softens and mellows the flavors. Add wide noodles and steamed French green beans for a satisfying meal. Be sure to serve the hare with red currant jelly to complement the flavors. Pour the same Cabernet Sauvignon or Pinot Noir used for cooking.

2 tablespoons unsalted butter

1 tablespoon olive or canola oil

3 tablespoons all-purpose flour

1 hare, cut into 6 or 8 pieces and blotted dry

Coarse salt and coarsely ground black pepper to taste

1 cup duck and veal demi-glace (see page 33), or 2 cups veal stock reduced by half

1 large onion, cut in half and sliced crosswise, plus 1 medium onion, studded with 8 cloves

24 black peppercorns

3 large bay leaves

1 cup hearty red wine, such as Cabernet Sauvignon or Pinot Noir, plus ⅔ cup water

2 tablespoons tawny port

1 tablespoon red currant jelly, plus jelly to serve along with the cooked hare

1 bouquet garni

1 teaspoon Worcestershire sauce

¼ teaspoon sweet paprika

3 dashes Tabasco

Minced parsley, to garnish

1. Preheat oven to 325°F.

2. Heat butter and oil in a large heavy casserole over medium-high heat until hot. Sprinkle flour on hare and cook until lightly browned, 3 to 4 minutes per side, stirring often. Season with salt and a generous amount of black pepper.

3. Pour in demi-glace and stir, scraping up any browned cooking bits. Add sliced onion and cook for 3 minutes, then add clove-studded onion, peppercorns, bay leaves, diluted wine, port, 1 tablespoon of red currant jelly, the bouquet garni, Worcestershire sauce, paprika, and Tabasco. Bring liquid to a boil, then cover casserole and braise in oven until meat is very tender when pierced with a fork, about 1½ hours. Remove from oven, discard bay leaves and bouquet garni. Arrange pieces of hare on a platter, ladle sauce over meat, sprinkle on parsley, and serve. Pass red currant jelly at the table.

Adapted from Stephen Day, avid hunter, bon vivant, and cook, Washington, D.C.

ragù of hare with peas
over homemade gnocchi

SERVES 4 TO 6

In Italian *ragù* usually refers to a rich sauce flavored with meat or poultry. Indeed, one could make this rustic dish with small amounts of leftover parts of rabbit and hare, and serve it as a sauce for gnocchi or pasta. However, here the entire hare is braised in the sauce until every morsel is easily pulled from the bones. It is especially pleasing when ladled over potato gnocchi, small potato dumplings. In keeping with the Italian flavor, savor a glass of Barolo.

4 tablespoons olive oil

1 hare, cut into 6 or 8 pieces and blotted dry

Salt and freshly ground black pepper to taste

1 *each* small onion, small carrot, small rib celery, finely chopped

1 teaspoon finely chopped garlic

4 ounces thickly sliced prosciutto or other unsmoked, dry-cured bacon, chopped

¾ cup chopped flat-leaf parsley, plus 2 tablespoons chopped parsley, to garnish

1 tablespoon chopped fresh basil leaves, or 1 teaspoon dried basil

1 (28-ounce) can crushed plum tomatoes

1 cup hearty red wine

½ cup beef or chicken stock

Homemade Gnocchi (recipe follows), or purchased gnocchi or pappardelle

1 cup shelled peas or petit frozen peas, defrosted

Freshly grated Parmigiano-Reggiano

1. Preheat oven to 350°F.

2. Heat oil in a large heavy pot over medium-high heat until hot but not smoking. Add hare and brown on both sides, about 4 minutes each side. Take care not to crowd; do this in batches if necessary. Remove pieces with a slotted spoon to a platter. Season with salt and a generous amount of pepper.

3. Add onion, carrot, celery, and garlic to pot and sauté until wilted, 5 to 6 minutes. Stir in prosciutto, ¾ cup parsley, basil, and

tomatoes, scraping up all browned cooking bits. Pour in wine and stock and bring to a boil. Return hare to pot, cover, and braise in oven until tender, 1¾ to 2 hours.
4. Meanwhile, prepare Homemade Gnocchi.
5. Lift hare from sauce with a slotted spoon and allow to rest on a platter until cool enough to handle. Remove meat from bones, discarding bones. Chop meat into small pieces and return to sauce. *Recipe may be made to this point several days ahead and refrigerated.* Add peas, cook until tender, then taste to adjust seasonings. Spoon gnocchi onto a large warm platter. Ladle on ragù, sprinkle on parsley, and serve. Pass Parmesan cheese at table.

homemade gnocchi

¾ pound mature boiling potatoes, quartered

1 to 1½ cups all-purpose flour

1. Put potatoes in a large pot of cold water, bring to a boil, and cook until tender, 12 to 14 minutes. Drain and, when cool enough to handle, peel. Lightly sprinkle a large wooden board with flour. Press potatoes through a potato ricer or food mill, and spread out on the board to cool.
2. Begin incorporating flour by ½ cupfuls into potatoes, dusting hands, board, and potatoes repeatedly as you knead potatoes into a smooth, uniform, slightly sticky dough. When smooth, knead 3 to 4 minutes more, then form dough into a cylinder about 4 to 5 inches in diameter.
3. Cut off slices about 1 inch thick. Cut slices into 1-inch widths, then roll into

strands about ¾ inch in diameter. Cut into 1-inch lengths. Allow gnocchi to dry on floured board.
4. Bring a large pot of salted water to a boil. Add about a quarter of the gnocchi at a time. After water returns to a boil, continue cooking for 30 to 40 seconds, then remove with a skimmer or slotted spoon to a warm platter. Repeat with remaining gnocchi.

Inspired by a chicken dish prepared by Mita Antolini, Cortona, Italy

hare cooked two ways, with red wine and cherries

SERVES 4

Surely a showstopper for lovers of great game dishes. Tangy cherries and spiced red wine, port, and Armagnac permeate the assertively flavored hare to the point that it's positively tame. The legs become a juicy, meaty sauce, while the loins are seared and sliced. The simplest wild rice, pasta, or spaetzle will soak up all the delicious sauce. If you want to serve a vegetable with this dish, choose one that is bright green, such as green beans or broccoli florets.

4½ cups red wine, such as a Rioja or Madiran

1½ cups dried cherries

1 hare

¼ cup tawny port

2 tablespoons Armagnac, Cognac, or brandy

2 tablespoons red wine vinegar

1 tablespoon coriander seeds

1 tablespoon juniper berries, bruised

½ tablespoon black peppercorns

3 bay leaves

4 tablespoons plus ½ teaspoon canola oil

1 tablespoon unsalted butter

2 medium onions, coarsely chopped

2 medium carrots, coarsely chopped

2 large heads garlic, coarsely chopped

1 tablespoon all-purpose flour

5 cups veal, chicken, or game stock

Salt to taste

Finely chopped flat-leaf parsley, to garnish

1. One day prior to cooking, combine 1½ cups of the wine with 1½ cups of the dried cherries. Cover and refrigerate overnight.

2. Cut up hare by removing front and hind legs. Remove loins from saddle in one piece from either side of the backbone, and carefully remove white membrane from surface of loin. Save all trimmings. Chop bones into 2- to 3-inch pieces. Combine hind legs, front legs, loin meat, bones, and trimmings with the remaining 3 cups of red wine, the port, Armagnac, vinegar, coriander seeds, juniper berries, peppercorns, and bay leaves in a nonreactive bowl. Cover and refrigerate overnight.

3. Next day, remove legs and loins from marinade. Dry them well and set aside. Return loins to refrigerator until needed.

4. Heat 2 tablespoons of the oil and the butter in a large casserole over medium-high heat until hot. Add onions, carrots,

and garlic, and sauté until lightly browned, 5 to 6 minutes. Sprinkle on flour and continue cooking until flour is light brown, 30 seconds. Add all of the marinade from the cherries and about 1 cup of the cherries, reserving about ½ cup. Add the hare marinade mixture along with remaining trimmings and bones. Stir well and bring to a boil. Reduce heat and simmer for 20 minutes.

5. Meanwhile, heat 2 additional tablespoons of oil in a large skillet over high heat. When smoking, add front and rear hare legs, and brown well, 3 to 4 minutes per side. When legs are brown, transfer to pot of simmering marinades. Discard oil in skillet, and, over high heat, deglaze pan with a little of the simmering marinade, stirring to incorporate any browned cooking bits. Pour deglazing juices into casserole.

6. Pour stock into casserole and bring to a boil. Reduce heat and skim fat from mixture. Cover and continue to simmer until hare legs are tender, approximately 1¾ to 2 hours, stirring occasionally. (Note: front legs will be done first and should be removed when tender; lightly cover and set aside.)

7. When all legs have been removed, raise heat and allow sauce to boil gently for 30 to 40 minutes. Strain liquid into a clean pot, pressing hard on solids to extract as much flavor as possible. Reduce liquid over high heat until lightly thickened and flavorful, about 20 minutes. Season with salt.

8. Remove meat from legs, pulling it off in large pieces, add to sauce along with remaining cherries, and simmer gently for 15 minutes.

9. Meanwhile, heat remaining ½ teaspoon oil in a sauté pan until very hot. Blot loins dry, then brown on all sides, 2 to 3 minutes total cooking time. Do not overcook; they should be quite rare.

10. Spoon some of the hare leg stew onto 4 warmed plates, adding a little extra sauce to put the loins on. Slice loins crosswise and divide among plates. Scatter a little parsley on top and serve.

Adapted from David Waltuck, chef-owner, Chanterelle, New York City

lièvre à la royale garnished with ziti in wine-cream sauce and beet mousseline

SERVES 8

Truly a dish for royalty, and one of Ariane's favorite foods: boned hares stuffed with foie gras and forcemeat. Rolled and braised in wine and stock, the hare is then sliced and presented surrounded with wine-and-cream-bathed ziti and ovals of puréed beets. Yes, it's time-consuming, but most of the work is done ahead. You and your guests will marvel at the dramatic results; it's indeed a dish fit for nobles. Accent it with the richness of a fine Bordeaux, such as Château Lynch Bages.

2 Scottish hares, or 8 hare hind legs

2 tablespoons olive oil or unsalted butter

6 ounces wild mushrooms such as chanterelles, cèpes, morels, cleaned, stems removed if necessary, cut into small dice

3 ounces shallots, minced, plus 2 ounces shallots, finely chopped

¼ cup Armagnac or brandy

8 ounces ground pork

1½ teaspoons fresh thyme leaves, plus 1 bunch thyme

1 teaspoon plus 1 tablespoon chopped fresh sage leaves

2 teaspoons salt or to taste

1 teaspoon pepper or to taste

8 ounces Grade B foie gras (see page 255)

1 *each* onion, carrot, and celery rib, coarsely chopped

3 (750-ml) bottles full-bodied, fruity red wine

1 tablespoon all-purpose flour

12 juniper berries

1 stick cinnamon

1 large bay leaf

2 to 4 tablespoons red currant jelly

1 cup heavy cream

1 pound fresh beets

2 tablespoons unsalted butter

40 pieces (about 4 ounces) dried ziti or other large tubular pasta

QUICK MEASURING STICK

When boiling liquids to reduce them, a simple way to estimate how much evaporation takes place is to dip a wooden stick, such as a chopstick, into the liquid and mark how deep it is at the start. As the liquid cooks down, you can gauge the progress without pouring it into a measuring cup each time.

1. Cut up hare into legs, saddles, and flaps. Carefully debone hind legs and saddles, and set meat aside. Scrape meat from front legs and from the inside of the saddles (tenderloins). Combine with flap meat in a food processor and pulse until fairly finely chopped. Reserve all bones.

2. Heat oil in a skillet over medium-high heat. Add wild mushrooms and the 3 ounces minced shallots. Sauté until tender, 2½ to 3 minutes, then pour in Armagnac and deglaze pan over high heat until liquid evaporates. Allow to cool, then scrape mixture into food processor with chopped hare. Add pork, the 1½ teaspoons thyme leaves, 1 teaspoon sage, salt, and pepper. Pulse until blended. Do not overmix.

3. Line a 3 x 5 x 10-inch loaf pan with plastic wrap. Lay 2 of the boned legs on the bottom, pressing into place to cover bottom as completely as possible. Place loins against sides of pan. Put half the forcemeat in pan. Cut foie gras into chunks the size of your thumb, and lay them down center of forcemeat. Add remaining forcemeat, and cover with remaining 2 legs, pressing them gently into forcemeat. Wrap plastic wrap

over terrine and refrigerate until firm, preferably overnight.

4. Preheat oven to 400°F.

5. Place bones, onion, carrot, and celery in a deep pot, large enough to hold hare terrine along with braising liquid. Roast bones and vegetables uncovered until bones are a rich mahogany color, about 1 hour, stirring occasionally.

6. Meanwhile, lay out a 24-inch square of cheesecloth. Remove terrine from refrigerator and unmold onto cheesecloth. Remove plastic wrap and roll up terrine snugly in cheesecloth. Secure ends with string. Tie string around width of terrine, every 1 to 1½ inches, using butcher's knots.

7. Remove pot with roasted bones from oven. Adjust temperature to 350°F.

8. Pour in 2½ bottles wine (pour yourself a glass of the remainder), add the flour, juniper berries, cinnamon, bay leaf, and bunch of thyme. Bring to a boil, then reduce to a simmer. Lower terrine carefully into liquid, cover pan with aluminum foil and a lid, and return to oven. Cook until an instant-read thermometer inserted into the center reads 135°F, 50 to 70 minutes.

THE WAY TO GO, ROYALLY

ARIANE: Jean-Michel Cazes, the owner of Château Lynch Bages, in Pauillac, was planning to visit New York a few years ago. We decided to have a series of game dinners at the Waldorf Astoria. Of course, it would be with D'Artagnan's game and Cazes's wine. At that time Laurent Manrique, another Gascon, was the chef of the hotel's restaurant, Peacock Alley. Among the many dishes he suggested was Lièvre à la Royale, which Laurent executes magnificently.

Jean-Michel arrived in New York with strict orders from his doctors and, more significantly, his wife, Teresa: NO MORE RICH FOOD. He was firmly intending to follow this edict until he took a look at the menu. For each of the subsequent four nights of the series, we ate double portions of Lièvre à la Royale, and both Jean-Michel and I decided this was the dish that, if given the opportunity, we would choose to enjoy as our last supper.

If liquid does not completely cover terrine, turn terrine over halfway through the cooking time. Cool overnight in the liquid.

9. Remove terrine from braising liquid. Strain liquid into a clean pan, bring to a boil, and reduce by half. Stir in jelly and adjust seasonings.

10. Combine remaining 2 ounces of shallots with the reduced braising liquid and bring to a boil. Reduce by half, then pour in all but 1 tablespoon of the cream and, over medium-high heat, reduce to the consistency of light cream, stirring occasionally. Stir in chopped sage leaves and keep warm.

11. Cook beets in salted water until tender when pierced with a knife. Drain, peel, and purée in a food processor. Add remaining tablespoon of cream, the but-ter, and salt and pepper. Pulse to blend, then keep warm in a small saucepan.

12. Bring a pot of salted water to a boil. Add ziti and cook until al dente.

13. While ziti are cooking, remove cheese-cloth from terrine and cut terrine into 1-inch slices. Carefully place slices in a large skillet, with a little braising liquid, to reheat over medium-high heat.

14. Drain ziti and toss with wine-cream sauce. Arrange 5 ziti around the outside of each of 8 heated plates. Place 3 small ovals of beet mousseline on pasta. Place 1 slice of terrine in the center of each plate and spoon about $1/4$ cup of sauce on top. Pour yourself one more glass of reserved red wine, and relax.

Adapted from Philippe Boulot, chef de cuisine, Heathman Hotel, Portland, Oregon

These are the beasts which ye shall eat . . . the hart, and
the roebuck, and the fallow deer.

— Deuteronomy 14:4–5

venison

Talk about a culinary superstar: venison easily claims the title of "a red meat for the millennium"! Walk into most better restaurants and there it is on the menu. Cruise down progressive supermarket aisles and, chances are, venison fillets and sausages are featured. The meat is being showcased in food magazines and heralded on talk shows.

Why the change from outcast to darling?

GEORGE: Because finally, in a climate where a desire for healthful eating has sometimes eclipsed even the demand for taste, there's a flavorful and tender red meat that has all the right attributes: it's low in cholesterol, calories, and fat, and raised without hormones or steroids. Venison is also versatile and easy and quick to prepare. The quality is consistent, it's readily available in manageable cuts the year around, and there's little waste and shrinkage.

Obviously, there are a lot of wannabe meat eaters out there, since D'Artagnan's venison sales are up 20 percent compared with last year. Also, I think Bambi has lost some sympathy recently. Many mild-mannered urban homeowners are aggressively seeking ways to protect their gardens from deer. It's making eating them less distasteful.

The word "venison" comes from the Latin verb *venari,* to hunt. It refers to the meat of several species of the deer family, from small roe and axis deer, through fallow, white-tailed, and red deer, to large elk and moose. All have fine-grained and supple flesh that varies in color from pale (axis) to dark red (roe) with the species of animal.

ARIANE: The flavor of the meat ranges from sweet and subtle to strongly gamy. Eighty-five percent of venison sold in the United States is farmed deer from New

Zealand, primarily marketed under the appellation Cervena. Between fallow and red Cervena deer there are subtle taste and color differences, but the carcass of the red deer is appreciably larger. These animals graze exclusively on grasses, so they taste milder than the roe deer from Scotland that forage for berries, leaves, and heather. Americans, just learning to appreciate deer meat, like this mildness.

The variable conditions under which wild animals live make finding a good piece of roe deer a hit-or-miss affair. When conditions are favorable, it can be sublime and exceptionally tender, and devotées crave the meat.

GEORGE: Within the last 10 years, we've seen some of the best young chefs and adventuresome diners turn venison's future around. Before that, for a good part of this century, venison ranked fairly low on most Americans' list of epicurean favorites. In restaurants, venison was served sporadically during winter months. It tended to be over-marinated, oversauced, and overpriced. Who knew how delicious the meat could be if prepared simply, to allow the true taste to be savored?

Home cooks who weren't hunters, and even some friends and family of those who were, thought of the meat as a gastronomic pariah. And no wonder. Its arrival was generally signaled by a car pulling into the driveway with a bloody carcass — field dressed if you were lucky — tethered to the hood. Or it came as irregular, butcher-paper-wrapped parcels of uneven or inedible quality that often emerged as massive blocks of freezer-burned meat.

Basically, there were hunters and a few specialty outlets from which to obtain venison. Not surprisingly, a lot of stews and chili dishes were made from the poorly handled

Farm-raised deer in New Zealand ∧

meat. Of course, deer hunting with bow and arrow or guns continues to be a venerated sport. Fortunately, hunters today better understand how to handle their quarry.

The earliest mentions of deer occur about 500,000 years ago in the Far East. The Latin name of the exotic sika deer is *Cervus sika nippon,* referring to Japan. Pictorial records of the animals have been discovered in prehistoric French caves and Egyptian tombs, as well as Mesopotamian bas-reliefs. For Native American Indians, white-tailed deer were not only an important dietary staple; their faces were represented on masks worn by shamans in ritual ceremonies.

At medieval feasts, roasted roe deer was a worthy offering for the lord of the manor. If you ate "humble pie," you were a servant, as no part of the animal was to be wasted. Your pastry-enclosed dish was made with the deer's "umbles" — the heart, liver, and kidneys — mixed with sweetmeats, such as dried fruits and nuts, and baked. Venison was a medieval estate's most treasured comestible.

Today's popular idea of serving fruited or spiced condiments with venison was already much favored during the Middle Ages. In fourteenth-century Paris, housewives could buy ready-made "yellow sauce" infused with ginger and saffron, and "green sauce" made of sweet spices like clove and cardamom blended with green herbs, and a cinnamon-based sauce. Even late in the nineteenth century, deer was respected fare for celebrations throughout Europe and America.

Farm-raised red deer is shipped either vacuum-packed fresh or occasionally frozen from New Zealand. The animals are brought to market at 18 to 30 months to maintain consistent size and texture. The meat arrives with skin and sinews removed, separated into easy-to-use portions, and ready to use like beef, pork, or lamb. It's simple to cook well (though you'll want to review the guidelines on pages 167–168 when preparing to cook venison) and, despite old beliefs, doesn't need to be marinated.

THE ACCENT WOULD NOT BE THE SAME

GEORGE: In the United States, the only way to get certification to sell any meat is to have an inspector from the Department of Agriculture on hand to check the animals live, before they are killed (it's called antemortem inspection). On the other hand, it is all right to sell meat imported from Great Britain, provided it is certified wholesome by the British government. In England, though, the inspection, as it is everywhere in Europe, is made postmortem (after death). Thus, we are allowed to bring in and sell roe deer, pheasants, wood pigeons, partridges, grouse, and hare all shot in the wild in Scotland, while we can't sell them if they were shot in America. Maybe if we invited a USDA inspector to hunt with us, he would check the animals right there in the woods and let us know if they're OK to shoot. Would that be considered antemortem inspection? Would he need electronic binoculars? And would he have to wear his white lab coat, or would we be allowed to cover him in camouflage gear?

ARIANE: Marinating was done in the past to mask problems in game meats like venison, particularly when the animal was older or tougher, or if it was not as fresh as it should be. Another reason marinades were popular until recently was that venison was often sold frozen or was obtained from a friend's freezer. Marinating was an attempt to put moisture back into defrosted meat. Unfortunately, it doesn't work. In fact, long marination only serves to break down the tissue, rendering it mushy.

When the quality is consistently the finest and freshest, covering up bad flavors and tenderizing aren't necessary. Still, you might want to marinate your venison for a short period of time (1 to 2 hours) to add another flavor component to the meat. In this chapter you will find both traditional and unconventional marinades.

risotto con cervo

SERVES 6

This substantial main course marries slowly simmered venison, perfumed with rosemary and Barolo wine, with creamy risotto. For lovers of game and Italian food, it's an incomparable match. Before serving, a generous spoonful of the tender meat and rich sauce is ladled on top of the risotto. Slowly adding hot liquid to risotto while stirring allows the starchy outer coat of each grain of arborio rice to absorb the broth while thickening it. When done al dente, the grains are creamy with a small firm center. A couple of tricks: Add the liquid in small amounts, stir pan thoroughly and continuously, and adjust the heat to keep the liquid bubbling briskly, but not too fast, so it evaporates slowly enough to soften the rice without making it pasty. Usually this takes about 30 minutes.

½ cup dried porcini mushrooms

½ cup olive oil

1 onion, minced

½ cup minced pancetta or bacon

Salt and freshly ground black pepper to taste

2 pounds venison stew meat, well trimmed and silver skin removed, cut into 1-inch cubes, blotted dry

2 bay leaves

1 sprig rosemary, plus small sprigs to garnish, if desired

2 whole cloves

½ cup dry red wine, preferably Barolo

2 tablespoons tomato paste

2 quarts chicken stock

1 shallot, minced

2 cups arborio rice

½ cup dry white wine

2 tablespoons unsalted butter, cut into small pieces

½ cup freshly grated Parmigiano-Reggiano

1. Soak porcini in 2 cups of hot water until softened, about 20 minutes. Meanwhile, heat ¼ cup of the olive oil in a large casserole over medium-high heat. Add all but 2 tablespoons of the minced onion and all of the pancetta to the pan, and sauté until golden, about 8 minutes. Season lightly with salt and pepper, add the venison, and cook until all the meat liquids have evaporated, about 15 minutes.

2. Pick porcini out of soaking water and chop them coarsely, reserving the liquid except for the last 2 tablespoons of gritty sediment. Add porcini to casserole, along with bay leaves, 1 sprig rosemary, cloves, and red wine, and cook, stirring, for 5 minutes, until the wine has nearly evaporated. Stir in tomato paste and season lightly with salt and pepper.

3. Add 2 cups of the chicken stock slowly, then the reserved mushroom liquid. Bring to a boil, then reduce heat to medium low and simmer partially covered until meat is tender and the sauce is thickened, about 1½ hours. Remove bay leaves and rosemary, adjust seasoning, and set aside. *Recipe may be made several days in advance, covered, and refrigerated. Reheat gently before continuing.*

4. Heat the remaining 6 cups of chicken stock and keep hot. Heat remaining ¼ cup olive oil in a medium casserole over medium-high heat. Add the reserved 2 tablespoons of onion and the shallot and sauté until golden. Stir in rice, turning to coat with oil. Pour in white wine, stir well, then add ½ cup of the hot stock and season with about a teaspoon of salt. Cook, stirring constantly, until all liquid has been absorbed.

5. Stir in half the venison and sauce. Continue to add hot stock in small batches, and cook until each successive batch has been absorbed, stirring constantly, until rice mixture is creamy and al dente. Remove from heat, stir in butter and cheese, and season with pepper. Ladle risotto onto 6 large warmed plates. Spoon the remaining venison and sauce over each portion, add a small sprig of rosemary, and serve.

Adapted from Lidia Bastianich, chef-owner, Felidia, Becco, and Frico Bar, New York City, and Lidia's, Kansas City, Missouri

MAIR VENISON AND CERVENA

Settlers from Scotland first introduced deer into New Zealand in the mid-1850s for sport. The idea was good for sportsmen, but by the 1900s, because there were no natural predators and the climate was temperate, herds had multiplied to epidemic proportions. The results were extensive damage to native bush and depletion of food supplies for livestock and deer. As a means of control, bounty hunting was established and commercial sale of the meat encouraged. During the 1960s much of the meat was exported to Europe's traditional game markets.

By 1972, when the pendulum began to swing back in the other direction, exports had peaked at almost 4,500 tons of meat annually. Hunters couldn't hope to sustain such volume from the rapidly diminishing wild deer population. Rifles and bullets changed to dart guns for live capture, and a budding deer farming industry began to evolve, in order to ensure a regular future supply of venison.

Today the farmed deer population is about 1.6 million head, held on 4,500 farms. The industry prides itself on the fact that the deer are raised free-ranging on grass, without the use of hormones or growth stimulants.

The name Cervena is used like an appellation in New Zealand, much the way Champagne is used in France. It refers to the finest fresh farm-raised red deer and fallow deer from New Zealand. All Cervena venison must be between 18 and 30 months of age to guarantee proper sizing and texture. The name is derived from a combination of *Cerv*idae, the scientific name for the deer family, and *veni*son, which comes from the Latin word for hunting.

Twenty percent of all New Zealand's venison comes from Mair Venison, D'Artagnan's supplier. A pioneer in export marketing of venison, Mair became involved with the industry in the 1960s, when it was appointed one of the first licensed companies to process feral deer. From the original plant on the North Island of New Zealand, today Mair Venison has three state-of-the-art, internationally accredited facilities, and ships extensively into Europe, Asia, and the United States.

southwestern venison kebabs
with tomato salsa

SERVES 4 GENEROUSLY

With a paint box full of colors, and flavor to knock your socks off, these venison kebabs will satisfy a huge hunger. If you thought venison was exclusively a winter meat, you're about to learn how satisfying and light it can be. The recipe for salsa is copious; you'll enjoy it with red beans and rice or black beans as well. Mexican beer, sangria, margaritas, or iced tea will all solve the drink question.

(8 bamboo skewers, soaked overnight in water)

3 Yukon Gold potatoes, peeled and cut into 1 x 2-inch pieces

2 to 3 tablespoons olive oil

8 medium-large white mushrooms, stems trimmed, wiped clean, cut in half

Tomato Salsa (recipe follows)

1½ pounds venison cut from leg, well trimmed and silver skin removed, cut into 1 x 2-inch pieces, blotted dry

1 *each* green and yellow bell pepper, seeded, cut into 1 x 2-inch pieces

16 cherry tomatoes

Salt and freshly ground black pepper to taste

2 tablespoons *each* ground cumin and chili powder

1. Cover potatoes with cold water in a saucepan. Bring water to a boil and cook for 10 minutes. Drain, and plunge potatoes into very cold water to stop cooking.

Blot dry and reserve. Heat 1 tablespoon of the oil in a skillet over high heat. Add mushrooms and sauté until lightly colored but still firm inside, 4 to 5 minutes, shaking pan to turn and cook evenly.

2. Light a gas or charcoal grill and heat until medium hot. Or heat a broiler. Prepare Tomato Salsa.

3. Thread venison, peppers, mushrooms, tomatoes, and potatoes onto skewers. Brush each with a little olive oil, season with salt and pepper, and dust with cumin and chili powder. Grill until meat is rare or medium rare, 2 to 3 minutes per side.

4. Spoon mounds of rice (if serving) onto 4 plates. Add a generous amount of salsa, and 2 kebabs per plate. Serve at once.

tomato salsa

1 (28-ounce) can crushed tomatoes

2 to 3 tablespoons chopped cilantro leaves

2 jalapeños, seeds and membranes removed, chopped

2 tablespoons ground cumin

1 bunch scallions, chopped

1 red onion, chopped

1 tablespoon minced garlic

Lime juice to taste

Salt and freshly ground black pepper to taste

Combine tomatoes, cilantro, jalapeños, cumin, scallions, red onion, and garlic in an electric blender or food processor, and purée until almost smooth. Season with lime juice, salt, and pepper.

‹ Barbecued wild game on the grill, including Southwestern Venison Kebabs, Grecian Quail on the Grill (page 109), and Grilled Magret with Peaches (page 47)

venison chili
with apples

Think you've tasted all the great chilies? Guess again. Unless you've sampled this one with perfectly balanced heat — hot and savory flavors played against tart green apples — your research is incomplete. Eat it out of a bowl, or slather it over toasted sourdough bread with melted Cheddar or Monterey Jack cheese.

2 tablespoons vegetable oil

1¼ pounds venison stew meat, trimmed, roughly ground or cut into small dice

2 medium yellow onions, finely diced

2 tablespoons ground cumin

2 teaspoons chili powder

2 tablespoons chopped garlic

2 jalapeños, seeded and finely chopped

3 Granny Smith apples, peeled, cored, and cut into ½-inch dice

Salt to taste

1 teaspoon ground black pepper

1½ cups chopped canned tomatoes in juice

¼ cup tomato paste

1 cup or more chicken broth

½ cup red wine

Sourdough baguette, sliced ½ inch thick (optional)

Cheddar or Monterey Jack cheese (optional)

Chopped scallions, to garnish (optional)

1. Heat oil over medium-high heat in a heavy pot large enough to hold all ingredients. Add venison and onions, and brown for approximately 5 minutes.
2. Add cumin, chili powder, garlic, jalapeños, apples, salt, and black pepper, and cook for 5 minutes longer.
3. Stir in tomatoes, tomato paste, chicken broth, and red wine. Bring to a boil, and simmer partially covered for 2 hours, stirring occasionally, adding more broth if mixture becomes dry. Taste to adjust seasonings, and serve.
4. As an hors d'oeuvre, top each bread slice with a little sharp Cheddar or Monterey Jack cheese, and melt. Spoon on some chili and chopped scallions, and serve.

Adapted from Waldy Malouf, chef-owner, Beacon, New York City

venison
carpaccio salad
with blood oranges, parmesan cheese, and pecans

Elegant and sophisticated, this room-temperature main course salad is simple to make, especially if your butcher slices the venison for you. The lean, raw venison is set off by crunchy greens, tangy Parmesan, and a citrus mayonnaise. Don't despair if your slices aren't as thin as you'd like. Place them between sheets of wax paper and pound until even. We suggest a Côtes du Rhône to drink.

2 blood or navel oranges, zested

½ cup homemade or best-quality purchased
  mayonnaise

¼ cup orange-scented or extra-virgin olive oil

2 tablespoons small capers, drained

6 to 8 ounces baby romaine or mesclun salad

1 small bunch watercress, tough stems
  removed

1 to 1½ pounds strip loin of red venison,
  well chilled and sliced paper-thin

2 to 3 ounces Parmigiano-Reggiano

¼ cup coarsely chopped pecans, toasted

Salt and coarsely ground black pepper
  to taste

1. Mince orange zest. Using a sharp paring knife, remove pith from oranges and discard. Working over a bowl to catch any falling juice, remove segments from oranges by cutting between membranes. Reserve 2 tablespoons of juice.
2. Combine the 2 tablespoons orange juice and the zest with mayonnaise and olive oil in a small bowl. Mince ½ tablespoon of the capers and stir into mayonnaise.
3. Divide romaine and watercress among 4 dinner plates. Lay venison slices over greens, then add orange segments around outside of plates. Shave Parmigiano-Reggiano over venison. Sprinkle on remaining capers. Drizzle mayonnaise over salad, add pecans, salt, and pepper, and serve.

venison daube
à l'armagnac

SERVES 6

This hearty Gascon stew, or daube, is everything you'd want from a dish of comfort food. It's full-flavored and well seasoned without being pretentious or overly complex. It gets better as it sits, so you can prepare it a couple of days before you need it. Keep it as long as possible over a slow simmer and let it perfume your house. Serve with boiled potatoes or wide buttered noodles.

CHILLING AND SLICING MEAT FOR CARPACCIO

The best way to slice meat paper-thin is to become friendly with your butcher, or anyone with a meat slicer. The meat should be well chilled in the freezer until it is very firm but not frozen, and then cut across the grain. Chilling time will vary with the cut of meat.

If you don't have a friendly butcher, an electric knife will greatly assist in slicing the well-chilled meat, or use a sharp carving knife. The chilled venison should be sliced as thin as possible. Place pieces between 2 sheets of wax paper and, using a meat pounder or the palm of your hand, strike the meat in the center, and slide it outward. Continue working around the meat, as spokes of a wheel, until it is quite thin and even. Do not pound it so hard as to make holes, but rather press and stroke it.

Note that you should serve the carpaccio the same day it is sliced and pounded. Otherwise, the meat may turn darker in color. It is not dangerous, only less attractive.

3 tablespoons rendered duck fat or canola oil

3 pounds venison stew meat, well trimmed, cut into 2-inch cubes, and blotted dry

Salt and freshly ground black pepper to taste

6 tablespoons all-purpose flour

¾ cup plus 2 tablespoons Armagnac

3 tablespoons rendered duck fat or unsalted butter

½ pound prosciutto or Jambon de Bayonne, finely chopped

3 medium carrots, finely chopped

1 large onion, finely chopped

1½ tablespoons finely chopped garlic

1 (750-ml) bottle full-bodied red wine

1 quart water

1 bouquet garni: 5 sprigs parsley, 1 bay leaf, 1 sprig thyme, and several celery leaves, if you have them, tied in cheesecloth

6 slices good-quality white bread

1. Heat 3 tablespoons duck fat in a large skillet over high heat. Season venison with salt and pepper, and sprinkle with flour. Sear venison until brown on all sides. Do this in batches if necessary, to prevent steaming the meat.

2. Transfer venison to a large heavy casserole. Pour the ¾ cup of Armagnac over the meat and carefully ignite. Cook until flames subside. Be careful, Armagnac can produce high flames.

3. Heat 1 tablespoon duck fat or unsalted butter in a skillet over high heat. Sauté prosciutto, carrots, onion, and garlic until golden, about 5 minutes, stirring often. Scrape into casserole with venison, stirring

to blend. Add wine, water, bouquet garni, salt, and pepper. Bring liquid to a boil over high heat, then lower heat to a slow simmer and cook, covered, for at least 1½ hours. Remove from heat and cool to room temperature. Refrigerate until shortly before serving time.

4. When ready to serve, bring stew slowly to a boil over medium heat. Cut each bread slice diagonally to form 2 triangles. Heat remaining 2 tablespoons duck fat or butter in a small skillet over medium heat, and sauté bread until golden, 2 minutes on each side. Keep warm.

5. Just before serving, stir the remaining 2 tablespoons Armagnac into hot stew, and serve immediately with the fried bread triangles.

venison osso buco
with orange-fennel broth
with celery root purée

SERVES 4

A lively new version of an Italian classic, made with venison rather than veal. Served over a luscious celery root purée, and topped with a full-flavored reduced broth, the dish is handsomely presented, with glazed pearl onions and macerated dried cherries. Add a generous spoonful of minted baby peas for color. Drink Italian: try a Dolcetto d'Alba

8 small venison shank pieces, about 3¾ to 4 pounds total weight (see Note)

3 carrots, chopped

3 ribs celery, chopped

2 onions, chopped

1 large fennel bulb with fronds, chopped (reserve 4 small fronds for garnish)

Grated zest of 1 orange

1 bay leaf

1 sprig thyme, or 1 teaspoon dried thyme

12 black peppercorns

1 (750-ml) bottle full-bodied red wine

Salt and freshly ground black pepper to taste

1½ tablespoons olive oil

2 cups orange juice

1 quart venison or chicken stock

¼ cup venison demi-glace or duck and veal demi-glace (see page 33), optional

¼ cup sun-dried cherries soaked in 2 tablespoons brandy for 1 hour, to garnish

20 pearl onions, blanched, peeled, and sautéed with 2 tablespoons butter and 1 tablespoon sugar until caramelized, to garnish

Celery Root Purée (recipe follows)

1. Combine venison shanks, carrots, celery, onions, fennel, orange zest, bay leaf, thyme, black peppercorns, and red wine in a large nonreactive container. Cover and refrigerate overnight.

2. Separate shanks, vegetables, and wine (leave zest, bay leaf, thyme, and peppercorns with the wine). Blot shanks dry and season with salt and pepper.

3. Place olive oil in a large deep pan with a tight-fitting lid and heat over high heat until almost smoking. Sear shanks until brown on all sides, 3 to 4 minutes. Remove from pan. Add vegetables and sauté until

brown over medium-high heat, about 7 minutes.

4. Pour orange juice and reserved red wine into pan, scraping up any browned particles. Bring to a boil and reduce by half. Return shanks to pan and add enough stock to just cover. Add demi-glace, if using. Bring liquid to a boil, then cover pan and reduce heat so liquid barely simmers. Cook gently until shanks are tender, approximately 1½ hours.

5. Meanwhile, prepare garnishes and Celery Root Purée.

6. Remove shanks and cover loosely. Bring braising liquid to a boil, and reduce by half, about 15 minutes. Strain and check seasonings.

7. Spoon Celery Root Purée in the center of 4 warmed dinner plates. Put 2 shanks on purée, and spoon a little broth over shanks. Pour the remainder around the outside of plate. Garnish with cherries and pearl onions. Add reserved fennel fronds, and serve.

NOTE:

Venison hind shanks are larger and meatier than the foreshanks. Either will work in this recipe: 2 small shanks or 1 large shank per person. However, all shanks should be about the same size and weight, so that they cook evenly. Ask your butcher to saw the shanks for you if they are not precut.

celery root purée

1½ pounds *each* baking potatoes and celery root, peeled and cut into cubes

1 to 2 tablespoons unsalted butter

Salt and white pepper to taste

Cover potato and celery root with salted water. Bring to a boil and cook until completely tender, 10 to 12 minutes. Drain, and pass through a food mill or potato ricer. Because of the celery root, you can also pulse this in a food processor, but be careful not to overprocess. Add butter and season with salt and pepper. Keep warm until ready to serve.

Adapted from Stu Stein, chef-instructor, The California Culinary Academy, former chef, The Oval Room, Washington, D.C.

grilled venison chops with tomato-watercress relish and red wine jelly

with warm new potato and preserved shallot salad

SERVES 4

Venison needn't be limited to winter menus. When the weather is sultry, try these juicy grilled chops accompanied by a refreshing chilled relish. Most of the work for this tempting meal (minimal in any case) is done a day ahead. A quick sear on the grill and the chops are ready to serve, along with a warm salad of new potatoes and preserved shallots.

½ cup olive oil

¼ cup chopped garlic

¼ cup chopped fresh thyme leaves

Salt and freshly ground black pepper to taste

8 venison rib chops, 1 inch thick

½ bunch fresh watercress, washed, coarse stems removed, roughly chopped

1 large ripe tomato, peeled, seeded, and diced

1 tablespoon chopped fresh mint leaves

¼ cup extra-virgin olive oil

½ cup currant jelly

1 cup good-quality red wine

1 tablespoon chopped shallots

Warm New Potato and Preserved Shallot Salad (recipe follows)

1. THE DAY BEFORE SERVING: Combine olive oil, garlic, thyme, salt, and pepper and rub into chops; cover and refrigerate overnight. Combine watercress, tomato, mint, and extra-virgin olive oil in a bowl; cover and refrigerate overnight. Combine jelly, red wine, and shallots in a small saucepan; bring to a boil and reduce by half. Pour into a container, cover, and refrigerate overnight.

2. ON SERVING DAY: Prepare Warm New Potato and Preserved Shallot Salad.

3. Grill the chops on a fairly hot grill, or broil close to the heat for 2 minutes per side, or until rare or medium rare. Season with salt and pepper. Serve immediately, 2 chops per person, with a teaspoon of red wine jelly on each chop and a large spoonful of watercress relish on the side. Accompany with the warm potato salad.

warm new potato and preserved shallot salad

12 to 15 small red-skinned new potatoes, scrubbed

¼ cup dry white wine

¼ cup chicken stock

6 tablespoons extra-virgin olive oil

1 tablespoon white wine vinegar

2 tablespoons Shallots Preserved in Red Wine (recipe follows)

1 tablespoon *each* chopped chives and chervil

Coarse salt and freshly ground black pepper to taste

Boil potatoes in salted water until tender, then drain. Bring wine, stock, oil, and vinegar to a boil in a skillet. Adjust heat down to low. Slice warm potatoes ¼ inch thick into pan. Add preserved shallots, herbs, and salt and pepper. Toss gently to combine. Taste to adjust flavors, adding more vinegar if needed. Transfer to a bowl and serve.

shallots preserved in red wine

MAKES 1 CUP

½ cup finely diced shallots

1½ cups dry red wine

1½ tablespoons red wine vinegar

½ tablespoon olive oil

Plenty of freshly ground black pepper

Combine shallots, wine, and vinegar in a saucepan and bring to a boil. Boil uncovered until all liquid evaporates, about 30 minutes. Watch carefully toward the end of boiling time, to be sure shallots don't burn. Stir in oil, and season liberally with pepper. *Recipe may be made ahead of time. Shallots will keep, covered, for 4 weeks in refrigerator.*

Adapted from Waldy Malouf, chef-owner, Beacon, New York City

rack of venison on quince purée with quince sauce

SERVES 4

After sampling the double whammy of quince on this rack of venison, you might just fall in love with this often overlooked fruit. Its slightly astringent, apple-pear taste adds intense, full-bodied flavor to complete this elegant dish. Serve with asparagus or sautéed green beans.

1 rack of venison, 8 or 9 ribs, frenched and blotted dry

1 tablespoon chopped fresh rosemary leaves

½ tablespoon chopped fresh sage leaves

½ tablespoon crushed black pepper

3 tablespoons olive oil

3½ tablespoons sugar

½ cup plus 3 tablespoons red wine vinegar

CONSIDER THE QUINCE

Quinces have become a rarity of late — a pity, to be sure. Once they were highly valued both for making preserves, because of the high percentage of pectin they contain, and for the lush, sweet-tart flavor they impart to stews. The firm flesh and taste hold up well in slow cooking, adding flavor and texture. Perhaps quinces have an image problem. They can be irregularly shaped. Furthermore, the dry flesh is inedible when raw, and removing the peel and stone-hard core from quinces takes careful work. They are still widely used in Gascony, where by tradition quince trees serve as territorial markers between neighbors. The fruit has an ideal sweet-sour balance of taste that complements foie gras.

3 quinces, Granny Smith apples, or firm
Bartlett pears, peeled, cored, and diced
(reserve peelings)

½ cup vegetable or chicken stock

Salt to taste

½ cup duck and veal demi-glace (see page 33)

1. Marinate venison with rosemary, sage, black pepper, and olive oil, in a resealable plastic bag or covered bowl. Prepare quince purée and sauce at least 1 hour ahead of cooking time for venison.

2. Meanwhile, heat 2 tablespoons of the sugar in a heavy saucepan over medium heat until lightly caramelized. Stir in ½ cup of the vinegar and cook over high heat until reduced by half, about 2 minutes. Add diced quince, stock, and salt, and partially cover. Adjust heat to low and cook until fruit is tender, 25 to 30 minutes, stirring occasionally. Purée in an electric blender or with a hand mixer until smooth. Return to the pan and keep warm.

3. Heat the remaining 1½ tablespoons sugar in a small saucepan over medium heat until lightly caramelized. Add the remaining 3 tablespoons vinegar and reduce by half. Add quince peelings and demi-glace. Infuse sauce over low heat for 30 minutes, strain, and keep warm.

4. Preheat oven to 375°F.

5. Heat a 10-inch skillet over medium-high heat. Gently sear the rack just to seal the exterior, 2 minutes. Roast, ribs down, until rare or medium rare, approximately 20 minutes, or to an internal temperature of 120° to 125°F. Remove from oven and allow to rest at least 5 minutes.

6. To serve, place a small amount of purée in the center of each of 4 warmed plates. Cut rack into double-bone chops and place on the purée. Spoon a small amount of infused quince sauce around the meat. Serve at once.

Adapted from Todd Gray, chef-owner, Equinox, Washington, D.C.

rack of venison rubbed with szechuan pepper
with spicy fruit chutney

SERVES 4

The zingy blend of spicy hot-sweet chutney paired with succulent venison is like a breath of fresh air. It's modern cuisine at its best: exquisitely blended tastes and textures from the East and West that satisfy all the senses. A perfect year-round choice for entertaining. Serve over japonica rice.

1 rack of venison, 8 or 9 ribs, frenched and blotted dry

3 tablespoons Szechuan peppercorns, cracked

4 Thai chilies, seeded and chopped (see Note 1)

3 kaffir lime leaves (see Note 2)

2 teaspoons crushed garlic

1 stalk lemongrass, coarse outer stems removed, lower 6 to 8 inches finely chopped

1 tablespoon peanut oil

2 teaspoons fish sauce (*nam pla,* available in Asian groceries and some supermarkets)

Spicy Fruit Chutney (recipe follows)

1. Rub venison with Szechuan peppercorns. Combine chilies, lime leaves, garlic, and lemongrass with peanut oil and fish sauce in a large resealable plastic bag or bowl. Add venison and turn to coat, then seal or cover and refrigerate overnight.

2. Prepare Spicy Fruit Chutney. Preheat oven to 375°F.

3. Heat a 10-inch skillet over medium-high heat. Remove venison from marinade and lightly sear on all sides, then roast until rare or medium rare, approximately 20 minutes, or until internal temperature is 120° to 125°F, turning a couple of times. Remove to a carving board and let rest for 5 minutes before cutting.

4. Cut venison between bones into chops, top with chutney, and serve.

NOTES:

1. Thai chilies can be found in Asian markets in both red and green. Thin and only about 1¼ inches long, they are fiery and retain their heat even after cooking.

2. Kaffir lime leaves are a popular flavoring in Southeast Asia, where the small trees are native. The fruit is pear-shaped with a bumpy rind and a bitter taste. The leaves have a clean, herbaceous taste. They are best when fresh, but dried leaves may be used. If neither is available, use lime zest, lemon zest, or lemongrass.

spicy fruit chutney

1 cup rice vinegar

¼ cup sugar

4 Thai chilies, seeded and chopped

1 teaspoon turmeric

1 tablespoon julienned gingerroot

½ cup diced pineapple, fresh or juice-packed canned

1 green apple, cored and diced

1 pear, cored and diced

1 red bell pepper, seeded and diced

½ cup dark raisins

1 tablespoon chopped cilantro

1. Combine vinegar, sugar, chilies, turmeric, and ginger in a saucepan, and bring to a boil to dissolve sugar. Turn off heat and let stand, to infuse flavors, for 10 minutes.

2. Add pineapple, apple, pear, bell pepper, and raisins, and cook gently over medium-low heat for 10 minutes. Let cool to room temperature. Stir in cilantro and serve.

Adapted from Jean-Georges Vongerichten, chef-owner, Vong, Jo Jo, Jean-Georges, New York City

pan-fried venison steaks with mushrooms
and red pepper butter

SERVES 4

This supersimple and quick recipe for venison steaks paired with fiery-colored (but sweet-tasting) Red Pepper Butter makes an everyday meal exceptional. The combination of the warm seared steaks and cool butter creates a mouthwatering sensation.

Red Pepper Butter (recipe follows)

2 tablespoons rendered duck fat or unsalted butter

1 clove garlic, split

¾ pound cremini or white mushrooms, wiped clean, trimmed, and sliced

Salt and freshly ground black pepper
    to taste

4 venison strip loin or leg fillet steaks, about
    1 inch thick, well trimmed and blotted dry

Chives, for garnish

1. Prepare Red Pepper Butter.

2. Melt fat or butter in a large skillet over medium-high heat. Add garlic and mushrooms, and sauté until they start to wilt, 2 minutes, shaking pan to cook evenly. Remove mushrooms with a slotted spoon, leaving the garlic. Liberally season mushrooms with salt and pepper. Keep warm.

3. Add venison fillets to pan and sauté for 1 to 1½ minutes on each side. If crowded, do this in batches so meat does not steam. Remove to a heated platter and season with salt and pepper.

4. Serve fillets topped with a rosette or spoonful of Red Pepper Butter and crisscrossed with a pair of chives. Spoon mushrooms around steaks.

red pepper butter

1 red bell pepper, peeled, seeded, and membranes removed, or 1 pepper from a jar packed in water (not oil and vinegar), drained and patted dry

1 large clove garlic

3 tablespoons unsalted butter, at room temperature

1 teaspoon Worcestershire sauce

⅛ teaspoon salt or to taste

1. Purée pepper and garlic in an electric blender until smooth. Add softened butter, Worcestershire sauce, and salt and,

with an on-off motion, process until smooth, scraping down sides as needed.

2. Fill a pastry bag fitted with a star tip with the butter, and pipe 4 large rosettes onto a sheet of wax paper. Or scrape butter into a small bowl and cover. Refrigerate until needed.

venison medallions
with baked celery root and gingerbread sauce

SERVES 6

Contemporary cooking has some inspired food pairings. For sweet venison and earthy celery root, the mildly spicy reduced wine and orange juice sauce is unique. Surprise! Gingerbread scents the sauce with myriad spices.

Celery root, also known as celeriac, is a relative of the familiar rib celery. However, it's grown especially for its bulbous root. It is not the most attractive vegetable, with knobby rough brown skin, but the firm creamy flesh tastes like a blend of parsley and celery. Look for firm ones with no soft spots. Once raw celery root is cut, drop it into acidulated water to keep it from browning.

1 celery root, 2½ to 3 pounds, wrapped in aluminum foil

1 (750-ml) bottle Côtes du Rhône or other red wine

1¼ cups duck and veal demi-glace (see page 33)

1 cup tawny port

Juice of 1 orange

4 ounces purchased gingerbread (not cookies)

Salt and freshly ground black pepper
   to taste

5 tablespoons unsalted butter

12 venison leg fillet steaks, 2½ to 3 ounces each,
   well trimmed and about 1 inch thick,
   blotted dry

10 juniper berries, crushed

2 tablespoons grapeseed or canola oil

1. Preheat oven to 300°F. Bake foil-wrapped celery root until tender, about 3½ hours. Unwrap, peel, and cut into 1-inch slices. Cover and set aside. *Celery root may be cooked several hours ahead.*

2. Reduce 1½ cups of the wine in a non-reactive saucepan by half. Add the demi-glace, bring to a boil, and set aside.

3. Combine port, orange juice, and remaining wine in a nonreactive saucepan and reduce by half over high heat. Add gingerbread, remove from heat, let sit for 15 to 20 minutes, then strain. Combine strained liquid with demi-glace. Bring to a boil and reduce to sauce consistency, at least by half, then season with salt and pepper. Off the heat, whisk in 1 tablespoon of the butter. Keep warm.

4. Melt 2 tablespoons of the butter in a large skillet. Add sliced celery root and sauté over medium-high heat until warmed and lightly browned, 6 to 7 minutes. Season with salt and pepper. Keep warm.

5. Season medallions with juniper berries, salt, and pepper. Heat the remaining 2 tablespoons of butter with the oil in a large skillet over high heat until hot. Add

venison and cook approximately 2 minutes per side for rare to medium rare. Do this in batches if necessary, so meat sears rather than steams. Arrange celery root and venison on 6 plates. Spoon over sauce and serve.

Adapted from Guenter Seeger, chef-owner, Seeger's, Atlanta, Georgia

medallions of venison with a mélange of dried and fresh fruit
with puréed pan-roasted beets and puréed sweet potatoes

SERVES 4

The juxtaposition of dried and fresh fruits against the rich, reduced wine sauce with its magical hint of bittersweet chocolate will dance on your tongue and enhance the sweet venison medallions. Jewel-toned roasted beet purée and sweet potato purée add visual glamour to this noble meal. Most of the work in this somewhat demanding preparation can be done ahead of time. You will savor every morsel when it's served.

1 medium onion, quartered

1 medium carrot, coarsely chopped

4 cups hearty red wine

1 cup plus 2 tablespoons red wine vinegar

12 black peppercorns

8 venison strip loin medallions, 1 inch thick,
   blotted dry

¾ cup duck and veal demi-glace (see page 33)

4 tablespoons unsalted butter

2 firm ripe pears, peeled, cored, and cut into
½-inch dice

2 Granny Smith or other tart apples, peeled,
cored, and cut into ½-inch dice

4 tablespoons sugar

Puréed Pan-Roasted Beets and Puréed Sweet
Potatoes (recipes follow)

Salt and freshly ground black pepper to taste

½ ounce extra-bitter chocolate, finely grated

8 *each* dried apricots and pitted prunes, softened
in water if necessary, quartered

2 tablespoons dried sour cherries, softened in
water if necessary

Chervil or flat-leaf parsley sprigs, to garnish

1. Combine onion, carrot, red wine, 1 cup
of the wine vinegar, and the peppercorns
in a flat nonreactive dish or resealable
plastic bag. Add venison loin, cover or
seal, and marinate for 1 hour. Remove
medallions from marinade and set aside.
Strain marinade into a nonreactive saucepan, bring to a boil over high heat, and
reduce to 1 cup liquid. Stir in demi-glace
and set aside.

2. Meanwhile, melt 2 tablespoons of
the butter in a large skillet over high heat.
Add pears and apples, and sprinkle on
about 1 tablespoon sugar, turning to coat
the fruit pieces. Add about 1 tablespoon
of water and continue cooking until fruit
is lightly caramelized, 2 to 3 minutes. Set
aside. *Recipe may be done ahead to this point.*

3. Prepare Puréed Pan-Roasted Beets and
Puréed Sweet Potatoes.

4. Turn oven to warm. Blot venison dry
on paper towels. Season generously with
salt and pepper.

5. Melt the remaining 2 tablespoons butter in a large heavy skillet (or 2 smaller
pans) over high heat. Add venison and
cook for about 2 minutes each side for
medium rare. Do not crowd meat or it will
steam. When cooked, transfer to a platter
and keep warm in oven.

6. Discard almost all fat, and add the
remaining 3 tablespoons of sugar to pan.
Cook over medium-high heat until caramelized, watching that it does not burn,
about 1 minute. Combine remaining
2 tablespoons vinegar with the reduced
marinade and stir into pan. Bring to a full
boil, then reduce heat and cook over
medium-high heat for 3 minutes. Stir in
chocolate and fresh and dried fruits.
Arrange 2 medallions on each of 4
warmed dinner plates and spoon on sauce
and fruits. Either pipe rosettes of vegetable purées onto plates or, using 2 large
soup spoons, create oval mounds of each.
Top with a sprig of chervil.

puréed pan-roasted beets

3 tablespoons unsalted butter

1 medium onion, thinly sliced and separated
into rings

1½ pounds beets, peeled and cut into 1-inch
cubes

3 cloves garlic

Salt and freshly ground black pepper to taste

Melt butter in a heavy skillet over medium-
low heat. Add onion rings and sweat until
tender but not colored, 5 minutes. Add
beets, garlic, and 1 teaspoon salt. Cook
over low heat, stirring often, until beets
are fully cooked. Scrape into a food
processor and purée until smooth. Season

with salt and pepper. *Recipe may be made ahead and held over low heat or reheated over medium heat, stirring often.*

puréed sweet potatoes

½ cup honey

1 pound sweet potatoes, peeled and cut into 1-inch cubes

Juice of 1 lemon and 1 orange

6 tablespoons cold unsalted butter, cut into pieces

Salt and freshly ground black pepper to taste

1. Lightly caramelize honey in a heavy-bottomed pot over medium-high heat. Add sweet potatoes and cook for 2 minutes over medium heat, turning to cover potatoes with honey. Stir in fruit juices, cover pan, reduce heat to low, and cook, stirring often, until potatoes are completely tender, 13 to 15 minutes.

2. Scrape mixture into a food processor. With motor running, add butter through feed tube. Season with salt and pepper. *Recipe may be made ahead and held over low heat or reheated over medium heat, stirring often.*

Adapted from Gérard Pangaud, chef-owner, Gérard's Place, Washington, D.C.

A FORMAL MEETING

ARIANE: The first time I met Gérard Pangaud, he was the chef at Aurora, in New York City. We sat down in his office, and as we were talking, I noticed little drips of fat falling in front of us. I looked up to see curing duck breasts hanging from the ceiling. Pangaud was making his own duck prosciutto. You can make your own too (see page 289), but not necessarily in your office.

grilled hoisin-marinated venison loin

SERVES 6

Total simplicity to prepare, this venison becomes crunchy on the outside and tender inside. Be sure to use rice vinegar that is not seasoned. To broil instead of grill, position your broiler pan about 4 inches from heat, and cook for the same length of time. Drink a Pinot Noir or fruity Merlot.

⅓ cup hoisin sauce

3 tablespoons rice vinegar

2 tablespoons soy sauce

2 tablespoons minced garlic

¼ cup minced scallions, including about 2 inches of green parts

1 tablespoon honey

½ teaspoon salt

3 tablespoons olive oil

1 boneless venison strip loin, 2½ to 3 pounds, well trimmed, silver skin removed

1. Whisk together hoisin, vinegar, soy sauce, garlic, scallions, honey, salt, and oil, and scrape into a large resealable plastic bag. Add venison and seal, turning to coat evenly. Marinate in refrigerator for at least 4 hours.

2. Remove venison from refrigerator and return to room temperature before cooking. Light a gas or charcoal grill and heat to medium. Grill for 15 minutes per side, turning once, for medium rare.

Adapted from Rhonda Thomson, passionate cook and professional potter, Lakenheath, England

venison wellington

SERVES 8 TO 10

A truly spectacular main course to celebrate a grand event. This modern version of a French classic is placed on crunchy pastry after cooking, rather than being entirely enclosed in what often becomes soggy dough. The full-flavored, tender venison is highlighted by the robust mushrooms and rich crust. It's a showstopper that is truly easy to prepare. The mushroom ragout is made ahead of time, and you can purchase excellent all-butter puff pastry. Don't stint with the mushrooms, however. You and your guests will swoon over them. Serve with glazed carrots and asparagus, and a rich French Burgundy or California Pinot Noir.

FOR THE VENISON AND MARINADE:

1 boneless venison strip loin roast, 2½ to 3 pounds, well trimmed, silver skin removed

3 cups good-quality hearty red wine

½ cup Cognac or brandy

1 carrot, coarsely chopped

1 onion, coarsely chopped

1 large rib celery, coarsely chopped

1 sprig thyme

12 black peppercorns

6 juniper berries, bruised

FOR THE MUSHROOM MIXTURE:

1 stick unsalted butter

1 carrot, finely chopped

¾ cup finely chopped celery root

⅓ cup finely chopped shallots

2 pounds mixed wild mushrooms (such as shiitakes, oysters, chanterelles, and morels), wiped clean, coarse stems removed if necessary, and cut into thick slices

3 tablespoons minced garlic

1½ cups good-quality hearty red wine

⅓ cup Armagnac or Cognac

2 sprigs thyme

1 tablespoon cornstarch

Salt and coarsely ground black pepper to taste

FOR THE PASTRY:

2 pounds all-butter puff pastry, defrosted according to package directions if frozen

All-purpose flour for dusting work surface

1 egg beaten with 1 tablespoon water

TO FINISH:

Salt and freshly ground black pepper to taste

2 tablespoons unsalted butter

Chervil or flat-leaf parsley sprigs, to garnish

1. MARINATE THE VENISON: Combine venison with 3 cups red wine and ½ cup Armagnac in a large bowl or resealable plastic bag. Add the carrot, onion, celery, thyme sprig, peppercorns, and juniper berries. Cover or seal, and refrigerate for at least 4 hours.

2. PREPARE THE MUSHROOM MIXTURE: Melt 1 stick butter in a large saucepan over medium-high heat. Add the finely chopped carrot, celery root, shallots, and mushrooms, and sauté until wilted, about 5 minutes, stirring often. Stir in garlic and cook for 30 seconds longer.

3. Pour in wine and Armagnac. Add 2 sprigs thyme and bring liquid to a boil over

high heat. Reduce heat and simmer for 20 minutes. Mix cornstarch with a little of the liquid until smooth, then stir into mixture, and continue cooking for 5 minutes. Season with salt and pepper, then set aside, or cover and refrigerate until needed.

4. MAKE THE PASTRY CRUSTS: Preheat oven to 350°F. Line 1 or 2 baking sheets with parchment.

5. Roll out pastry on a floured board to a thickness of ⅛ inch. Cut out 8 or 10 circles or squares approximately 4 inches across. Brush with egg wash. Using a sharp paring knife, make a few *shallow* crisscross cuts in dough. Put on prepared baking sheets and place in freezer for 10 minutes. Transfer to oven and bake until puffed, rich golden brown, and baked through, 15 to 20 minutes. The pastry should be very dry. Remove and carefully split each circle (or square) into a top and a bottom crust, using a sharp serrated knife. Separate and allow to dry completely. Set aside. *You can bake, split, and dry the puff pastry circles a day ahead and store them in an airtight plastic container, separated with pieces of parchment paper.* Leave oven at 350°F.

6. TO FINISH: Remove venison from marinade, blot dry, and season generously with salt and pepper. Melt butter in a large roasting pan. When it is very hot, add meat and sear on all sides, 4 to 5 minutes. Transfer pan to oven, and roast approximately 20 minutes for medium rare, or to an internal temperature of 120° to 125°F. Remove and let stand for 5 minutes.

7. Meanwhile, reheat mushroom mixture. Return pastry to oven for a few minutes to warm. Put bottom crusts on warmed plates or a platter. Slice meat into 8 or 10 slices, and lay on top of crusts. Spoon a generous amount of mushrooms over venison, and add top crusts. Garnish with chervil or parsley and serve.

roast loin of venison with spiced date glaze
with braised white root vegetables

SERVES 6

Puréed spiced dates lend an intoxicating, exotic fragrance to this venison loin. Once roasted, the meat is sliced and glazed with the perfumed mixture before serving. Earthy root vegetables are a nice counterpoint.

1¾ teaspoons cinnamon

¾ teaspoon nutmeg

1 teaspoon ground star anise

1 boneless venison strip loin, 2½ to 3 pounds, well trimmed, silver skin removed

1½ cups orange juice

3 tablespoons extra-virgin olive oil

2 teaspoons crushed garlic, plus 1 whole garlic clove

2 sprigs thyme

1½ teaspoons freshly grated orange zest

¼ teaspoon black peppercorns

¾ pound fresh dates, or approximately ½ pound dried dates

1 tablespoon sherry wine vinegar

½ teaspoon salt, plus salt to taste

Braised White Root Vegetables (recipe follows)

Freshly ground black pepper to taste

1. Stir together cinnamon, nutmeg, and star anise, and set spice mix aside (reserve ½ teaspoon mix for root vegetables).

2. Combine venison with ½ cup of the orange juice, 2 tablespoons of the oil, 2 teaspoons of the spice mix, 2 teaspoons crushed garlic, 1 sprig thyme, 1 teaspoon orange zest, and peppercorns in a resealable plastic bag or bowl. Seal or cover and refrigerate overnight, or for at least 4 hours.

3. Soak dates in enough warm water to cover until skins peel off easily, 15 to 20 minutes. Pit dates and combine them in a small saucepan with the remaining cup of orange juice, the vinegar, 1 teaspoon of the spice mix, the garlic clove, 1 thyme sprig, ½ teaspoon of the orange zest, and ½ teaspoon salt. Bring liquid to a simmer over medium heat and poach dates until they are quite tender and resemble a compote, about 30 minutes. Discard garlic and thyme. Purée dates and poaching liquid in a food processor or electric blender until smooth. Taste to adjust seasonings. Scrape into a container, cool, cover, and refrigerate if not using right away. *Sauce may be made several days ahead, and refrigerated until needed.*

4. Prepare Braised White Root Vegetables.

5. Preheat oven to 350°F.

6. Drain venison from marinade, blot dry, and season with salt and pepper. Heat the remaining tablespoon oil in a roasting pan over high heat. When it is almost smoking, turn heat down slightly, add venison, and sear both sides for 1½ to 2 minutes. Transfer to oven, and roast for about 20 minutes for medium rare, or until internal temperature is 120°F. Turn meat occasionally during cooking.

7. Remove venison from oven and pan, and allow to rest a few minutes while you preheat broiler. Generously coat roast with date sauce and run under broiler for 2 to 3 minutes.

8. Place vegetables in the center of a warm platter. Cut venison into 12 slices and arrange on top of vegetables. Serve remaining date sauce on the side.

braised white root vegetables

Zest of ½ orange, julienned

1 tablespoon lemon juice

3 medium turnips, quartered

3 salsify roots, cut into 1½-inch segments

1 small celery root, cut into ½-inch dice

2 tablespoons extra-virgin olive oil

12 pearl onions

½ teaspoon spice mix, reserved from recipe above

1 clove garlic

1 sprig thyme

Salt and freshly ground black pepper to taste

12 icicle radishes, cleaned and greens removed (optional)

3 heads Belgian endive, quartered lengthwise

½ cup chicken stock

1. Bring a small pot of water to a boil and add julienned orange zest. Boil for 2 minutes, drain, and blot dry. Set aside.

2. Sprinkle lemon juice over turnips, salsify, and celery root, and toss to prevent discoloration.

3. Heat oil in a large skillet over medium heat. Add turnips, salsify, celery root,

onions, spices, garlic, thyme, orange zest, salt, and pepper, and sweat for 5 minutes without letting them take color. Add radishes and endive, and sweat 5 minutes longer.

4. Pour in stock, bring to a boil, cover pan, adjust heat down, and braise vegetables at a simmer until turnips and celery root are tender when pierced with a knife, about 15 minutes. Remove cover, raise heat, and toss vegetables until all liquid evaporates from the pan, about 5 minutes. Taste to adjust flavors.

Adapted from Daniel Boulud, chef-owner, Restaurant Daniel and Café Boulud, co-owner, Payard Pâtisserie & Bistro, New York City

grilled elk short loin with porcini sauce
with pumpkin-semolina gnocchi

SERVES 4

Grilled sweet elk steaks glazed with reduced balsamic vinegar are a lusty partner for earthy pumpkin gnocchi scented with Parmesan cheese. Accent the rich, dark colors of this dish with a bright vegetable. Finish the sauce and shape the gnocchi before (even the day before) turning your attention to the meat or lighting the barbecue or broiler.

Pumpkin-Semolina Gnocchi (recipe follows)

3 cups balsamic vinegar

1 tablespoon juniper berries, crushed

1 tablespoon olive oil

3 cups sliced fresh porcini mushrooms

½ teaspoon minced garlic

1 quart chicken stock

¼ cup duck and veal demi-glace (see page 33)

6 sprigs thyme

1 tablespoon cracked black pepper

1½ pounds elk or venison short loin, well trimmed and silver skin removed, cut into 4 steaks, blotted dry

Salt to taste

¼ cup peeled, seeded, and finely diced tomato

2 tablespoons finely chopped flat-leaf parsley

1. Prepare Pumpkin-Semolina Gnocchi through Step 3.

2. Combine balsamic vinegar and juniper berries in a nonreactive saucepan and reduce over medium-low heat to slightly more than ½ cup. Strain, and set vinegar aside to cool; reserve juniper berries.

3. Heat olive oil in a large skillet over medium heat. Stir in porcini and cook until mushrooms are just cooked through, then add garlic and cook 30 seconds more. Pour in chicken stock and simmer for 10 minutes. Remove mushrooms from stock with a slotted spoon and reserve. Continue simmering stock over medium heat until reduced to a thin sauce consistency. Add demi-glace, 1½ tablespoons of the reduced balsamic vinegar, and 2 of the thyme sprigs, and simmer another 5 minutes. Strain through a fine strainer and keep warm.

4. Light a gas or charcoal grill and heat to medium hot. Or preheat oven to 375°F.

5. Combine remaining scant ½ cup of reduced vinegar, the black pepper, and reserved juniper berries in a small bowl.

Brush elk steaks with mixture, season with salt, and grill to desired doneness, preferably medium rare, 5 to 6 minutes per side. Remove and allow to rest while finishing porcini sauce. Alternatively, quickly sear both sides of the steaks in a heavy skillet over medium-high heat, then bake in oven for 5 minutes for medium rare.

6. Return porcini sauce to a skillet and heat reserved mushrooms, diced tomato, and parsley in sauce just until it simmers.

7. Finish gnocchi.

8. Slice each steak on the diagonal into 2 pieces. Spoon sauce and mushrooms into the center of 4 warmed plates. Place 3 gnocchi around each plate and place sliced elk, cut side up, on top of mushrooms. Garnish each plate with a sprig of the remaining thyme, and serve.

pumpkin-semolina gnocchi

MAKES 12 LARGE GNOCCHI

½ cup pumpkin purée, fresh or canned

2 cups whole milk

2 tablespoons unsalted butter, at room temperature

1½ teaspoons salt

½ freshly ground black pepper

¼ teaspoon ground nutmeg

1 cup semolina flour

3 egg yolks

¾ cup grated Parmesan cheese

1 tablespoon olive oil, plus oil for sheet pan and for frying gnocchi

Salt and white pepper to taste

1. Combine pumpkin, milk, butter, 1½ teaspoons salt, black pepper, and nutmeg in a medium saucepan, and whisk until smooth. Set over medium heat and bring mixture to a simmer. Slowly add semolina, whisking quickly to avoid lumps. Once semolina is incorporated, reduce heat to low and stir continuously with a wooden spoon for 8 minutes.

2. Remove pot from heat and add egg yolks, one at a time, mixing well between each addition. Fold in Parmesan cheese and 1 tablespoon olive oil, and season well with salt and white pepper. Spread mixture approximately 2 inches thick on an oiled sheet pan, and refrigerate until chilled.

3. Form batter into 12 ovals, using large soup spoons. Place on a lightly oiled dish, cover, and refrigerate until chilled. *Prepare to this point ahead of venison.*

4. Pour oil into a large skillet, to a depth of 1 inch, and heat over medium-high heat until hot. Slide gnocchi into skillet and cook until golden brown, carefully turning to brown both sides. Remove, blot on paper towels, and serve.

Adapted from David Walford, executive chef, Splendido at the Chateau, Beaver Creek, Colorado

foie gras, sausages, and charcuterie 3

Foie gras, sausages, and charcuterie not only taste great; when properly stored and cooked, they are also the ultimate fast foods.

FOIE GRAS

At one end of the perishable foods spectrum is fresh foie gras, the most fragile and the most luxurious. It's worth saying again and again, use foie gras as quickly as possible, certainly within a week. Order foie gras from a reputable dealer who does a high volume in foie gras, or directly from D'Artagnan. Buy it as close to the date you will prepare it as possible. And *never* freeze foie gras. The longer you keep a foie gras before cooking it, the more the internal structure breaks down and becomes spongy.

Cooking foie gras that is served hot is simple. There are a couple of things to remember. Season the slices generously. As the fat melts, some of the seasonings flow away. The pan must be very hot, almost smoking. How long it will take to sear a ¾-inch-thick slice depends on what kind of pan you use. In a cast iron skillet, it will take about 30 seconds on each side. In a heavy stainless steel skillet, it takes about 1 minute. Ideally, you want the liver to be uniform in color (beyond its seared exterior) and just cooked through. It should be warm in the center, not raw or cool. Serve at once, if possible, on very hot plates. The sauce, too, should be very hot.

When cooking foie gras in batches, make sure all burned fat is discarded and the pan is wiped out between batches. Cooked foie gras should be put on paper towels next to the stove while cooking the second batch. If you are cooking foie gras for several people, it's advisable to have two pans.

◄ Roasted Foie Gras with Garlic Confit (page 278)

For recipes that are to be served cold, a little more care is needed. First the liver has to be deveined. Detailed instructions for cleaning and deveining a foie gras are on page 255.

Once foie gras is cooked and cooled in a terrine — for example, the Classic Terrine on page 257 — it will last for at least 2 weeks under refrigeration. ("Terrine," by the way, refers both to the container and to the pâté mixture or foie gras cooked in it.) To ensure its shelf life, wrap a cooked pâté or foie gras tightly with plastic wrap, pressing out any air. Then cover again with aluminum foil to protect it from the light. If the contents remain in a porcelain terrine, press the plastic wrap over the cut surfaces and cover top with foil. Each time you open it, change the plastic wrap.

SAUSAGES AND CHARCUTERIE

On the opposite end of the perishability spectrum is charcuterie. These preserved meats — pâtés, confits, dried and smoked products — are meant to endure. The only suggestions we have are logical and basic good sanitation practices. When eating a piece of confit or dried meat, wrap the rest well immediately after each use, and keep them refrigerated. Exposure to air causes deterioration.

There are three basic types of sausages, cooked, dry-cured, and raw. Cooked sausages, like D'Artagnan's Chicken Mediterranean sausages, are fully cooked when you buy them. Sauté them whole or in slices if you want to serve them hot. Like *saucisson à l'ail* (garlic sausage), they are sometimes eaten at room temperature or warmed in casserole dishes like cassoulet. These sausages come with a use-by date, generally 2 to 3 weeks after purchase, or even 5 to 6 weeks for the garlic sausage. Dry-cured sausages, like *saucisson sec* (dry sausage) and *sopressata* (salami), are sliced and eaten as is. When you cut off a part, carefully rewrap the remainder, or hang the sausage in a cool place, as it is already dry. Dried cured sausages last a very long time.

Raw sausages have the shortest shelf life. They should be used within a week of purchase. They may be tightly wrapped and frozen for up to 4 months. Defrost them slowly in the refrigerator or in a microwave. Quick ways of preparing fresh raw sausages include pricking them a couple of times, then sautéing them in a skillet or grilling them on the barbecue. You can parboil them briefly to remove some of the fat before sautéing, if you prefer. Or remove them from their casing and use in other dishes, like the stuffing for squab with mole sauce (page 135).

My idea of heaven is eating pâté de foie gras to the sound
of trumpets.

— Sydney Smith,
British author and wit, 1771–1845

foie gras ⤴

ARIANE: In the introduction to the duck chapter we give a historical account of how duck and goose foie gras developed. You also know that foie gras is the cornerstone of D'Artagnan. It's our passion and our life. What we haven't shared yet are the basics of cleaning and cooking foie gras, how creatively foie gras can be used, and most important, how it tastes and invariably affects people who eat it.

Ruth Reichl, the former *New York Times* food critic, described in a column a friend's first bite of foie gras: "'Oooh,' she began to moan. 'This is so good!' Her face went pink with pleasure. . . . 'It feels fabulous. Why have I spent my whole life without this?' Each bite brought a new sigh of ecstasy. . . . It was like being in the middle of that scene from *When Harry Met Sally,* but [my friend] wasn't faking a thing."

Chefs love foie gras because it invariably seduces diners. They serve the delicacy from morning (with French toast), to noon (consommé with foie gras ravioli), to late-night snacks of pizza and — yes — even a foie gras peach surprise. In our collection of recipes, we start with the most basic and, for purists, the ultimate cold foie gras experience: the liver cooked whole in Sauternes. Then we take you on an odyssey of classic and contemporary dishes, ending up with a sensational red snapper with foie gras. We've included creative pairings where they work, but nothing outright weird.

Be as creative as you like in what you pair with foie gras, as long as you observe one fundamental rule. The richness of foie gras needs to be complemented by a sweet and acidic balance in the dish as a whole. This can be accomplished with the garnish or wine for cold foie gras. Thus, a Sauternes or a late-harvest wine having that balance is the ideal partner. With hot foie gras, the garnish or sauce provides the counterpoint. In classic dishes, fruits like apples or grapes add both sweetness and acidity. Adding a touch of sugar when too sour or a splash of vinegar when too sweet will help achieve the perfect result. Once that balance is achieved in warm dishes, you can serve something like a light red wine, such as a Pomerol or a Merlot, that will stand up to the acidity. If you understand this fundamental principle, even adding the simplest reduction of port and balsamic vinegar makes sense in achieving the optimum flavor equilibrium.

When you buy a foie gras, look for a smooth-textured, firm-to-the-touch liver with no brown edges or spots. Refrigerate the liver immediately if you are not going to prepare it at once. Vacuum-packed raw foie gras has a shelf life of up to a week, but we *strongly* recommend that you use it as quickly as possible.

A CHARCUTERIE PRIMER

To help you know more than the gourmet store counter person, here are some of the terms commonly used to describe cooked foie gras and charcuterie (pâtés, mousses, rillettes . . .).

- **TERRINE OF FOIE GRAS**
- **WHOLE FOIE GRAS**
- **FOIE GRAS ENTIER**
  The whole foie gras deveined, cleaned, and cooked. Served chilled. It is the best.

- **MOUSSE OF FOIE GRAS**
- **BLOC OF FOIE GRAS**
- **PURÉED FOIE GRAS**
  Foie gras blended with water or wine and baked. This product will be less expensive than the terrine of foie gras. Check the ingredients list to make sure that the meat is 100 percent foie gras, with no chicken, no pork liver, no regular duck liver added.

- **PÂTÉ DE FOIE GRAS**
  Here the foie is mixed with other meats (pork or poultry). To be avoided.

- **PÂTÉ**
  Mixture of ground meats, spices, and liqueurs put in a mold, then slowly cooked. Check the ingredients list for quality.

- **TERRINE**
  Same principle as the pâté, but often with more noble ingredients (pheasant, duck, venison, quail, or with inlays of foie gras, truffle, and whole fillets of game).

- **RILLETTES**
  Shredded meat that has been stewed in seasoned stock and fat until it falls off the bones. D'Artagnan's rillettes are pure duck; they also can be made with goose, rabbit, or pork.

- **GALANTINE**
  A totally deboned bird stuffed with a pâté or mousse and inlays of whole foie gras, truffles, and/or fillets of meat. The galantine is gently cooked in stock and then chilled before serving.

- **CANNED VS. VACUUM-PACKED**
  Whenever possible, canned pâté and foie gras should be avoided. They must be cooked to an internal temperature of at least 212°F for a long period of time in order to be shelf stable. Vacuum-packed pâtés, foie gras, and mousses are cooked to 165°F internal temperature. They have a shorter shelf life and must be kept refrigerated, but the taste is dramatically superior.

At D'Artagnan, we use and sell three grades of foie gras:

Grade A — These are the largest, firmest, most perfect livers. They weigh from 1¼ to 1½ pounds and serve from 8 to 10 people as a first course. They are especially recommended when you want to use the liver whole, as in a terrine, and when the appearance is essential. We also sell them presliced, vacuum-packed, for times when a smaller amount is needed.

Grade B — These are smaller, more veined or bruised than the Grade A's, and will develop a slightly grainier texture during cooking. We use them to make our mousses of foie gras or cubed for stuffings.

Grade C — These are sporadically available; chefs usually use them to flavor and thicken their sauces.

CLEANING AND COOKING A FOIE GRAS

When working with raw foie gras, let it first sit at room temperature for about 20 minutes before separating it into lobes and removing the veins. Otherwise it can easily crack into pieces. If the foie gras is to be used in a hot preparation, deveining is unnecessary.

Here is how to clean and devein a foie gras:

1. Place the smooth side of the foie gras down on a cutting board, with the smaller lobe to your right. Separate the 2 lobes at A and B with your hands (see diagram). If the surface membrane is beginning to show, peel it off with your hands or a small knife. If the crooked piece that's between the lobes comes off, so be it.

2. From B, pull gently to take off as many of the small veins that are attached as possible. Then look for the main vein of the small lobe at C. Lift the vein up gently while holding the foie gras down with the fingers of your other hand so you don't pull away pieces of the liver, and detach it, working toward D. Toward the top, about three-quarters of the way up, feel and detach the branches one by one. As each one breaks, stop working on it and go on to the next.

3. In the large lobe, cut off green-colored flesh, if any, at A. Pull from A to small veins at E, then find the main vein at F and proceed to G as in C to D. The back of the lobes should stay intact. Remove any bloody spots.

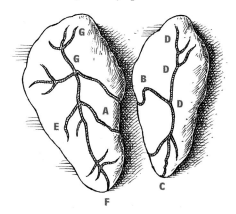

Because there is such a high percentage of fat in the liver, cooking it correctly is important. Either sear it over high heat very briefly or cook it very slowly over low heat. There's no middle ground. When cooking a terrine in a water bath, or *bain-marie,* the water you pour in should be hot, not boiling. Also, when poaching a foie gras, do not use an aluminum pan, as it will discolor the liver.

FOIE GRAS A HEALTH FOOD?

Amazingly enough, not only is foie gras one of the great combinations of taste and texture in the world of food, there is also good news on health from Gascony. Foie gras may actually aid the heart and promote long life. What? you may ask. How can this morsel of pleasure be good for us?

According to a ten-year epidemiological study in Gascony led by Dr. Serge Renaud, the director of research at the National Institute of Health and Medical Research in Lyons, the facts are these: In the southwest of France, where foie gras is a weekly way of life and duck fat is used to cook absolutely everything, Gascons have the lowest rate of death from cardiovascular disease in the country. In spite of a diet richer in fat than that of any other group of people in the industrialized world, Gascony boasts an impressive number of healthy ninety-year-olds.

Dr. Renaud analyzed duck and goose fat to evaluate its chemical composition. Unlike other animal fats, such as butter or lard, the fat of these web-footed birds is closer to olive oil, with a high combination of poly- and monounsaturated fats. This diet, along with the red wine that is readily consumed in the region, promotes HDL, the "good" cholesterol.

Some American doctors discount these facts. However, they admit to being stumped by the statistics, and have called the phenomenon "the French paradox." Further studies are being conducted. Stay tuned. Your newest health food just might be foie gras.

ARIANE: There is one thing I'm asked a lot: Which is better, a goose foie gras or a duck foie gras? In Gascony we have a saying: "A good goose foie gras is a duck foie gras." The fuller flavor of duck foie gras makes it the overwhelming Gascon favorite. Additionally, ducks take less time to mature, the liver is a more manageable size, and it loses less fat as it cooks. Still, some people prefer the more delicate flavors of goose foie gras. D'Artagnan sells duck livers all year. Fresh goose livers, imported from France, are available as well, but in limited quantities.

Back to using foie gras. I suggest you use it as a flavoring in zucchini flowers, to thicken or bind a sauce, to perfume a soup or stuff a quail, in scrambled eggs, pasta, salads, and on pizza. Get the picture? Foie gras makes anything tastier and more luxurious.

classic terrine of foie gras

SERVES 10

One of life's greatest pleasures is a whole foie gras, Grade A, of course, slowly cooked in a terrine with Sauternes, the wonderful sweet white wine from France. Serve chilled with slices of peasant bread and drink a glass of Sauternes, late-harvest Jurançon, or Côtes de Gascogne.

1 whole Grade A foie gras, about 1½ pounds, at room temperature, cleaned and deveined

Salt and freshly ground white pepper to taste

⅔ cup Sauternes

1. Preheat oven to 200°F.

2. Season liver generously all over with salt and pepper. Place the large lobe smooth side down in a rectangular or oval porcelain terrine mold about the same size as the foie gras. Pour a little of the Sauternes over it. Add the small broken pieces of liver, a little more Sauternes, and finally the smaller lobe, smooth side up, and the rest of the wine. Cover the terrine with its lid or, since cooking at such a low temperature, use microwavable plastic wrap.

3. Put a folded kitchen towel or 6 paper towels layered together in the bottom of a pan large enough to hold the terrine, and set the terrine on top. Fill the pan halfway up the sides of the terrine with hot, not boiling, water, transfer to oven, and cook until internal temperature measures 120°F on an instant-read thermometer, about 1 hour, depending on the thickness of the terrine or mold.

4. Remove terrine from water bath and place in a deep dish. Invert lid to exert a light pressure on liver; this will force rendered fat to the surface. If the terrine does not have a lid, or the lid has a handle, cut a piece of cardboard slightly smaller than the mold and wrap it in several layers of

---

FOIE GRAS NOTIONS: TRUE AND FALSE

FALSE

- Raw foie gras needs to be soaked in salted milk or salted water before it is cooked.

- Ducks and geese have their feet nailed to the ground to be force-fed.

- Foie gras is unhealthy.
- Foie gras should be dipped in flour and then cooked in butter.

- Terrines of foie gras are best made with brandy.

TRUE

- Most of the blood is removed when icing and then vacuum-packing, so soaking is superfluous.
- This tale never happened, because when web-footed birds are mistreated they stop eating and die.
- Foie gras is low in saturated fat.
- Foie gras should be quickly seared in a very hot, dry pan without any flour or butter. It is easier and better.
- Fortified and late-harvest wines are the best spirits to pair with foie gras to achieve a balance of sweetness and acidity. Brandy is too strong; it will overpower the delicate flavor of the liver.

plastic wrap. Place inverted lid (or cardboard) on liver and weigh it down with a *full* bottle of Armagnac (or two 1-pound cans from your pantry) for 20 minutes at room temperature. Then remove the weights and cover the terrine with the fat that was forced out.

5. When foie gras is entirely covered by its fat, wrap terrine tightly, and refrigerate for at least 3 days before serving. To serve, unmold by dipping terrine briefly in hot water and, using a hot knife, cut into serving slices.

foie gras
poached in madeira

SERVES 10

Gently poaching foie gras is an excellent way to cook the liver. Because it pairs so well with sweet fortified wines, we use the sweetest Madeira, a Malmsey, along with aromatic vegetables and spices in the court bouillon, or poaching liquid. It is important to tie the foie gras tightly so it stays together as it's poached.

3 cups sweet Madeira

2 cups water

1 onion studded with 3 whole cloves

1 clove garlic

1 carrot, chopped

½ teaspoon dried thyme

8 black peppercorns

Salt to taste

1 whole Grade A foie gras, about 1½ pounds, at room temperature, cleaned and deveined

Freshly ground white pepper to taste

1. Combine Madeira, water, onion, garlic, carrot, thyme, and peppercorns in a deep enamel or copper pot (do not use aluminum). Bring to a boil, then simmer for 15 minutes. Add salt to court bouillon until liquid tastes slightly salty. Season liver all over with salt and pepper, wrap in a double layer of cheesecloth, and tie the ends tightly to hold it together. Slide foie gras into court bouillon and simmer for 20 minutes, covered, until it reaches an internal temperature of 120°F.

2. Carefully lift liver from liquid onto a plate. Pour court bouillon through a fine strainer into a clean bowl. Wipe out pan and return liver to it. Pour enough poaching liquid over liver to cover. Liver will finish cooking as it cools. The fat of the liver will rise to the surface and form an airtight seal as it cools. Cover foie gras and refrigerate. *Foie gras will keep for at least a week in the refrigerator. When ready to serve, remove foie gras from court bouillon and unwrap and discard cheesecloth.*

lobster and foie gras salad
with mango-habanero ketchup

SERVES 4

It's hard to surpass lobster and foie gras for a luxury partnership. When field greens and mangoes are added to the plate, along with a vinaigrette and spicy fruit ketchup, the effect is dazzling. The important trick to making this work is to balance the sweet lobster and foie gras with the acidity of mangoes and vinaigrette, along with the heat of the ketchup. Although Gewürztraminer, Pinot Gris, and Grand Cru Riesling work wonderfully with this dish, our favorite partner is the sweet late-harvest Jurançon from Gascony.

Mango-Habanero Ketchup (recipe follows)

2 tablespoons finely chopped shallots

2 tablespoons *each* white wine vinegar and lemon juice

¼ teaspoon Dijon mustard

½ cup plus 1 tablespoon olive oil

Coarse salt and freshly ground black pepper to taste

2 lobsters, 1¼ pounds each, steamed and cooled

4 slices Classic Terrine of Foie Gras (page 257), about ¾ inch thick, sliced just before serving

1 head frisée lettuce, broken into leaves

6 to 8 ounces mesclun

1 tablespoon chopped mixed herbs, such as parsley, tarragon, chives, and chervil

½ ripe mango, cut into slivers

4 sprigs chervil

1. Prepare Mango-Habanero Ketchup. Combine 1 tablespoon of the shallots and the vinegar, lemon juice, and mustard in a small bowl. Whisk in the ½ cup olive oil, season with salt and pepper, and set vinaigrette aside.
2. Remove lobster meat from tails in 1 piece and split in half lengthwise. Remove

meat from claws in a single piece, and from knuckles. Heat remaining tablespoon olive oil in a skillet over medium heat. Add lobster meat and sauté for 30 seconds to 1 minute. Do not overcook.
3. Lay foie gras slices in the center of 4 plates. Toss frisée, mesclun, herbs, and remaining tablespoon shallots in a bowl with just enough vinaigrette to moisten slightly. Divide greens, piling them in a stack over the foie gras. Arrange mango and lobster knuckle meat around foie gras. Place 1 lobster tail half and 1 claw inter-linked on top of greens on each plate. Drizzle plate and salad with vinaigrette and Mango-Habanero Ketchup. Garnish top with a sprig of chervil and serve.

mango-habanero ketchup

MAKES 1½ TO 2 CUPS

1 tablespoon olive oil

1 small onion, sliced

½ pound yellow tomatoes, diced

1 red habanero or other small hot chili, seeded

1 yellow bell pepper, seeds and membranes removed, chopped

1 small mango, diced, about 1½ cups

¼ cup rice wine vinegar

¼ cup *each* golden raisins and orange juice

1½ tablespoons sugar

Coarse salt to taste

Heat a large saucepan over medium heat. Add olive oil and onion, and cook until translucent, about 5 minutes. Do not brown. Add tomatoes, chili, bell pepper, mango, vinegar, raisins, orange juice, and

HUDSON VALLEY FOIE GRAS

Izzy Yanay, of Hudson Valley Foie Gras, is tenacious, hardworking, and long on what's called chutzpah, or nerve, in his native Israel. He's also a successful entrepreneur who has watched American foie gras become a culinary celebrity. The story of Hudson Valley Foie Gras and its predecessor, Commonwealth Farms, is inextricably knitted together with D'Artagnan's own story, and forms the cornerstone of our success. In Israel, Yanay worked on a small goose cooperative. He dreamed of a big farm that did everything from breeding to hatching to feeding, which would be much more economical than the way it was traditionally done in France and Israel.

Through contact with an American investor, Reuben Joseph, Yanay arrived in the United States in 1981 ready to implement his ideas, although with ducks rather than geese. Full of bravado and naïveté, Yanay thought that he and his partner, Howard Joseph, Reuben's son, could strike out by themselves, open a duck farm in Sullivan County, New York, and win over the culinary world. They built the farm, attended to every aspect from breeding and feeding to packaging and labor issues. They did everything except figure out where and how to sell the livers.

IZZY YANAY: I came down from the farm after work, arriving at Lutèce at 6 P.M., in the heat of preparing for the dinner service. Were they interested in talking to me, Mr. Foie Gras? Not at all. Nor, as it turned out, would a lot of other chefs. We were going to have about 2,000 livers a week to sell. As breeders, that was the number that we had calculated was the right ratio of birds to land size. Sadly, more than half of them were thrown in the garbage. After a lot of sweat and nothing else to show, in 1983 we decided to revise our game plan.

Our next idea was to get names from *New York* magazine. The fancy food industry was just starting to explode, and here we had fresh duck livers that were vacuum-packed and not frozen. After a few more disappointing sales calls, we came to the realization that we couldn't do it alone. My partner was rich but not a food maven; he didn't know anything beyond barbecue on the weekend. We started visiting distributors like the Three Little Pigs and others. Which is how I met Ariane Daguin.

ARIANE: When he walked into the Three Little Pigs, where George and I were working at the time, he showed me this absolutely gorgeous foie gras. He asked to meet the company's principals. As we chitchatted, he promised that the liver hadn't been smuggled from France, but had been raised on an American farm.

With my employers' blessing, I started negotiating, and I drafted an agreement for the Three Little Pigs to become the sole distributor of these superb livers and all of the ducks. Just on the verge of signing, my two bosses got cold feet. I decided that I would do this myself, and I convinced George to join me.

In the meantime, Commonwealth Farms, as Izzy's company was then called, had gotten panicky and had started distributing through no fewer than five meat wholesalers. We had to persuade them to sell to us: two young would-be entrepreneurs with a shoestring budget.

IZZY YANAY: Ariane and George came up several times to the farm. They had to convince my then-partner, Howard Joseph, to take them on as an additional distributor. After much begging, Reuben and Howard agreed, half believing what Ariane was telling them — that given her background she was the only one in America who would and could utilize the rest of the duck to make terrines, rillettes, confits, smoked breasts, and so forth.

sugar, and bring mixture to a boil. Reduce heat and simmer until all ingredients have melted together, about 1 hour. If mixture becomes too dry, add a little water. Season with salt, then purée in a food processor or blender until smooth. Pass through a fine strainer, taste to adjust seasonings, and cool. *Excess ketchup may be covered and refrigerated for a few weeks for future use.*

Adapted from Tim Keating, executive chef, Four Seasons Hotel, Houston

pumpkin surprises:
foie gras in a pumpkin "terrine" and foie gras mousse in baby pumpkins

The following two recipes are perfect for autumn because a pumpkin is a perfect container in which to cook foie gras terrine style or to serve mousses of foie gras. Banyuls is a sweet red wine from the Languedoc-Roussillon region of France. If it is unavailable, use tawny port. Banyuls would be the ideal partner for either of these foie gras dishes.

foie gras in a pumpkin "terrine"

SERVES 8 TO 10 AS AN APPETIZER

To keep all of the flavors of the foie gras in the terrine, it shouldn't be exposed to air during cooking. When the pumpkin is wrapped in aluminum foil it is airtight, and no outside flavors can mingle with the liver. Once the foie gras has been consumed, use the cooked pumpkin flesh to make the delectable soup on page 262.

1 whole Grade A foie gras, about 1½ pounds, at room temperature, cleaned and deveined

Coarse salt and freshly ground white pepper to taste

1 pumpkin, 3 to 4 pounds, top, seeds, and membranes carefully removed

1 cup Banyuls or tawny port

ARIANE: So they agreed, not having much to lose because they kept us on COD terms. I projected that within 6 months we'd be their sole distributor. To make this come true — which it did — I went there at 4 A.M. to choose the best livers (before the other wholesalers got there). George took the subway to New York and peddled the livers on foot. A few sidesteps and four years later, Izzy and Commonwealth Farms parted ways. I introduced Izzy to Michael Ginor, and Hudson Valley Foie Gras was born. Within a year, he and Ginor bought out Commonwealth Farms.

IZZY YANAY: True to her promise, Ariane did — and does — a good job for us. We helped one another early on with our superb quality and her flair for marketing. The business started to grow. Ariane was already dreaming her future: a USDA kitchen to make mousses and terrines. Again we worked together.

When Ariane Daguin said she could "move this stuff," she wasn't kidding.

Postscript: In December of 1998, the USDA lifted its ban on the importation of French poultry. D'Artagnan was the first American company to import fresh duck and goose foie gras from France and has been offering a choice of French and American livers ever since.

1. Preheat oven to 275°F. Cover a baking sheet with *wrinkled* aluminum foil so pumpkin will rest securely flat on it.

2. Season foie gras with salt and pepper. Pour wine into pumpkin shell and sprinkle with salt and pepper. Place foie gras in pumpkin, the large lobe underneath the smaller lobe, cover with pumpkin top, and wrap pumpkin securely in aluminum foil. Bake until internal temperature of liver reaches 120°F, about 2 hours. Remove pumpkin from oven, discard foil, and cool to room temperature. Refrigerate overnight.

3. Remove pumpkin from refrigerator 30 minutes before serving. Serve at table, using a hot spoon to scoop out foie gras. Serve with slices of crusty French bread.

foie gras mousse in baby pumpkins

SERVES 8 TO 10 AS AN APPETIZER

1 whole Grade B foie gras, about 1 pound, cleaned, cut into pieces, and chilled

2 tablespoons water, chilled

2 tablespoons Sauternes, chilled

1½ teaspoons salt

½ teaspoon white pepper

¼ teaspoon sugar

8 to 10 baby pumpkins

Coarse salt and freshly ground white pepper to taste

8 to 10 tablespoons Banyuls or tawny port

1. Preheat oven to 250°F.

2. Combine foie gras, water, Sauternes, 1½ teaspoons salt, ½ teaspoon white pepper, and the sugar in a food processor, and purée until an even consistency, about

30 seconds. Pour mixture into a glass or porcelain terrine mold or a 9 x 5 x 3-inch glass loaf pan. Close the lid, or cover with parchment, and place terrine in a larger pan on top of a folded kitchen towel. Fill larger pan with enough hot water to come halfway up the side of the terrine. Place in preheated oven and cook in the water bath until the internal temperature reaches 145°F, about 1 hour. Remove terrine from water bath and let cool. Wrap terrine mold in plastic wrap and refrigerate for 2 or 3 days.

3. Cut off tops of pumpkins and scrape out seeds and membranes, taking care not to pierce the skin. Season each with salt, pepper, and a tablespoon of Banyuls. Replace tops on pumpkins, set them in a shallow baking pan, and bake until tender but still firm, 20 to 30 minutes. Pour out wine and cool. Fill pumpkins with foie gras mousse and serve. *This dish may be prepared 1 to 2 days ahead and refrigerated until 30 minutes before serving time.*

pumpkin soup with brussels sprouts, chanterelles, duck magret, and foie gras

SERVES 4 TO 5

So you just ate the foie gras out of the pumpkin terrine on page 261 and now have a leftover cooked pumpkin. Here is the perfect way to "recycle" it. (You can also start with raw pumpkin or butternut squash.) This is anything but mundane fare, with its delicious bits of duck, foie gras, wild mushrooms, and a host of complex tastes and textures.

¾ cup rendered duck fat (see Note)

2 medium onions, sliced

Salt to taste

Flesh from a 3- to 4-pound pumpkin, chopped,
    or 3 to 4 pounds butternut squash, peeled,
    seeded, and chopped

7 ounces smoked bacon, chopped

2 tablespoons chopped garlic

1 sprig thyme

4 cups chicken stock

3 Idaho potatoes, peeled and chopped

8 ounces Moulard duck breast (magret)

6 ounces Grade B foie gras, cleaned and cut
    into ½-inch cubes

12 chanterelles, quartered

8 brussels sprouts, blanched and separated
    into leaves

3 tablespoons crème fraîche

2 tablespoons unsalted butter

Freshly ground black pepper to taste

1. Heat duck fat in a saucepan over medium heat. Add onions and salt, cover, and cook until onions are tender, 8 to 9 minutes. Add pumpkin, bacon, garlic, and thyme. Replace cover and cook for 15 minutes if using raw pumpkin, 3 minutes if using cooked. Add chicken stock and bring to a boil. Add potatoes and taste to adjust seasoning. Cover and cook until vegetables are tender, about 30 minutes.

2. Purée soup in a food processor or electric blender until it is a coarse purée. Return to pot, bring to a boil, then remove from heat and set aside. Skim off any fat that rises to the surface.

3. Sauté duck breast in a skillet over medium-high heat until medium rare, 7 to 8 minutes on skin side, 3 to 4 minutes on flesh side. Remove and cut into ½-inch cubes, discarding skin if desired. Remove fat and wipe out skillet, heat to medium, and sauté foie gras cubes until golden brown, 30 to 60 seconds. Remove and blot on paper towels. Set aside and keep warm. Add chanterelles and brussels sprouts to

LE CHABROT, TAUGHT BY A MASTER

Le chabrot is the last sip of soup left in a bowl mixed with a little wine, a peasant tradition in the southwest of France. For the uninitiated, it takes a master's lesson to learn the proper posture, procedures, and sounds.

ARIANE: Christian Delouvrier, chef at Lespinasse in New York, and I were visiting the farm of friends in Connecticut. After a very good duck bouillon, Delouvrier — a Gascon — announced that he had come prepared to teach the gathered guests this fine art.

First, he passed out black berets to all the guests because, he said, real farmers wear them from morning to night. He also showed how, with two fingers, one makes the perfect point in the beret after putting it on. Then he explained that one has to know when to stop eating the soup (technically, when approximately ⅛ inch of liquid is left in the bowl; however, rulers are *not* allowed).

Finally, just the right splash of red wine is added, and the bowl is swirled vigorously and authoritatively, without having the soup fly out. The last movement may require a little practice. Both elbows are placed on the table. You hold the bowl by both edges, lift it to your mouth, and *SLURP*.

same skillet, and sauté them for 5 minutes. Set aside and keep warm.

4. Return soup to a boil. Off heat, stir in crème fraîche and butter. Season with salt and pepper. Divide magret, foie gras, chanterelles, and brussels sprouts leaves among 4 to 5 heated soup plates. Ladle soup over garnish and serve immediately.

NOTE:

Use duck fat that you have rendered and saved in the freezer (it keeps up to 6 months), or order from D'Artagnan or from a local purveyor of fine meats and poultry.

Adapted from Christian Delouvrier, chef, Lespinasse at the St. Regis Hotel, New York City

potato pancakes with foie gras and apples

SERVES 12 AS AN APPETIZER

Here's an extravagant hors d'oeuvre or first course for a dinner party that will certainly win all kinds of kudos. We know everyone loves crusty potato pancakes (you don't have to be a gourmet for that). But when the potatoes are cooked in duck fat and the pancake is topped by a silken medallion of foie gras and sweetly acidic apple, you're a long way from a breakfast staple. Come to think of it, what a great Sunday brunch. In that case, a mimosa or a Bellini would be perfect. (Try the pancakes alone with a dollop of sour cream and the peach-chili relish on page 273.)

PERONA FARMS GAME DINNER

GEORGE: For the past twelve years, the second Tuesday of January has been a special evening for more than 200 lovers of good game and 40 chefs who are fortunate enough to get into the Annual Perona Farms Game Dinner and Benefit.

Perona Farms, a respected restaurant and catering facility (and producer of our favorite smoked salmon) in Andover, New Jersey, plays host to a smorgasbord of game meats, game birds, and wild fish that are collected from local hunters (yours truly included) throughout the fall. These wild, wonderful meats are prepared by the finest chefs from around the country, who fly in just to participate.

Each chef strives to outdo everyone else. I've sampled raccoon pot pies served in individual pastry tarts garnished with rosemary sprigs; chipotle pepper–flavored opossum bruschetta; snapping turtle soup with locally foraged yellow morels — a yearly favorite — and grilled trout with a sauce of wild watercress harvested that morning from springs in the Kittatinny Mountains. My all-time favorite is usually served at the very end: woodcock breasts on top of foie gras–coated croutons.

Feathers from woodcock breasts, duck tails *(cul de canard),* and pheasant necks are carefully collected and sent to experts who tie flies for next spring's trout season. Grouse, woodcock, and pheasant wings are kept for the game bird hunters in order to sharpen up their dogs' noses. Bones and carcasses become the stocks used for the sauces and consommés. Hearts and livers are seasoned and ground for pâtés. Nothing, absolutely nothing, is wasted, as this evening represents for every contributing hunter the opportunity to show the respect they feel for the animals they pursue.

2 medium Granny Smith or other tart green
apples, peeled, cored, and cut crosswise in
⅛-inch slices (reserve trimmings)

⅔ cup simple syrup (see Note 1)

1 tablespoon Armagnac or brandy

1¼ cups duck and veal demi-glace (see page 33)

2 medium-large baking potatoes (about 1¼
pounds), peeled

1 small Red Delicious or other sweet apple,
peeled

1 small onion

1 tablespoon minced flat-leaf parsley

1 egg, beaten

6 or more tablespoons all-purpose flour

Salt and freshly ground white pepper to taste

Rendered duck fat for frying (see Note 2)

1 large Grade A foie gras, about 1½ pounds,
cut into 12 slices ¾ inch thick

24 chives

1. Combine sliced apples with simple
syrup and Armagnac in a bowl and soak
for 8 hours or overnight.
2. Add apple trimmings to demi-glace,
bring to a boil, then simmer for 30 minutes. Strain and keep warm.
3. Grate potatoes, red apple, and onion.
Gently stir in parsley, egg, and flour, and
season with salt and pepper. Heat enough
duck fat to measure about ½ inch deep
in a large heavy skillet. Form mixture into
12 pancakes. If too moist, add a little
more flour. When fat is hot, about 375°F,
add only as many pancakes as will comfortably fit in pan without crowding, flat-
tening them slightly. Cook until browned

and crispy on both sides, turning once.
Remove with a slotted spatula, blot on
paper towels, and keep warm in a warm
oven. Discard fat and wipe out pan.
4. Heat pan until very hot. Season foie
gras with salt and pepper, and sauté until
lightly browned and medium rare inside,
about 30 seconds per side.
5. On 12 warmed plates, place a potato
pancake, then add an apple slice and a foie
gras medallion on top of each. Add 2
chives, crisscrossed in the center, spoon
on sauce, and serve.

NOTES:
1. To make simple syrup, boil ⅓ cup
sugar in ⅔ cup water until sugar dissolves,
and let cool.
2. Use duck fat that you have rendered
and saved in the freezer (it keeps up to 6
months), or order from D'Artagnan or
from a local purveyor of fine meats and
poultry.

Adapted from Kirk Avondoglio, executive chef–owner,
Perona Farms, Andover, New Jersey

baked potato
with foie gras and
white truffle

SERVES 4

What a heavenly match: the ultimate comfort of baked potatoes (splendidly laced
with white truffles and truffle oil, then
spooned into the potato shell) and seared,
crunchy-custardy slices of foie gras. Don't
skimp here. Along with the luxury items,
use the best butter and potatoes you can
find. Firm yellow-fleshed potatoes, like

Belle de Fontenoy, Ratte, Yellow Finn, or Yukon Gold, would be ideal. You will be rewarded. As for shaving truffles, use a very sharp paring knife, a potato peeler, or a truffle slicer.

4 large potatoes, scrubbed (see headnote)

4 ounces unsalted butter

¼ cup white truffle oil, plus extra oil to drizzle over potatoes

Salt and freshly ground white pepper to taste

4 slices Grade A foie gras, ¾ inch thick (2½ to 3 ounces each)

1 medium white truffle

1. Preheat oven to 350°F.
2. Bake potatoes until cooked, about 45 minutes. Cut in half lengthwise and remove potato flesh with a spoon, being careful not to break skins. Keep skins warm.
3. Mash potatoes with a fork, add butter, ¼ cup truffle oil, and salt and pepper. Keep warm.
4. Heat a large skillet over medium-high heat until hot. Season both sides of foie gras with salt and pepper, and sear until both sides are brown and cooked, about 30 seconds per side. Blot on paper towels and keep warm.
5. Slice truffle very thin and set aside. Chop ends and any extra scraps finely, and add to potato mixture.
6. Fill potato shells with potato mixture and place in center of plates. Top with foie gras and cover completely with truffle slices. Season with salt and pepper, and drizzle with white truffle oil.

Adapted from Sottha Khunn, executive chef, Le Cirque 2000, New York City

foie gras pizza with caramelized onions and balsamic vinegar

MAKES 1 PIZZA WITH 8 SLICES

Pizza has come a long way since its supposed humble beginnings in Italy. After a long run with mozzarella and tomato sauce, it took a detour to California and became chic, with an "anything goes" style. Well, in the spirit of the best of anything, here is an exuberant pizza to inspire awe in anyone with a taste for the refined. Want almost the same results but faster? Buy ready-made pizza dough. The dough recipe makes enough for 4 crusts. The dough freezes well, so hopefully you'll be inspired to create other wild game pizza fantasies.

FOR THE DOUGH:

½ tablespoon honey

½ tablespoon sugar

1 to 2 tablespoons extra-virgin olive oil

½ ounce dry yeast

¾ cup cold water, or as needed

1 pound all-purpose flour, about 3¾ cups

2 ounces whole wheat flour, about ½ cup

½ tablespoon salt

FOR TOPPING AND FINISHING:

2 tablespoons unsalted butter

½ bay leaf

2 medium onions, thinly sliced lengthwise

Sea salt and white pepper to taste

3 to 4 tablespoons chicken stock, as needed

Foie Gras Pizza with Caramelized Onions and Balsamic Vinegar ❯

½ teaspoon fresh thyme leaves

2½ ounces sweet Provolone cheese, thinly
sliced or finely grated

1 whole Grade B foie gras, ¾ to 1 pound,
cleaned

2 teaspoons balsamic vinegar

8 small sprigs chervil

1. PREPARE DOUGH: Mix honey, sugar,
olive oil, yeast, and water together in a
bowl until well blended. In the bowl of a
standing mixer, combine both flours and
salt, and gradually add the liquid ingredients at slowest speed. Mix for 10 minutes,
then raise to second speed for 5 minutes,
then finally mix at slowest speed again for
5 minutes. Dough should be shiny and
elastic.

2. Remove dough from mixer, cover, and
allow to rise in a warm, draft-free spot for
2 hours. Punch down dough, form into
4 individual balls, cover, and allow to rise
again for 1 hour. Use 1 of the balls of
dough for this recipe. *Punch down remaining
3 balls of dough, wrap individually in plastic
wrap, and freeze for future use.*

3. PREPARE TOPPING: While dough is
rising, melt 2 tablespoons of the butter
in a medium-size saucepan over medium
heat. Add bay leaf, onions, salt and pepper to taste, and 2 tablespoons of the
chicken stock. Cover and stew onions until
tender. Remove lid, cook until onions are
dry and begin to caramelize. Gradually
add more chicken stock. Be sure that
onions continue to caramelize, becoming
dark brown and quite dry, but do not
burn. Remove from heat, remove bay
leaf, and fold in thyme leaves.

4. ASSEMBLE AND FINISH: Roll dough
on a floured board to a thickness of ⅛

QUICK IDEAS FOR SAUTÉED FOIE GRAS

As we have said, the perfect complement to
the taste of foie gras is a mix of sweetness with
acidity. Here are three serving suggestions
using sautéed slices of foie gras. First prepare
the sauce, and keep it warm while you cook the
foie gras. Cut the liver into ¾-inch slices, season both sides liberally with salt and freshly
ground black pepper, and sear in a hot skillet
about 30 seconds on each side. Before serving,
sprinkle a pinch of coarse salt over each slice.

SERVES 4

• Reduce ½ cup port and ½ cup balsamic vinegar by half, or to a syrupy consistency. Place
slices of sautéed foie gras over mixed baby
field greens, drizzle on port-balsamic reduction, and serve.

• Heat ¾ cup fresh unsweetened applesauce
(without cinnamon) with a splash of balsamic
vinegar. Peel and slice 1 green apple. Sauté
the slices in 1 tablespoon each butter and
sugar until the sugar caramelizes. Spoon
the applesauce onto a plate, add slices of
sautéed foie gras, and top with apple slices.

• Purée about 20 seedless green grapes with
½ cup sweet vermouth. Strain into a saucepan
and boil until reduced to ½ cup. Add 2 to 3
tablespoons duck and veal demi-glace (see
page 33). Taste and adjust balance of acid
or sweet, adding a touch of vinegar for acid,
a touch of sugar for sweetness. Drizzle over
slices of sautéed foie gras.

inch and about 9 inches across. Cover with Provolone cheese and caramelized onions, and let sit while roasting foie gras.

5. Preheat oven to 400°F.

6. Season foie gras with salt and pepper. Heat a large heavy skillet over medium-high heat until hot, then add foie gras. Sauté until golden brown, about 1 minute, then roast in oven until just cooked through, 10 to 12 minutes, or to an internal temperature of 120°F. Do not overcook. Remove from oven and drain excess fat. Adjust oven temperature to 550°F.

7. Bake pizza on a baking sheet or pizza pan in hottest part of oven until crust is crisp and golden brown, 8 to 10 minutes. Remove from oven, cut into 8 wedges while still on pan, then arrange on a serving platter. Keep warm.

8. Cut foie gras into 4 slices, then again on the diagonal to create 8 triangular segments of foie gras. Arrange 1 slice of foie gras on each wedge of pizza. *Alternatively, cut foie gras into large pieces and scatter over pizza.* Drizzle balsamic vinegar over foie gras, garnish each slice with chervil, and serve.

Adapted from Paul Bartolotta, chef, Spiaggia, Chicago

hatikva charcoal-grilled foie gras and duck
with fig jam

SERVES 4

The inspiration for this dish comes from the outdoor tavernas near Israel's foie gras region. The best livers are exported, leaving lesser-grade livers to be cubed, skewered, and charcoal-grilled. Pomegranates and figs, which are indigenous to the region, provide the sweet acidity necessary to balance the liver's richness. Duck prosciutto, a natural complement to figs, adds depth and the salty edge. Infusing the fig jam with cardamom and ginger incorporates an exotic Middle Eastern essence into the dish.

(8 bamboo skewers, soaked overnight in water)

Fig Jam (recipe follows)

1 whole Grade B foie gras, ¾ to 1 pound, at room temperature, cleaned

Coarse salt and freshly ground black pepper to taste

1 whole Moulard duck breast, skinned and cut into 16 (1½-inch) cubes

1 pita bread, cut into 4 wedges, to garnish

2 tablespoons rendered duck fat

4 fresh figs, to garnish

1 cup sweet pomegranate concentrate, reduced to a glaze

1. Prepare Fig Jam. Heat a charcoal or gas grill until hot.

2. Separate foie gras into 2 lobes. Using a knife warmed in hot water, cut foie gras into 16 (1½-inch) cubes. Season generously with salt and pepper. Arrange 4 cubes of foie gras on each of 4 skewers, and grill, turning once, while controlling flare-ups by using a spray water bottle. Cook until rare, 1 to 2 minutes total time, turning frequently. Set aside and keep warm.

3. Season duck cubes with salt and pepper, arrange 4 cubes each on remaining 4 skewers, and grill until rare, about 5 to 7

minutes, turning often. Set aside and keep warm.

4. Brush pita wedges with some of the duck fat, sprinkle with salt and pepper, and grill on both sides. Slice each fig in half. Brush 4 halves with duck fat, and grill lightly. Leave other fig halves cool.

5. Spoon a dollop of Fig Jam into the center of each of 4 plates. Place a pita wedge partially over jam, and a cool and warm fig half on the pita. Add a skewer each of duck and foie gras, drizzle on pomegranate glaze, and serve.

fig jam

1 pound fresh figs, preferably Calimyrna, or ¾ pound dried figs, diced

½ cup diced red onion

3 tablespoons minced fresh gingerroot

Seeds from 10 cardamom pods, crushed

2 cups tawny port

Juice of 2 lemons

4 ounces duck prosciutto (see page 289), finely diced

Combine figs, onion, ginger, cardamom, and port in a saucepan, and bring to a boil over high heat. Reduce heat and cook until mixture reaches the consistency of a jam, stirring occasionally. Remove from heat and stir in lemon juice. Cool to room temperature, then stir in prosciutto.

Adapted from Michael Ginor, partner, Hudson Valley Foie Gras, Ferndale, New York.

quinoa and black pepper–crusted foie gras
with roasted peach on corn galette

SERVES 4

This dish encompasses contemporary style with dramatic flair. You'll fall in love with the tender corn pancake and roasted peach set against the crisp-crusted warm-cool foie gras. The tangy sauce swirls around to blend the tastes into a seductive whole.

2 ripe freestone peaches, peeled and cut in half

3 tablespoons honey

1 large baking potato

1½ tablespoons olive oil

1 large shallot, thinly sliced

¼ cup red wine vinegar

2 tablespoons peach schnapps

1½ cups duck or chicken stock

1 teaspoon unsalted butter

Salt and freshly ground black pepper to taste

1 large ear Silver Queen or other sweet corn, cooked and kernels removed, or ¾ cup defrosted frozen petite kernel corn, blotted dry

2 tablespoons minced chives

1 egg

¼ cup milk

⅓ cup all-purpose flour

4 slices foie gras, ¾ inch thick (about 3 ounces each)

½ teaspoon coarsely ground black pepper

6 to 8 tablespoons quinoa

4 small sprigs chervil, to garnish

1. Preheat oven to 400°F.

2. Put peach halves, cut side down, in a flat baking dish. Drizzle 1 tablespoon of the honey over them. Bake peaches and potato in oven. After 10 to 15 minutes, remove peaches, and let cool. Peach should be tender when a knife point is inserted. Continue baking potato until soft, about 1 hour total time, then remove and let cool.

3. Meanwhile, heat ½ tablespoon of the oil in a small skillet. Add shallot and sauté over medium heat until tender, 1 minute. Pour in vinegar and boil until liquid has evaporated. Add the remaining 2 tablespoons honey and the peach schnapps, and reduce by half, then stir in stock. Slowly boil until liquid is reduced to ½ cup, about 20 minutes. Strain sauce, stir in butter, and season with salt and pepper. Keep warm.

4. Peel potato and grate or mash flesh with a fork until almost smooth. Add corn. *Recipe may be done a couple of hours ahead to this point.* Combine potato-corn mixture with chives in a bowl. Blend egg and milk together and pour over potato mixture, season with salt and pepper, and stir to blend. Sprinkle on flour and mix just to blend. Form into 4 round cakes (galettes) about ¾ inch thick. Mixture will be slightly sticky.

5. Season foie gras with salt and coarsely ground black pepper, and coat with quinoa, patting to cover all sides.

6. Heat the remaining tablespoon oil in a nonstick skillet over medium-high heat. Slide in corn galettes and cook until brown on first side, about 3½ minutes, then turn and cook second side until browned, 2 to 2½ minutes. Remove and keep in warm oven.

7. Discard any oil and make sure pan is hot. Sauté foie gras over medium-high heat until quinoa is lightly browned and crisp, 2½ minutes. Turn with a spatula, and cook second side until browned, about 1½ minutes. Center of slices should just be warmed. Remove and blot on paper towels. Quickly sauté peach halves to rewarm.

8. Place a corn galette in the center of each of 4 plates. Top with a slice of foie gras, then a peach half. Pour sauce around galette, add a sprig of chervil, and serve.

Adapted from Jean-Robert de Cavel, chef, Maisonette, Cincinnati

seared foie gras
on puréed cannellini

SERVES 6

In southwest France, foie gras isn't usually combined with beans, says Ariane. Why not? Because that's how it's been for centuries. But this is America, so in this dish, a little red wine vinegar is added to white beans to balance the rich liver, and — *voilà!* — the two foods blend together in perfect harmony.

1 pound dried cannellini or Great Northern beans, soaked overnight

2 quarts water

1 tablespoon duck and veal demi-glace (see page 33)

1 medium onion, coarsely chopped

2 medium carrots, coarsely chopped

½ large head garlic, stuck with 4 cloves

6 black peppercorns

Pinch dried thyme

Pinch grated nutmeg

1 tablespoon rendered duck fat

Coarse sea salt to taste

6 young, thin leeks, trimmed and well washed

Red wine vinegar

White pepper to taste

1 whole Grade A foie gras, about 1½ pounds, at room temperature, cleaned and cut into ¾-inch slices

1. Combine beans, water, demi-glace, onion, carrots, and garlic in a large pot. Bring liquid to a boil over high heat, then adjust heat down so liquid just simmers, and skim off any sediment that rises to the top. Add peppercorns, thyme, and nutmeg, and cook until beans are tender but still slightly al dente, 30 to 45 minutes. Remove and set aside about 1 cup of the beans.

2. Transfer remaining beans, onions, and carrots with a slotted spoon to a food processor or electric blender, discarding the garlic. Add about ½ cup of the cooking liquid and the duck fat, and purée until smooth, adding more liquid if needed, until the mixture is the consistency of mashed potatoes. Season with salt.

3. While beans are cooking, bring a pot of water large enough to hold the leeks to

a boil. Add about 1 teaspoon of vinegar to the water, then adjust heat to medium, add leeks, and blanch them just until tender, 4 to 5 minutes. Drain well and set aside.

4. Heat a large skillet over high heat until almost smoking. Lightly salt and pepper foie gras slices and cook them just until well seared on the outside, 30 seconds each side. Remove and blot them with paper towels.

5. Divide bean purée among 6 heated plates. Place a couple slices of foie gras on purée and season with a little salt. Top with some of the whole beans, add a leek on the side, drizzle vinegar all over, and serve immediately.

pan-roasted foie gras and white peach–chili relish

SERVES 4 TO 6 AS AN APPETIZER

Foie gras takes a modern turn when served on a bed of tangy peach relish with the bite of jalapeño. It is one more example of how versatile this liver is. Just as green bell peppers turn red as they ripen, jalapeños do the same. Look for them in your market or at ethnic groceries.

¼ cup white vinegar

¼ cup loosely packed light brown sugar

¼ cup finely chopped, seeded, and deveined red jalapeños

2 tablespoons finely chopped shallots

2 tablespoons golden raisins

1 tablespoon finely chopped garlic

1 tablespoon grated gingerroot

½ teaspoon salt

6 firm white or yellow fresh peaches, blanched
to remove skin, pitted and sliced

1 lobe Grade A foie gras, about 1 pound,
cleaned and cut into ¾-inch slices

Salt and freshly ground black pepper to taste

12 slices French baguette, brushed with olive
oil and toasted in hot oven until light brown

1. Bring vinegar and sugar to a boil in a
nonreactive saucepan. Add jalapeños, shallots, raisins, garlic, ginger, and the ½ teaspoon salt, and simmer for 5 minutes. Add
peaches, simmer 5 more minutes, and
remove pan from heat. Cool for 15 minutes, then divide among 4 or 6 plates. Or
transfer to a clean jar, cover, and refrigerate for up to 1 week.

2. Heat a large heavy skillet over high
heat. Season foie gras with salt and pepper,
and sear quickly on both sides, about 30
to 45 seconds per side. Serve over peach-
chili relish, accompanied by sliced
baguette toasts.

Adapted from Michael Lomonaco, executive chef, Windows on the
World and Wild Blue, New York City

sautéed foie gras
with grape sauce

SERVES 8 TO 10

This scrumptious yet very simple foie
gras dish will make a liver lover of even a
vegetarian. Ariane says, "It's vital that
everyone get equal portions of foie gras
and sauce. Several European wars started

because one of the kings got a smaller
portion of foie gras than his colleagues
during a banquet." Serve with French
Sauternes wine or demi-sec Champagne.

1 tablespoon rendered duck fat

40 seedless green grapes, peeled if you have
time

1 tablespoon sugar

½ cup fine red wine or balsamic vinegar

¼ cup duck and veal demi-glace (see page 33)

1 whole Grade A foie gras, about 1½ pounds,
cleaned and cut into ¾-inch slices

Salt and freshly ground white pepper to taste

1. Heat a heavy skillet over high heat until
hot. Add duck fat to pan, then add grapes
and sprinkle sugar over them. Allow
grapes to caramelize a little, then add vinegar and reduce by half. Add demi-glace
and let reduce again, until sauce is thick
enough to coat grapes. Keep warm.

2. Sprinkle foie gras with salt and pepper.
When pan is very hot and almost smoking,
put in foie gras slices and cook for 30
seconds on each side. Remove from pan,
place on paper towels.

3. Serve slices of foie gras on warmed
plates with grapes and sauce poured over
them.

GASCON SUSHI

East meets southwest France when it
comes to Gascon sushi. Take a slice of
duck prosciutto and spread it with a
spoonful of mousse of foie gras. Roll up
and fasten with a toothpick.

roasted foie gras with sauternes sauce
with madeira figs

SERVES 8 AS AN APPETIZER

One of the greatest partners for foie gras is Sauternes — the sweet, rich, fruity, golden wine with an *s* at the end of its name, produced in southwestern France. Here the combination is at its pinnacle. Whole foie gras roasted over aromatic vegetables and then browned in the oven is sauced with Sauternes and accented with a roasted fig. Serve each guest a shimmering, seductive slice from both the large and small lobes. Drink a small glass of Sauternes and go to heaven.

Madeira Figs (recipe follows)

3 tablespoons unsalted butter

1 cup *each* sliced mushrooms, shallots, leeks

1 whole Grade A foie gras, about 1½ pounds, cleaned

Salt and freshly ground black pepper to taste

1⅔ cups Sauternes

½ teaspoon black peppercorns

4 cups duck and veal demi-glace (see page 33)

1. Prepare Madeira Figs.
2. Preheat oven to 325°F. Melt 1 tablespoon of the butter in a heavy medium saucepan over medium heat. Add mushrooms, shallots, and leeks and sweat until tender, stirring occasionally.
3. Season foie gras with salt and pepper. Place foie gras on top of warm vegetables in same pan, and roast in oven for 20 minutes, or until internal temperature of foie

gras reaches 120°F. Remove foie gras from the pan with a spatula; do this carefully, as it is very delicate.
4. Increase oven temperature to 450°F and preheat a sheet pan in oven.
5. Meanwhile, return saucepan to top of stove and continue cooking vegetables until lightly browned. Pour off fat, then add Sauternes and carefully ignite. Add peppercorns and demi-glace, and reduce sauce by one-third over high heat. Add butter, and strain sauce through cheesecloth. Season with salt and pepper and keep warm.
6. Place foie gras on sheet pan and roast for 3 to 4 minutes, until foie gras turns brown, then remove from oven. Cut large and small lobes of foie gras into about ½-inch-thick slices. Place a slice from each lobe on each of 8 plates. Ladle with sauce, garnish with a fig half, and serve hot.

madeira figs

1 tablespoon butter

4 large fresh figs, split lengthwise

½ cup ruby port

½ cup good medium Madeira

2 tablespoons sugar

¼ cup duck and veal demi-glace

1. Preheat oven to 350°F.
2. Butter a shallow baking dish, and place figs cut side down in dish.
3. Add port, Madeira, sugar, and demi-glace, cover with aluminum foil, and bake until figs are tender, about 30 minutes.
4. Remove figs and reduce liquid to a syrup. Pour syrup on figs and reserve.

Adapted from Georges Perrier, chef-owner, Le Bec Fin, Philadelphia

red snapper and foie gras with artichokes and black truffle sauce

SERVES 4

This dish should be considered among the ultimate surf-and-turf combinations. Splendid fish and sublime foie gras. The luxurious ingredients and elegant presentation make it fare for a very special event. Most of the preparation can be done ahead of time. A gentle Pomerol, like a Château La Conseillante 1985, would be exceptional with this meal.

(2 heavy 10-inch nonstick skillets)

1 lobe Grade A foie gras, about 1 pound, cleaned

Juice of 1 lemon

1 tablespoon extra-virgin olive oil

4 large artichokes

1 ounce black winter truffle (fresh, frozen, or canned)

½ cup duck and veal demi-glace (see page 33)

½ cup truffle juice

½ cup shrimp stock or clam broth

5 tablespoons unsalted butter, cut in pieces

4 fillets of red snapper, 8 ounces each, skinless

Fine sea salt and freshly ground white pepper to taste

1 tablespoon balsamic vinegar

1 tablespoon canola oil

1. Cut 4 slices about ½ inch thick from foie gras lobe, then cut remainder into cubes. Set aside.

2. Bring a large saucepan of salted water to a boil. Add lemon juice and olive oil. Stem artichokes, cut off leaves, and trim around hearts. Cook hearts until tender, about 30 minutes. Set aside to cool in liquid. *The recipe can be made to this point up to 1 day ahead; refrigerate artichokes in their liquid.*

3. Use a spoon to scoop choke out of artichoke hearts, and cut hearts into pie-shaped wedges, ¾ inch at thickest part, and pat dry. Set aside. Cut half of truffle into julienne and finely chop the rest. Cover and set aside.

4. Combine demi-glace, truffle juice, and shrimp stock in a medium saucepan and bring to a simmer over medium heat. Adjust heat so liquid is just below a simmer. Gradually add 4 tablespoons of the butter and the foie gras pieces, whisking constantly, so that foie gras melts into the sauce. Strain through a fine mesh sieve into another saucepan. Stir in chopped truffle and set aside. *Recipe can be made to this point the morning before serving; cover and refrigerate sauce.*

5. Season foie gras slices and snapper fillets on both sides with salt and pepper. Place 1 of the skillets over high heat until very hot. Put foie gras in skillet and sear until browned, about 30 seconds per side. Remove foie gras from skillet and keep warm. Pour off fat and wipe pan. Add remaining tablespoon butter to skillet and when hot put in drained artichoke wedges and sauté until lightly browned, about 1 minute. Stir in balsamic vinegar and cook for 10 seconds. Set aside and keep warm.

6. Heat oil in other skillet over high heat until just smoking. Add snapper and sauté until browned on bottom, about 2 minutes. Turn and sauté 1½ to 2 minutes more.

7. Bring sauce just to a simmer. Taste and adjust seasoning with salt and pepper. Arrange artichokes in the center of 4 large warmed plates. Lay snapper over artichokes and set a slice of foie gras over snapper. Spoon sauce around artichokes, making sure truffle is evenly distributed. Scatter the truffle julienne over everything and serve immediately.

Adapted from Eric Ripert, chef, Le Bernardin, New York City

roasted foie gras
with garlic confit

SERVES 4 TO 6 AS A MAIN COURSE

Gascony is known for its garlic as well as its foie gras. In this wintry dish, the two are paired. It is a variation on an old Gascon tradition of pairing poultry with a lot of mild garlic. Slow-cooking the cloves in duck fat tones down their bite and makes a garlic confit. Roasting a foie gras whole gives it an unbeatable flavor. In southwest France, quatre épices — equal parts of clove, nutmeg, cinnamon, and black pepper ground together — is often used by chefs for seasoning pâtés and confits. Serve with a light red from Gascony, such as Côtes de St.-Mont or Buzet, or a California Merlot.

1 whole Grade A foie gras, about 1½ pounds, cleaned

Coarse salt and freshly ground white pepper to taste

1 pound rendered duck fat (see Note)

46 cloves garlic, peeled

Pinch dried thyme

¼ teaspoon quatre épices (see headnote)

¼ cup heavy cream

1 tablespoon unsalted butter

12 baby carrots, steamed until tender

Pinch sugar

1. Preheat oven to 375°F.

2. Season foie gras generously with salt and pepper. Place foie gras in a small porcelain or copper baking dish that is only slightly larger than the liver itself. Roast until medium rare, 20 to 25 minutes, or until internal temperature of foie gras reaches 120°F. Remove from oven and keep warm.

3. Meanwhile, melt duck fat in a medium saucepan over medium heat. Add garlic, thyme, quatre épices, and salt and pepper to taste (about 1½ teaspoons salt), and simmer until garlic is soft. When done, remove 30 cloves and purée them in a food processor or electric blender until smooth. Return purée to a small saucepan, mix with heavy cream, and cook over low heat for 5 to 6 minutes. Remove from heat and keep warm. Reserve remaining garlic cloves, covered, to keep warm.

Sauce and garlic cloves may be done to this point 1 day ahead of time and stored covered in the refrigerator. Reheat gently before serving.

4. Melt the butter in a small skillet over medium heat. Add steamed carrots, sugar, salt, and pepper, and heat through, shaking pan to coat carrots. Keep warm.

5. Carefully remove whole foie gras to a cutting board and cut each lobe into 4 to 6 slices. Garnish plates with the reserved garlic cloves and carrots. Place a spoonful of garlic purée in the middle of each plate.

Place 2 slices of foie gras, one from each lobe, on top of the purée, season with salt and pepper, and serve.

NOTE:

Use duck fat that you have rendered and saved in the freezer (it keeps up to 6 months), or order from D'Artagnan or from a local purveyor of fine meats and poultry.

Lawsuit, n. a machine which you go into as a pig
and come out as a sausage.

— Ambrose Bierce,
The Devil's Dictionary, 1906

There are one or two foods that I trust,
And another which I deeply lust.
It's charcuterie,
That grand potpourri
Of meats both well spiced and robust.

— Gene Kofke, poet,
Montclair, New Jersey, 1999

sausages and charcuterie

Smoking, curing, and drying have been used to preserve food supplies since prehistoric times. The availability of game birds and meats was always greater in the fall than the winter. Thus, it was essential to develop ways to make meats last. Sausages, too, have a long lineage. They have been known at least since early Greece, when Homer wrote about them in the *Odyssey.* The early Romans indulged in sausages and spirits so actively during wild feasts that when Constantine became emperor he banned the celebrations along with the favored food. By the time the Gascons started cooking and preserving duck in its own fat, perhaps things were a little more tame . . . *not!*

SAUSAGES, CONFIT, AND DUCK PROSCIUTTO

At D'Artagnan, we love sausages, terrines, pâtés, and all kinds of charcuterie. And so do a whole lot of today's cooks. These products are not only satisfying and flavorful, but easily transformed into almost instant meals.

Grilled sausages on mashed potatoes, for instance, is a supereasy supper. With sausages made from ingredients as varied as venison and cherries, wild boar and sage, and chicken and truffles — not to mention the different kinds of potatoes available — the possibilities are endless. Dress them up a bit by adding a tangle of golden sautéed onions or a rich reduced wine sauce. We give you a couple of recipes to start you thinking. Because of the vast array of sausages in today's markets, many that are reduced in fat and/or seasoned with ethnic flavors, we focus on how to use them in this chapter. (All of the sausages used in these recipes are available from D'Artagnan. Feel free to interchange them or substitute your own favorites.)

While preserved meats like confit and duck prosciutto can be bought, making them is fun and, although somewhat time-consuming, quite simple (see our recipes on pages 291 and 289). Once a confit is slowly cooked or a prosciutto air-dried, it patiently awaits your hunger and creative thoughts for months on end in the refrigerator. We use prosciutto on sandwiches, salads, as a garnish for soups, and for Gascon Sushi (wrapped around mousse of foie gras and secured with a toothpick).

Fork-tender duck confit is the best fast food in the larder, so moist and richly scented that it's hard to resist taking bites straight out of the pot. George and Ariane's favorite ways to eat confit are on page 292. Throughout this book, you will find some regional American interpretations for seasoning and serving confits, too. But surely this centuries-old method of preserving duck and other birds in their own fat, once tasted, will inspire your own ideas. One of the most treasured ways of using confit is in cassoulet. Try Ariane's personal version from Gascony (page 293); you will not be disappointed.

TERRINES AND PÂTÉS

Of all the recipes in this chapter, the most traditional are those near the end, the game terrines and pâtés. That's because although we've changed some of the seasonings, certain things are immutable. First and foremost, pâtés need fat — at least one-third. If you skimp, you'll end up with a dry meat loaf of expensive ingredients. Since most game is so lean, we add pork fat to the mixture. It is saturated, so it doesn't readily melt and drain out during cooking. If using duck fat, you have to add something to bind it, like bread, to keep it within the mixture. Second, pâtés need to be highly seasoned. Since we don't advocate eating raw meats, cook a little ball of the mixture and let it cool to verify how it will taste. Adjust the ingredients at this point, bearing in mind that flavors will develop further as the pâté sits.

One place we have gone modern is when lining terrines or molds. We don't use the traditional pork fat or caul fat. Instead, we find that blanched Savoy cabbage or grape leaves retain all the moisture and flavor of the meat mixture without compromising the finished product. Although today's nonstick materials make pastry unnecessary for easy unmolding, there is nothing more luxurious than a crunchy crust as a contrast to the moist filling. We also have what we think is a terrific way to use up leftover bits of cooked game meat and birds. Look on page 307.

CONFIT STORAGE

In the days prior to improved refrigeration and vacuum packing, confit was placed in crockery pots or jars filled with duck fat, then covered with a layer of pork fat and stored in a cellar. This impenetrable top protected the confit throughout the long winter and on into the spring. In today's Gascon cellars, you'll find many small jars filled with confit. Since the entire small container can be used at one time, the confit isn't exposed to the outside air for long and can't spoil.

salad of duck sausages, green beans, and walnuts

SERVES 2 AS A MAIN COURSE SALAD

This salad was inspired by several composed salads served throughout the Dordogne region, in the southwest of France, where walnuts and duck are frequently paired. The rich sausages are scented with Armagnac, also from this area. Toasting walnuts intensifies their taste and adds crunch. For a more luxurious version of this salad, substitute a spoonful of truffled mousse of foie gras (about 4 ounces for 2 portions) for the sausages. Alternatively, if you have a little leftover cooked foie gras (although we've never heard of that happening), cut it in small cubes and add it to this salad.

4 ounces mesclun

1 teaspoon rendered duck fat or canola oil

4 links (8½ ounces) duck and Armagnac sausages

1 large shallot, minced

3 tablespoons tarragon vinegar

4 tablespoons walnut oil

Salt and freshly ground black pepper to taste

4 ounces thin green beans, tipped and cooked until crisp-tender

⅓ cup walnut pieces, lightly toasted

2 teaspoons minced flat-leaf parsley

1. Divide mesclun between plates. Heat duck fat in a large skillet over medium-high heat. Add sausages and brown on all sides, pricking to allow excess fat to run out. Reduce heat and cook until sausages are no longer red in center. Remove from pan and set aside. Discard all but ½ teaspoon of fat from skillet. Stir in shallot and cook over medium heat until soft, about 2 minutes. Add vinegar, stir up any browned cooking bits, and allow to reduce for about 30 seconds. Stir in walnut oil. Season with salt and pepper.
2. Cut sausages on the diagonal into 1-inch slices and divide between plates. Add green beans. Spoon on warm vinaigrette, then sprinkle on walnut pieces and parsley, and serve at once.

split pea soup
with merguez

SERVES 8

Pea soup is a traditional favorite for all ages. Adding chunks of sausages to this hearty soup and serving it with thick slices of garlic bread makes a perfect supper. Spicy Moroccan lamb sausages, *merguez*, infuse the soup with tantalizing, exotic perfumes. If you prefer, any relatively flavorful sausage may be substituted. The soup freezes beautifully. Defrost first, then stir in sausage.

2 medium carrots

2 medium ribs celery

2 medium parsnips

1 large onion

2 tablespoons vegetable oil

1 pound green split peas, rinsed and picked over

A picnic featuring an assortment of charcuterie, including Duck Rillettes (page 292), ❯
Festive Terrine of Rabbit (page 296), and Salad of Duck Sausages, Green Beans, and Walnuts

4 cups chicken or vegetable stock

3 to 4 cups water

1 teaspoon dried thyme

1 bay leaf

Salt and freshly ground black pepper to taste

6 to 8 links merguez sausages (10 to 12 ounces), cooked and cut into 1-inch pieces

1. Finely chop carrots, celery, parsnips, and onion either by hand or in a food processor. If using a processor, pulse vegetables so you don't overchop them.
2. Heat oil in a large heavy pot over medium-high heat. Stir in vegetables, reduce heat to medium, and sauté until softened, 6 to 8 minutes, stirring occasionally. Add split peas, stock, 3 cups of the water, thyme, bay leaf, and salt and pepper. Bring mixture to a boil, cover, and reduce heat so liquid is simmering. Cook until peas are very tender, about 1 to 1¼ hours.
3. Remove bay leaf. Transfer mixture to a food processor and pulse until almost smooth. Return to pot, stir in sausage pieces, and simmer until sausages are warmed through. Soup should be rather thick. However, add more water if needed.

potato and olive oil broth with littleneck clams and chorizo

SERVES 6 TO 8

This tasty potato soup, inspired by Portuguese caldo verde, has accents of garlic, bacon, and jalapeño that play against briny clams, spicy chorizo, and earthy kale. Serve with toasted slices of French or Italian bread. Chorizo is a sausage staple in Spanish cooking, often turning up in thin slices as snacks, or tapas, and served with a glass of wine. It's made with coarsely ground pork and garlic, and has a lively red color and hot taste from the ground chilies characteristically used to season it.

¼ pound slab bacon, cut into ¾-inch cubes

2 jalapeños, seeded, if desired, and chopped

1 onion, chopped

1 large head garlic, peeled and smashed

3 quarts chicken stock

4 large russet potatoes, peeled

½ head napa cabbage, shredded

2 bay leaves

¾ to 1 cup fruity olive oil

½ pound chorizo, sliced

48 littleneck clams, scrubbed

½ pound kale or Swiss chard, cut into thin shreds

Salt and freshly ground black pepper to taste

1. Combine bacon, jalapeños, onion, and garlic in a large saucepan, cover, and sweat over medium heat until onion is soft, 6 to 8 minutes. Add stock, potatoes, cabbage, and bay leaves, and simmer until potatoes are tender when pierced with a knife. Remove potatoes with a slotted spoon and set aside. Bring stock to a gentle boil and reduce to 2 quarts. Strain and set aside.
2. Heat ¼ cup of the oil in a large skillet over high heat. Add chorizo and sauté

for 1 to 2 minutes, shaking pan to turn pieces. Add clams and reduced broth, cover, and steam until clams are opened. Remove clams and divide among 6 to 8 large heated soup bowls. Discard any clams that don't open.

3. Reduce broth by one-third. Grate cooked potatoes and whisk into broth. Add kale, whisk in ½ cup or more olive oil, season with salt and plenty of black pepper, and pour over clams. Serve at once.

Adapted from Andy D'Amico, executive chef, The Santo Family Restaurant Group, New York City

bangers and bubble and squeak with pinot noir–thyme sauce

SERVES 2

Anyone who has eaten English boarding school food knows bubble and squeak as a cafeteria mainstay that's made with left-over mashed potatoes and cabbage. The name supposedly comes from the sounds the mixture makes as it's reheated in the skillet. (Other explanations say it's the sound your stomach makes when digesting.) Here we update the combination and top it with sausages, known colloquially as bangers in England. D'Artagnan's venison sausages are just a little hot and smoky, from dried ancho and chipotle chilies, and sweet from dried bing cherries. The combination, with a rich, thyme-infused wine sauce, makes this a comfort food from gastronomic heaven.

2 teaspoons sugar

¼ cup finely chopped shallots

4 black peppercorns

2 large sprigs thyme, plus 2 small sprigs, to garnish

¾ cup Pinot Noir or other full-bodied red wine

1 cup duck and veal demi-glace (see page 33)

2 teaspoons unsalted butter

Salt and freshly ground black pepper to taste

1 pound potatoes, peeled and cut into pieces, or 2 cups leftover mashed potatoes

¼ cup chicken or vegetable stock

¾ pound cabbage, cored and shredded

2 tablespoons rendered duck fat or canola oil, plus a little extra to sauté sausages

1 large onion, chopped

4 links (12 ounces) venison and cherry sausage

1. Combine sugar, shallots, peppercorns, 2 large sprigs thyme, and Pinot Noir in a small saucepan. Bring to a boil over high heat and boil until liquid is almost completely evaporated, 10 to 12 minutes. Pour in demi-glace and gently boil until reduced to a rich sauce, about ½ cup when strained. Whisk in butter, and season with salt and pepper if needed. Keep warm. *May be prepared ahead, covered, and refrigerated for several days.*

2. While sauce reduces, cover potatoes with cold water in a saucepan and boil until tender. Drain, and pass through a food mill or potato ricer, and stir in stock. Set aside. Meanwhile, bring a large pot of salted water to a boil. Add cabbage and blanch until bright green and wilted, 1½ to 2 minutes, drain, shock under cold water, and drain again.

3. Heat duck fat in a large skillet over medium-high heat. Add onion and drained cabbage, and cook until light brown, 3 to 5 minutes, stirring often. Stir in potatoes, salt, and a generous amount of black pepper, and continue cooking until potatoes are heated through and lightly browned, turning occasionally. Keep warm. *Potatoes may be made ahead and reheated.*

4. Heat a little fat or oil in a skillet, add sausages and sauté over medium-high heat until browned and cooked through, turning once or twice. Divide potato mixture between 2 large plates. Add sausages and spoon Pinot Noir sauce over them. Add a sprig of thyme to each plate, and serve.

wild boar sausage lasagna

SERVES 6

Here is lasagna to bring forth memories — or create them — of elegant northern Italian cooking. A light hand layers the béchamel, two cheeses, woodsy porcini mushrooms, and sage-scented boar sausage. No one ingredient overwhelms the whole. Don't increase the quantities of sauces or cheese. It will take away the delicate quality and make the dish gloppy. While there are lusty flavors in this lasagna, it is actually light enough to serve as a first course. Most of this dish is prepared in advance. The sauces may be frozen as well. No-cook lasagna noodles

(see Note) are another shortcut. Serve a Chianti or other medium-bodied red.

1 ounce dried porcini mushrooms

1 tablespoon extra-virgin olive oil

1 *each* carrot, onion, celery rib, finely chopped

1 (28-ounce) can Italian plum tomatoes, puréed with liquid

½ teaspoon sugar

Salt and freshly ground black pepper to taste

1½ tablespoons unsalted butter

2 tablespoons all-purpose flour

1½ cups hot milk

Pinch freshly grated nutmeg

4 links (8½ ounces) wild boar sausage with sage

2 teaspoons minced garlic

6 sheets thin, no-boil lasagna noodles (see Note)

½ pound fresh mozzarella, grated

½ cup freshly grated Parmigiano-Reggiano

1. Soak mushrooms in enough hot water to cover until soft, about 20 minutes. Lift from water, strain water through paper towels or a coffee filter, and reserve. Repeat soaking mushrooms in clean water as needed, until water has no grit. Squeeze gently and chop.

2. Heat oil in a medium pot over medium-high heat. Stir in carrot, onion, and celery, reduce heat to medium, and gently sauté until softened and translucent, 5 to 6 minutes. Add chopped porcini and strained soaking liquid, and bring to a simmer. Add tomatoes and sugar, bring to a boil, and gently simmer, partially covered, until thickened, about 1 hour. Season with salt and pepper. *Sauce may be made ahead, covered, and refrigerated for up to 5 days, or stored frozen for 2 months.*

3. Heat butter in a medium-small saucepan over medium-high heat. Stir in flour, making a roux. Cook over low heat for 2 to 3 minutes, then remove pan from heat and whisk in milk. Return to heat and bring to boil, whisking constantly. Season with salt, pepper, and nutmeg, and simmer 5 to 10 minutes. Sauce should be consistency of heavy cream. If too thick, thin with a little milk. *Béchamel may be made ahead, cooled, covered, and refrigerated for 4 to 5 days, or stored frozen for several months. Stir before using.*

4. Remove sausages from casing and break into pieces. Sauté sausage meat in a large skillet over medium-high heat until all pink is gone, breaking it apart with a wooden spatula as it cooks. Stir in garlic, then combine with béchamel and set aside.

5. Preheat oven to 350°F.

6. Spread 1 to 2 tablespoons of the tomato sauce on the bottom of a 9- or 10-inch square baking pan, then lay 1 sheet of pasta on top. Thinly spread ¼ cup of the béchamel on the pasta, taking care to cover the edges. It's all right if there are spots not completely covered with sauce. The pasta will flatten and swell in size, so don't worry that the sheets seem too small.

7. Spread ⅓ cup of tomato sauce over béchamel, season with salt and pepper, remembering that the pasta and mozzarella have no salt. Sprinkle one-sixth of the mozzarella over sauce, then 1 tablespoon of the Parmigiano-Reggiano. Repeat layers, starting with another pasta sheet, laying it so ridges go in other direction. Add

béchamel, tomato sauce, mozzarella, and Parmigiano-Reggiano. Continue until you have 6 layers of pasta, and a layer of sauce and cheese on top.

8. Cover pan with aluminum foil and bake until heated through, about 20 minutes. Uncover, and continue cooking to brown top slightly. Let lasagna stand, covered, for 5 to 10 minutes before cutting and serving. *Lasagna may be made ahead and reheated in a microwave oven.*

NOTE:

Delverde and other brands of pasta now sell instant, no-boil lasagna noodles in approximately 8-inch square sheets.

Adapted from Sally Kofke, cooking teacher and consultant, Montclair, New Jersey

grilled game sausages on basil-flecked polenta with buried mozzarella
and chunky tomato sauce

SERVES 4

A favorite rustic Italian main course feast that's easy to prepare yet so pleasing. Use any sausages that take your fancy. This recipe is easily doubled or tripled to feed a crowd. Serve with a large salad, a platter of fruit and cheese, and a simple, hearty red wine.

2 cups Chunky Tomato Sauce (recipe follows) or purchased tomato sauce

1 teaspoon olive oil

8 to 12 rabbit, duck, or other well-seasoned game sausages of your choice

4 ounces small fresh mozzarella balls

1 quart chicken stock

Salt to taste

1 cup instant polenta

3 tablespoons unsalted butter, softened

3 to 4 tablespoons chopped fresh basil leaves, plus 4 sprigs basil, to garnish

Hot water, if needed

Freshly grated Parmigiano-Reggiano to taste

1. Prepare Chunky Tomato Sauce.
2. Heat oil in a skillet over medium-high heat. Or brush a grill with oil and heat. Add sausages and cook until hot, turning to cook all sides. Leave whole or cut into 1¼-inch pieces, and keep warm over low heat.
3. Meanwhile, divide mozzarella balls among 4 large plates or bowls.
4. Bring chicken stock to a boil in a saucepan. Add salt, sprinkle in polenta, and stir constantly for 5 minutes. Turn off heat. Stir in butter and chopped basil. Stir in a little hot water if polenta is too thick to pour. Pour polenta over mozzarella, spoon about ½ cup tomato sauce over each serving, arrange sausages on top of polenta, and sprinkle on Parmigiano-Reggiano. Add a sprig of basil to each plate. Serve at once.

chunky tomato sauce

MAKES ABOUT 4 CUPS

2 tablespoons olive oil

1 large onion, chopped

2 teaspoons minced garlic

1 (28-ounce) can imported Italian or finest-quality California chopped tomatoes

1 (6-ounce) can tomato paste, plus ½ cup water to rinse out can

2 tablespoons chopped fresh oregano leaves, or 2 teaspoons dried oregano

2 tablespoons chopped fresh basil leaves, or 2 teaspoons dried basil

1 bay leaf

1 to 2 teaspoons brown sugar, if needed

Salt and freshly ground black pepper to taste

Heat olive oil in a large saucepan over medium-high heat. Add onion and sauté until just beginning to brown, about 6 minutes. Stir in garlic and continue cooking for 1 minute. Stir in tomatoes, tomato paste, water from can, oregano, basil, bay leaf, brown sugar (if tomatoes are acidic or sharp), salt, and pepper, and bring to a boil. Reduce heat and simmer partially covered for 20 minutes, stirring occasionally. If sauce is too thick, add a little more water.

Adapted from Judith Epstein, attorney, Piedmont, California

duck prosciutto

MAKES 1 DUCK BREAST

Italians love the dry-cured ham from pork legs called prosciutto. But in Gascony we love ducks, and our prosciutto is made from their breasts. In fact, ours tastes better and is far easier to make, slice, serve, and store! You'll love how well the salty, paper-thin slices marry with fruits like cantaloupe, mango, or Bosc pear.

◄ Grilled Game Sausages on Basil-Flecked Polenta with Buried Mozzarella and Chunky Tomato Sauce (page 287)

1 Moulard duck breast (magret), about 1 pound

½ pound coarse salt

½ cup red wine vinegar

Ground white pepper

1. Score skin side of breast diagonally into small squares, taking care not to cut flesh of duck. Bury breast in salt overnight.
2. Rinse off salt by dipping breast in vinegar for 1 to 2 seconds. You do not want magret to regain moisture it lost in the salt. Cover breast generously with ground pepper on all sides.
3. Wrap in cheesecloth and hang in a dry, well-ventilated, cool (maximum 60°F) place for around 15 days; the basement, not too far from the boiler, is the ideal location. When the magret becomes firm, it is ready. Unwrap and cut on the diagonal into paper-thin slices. Serve with sliced cantaloupe, wrapped around breadsticks, or in a sandwich.

A PERFECT LUNCH . . .

. . . to savor along the Seine or the Arno, in Napa Valley, or anyplace you want a great sandwich: On a 6- to 8-inch length of baguette, layer chopped sun-dried tomatoes, sliced goat cheese, Boston lettuce leaves, paper-thin slices of duck prosciutto, and a sprinkle of olive oil and red wine vinegar.

gascon salad

SERVES 4 AS A LIGHT LUNCH

Gascons are known to always favor protein over fiber. This traditional salad well illustrates the tendency to eat duck rather than greens.

1 head Boston lettuce, torn into pieces

2 ounces duck prosciutto, finely diced
(see previous recipe)

2 ounces smoked duck breast, diagonally
sliced

1 tablespoon balsamic vinegar

2 teaspoons Dijon mustard

1 teaspoon minced garlic

3 tablespoons rendered duck fat

8 "white olives" (see sidebar)

4 ounces duck gizzards confit, sliced
(see next page)

Salt and coarsely ground black pepper
to taste

1. Combine lettuce, prosciutto, and smoked duck breast in a bowl. In another bowl whisk together vinegar, mustard, and garlic. Set aside.
2. Heat duck fat in a skillet over medium-high heat. Add "olives" and sauté until golden, 2 to 3 minutes, shaking to turn and cook all sides. Add gizzards and cook until heated through, about 2 minutes.
3. Pour vinegar mixture over salad and toss to blend. Add olives, gizzards, and duck fat, season with salt and pepper, toss again, and serve immediately.

confit of duck

SERVES 8

The easiest way to enjoy confit of duck legs and thighs is to order it from D'Artagnan. Yet any book about game cooking, especially with a Gascon involved, would be remiss if it didn't explain the centuries-old tradition of slowly simmering seasoned ducks (or other birds) in their own fat. The tender, flavorful duck meat is a splendidly useful staple to keep in your refrigerator for weeks on end.

8 Moulard duck legs plus 8 wings plus 1 pound duck gizzards, or 12 Moulard duck legs

1 cup water

1 cup coarse salt

1 tablespoon freshly ground black pepper

1½ teaspoons dried thyme

1½ teaspoons crushed dried rosemary

1 bay leaf, crushed

1 teaspoon quatre épices, or ¼ teaspoon *each* ground cinnamon, cloves, nutmeg, and black pepper

1 large head garlic

10 whole cloves

8 cups rendered duck fat (see Note 1)

1. Remove any *excess* skin and fat from pieces of duck; cut skin and fat into cubes, place in a deep pot with 1 cup water, and slowly render fat over medium heat. When water has evaporated and remaining liquid is strained, clear duck fat will remain. Use the fat in this recipe, or pour it into a clean container, cover, and refrigerate or freeze for future use.

2. Place duck pieces in a large mixing bowl. Combine salt, pepper, thyme, rosemary, bay leaf, and quatre épices, and rub mixture over duck pieces. Cut unpeeled head of garlic in half crosswise, stud with cloves, and add to bowl. Cover meat with plastic wrap, place a weight on it to press down on meat, and refrigerate for 1 day. (A bottle of Armagnac is a perfect weight unless you drink too much of it during the next 24 hours!)

3. The next day, melt 8 cups duck fat in a large heavy casserole over medium heat. Remove duck pieces from refrigerator and wipe off herb and salt mixture. Reserve garlic studded with cloves.

4. When fat is warm but not hot, add duck pieces to the pot along with clove-studded garlic. Put in legs first, bringing to a low simmer. Half an hour later, add wings; 15 minutes later, add gizzards; then cook slowly over low heat for another 45 minutes. Simmer until meat can be easily pierced with a fork. Remove pieces from pot and set aside.

A LOVE OF THREE OLIVES

Maurice Coscuella, chef-owner of Le Ripa Alta, in Plaisance de Gers (Gascony), serves a famous *amuse-gueule*, or cocktail snack: brochette of three olives. The little skewers have black, white, and green olives.

When patrons eventually stop eating them long enough to ask about this intriguing, delicious white olive in the middle of the skewer, Coscuella — who trained with celebrated master chef Ferdinand Point, along with fellow students Paul Bocuse and Roger Vergé — explains his source. "Oh, I get them from ducks. But only male ducks have them."

5. To store, use sterilized small wide-mouthed glass jars or crocks (see Note 2). Arrange duck pieces in jars. Pass duck fat through a fine sieve and completely cover duck pieces. Make sure there are no air bubbles trapped in the fat. Cover jars, cool to room temperature, then refrigerate. Confit will keep under refrigeration for several weeks.

NOTES:

1. Use duck fat that you have rendered and saved in the freezer (it keeps up to 6 months), or order from D'Artagnan or from a local purveyor of fine meats and poultry.

2. To sterilize jars, submerge clean jars and lids in boiling water for several minutes, then remove with tongs and allow to dry on clean towels.

ENJOYING CONFIT

ARIANE: The classic way to enjoy a duck leg confit is to warm it up in duck fat, skin side down, until crisp, and serve with garlic potatoes and cèpes cooked in the same fat.

GEORGE: My favorite way is to grill it just to warm it through and crisp the skin, and then serve it over a salad that has been tossed with a fairly acidic vinaigrette.

ARIANE: There is no wrong way to prepare confit. As a matter of fact, you can successfully confit anything you want, from garlic to quail, from young vegetables to chicken wings. The only trick is not to use a meat that is too lean, as it would become dry during the process. For instance, when using a rabbit or chicken, confit the legs, not the loin or breast.

duck rillettes

SERVES 6 TO 8 AS AN HORS D'OEUVRE

Rillettes made the old-fashioned way, using only duck, aromatic vegetables, and herbs, once again affirm that the best things in life are very often the simplest. Remove rillettes from the refrigerator at least 30 minutes before serving. Accompany with thinly sliced French bread and cornichons.

1¾ cups dry white wine

1 bouquet garni: 5 parsley sprigs, 3 celery leaves, 1 thyme sprig, 1 bay leaf, 5 whole cloves, and 10 peppercorns, tied in cheesecloth

½ head garlic, separated into cloves and peeled

3 carrots, cut into 4 chunks each

3 onions, quartered, studded with 16 whole cloves per onion

Pinch dried thyme

Pinch quatre épices (equal parts ground cinnamon, cloves, nutmeg, and black pepper)

6 Moulard duck legs

Salt and freshly ground black pepper to taste

1. Combine white wine, bouquet garni, garlic, carrots, onions, thyme, and quatre épices in a large stockpot and bring to a boil over high heat. Add duck legs, and water to cover meat if necessary. Return to a boil, skim off scum, reduce heat, and cook until most of the liquid has evaporated and been replaced by duck fat, and the duck is completely tender when pierced with a toothpick, about 3 hours.

2. Remove duck pieces with a strainer. The meat will fall off the bone. Discard skin and debone duck with a fork, shredding meat into thin strips.

3. In a large bowl, combine meat with fat and vegetables while still hot, discarding onions. Remove bouquet garni. Gently mix together. Season with salt and pepper. Scrape into a terrine, cover, and refrigerate at once. Let stand for at least 2 days.

4. Bring to room temperature before serving.

cassoulet

SERVES 8

This classic casserole of sausage, preserved duck or goose, and beans is at the heart of traditional Gascon cooking. While the ingredients vary according to who makes it, the kind of sausages and confit available, and regional and personal preference, it's important that cassoulet cook slowly so all of the ingredients have time to marry. Serve with thick slices of crusty country bread and a bottle of Madiran wine from Gascony.

THE MEXIFROST CONNECTION

ARIANE: Like many new businesses, D'Artagnan started on a shoestring. We were always trying to cut corners and do the most with the least. After getting caught a couple of times trying to smoke or cook meat in our own kitchens, we decided that it was time to become USDA approved. That's fine if you have the money to find a proper facility, which we didn't.

But as has been our fortune throughout the years, we got help when we needed it. A friend sent us to see a friend of his, Gonzalo Armendariz, who was making chimichangas, burritos, and other Mexican specialties at Mexifrost, his plant in Brooklyn. He had giant steam kettles but also an old steam oven that, with the exception of lunch hour, when his employees warmed their meals in it, went unused.

Asked if we might share space, Armendariz replied, "When I started, someone helped me. Now it's my turn." So from 1986 to 1987 we scheduled our confits, terrines of foie gras, and rillettes to cook between batches of black beans and heated burritos. In July of 1987,

when a butcher vacated a USDA shell in Jersey City, we moved on. But if it had not been for the Armendariz family, our prepared delicacies might never have come to market.

GEORGE: Burritos made with our rillettes are delicious. Take an 8-inch flour tortilla and spoon in 2 to 3 ounces rillettes, 1 tablespoon fresh tomato salsa, 1 to 2 ounces crumbled fresh goat cheese, and 1 tablespoon chopped cilantro. Roll up the tortilla around the ingredients and place seam side down on a rack or a baking sheet. Bake in a preheated 350°F oven for 20 minutes. Let cool, then serve whole or cut into 1-inch slices and skewered with a toothpick.

ARIANE: When Daniel Boulud — at that point the chef of Le Cirque — asked why our terrine of foie gras had *un arôme unique* — as if it were seasoned with cumin — we realized that our generous space-partner's seasonings perfumed our own endeavors.

1½ pounds dried navy, Tarbais, or
Great Northern beans

½ pound unsmoked bacon, ventrèche, or
pancetta, in one piece

6 ounces fresh pork rind or fatback, in one
piece, rinsed well

10 cloves garlic

2 medium onions, cut in half

1 carrot, coarsely chopped

1 bouquet garni: 5 parsley sprigs, 3 celery
leaves, 1 sprig thyme , 1 bay leaf, 5 whole
cloves, and 10 peppercorns, tied in
cheesecloth

10 cups water

½ pound duck gizzards confit (page 291)

4 duck legs confit (page 291)

3 cups duck and veal demi-glace (see page 33)
dissolved in 3 cups water

2 large tomatoes, peeled, seeded, and
chopped

Coarse salt and freshly ground black pepper
to taste

4 links (8½ ounces) duck and Armagnac
sausages, lightly browned, then cut in half
crosswise

½ pound fresh garlic sausage, cut into 8 slices

¼ cup rendered duck fat, melted

1. Cover beans with water and soak
overnight. Drain and put into a large heavy
casserole, preferably enameled cast iron,
with bacon, pork rind, garlic, 1 onion, the
carrot, and the bouquet garni. Cover with
the 10 cups of water and bring to a boil.
Simmer over low heat, stirring often, until
beans are barely tender, about 1 hour.
Drain and return to casserole, discarding
onion and bouquet garni.

2. Add remaining onion, the gizzard confit, duck legs, demi-glace mixture, and
tomatoes, and bring to a boil. Add a pinch
of salt and pepper, and simmer over low
heat for about 15 minutes.

CASSOULET WARS

ARIANE: My father often says, "Cassoulet
is not really a recipe, it's a way to argue among
neighboring villages of Gascony." Toward the
east, they add lamb (a no-no in the west).
Around Toulouse, they top the dish with bread
crumbs (if you serve that in Auch, your guests
will throw it out). They even disagree on the
type of beans. In the south, it is the *coco,* or
Tarbais, a big, somewhat flat white bean; in the
north, they use flageolets.

However, everybody agrees, come spring,
to make the last and best cassoulet of the season with freshly picked fava beans. That's an
extraordinary treat.

Here are some tips for cooking and serving
cassoulet:

- Mix the beans with the meat once all the
  beans are cooked and some of them start
  to burst.
- Use as many confit meats as possible. They
  will give the most flavor.
- Don't hesitate to cut open the upper crust
  to check if the casserole is drying out too
  much inside. If so, add some liquid, such as
  stock or demi-glace.
- Eat cassoulet very hot.
- Reheat leftovers. They will be even better
  than the original.

3. Drain bean mixture in a colander over a bowl; reserve 5 cups of the cooking liquid. Discard bacon and pork rind. Remove duck legs and cut each in half at the joint. Season beans with 1 teaspoon salt and a few grindings of pepper.

4. Preheat oven to 325°F.

5. Place half the bean mixture in casserole. Add duck legs, duck sausages, and garlic sausage, and cover with remaining beans. Add reserved cooking liquid and drizzle duck fat over top. Cover and bake until hot and bubbling, about 2 hours. *Cassoulet may be prepared ahead to this point, then cooled and refrigerated for up to 3 days. If refrigerated, bring to room temperature before proceeding with Step 6.*

6. Increase oven temperature to 400°F. Uncover casserole and bake until top is browned, about 20 minutes. Remove from oven and serve.

festive terrine of rabbit
with port-soaked prunes or french kisses

SERVES 8 AS A FIRST COURSE OR HORS D'OEUVRE

This fine-textured terrine, with rabbit loins adding a decorative circle in the center of each slice, is celebratory fare for a special occasion. The terrine's ingredients, including Black Forest ham, Armagnac, port, and spices, complemented by small marinated prunes, will entice even the most blasé diner. Instead of pork fat, this contemporary version is wrapped in blanched Savoy cabbage leaves. They are not only healthier but easier to work with. Prepare

the terrine at least 5 days ahead of time for the flavors to develop. Serve it cool, not cold, and pass thin slices of country peasant bread or whole wheat bread. For a sparkling meal, add a glass of champagne to the menu.

5 to 7 large leaves Savoy cabbage

1 young rabbit, 2½ to 3 pounds, boned, reserving 1 loin and liver

½ pound ground pork fat

1 egg, slightly beaten

1 teaspoon crushed garlic

1 teaspoon dried thyme

¼ teaspoon ground allspice

¼ teaspoon ground cardamom

½ tablespoon salt or to taste

Freshly ground black pepper to taste

2 tablespoons Armagnac

¼ pound Black Forest or other smoky ham, cut into ⅛-inch dice

1½ teaspoons green peppercorns packed in brine or vinegar, rinsed

3 teaspoons rendered duck fat or unsalted butter

¼ cup finely chopped shallots

1 tablespoon tawny port

1 large bay leaf

Port-Soaked Prunes (recipe follows) or French Kisses (see sidebar)

1. Bring a large pot of salted water to a boil. Add cabbage leaves and cook until bright green and wilted, about 4 minutes. Remove, blot very dry on paper towels, and use a sharp knife to pare down coarse center ribs until flat.

2. Line a loaf pan, approximately 8 x 4 x 2½ inches, with cabbage leaves, allowing leaves to drape over edges of pan. Reserve any extra leaves, cover with plastic wrap, and refrigerate.

3. Mix together rabbit (except reserved loin and liver), pork fat, egg, garlic, thyme, allspice, cardamom, salt, plenty of black pepper, and Armagnac in a large bowl. Set aside. Combine ham and green peppercorns in a small bowl.

4. Pat rabbit loin dry. Melt 2 teaspoons of the duck fat in a large skillet over medium-high heat. Add loin and liver and brown on all sides, 1½ minutes. Remove to a plate and set aside. Add the remaining teaspoon duck fat and the shallots, and sauté until limp, 2 minutes longer.

5. Pour in port, bring liquid to a boil for 30 seconds, scraping up all browned particles. Scrape into meat mixture and blend well. Chop cooled liver into pieces,

transfer along with meat mixture to a food processor, and process until almost smooth. Add diced ham and peppercorns, and pulse a couple of times to mix. Spoon half the meat mixture into prepared pan.

6. Place loin lengthwise in center of the terrine. Press down gently. Cover with remaining meat, packing it into corners of the pan, and mounding it slightly in the center. (This is easier done with wet hands.) It will be higher than the pan's edge. Fold cabbage over meat mixture, adding more cabbage leaves if top is not completely covered. Add bay leaf and a layer of parchment the size of the pan. Cover top of pan with a double layer of heavy foil and punch 3 holes to let steam escape.

7. Preheat oven to 350°F.

8. Put chilled terrine on a folded kitchen towel in a large deep pan and fill pan with boiling water halfway up the sides of the terrine. Bake in oven until juices run clear and an instant thermometer reads 160°F

FRENCH KISSES, OR HOW SUNSWEET FELL IN LOVE

ARIANE: French Kisses, a D'Artagnan original, are one step this side of paradise: prunes soaked in Armagnac and filled with foie gras. Yet these sublime treats were almost forced off the market until their own seductive powers came to our rescue.

For about five years, we had been producing French Kisses in small batches, mostly for Christmas and Valentine's Day, when we received a very official letter from the Sunsweet Company's lawyers. "Cease and desist!" it threatened. "That name is trademarked by the prune company."

Now, we loved that name and never thought we were doing anything to threaten the food

giant, and until then we had thought we were the first ones to have used the name French Kisses for something other than the original. So we wrote a very nice letter to the vice president of marketing and sales for Sunsweet, explaining that D'Artagnan was a small company and there was no way we would compete with them. In fact, we pointed out, we had used Sunsweet prunes exclusively for the past three years. Along with this letter, we enclosed three samples.

Shortly thereafter, we got a call back from the vice president saying it was absolutely OK to use the name, and by the way, those French Kisses are a great product. *Whew*.

when inserted in the center, 60 to 70 minutes. Remove from oven and water bath. Cover terrine with a piece of cardboard wrapped in aluminum foil, or a second pan the same size as the first, place a 1-pound weight on it, and let cool for 1 hour.

9. Remove weight and refrigerate, still covered with parchment and foil, for at least 2 days, and up to 5 days, to develop the flavors.

10. Prepare Port-Soaked Prunes.

11. Remove terrine from refrigerator at least 1 hour before serving. Dip in hot water to unmold. Wipe off any congealed juices or fat. Remove cabbage leaves, if desired. Slice with a serrated knife, and serve with a couple of soaked prunes or French Kisses. Drizzle reduced port sauce from prunes over slices.

port-soaked prunes

1 cup bite-size pitted prunes, cut in half

¾ cup tawny port

1 stick cinnamon (optional)

3 whole cloves

1. Combine prunes with port and spices in a bowl, cover, and refrigerate for several days.

2. Several hours before serving, lift the prunes from the liquid and set aside. Strain the liquid into a small saucepan. Retrieve the spices from the strainer and add to the saucepan. Bring the liquid to a boil over high heat, cook until reduced by half, then let cool. Remove cinnamon and cloves before serving.

partridge and foie gras terrine

SERVES 6

This union of partridge and foie gras produces a rich, elegant first course. The breast meat is left in long, thin strips, while the remaining meats are finely chopped. If you have a ceramic terrine mold, use it. Otherwise, a glass loaf pan is a perfect stand-in. Speaking of stand-ins, you can use other game birds, such as a pheasant, in this recipe.

1 partridge, 10 to 12 ounces, or other game bird

Salt and freshly ground black pepper to taste

¼ cup Armagnac

1 pound Grade B foie gras, cleaned

¾ pound fresh pork belly (or 1 pound if using a pheasant)

1 egg

EASY DOES IT

Putting a weight on a terrine or pâté fresh from the oven helps to solidify the shape. However, too much weight (you only need about a pound) or too long a time under the weight (an hour will do) forces the juices and flavor out, leaving the meat dry and underseasoned. Make sure weight is distributed evenly, or shape will be irregular.

2 teaspoons quatre épices, or ½ teaspoon *each* ground cinnamon, cloves, nutmeg, and black pepper

3 ounces unsmoked bacon, pancetta, or ventrèche, finely chopped

1. Bone partridge, removing as much meat from legs and wings as possible. Slice breasts lengthwise into thin strips, season with salt and pepper, combine with 2 tablespoons of the Armagnac in a bowl, and set aside.

2. Place the remaining partridge meat, the foie gras, pork belly, egg, quatre épices, salt, pepper, and remaining Armagnac in a food processor and process until fairly smooth. Do not overprocess. Add bacon, and pulse just to blend. Heat a nonstick skillet and cook a small ball of the mixture to test for seasonings. Adjust if necessary.

3. Preheat oven to 350°F. Bring a pot of water to a boil. Brush inside of a 9 x 5 x 3-inch terrine or glass loaf pan with a little water.

4. Spread a 1-inch-thick layer of force-meat mixture in the bottom of the terrine. Add a layer of breast meat. Repeat with layers of forcemeat and breast meat, ending with a layer of the forcemeat. It is easiest to do this with wet hands. Place a folded kitchen towel in the bottom of a pan large enough to hold the terrine, and set the terrine on top. Pour enough boiling water into the pan to come halfway up the sides of the terrine. Bake until top of terrine starts to brown, then cover with aluminum foil and continue cooking until an instant-read thermometer registers 160°F when inserted into the center of the terrine, about 1 hour total cooking time.

5. Remove terrine from oven and from water bath. Cover with a piece of cardboard wrapped in foil or with another terrine of the same size. Place a 1-pound weight on it, and let it cool for 1 hour. Remove weight, wrap in plastic wrap, and refrigerate for at least 1 week to allow flavors to develop.

winter pheasant pâté sur les plumes
with cranberry-apple chutney

SERVES AT LEAST 12

For entertaining a crowd, pâtés are dramatic and festive. The effect of this one may be heightened by serving the pâté on a smaller plate resting on a blanket of pheasant feathers. (See directions for drying the plumes on page 301.) In this classically inspired version, diced ham, pistachios, and Madeira are blended into the well-spiced mixture. A layer of sliced breast meat in the center adds visual appeal that tempts you even before the first bite. The spices are repeated in our Cranberry-Apple Chutney. To save time, you could buy prepared chutney.

5 to 7 large Savoy cabbage leaves

1 large pheasant, 3 to 3½ pounds, skinned (see sidebar) and boned

1 pound ground veal

12 ounces ground pork fat

3 eggs, beaten

6 ounces smoked ham or Canadian bacon, diced

⅓ cup shelled pistachio nuts

½ cup finely chopped shallots

10 juniper berries, crushed

1 teaspoon ground thyme

¼ teaspoon ground nutmeg

1 tablespoon salt, or to taste

Freshly ground black pepper

½ cup medium Madeira

¼ cup Armagnac or brandy

2 slices thick-cut bacon

2 bay leaves

Cranberry-Apple Chutney (recipe follows), or 1 cup purchased chutney

1 to 2 heads escarole, red leaf, or other decorative lettuce, separated, washed, and patted dry

1 pound purple or green seedless grapes, washed and cut into small bunches

Lightly toasted bread

1. Preheat oven to 350°F.

2. Bring a large pot of salted water to a boil. Add cabbage leaves and blanch until bright green and wilted, about 4 minutes. Remove, blot very dry on paper towels, and use a sharp knife to pare down the coarse center ribs until flat.

3. Line a loaf pan approximately 9 x 5 x 3 inches with cabbage leaves, allowing leaves to drape over edges of pan. Reserve extra leaves.

4. Reserve half of the breast meat. Add remaining pheasant meat, veal, pork fat, and eggs to a food processor, and pulse until a somewhat smooth texture is reached. *Do not overprocess* or pâté will be too uniform and compacted in texture. This may be done in batches if necessary.

PHEASANT SUR LES PLUMES: A DRAMATIC PRESENTATION

If you are able to get an unskinned pheasant and would like to present a pheasant pâté *sur les plumes* — on a blanket of its feathers — here is what to do:

Remove and discard head at top of neck. Using a sharp knife, cut off wings at the rib cage and spread open. Cut off the tail where it joins the body, and set aside. Slit bird down the breastbone and, using your fingers, slide the skin loose in one piece from the body, working the skin loose from the neck. Make a cut around the base of each leg, and slide off skin in one piece. Either bone out bird immediately or wrap and bone later. Refrigerate bird and use for pâté within one day.

Using a generous amount of coarse salt, sprinkle the inside of the body skin (not the feathers), as well as the cut parts of the wings and tail, liberally with salt. Lay on a flat surface, skin side up, and dry in a cool spot for at least several days or up to a week. Brush off salt before using.

Once you have this blanket, you can use and reuse it as a decorative base. Lay the body feathers on a large oval platter. Add wings on sides and tail extending from one end of platter. Small clusters of red or green grapes may be used as a garnish. Slice your pâté and serve it on a small plate, not directly on the feathers. Store feathers in a cool place.

◄ Winter Pheasant Pâté *Sur les Plumes* (page 299) and Foie Gras Mousse in Baby Pumpkins (page 262)

5. Transfer mixture to a large bowl. Add ham, pistachios, shallots, juniper berries, thyme, nutmeg, salt, pepper, Madeira, and Armagnac and stir with a wooden spoon. Spoon half the mixture into mold, patting it down into the corners. Cut reserved breast meat into thin strips and place them over pâté layer. Add remaining pâté mixture, lay bacon slices on top, and turn cabbage leaves over meat, adding additional leaves if necessary to cover. Place bay leaves over cabbage, cover with a piece of parchment the size of the pan, then a double layer of heavy foil, and punch a hole in the middle for steam to escape.

6. Place pâté mold on a folded kitchen towel in a larger pan and fill the larger pan with boiling water to a level halfway up the side of the mold. Bake in the middle of the oven for 1½ to 1¾ hours. When done, pâté will have shrunk slightly and juices will run clear.

7. Remove pan from oven. Lift pâté from water bath. Place about 8 ounces of weight evenly distributed on pâté (set the weight on a piece of cardboard cut to fit, or in a loaf pan the same size as the mold), and let it cool for an hour. Remove weight and refrigerate for at least 4 or 5 days. Prepare Cranberry-Apple Chutney.

8. Before serving, dip mold briefly into hot water to release pâté. Discard cabbage and bay leaves, wipe off any jellied liquids or fat, and allow to stand at room temperature for 1 hour. To serve without the bed of feathers, line a large platter with lettuce leaves. Put pâté in center, cut 2 or 3 slices, and arrange attractively on platter. Add grapes around edges. Serve with lightly toasted bread and Cranberry-Apple Chutney.

cranberry-apple chutney

MAKES 1 TO 1½ CUPS

1 cup chopped cranberries

½ Granny Smith apple, cored, peeled, and diced

½ medium onion, chopped

⅓ cup sugar

2 tablespoons honey

¼ cup chopped dried apricots

2 tablespoons apple cider vinegar

1 tablespoon orange juice concentrate

1 tablespoon finely chopped candied ginger

1 tablespoon brown sugar

1 teaspoon mustard seed

½ teaspoon salt

1 teaspoon Regime Blend spice mixture (see page 203)

Combine all ingredients in a saucepan. Cook over medium heat for 5 minutes. Adjust heat to medium high and gently boil for 8 to 10 minutes, until reduced and thick, stirring often.

squab game torte with red wine sauce

SERVES AT LEAST 10

This golden-domed game torte is reminiscent of days gone by, when magnificent molded domes of pastry covered everything from whole birds to chopped meat. A rich mousse of squab, foie gras, and cream is at the heart of this one. Diced morsels of squab and foie gras enhance its texture. The easy, foolproof pastry dough will form a perfect crust once it's cooked.

4 squab

1 tablespoon rendered duck fat or unsalted butter

6 large garlic cloves, sliced

4 ounces white mushrooms, wiped clean, trimmed, and sliced

2 large tomatoes, diced

2 ribs celery, sliced

1 large onion, sliced

1 carrot, sliced

¼ cup red wine vinegar

2 quarts hearty red wine

1 bouquet garni: 10 parsley stems, 8 black peppercorns, and 1 bay leaf, tied in cheesecloth

Egg Torte Dough (recipe follows)

1 whole Grade A foie gras, about 1½ pounds, cleaned

1 quart very cold heavy cream

Salt and freshly ground black pepper to taste

1 egg beaten with 1 tablespoon water

8 to 12 tablespoons unsalted butter, cut into pieces

1. Bone out squab breasts. Remove and discard skin, then refrigerate breasts.
2. Chop remaining squab for stock. Heat duck fat in a large heavy casserole over medium-high heat. Add chopped bones and legs and cook until richly browned, turning occasionally, about 15 minutes.

Add garlic, mushrooms, tomatoes, celery, onion, and carrot, and cook until vegetables are tender and lightly browned, about 8 minutes, stirring often. Deglaze the pan with vinegar, scraping up all browned bits, then add wine and bouquet garni. Turn heat down, and simmer stock uncovered for 4 to 5 hours, skimming frequently. Strain stock into a clean pan, bring to a gentle boil, and reduce until the consistency of a sauce, to about one-quarter of the original volume. *Stock may be made a day ahead and refrigerated. Reheat before finishing.*
3. While stock simmers, prepare Egg Torte Dough through Step 1.
4. FOR MOUSSE: Dice breast meat and reserve half. Remove small lobe of foie gras, devein, dice, and set aside. Purée half the diced breast meat and the large lobe of foie gras in a food processor until smooth, then pass through a strainer. Fold in cream, salt, and pepper. Cook a small ball of mousse to test for seasonings. Fold in reserved diced breast and foie gras.
5. Preheat oven to 350°F.
6. Finish Egg Torte Dough. Place small pastry circle on a baking sheet or a pie plate lined with aluminum foil. Mound mousse onto pastry, forming it into a dome, and leaving a ¾-inch pastry border. Brush border with egg wash. Place large pastry circle on top, and press edges together. Brush remaining egg wash over top, and bake in oven until crisp and golden brown, 35 to 40 minutes.
7. While torte finishes baking, reheat sauce, taste for salt and pepper, and then, off the heat, whisk in butter a little at a time. Slice torte at the table, and serve sauce on the side.

egg torte dough

8½ cups all-purpose flour, plus flour for dusting work surface

1 tablespoon salt

2½ sticks cold unsalted butter, cut into small pieces

5 egg yolks, beaten

2 cups plus 2 tablespoons ice water

1. Mix flour and salt together in a food processor. Add butter and pulse until the consistency of coarse meal. Add egg yolks and, with motor running, add water and process just until mixture pulls together. Turn onto a floured board and form into 2 balls, 1 slightly larger than the other. Cover with plastic wrap and refrigerate for 1 hour. **2.** Roll pastry out on a floured board into 2 circles, each ¼ inch thick. Trim to a 12-inch circle and a 10-inch circle.

Adapted from Jean-Marie Lacroix, executive chef, Four Seasons Hotel, Philadelphia

porcini terrine with wood pigeon, foie gras, and duck prosciutto with red wine emulsion

SERVES 10

Experience classic and modern elegance in this molded terrine wrapped in a rosy layer of duck prosciutto. Wood pigeon, porcini, and foie gras are bound by a jelly made with seasoned wood pigeon stock and red wine. The emulsified sauce has as its base the same stock reduced to its very essence, then puréed with foie gras, porcini, and a splash of balsamic vinegar. You will truly taste the quality of the red wine as it reduces.

4 wood pigeons

2 small tomatoes, coarsely chopped

4 shallots, coarsely chopped

1 *each* onion, carrot, celery rib, and small leek, coarsely chopped

1 small head garlic, coarsely chopped

2 (750-ml) bottles red wine from the Tannat grape, such as Madiran or Côtes de Gascogne

Pinch dried thyme, plus 1 tablespoon fresh thyme leaves

1 bay leaf

2 tablespoons unflavored gelatin powder

3 tablespoons rendered duck fat or unsalted butter

1½ pounds fresh porcini mushrooms, wiped clean, stems separated from caps

1 teaspoon minced garlic

Salt and freshly ground black pepper to taste

1 whole Grade A foie gras, about 1½ pounds, cleaned and separated into 2 lobes

1 to 2 duck prosciuttos (page 289), sliced by machine lengthwise paper-thin

1 tablespoon balsamic vinegar, or to taste

Chicken stock, as needed

1 pound mixed field greens or mesclun lightly dressed with olive oil and balsamic vinegar

1. Preheat oven to 350°F. Clean wood pigeons and bone out breasts, leaving them whole. Remove and discard skin, and refrigerate breasts. Chop bones and legs, and roast them in a flat pan along with the tomatoes, 2 tablespoons of the shallots, and the onion, carrot, celery, leek, and head of garlic until golden brown, about 20 minutes. Scrape into a stockpot, deglazing pan with a little water if necessary.

2. Pour in wine and add enough water to cover bones. Add dried thyme and bay leaf, bring liquid to a boil, then adjust heat down to a simmer, cook for 2 hours, then strain. Reserve 2 cups of the liquid and reduce the rest over medium-high heat to a thick syrup, lowering heat as it thickens so as not to burn it. Cover and refrigerate. Bring the 2 cups of stock to a boil, sprinkle on gelatin, and cook until dissolved. Set aside to thicken into jelly.

3. While stock reduces, heat 2 tablespoons of the duck fat in a heavy casserole over medium-high heat. Add porcini caps and stems, thyme leaves, and minced garlic, and sauté until cooked, about 8 minutes. Season with salt and pepper, drain on paper towels, and set aside.

4. Preheat oven to 300°F.

5. Season foie gras lobes with salt and pepper. Heat an ovenproof skillet over high heat. Add foie gras lobes and cook for 30 seconds on each side to lightly brown them, turning carefully. Transfer skillet to oven and roast foie gras for 12 minutes, then turn, add remaining 2 tablespoons shallots, and roast 8 minutes longer. Drain on paper towels and set aside.

6. Heat a skillet with 1 tablespoon of the duck fat over medium-high heat. Season wood pigeon breasts with salt and pepper and sauté them until medium rare, 1½ to

2 minutes per side. Remove and blot on paper towels. Coarsely chop wood pigeon, porcini caps and stems, and foie gras separately. Combine in a bowl, reserving about 3 tablespoons of the foie gras and mushrooms for the sauce.

7. Carefully line an 8 x 4½ x 2½-inch terrine with slightly overlapping slices of duck prosciutto, and add filling. Pour wine jelly over the filling, warming it up if it is too thick to pour. Cover with plastic wrap, and refrigerate for 20 minutes. Place another terrine of the same size on top, add about 1 pound of weight to it, and refrigerate for at least 24 hours. Remove weight and unmold terrine by dipping the bottom into hot water.

8. Combine reduced stock, reserved foie gras and mushrooms, and vinegar in an electric blender and purée until smooth. Add just enough chicken stock to thin mixture to a smooth sauce. Season to taste with salt and pepper. Cut terrine into slices and lay each portion on a small handful of salad. Drizzle on sauce, and serve.

Adapted from Jean-Louis Palladin, chef-partner, Napa Restaurant at the Rio Hotel, Las Vegas, and Restaurant Palladin and Restaurant Jean-Louis, New York City

venison and cherry
pâté en croûte

SERVES 10

A glorious pâté that is fairly easy to make with the benefit of frozen puff pastry. The results: the flavorful centerpiece that you may have only dreamed about in the past. If you have any venison trim left over from other dishes, use it here. Ask the butcher to grind the pork butt for you. The pork should not be too lean, since without enough added fat the venison will be dry.

½ cup dried cherries

4 tablespoons cherry wine or cherry liqueur

4 ounces mousse of foie gras (see page 262)

1 small black truffle, finely chopped (optional)

1 pound well-trimmed venison stew meat with fat and silver skin removed, plus 1 venison fillet

6 ounces duck or chicken livers

1 pound ground pork butt

1 egg white

1 teaspoon salt

Pinch white pepper

½ tablespoon lemon juice

2 tablespoons full-bodied red wine, such as Cabernet Sauvignon

½ tablespoon unsalted butter

2 pounds all-butter puff pastry, defrosted according to package directions

1 egg beaten with 1 tablespoon water

1½ cups water

2 tablespoons unflavored gelatin powder

2 tablespoons duck and veal demi-glace (see page 33)

1. Combine dried cherries with 2 tablespoons of the cherry wine. Set aside to soak.

2. Mix foie gras mousse with truffle and roll into a 9-inch log, using a piece of plastic wrap to help. Refrigerate until solid, about 1 hour, then remove plastic. Keep chilled.

3. Pulse venison stew meat and duck livers in a food processor until they are fairly finely ground. Add pork butt, egg white, salt, pepper, lemon juice, red wine, and remaining 2 tablespoons of cherry wine. Pulse until blended. Do not overmix. Transfer to a bowl, and blend in marinated cherries.

4. Preheat oven to 375°F.

5. Line a 9 x 5 x 3-inch loaf pan or terrine with aluminum foil and grease with butter. Roll 1 sheet of puff pastry to a thickness of ¼ inch. Place it in the loaf pan, working the pastry into the corners. Pastry should extend about ½ inch above all sides. Add one-third of the venison mixture, smoothing it down with a spatula. Lay foie gras log in the center, then one-third more venison mixture. Lay in venison fillet and add remaining venison mixture, smoothing it with a spatula or with wet hands. Flip pastry edges over meat and pat flat. Brush pastry with egg wash.

6. Roll out second sheet of puff pastry to a thickness of ¼ inch, and lay it over the venison terrine, trimming it to about ½ inch wider than pan. Carefully tuck top pastry into sides of terrine, using a small metal or rubber spatula. Use extra pastry to make cut-out designs, if desired, attaching pieces with egg wash. Make a 1-inch round hole in center of pastry for steam to escape. Brush surface of pastry with egg wash.

7. Bake in preheated oven until pastry is lightly browned, about 20 minutes. Reduce temperature to 300°F and continue baking until pastry is rich golden brown and internal temperature measures 160°F, 1 hour to 1 hour 15 minutes. Remove and let cool for 15 minutes, then refrigerate *uncovered* until cold.

8. Combine water, gelatin, and demi-glace in a small saucepan and bring to a boil. Once gelatin is dissolved, pour mixture into a glass measuring cup with a lip.

Carefully pour enough gelatin through hole in pastry to fill spaces between meat and pastry. Chill until firm. Allow pâté to rest uncovered in refrigerator for 5 to 7 days. Remove from refrigerator at least 1 hour before serving. Slice with a sharp serrated knife.

Adapted from Lee Hyman, executive chef, D'Artagnan, Newark, New Jersey

D & D GAME BIRD PÂTÉ

JOANNA: My father used to make crazy concoctions by puréeing together whatever leftovers he could find in the refrigerator. Every time those "dribs and drabs," little bits of this and that, were spread on crackers, they somehow tasted great. He'd add mayonnaise, mustard, onions, and who knew what else. The blender or meat grinder made these disparate foods into a special treat.

Imagining how wonderful leftover game would be, I stole the idea, and started putting scraps of cooked game in the freezer. Bits from different birds go in one resealable plastic bag, game meat scraps in another. Since I save duck and goose fat, too, the spread is almost free. Serve the "pâté" in a handsome crock or dish, elegantly garnished, and — Ssssh! — don't tell. Once you've tried this mixture, make up your own . . . almost anything goes.

MAKES ABOUT 2½ CUPS

½ pound boneless, skinless leftover cooked game bird

½ cup duck or goose fat or unsalted butter

2 minced shallots sautéed in a little duck fat or butter until tender

1 tablespoon Armagnac

1 tablespoon minced flat-leaf parsley

1 teaspoon fresh thyme leaves

½ teaspoon quatre épices (equal parts ground cinnamon, clove, nutmeg, and black pepper)

Salt and freshly ground black pepper to taste

¼ cup dried cranberries soaked in 1 tablespoon of port

1 to 2 teaspoons balsamic vinegar

Pulse everything except cranberries and vinegar together in a food processor until fairly finely chopped. Add cranberries and vinegar and mix briefly. Scrape into a decorative terrine or bowl, cover, and chill for at least 8 hours. Remove from refrigerator 30 minutes before needed and let come to room temperature. Serve with crackers or thinly sliced pieces of French bread. Chutney or cornichons would be a nice accompaniment.

appendix: charting game meat flavors

For people unfamiliar with many game birds and meats, this chart shows their relative "gaminess." If you're just starting out, you might want to try a meat with a rating of 5 or less. Bolder palates will want to explore the higher end of the spectrum.

	MILD FLAVOR						FULL FLAVOR			
	1	2	3	4	5	6	7	8	9	10
GAME BIRDS										
Capon		2								
Chicken, Free-Range Organic		2								
Duck, Mallard							7			
Duck, Moulard Magret					5					
Duck, Muscovy					5					
Duck, Pekin			3							
Goose, Farmed				4						
Goose, Wild						6				
Grouse, Scottish										10
Guinea Hen			3							
Ostrich						6				
Partridge, Farmed		2								
Partridge, Wild				4						
Pheasant, Free-Range			3							
Pheasant, Wild					5					
Poussin	1									
Quail			3							
Squab							7			
Turkey, Organic		2								
Turkey, Wild				4						
Woodcock									9	
Wood Pigeon								8		
GAME MEATS										
Boar				4						
Buffalo						6				
Hare										10
Rabbit		2								
Venison, Farmed/Cervena						6				
Venison, Scottish Red								8		
Venison, Scottish Roe								8		

index